Contributions To Phenomenology

In Cooperation with The Center
for Advanced Research in Phenomenology

Volume 88

Series Editors
Nicolas de Warren, KU Leuven, Belgium
Dermot Moran, University College Dublin, Ireland

Editorial Board
Lilian Alweiss, Trinity College Dublin, Ireland
Elizabeth Behnke, Ferndale, WA, USA
Rudolf Bernet, Husserl Archive, KU Leuven, Belgium
David Carr, Emory University, GA, USA
Chan-Fai Cheung, Chinese University Hong Kong, China
James Dodd, New School University, NY, USA
Lester Embree, Florida Atlantic University, FL, USA
Alfredo Ferrarin, Università di Pisa, Italy
Burt Hopkins, Seattle University, WA, USA
José Huertas-Jourda, Wilfrid Laurier University, Canada
Kwok-Ying Lau, Chinese University Hong Kong, China
Nam-In Lee, Seoul National University, Korea
Rosemary R.P. Lerner, Pontificia Universidad Católica del Perú, Peru
Dieter Lohmar, University of Cologne, Germany
William R. McKenna, Miami University, OH, USA
Algis Mickunas, Ohio University, OH, USA
J.N. Mohanty, Temple University, PA, USA
Junichi Murata, University of Tokyo, Japan
Thomas Nenon, The University of Memphis, TN, USA
Thomas M. Seebohm, Johannes Gutenberg-Universität, Germany
Gail Soffer, Rome, Italy
Anthony Steinbock, Southern Illinois University at Carbondale, IL, USA
Shigeru Taguchi, Hokkaido University, Japan
Dan Zahavi, University of Copenhagen, Denmark
Richard M. Zaner, Vanderbilt University, TN, USA

Scope

The purpose of the series is to serve as a vehicle for the pursuit of phenomenological research across a broad spectrum, including cross-over developments with other fields of inquiry such as the social sciences and cognitive science. Since its establishment in 1987, *Contributions to Phenomenology* has published more than 80 titles on diverse themes of phenomenological philosophy. In addition to welcoming monographs and collections of papers in established areas of scholarship, the series encourages original work in phenomenology. The breadth and depth of the Series reflects the rich and varied significance of phenomenological thinking for seminal questions of human inquiry as well as the increasingly international reach of phenomenological research.

The series is published in cooperation with The Center for Advanced Research in Phenomenology.

More information about this series at http://www.springer.com/series/5811

Dorothée Legrand • Dylan Trigg
Editors

Unconsciousness Between Phenomenology and Psychoanalysis

Springer

Editors
Dorothée Legrand
Archives Husserl, CNRS, Ecole Normale
 Supérieure
Paris Sciences et Lettres Research
 University
Paris, France

Dylan Trigg
School of Philosophy
University College Dublin
Dublin, Ireland

ISSN 0923-9545   ISSN 2215-1915 (electronic)
Contributions To Phenomenology
ISBN 978-3-319-55516-4   ISBN 978-3-319-55518-8 (eBook)
DOI 10.1007/978-3-319-55518-8

Library of Congress Control Number: 2017939707

© Springer International Publishing AG 2017
This work is subject to copyright. All rights are reserved by the Publisher, whether the whole or part of the material is concerned, specifically the rights of translation, reprinting, reuse of illustrations, recitation, broadcasting, reproduction on microfilms or in any other physical way, and transmission or information storage and retrieval, electronic adaptation, computer software, or by similar or dissimilar methodology now known or hereafter developed.
The use of general descriptive names, registered names, trademarks, service marks, etc. in this publication does not imply, even in the absence of a specific statement, that such names are exempt from the relevant protective laws and regulations and therefore free for general use.
The publisher, the authors and the editors are safe to assume that the advice and information in this book are believed to be true and accurate at the date of publication. Neither the publisher nor the authors or the editors give a warranty, express or implied, with respect to the material contained herein or for any errors or omissions that may have been made. The publisher remains neutral with regard to jurisdictional claims in published maps and institutional affiliations.

Printed on acid-free paper

This Springer imprint is published by Springer Nature
The registered company is Springer International Publishing AG
The registered company address is: Gewerbestrasse 11, 6330 Cham, Switzerland

Contents

Part I Within the Husserlian Framework

1 **Husserl's Layered Concept of the Human Person: Conscious and Unconscious**.. 3
   Dermot Moran

2 **Reflections on the Phenomenological Unconscious in Generative Phenomenology** 25
   Alexander Schnell

Part II From the Specific Perspective of Merleau-Ponty

3 **Merleau-Ponty's Conception of the Unconscious in the Late Manuscripts**... 41
   Emmanuel de Saint Aubert

4 **Repression and Operative Unconsciousness in *Phenomenology of Perception***.. 61
   Timothy Mooney

5 **Merleau-Ponty's Nonverbal Unconscious**... 75
   James Phillips

Part III At the Limit of Phenomenology

6 **Is There a Phenomenology of Unconsciousness? Being, Nature, Otherness in Heidegger, Merleau-Ponty, Levinas**................................ 95
   Dorothée Legrand

7 **Phenomenology of the Inapparent**.. 113
   François Raffoul

8	From the Night, the Spectre	133
	Joseph Cohen	
9	Phenomenology and the Problem of the Inhuman: Psychologism, Correlationism, and the Ethics of Absolute Materiality	141
	Drew M. Dalton	

Part IV With Phenomenology and Beyond

10	Hypnagogia, Anxiety, Depersonalization: A Phenomenological Perspective	163
	Dylan Trigg	
11	Merleau-Ponty's Non-Exclusively-Verbal Unconscious: Affect Figurability and Gender	181
	Thamy Ayouch	
12	The Unconscious and the Non-linguistic Mode of Thinking	209
	Dieter Lohmar	
13	A Broken Self-Possession: Responsive Agency in Habits	223
	Line Ryberg Ingerslev	

Part V Beyond Phenomenology

14	Surprise as a Phenomenal Marker of Heart-Unconscious	239
	Natalie Depraz	
15	This Immense Fascination with the Unconscious: Psychoanalysis and Surrealism	261
	Alphonso Lingis	

Index 279

Introduction

Context

What you are reading now is the fruit of an encounter not only between phenomenology and psychoanalysis but also between the editors. Out of our encounter grew something else, progressively – a friendship and now the book you are holding. If you hold it now, it is because we had too many questions, more than the two of us could unfold, more than we could even think of. We thus invited others to embark with us.

We first organized a conference, titled *Is there a phenomenology of unconsciousness?* Sponsored by both French and Irish institutions, the event took place at University College Dublin in February 2014. We are gratified that each of the nine speakers for the event has agreed to include their contributions in this volume. Alongside these chapters, we have solicited further contributions from leading figures in the field, expanding and strengthening our original scope. In bringing together thinkers from diverse backgrounds and with divergent interests, we have sought to preserve the differences between phenomenology and psychoanalysis rather than to efface or resolve those differences. Our task from the outset was neither to render phenomenology psychoanalytical nor to render psychoanalysis phenomenological, but instead to locate the shifting terrain in which each discipline appears and disappears. As Merleau-Ponty noted at the end of his life, the relation between phenomenology and psychoanalysis is not simply predicated on a mutual resistance to positivism. Much more than this, their rapport is grounded in a shared orientation, a mutual latency.

Our initial plan was to be fair, if not exhaustive – what a plan! As if (academic, linguistic, practical, conceptual, and so forth) frontiers could be easily crossed, we sought to invite both philosophers and psychoanalysts, to discuss both philosophy and psychoanalysis, and to cross these "fields" both theoretically and clinically. Here already, an asymmetry imposed itself: namely, if there is no psychoanalysis without patients, inversely, what is philosophy's clinical practice? By this question alone, our plan collapsed, not because there would be no philosophical practice, even less because philosophy would be clinically irrelevant, but because this question – is there a philosophical clinical practice? – if not heretical, is comparative. It soon leads, indeed, to question what a clinical practice would be, if philosophically relevant, by comparison with a clinical practice that would not be so and what a philosophy would be, if clinically relevant, by comparison with a philosophy that would not be so. In our own research, both of us work with "this and that" (here is not the place to detail this and that), but our approach has never been comparative; in this collective work, the same approach remains intact.

In particular, to work at once with philosophy and psychoanalysis does not impose a comparison between – say – the concept of unconsciousness in philosophy and the hypothesis of the unconscious in psychoanalysis. A comparison is rather sterile if it offers only the detection of redundancies or incompatibilities. The power of a comparison comes notably from its ability to size the scope of a given thought within its own field and in its primary context. In doing so, one ends up better understanding, for example, the specificity of Freud's unconscious, by comparing it with Merleau-Ponty's. But we aimed at something else: we proposed – to ourselves, to each other, to the contributors of this book, and now to its reader – to work beyond borders, so to speak, or between borders, rather. We didn't aim at erasing borders nor to work without borders, but proposed to displace borders, to displace a thought where it is not (yet) thought of and to impregnate or contaminate a thought with what it does not (yet) think.

What does occur to philosophy, if it thinks the unconscious which psychoanalysts work with; what does happen to the psychoanalytic unconscious if it is thought of by philosophy; what does occur to psychoanalysis if it is confronted with unconsciousness as it is conceptualized philosophically; how is a philosophical unconscious impacted if it is captured within a psychoanalytic frame? These are some of the questions that arise, as soon as we started to put together in a single sentence the words unconscious philosophy.

As we will not compare philosophy and psychoanalysis, so we will not launch this non-comparative book by comparing comparative approaches. We will not, for instance, list the manners in which, explicitly or not, philosophers may have discussed psychoanalysis, the manners in which philosophers may have made, toward what would become or what was already named psychoanalysis, movements of anticipation, foundation, integration, overshadowing, neglect, revelation, clarification, plagiarism, diversion, deconstruction, differentiation, immersion, etc. Neither "for" nor "against," neither exactly "with" nor entirely "without," neither "alike" nor "dislike," we here navigate "between" philosophy and psychoanalysis; for us, this work is interstitial.

Even unpronounced, psychoanalysis is on every page of this book – as an explicit or implicit reference to the split subject, to language, sex, others, dreams, symptoms, and so forth. Philosophically, the explicit reference here is a method which has often been abusively confused with a philosophy of consciousness, a philosophy which has indeed championed the study of the structure of consciousness – phenomenology. Within this background and because we hoped for a dialogue with philosophical thoughts which did not aim primarily to be practiced clinically, we do not do here what should be done elsewhere: a dialogue between psychoanalysis and phenomenological psychiatry, as clinical practices. For now, we just needed to pause a moment and ask: what are we talking about when we talk about unconsciousness?

This specific question arose from a strange realization: it is possible, or so it seems, to work phenomenologically with psychoanalysis, without encountering unconsciousness – the concept, the hypothesis. Does that mean we can get rid of it, as detractors of psychoanalysis think we should? Quite the contrary, we soon realized that unconsciousness, even if unpronounced, unnamed, and unthematized as such, has been unavoidable for phenomenology, so unavoidable that we could not dispense from detailing the multiple conceptualizations of unconsciousness offered within phenomenology. To do so, evidently, we could not retain unconsciousness imprisoned into psychoanalysis; we could not aim at educating psychoanalysis and reshape it with a proper philosophical logos; we could not purify the mind of its unconsciousness, immersing it into an enlarged ring of consciousness. Our project has been more simple and more ambitious too: to speak of "unconsciousness" as if the word could be said in more than one language at once, as if it could be worked on in more than one framework at once.

The unconscious, says Freud, is a hypothesis. Our starting point here is that unconsciousness is a concept. To conceive of unconsciousness as a concept is to be able to conceive of it as independent from its originary context: if unconsciousness is a concept, then it must be robust enough to be extracted from its native field, to support exportation, if not deterritorialization, to be modified by its contact with other concepts it didn't touch initially, without losing its defining core. In other terms, our project here is exterior to psychoanalysis, which does not mean that it is independent from it. Exteriority allows us to violate some acknowledged interpretation of the hypothesis of the unconscious, to reveal other dimensions.

To reveal other dimensions is not to aim at revealing all of them – how could such completeness ever be assessed? As our project does not aim at comparing a definition of unconsciousness against another, it does not aim either to capture unconsciousness into an integrative definition, which would be total, totalizing, totalitarian. If anything, unconsciousness is that which resists any complete definition, any firm grasp in any given framework, any clear definition under any monochromatic light.

To do justice to unconsciousness as a complex, we preserve here disparate voices. In the following (explicitly or not), all authors let themselves be informed by psychoanalysis and are oriented by phenomenology. But their manners to work with the concept of unconsciousness have led them either to embrace the core of phenomenology, to mix the latter with other perspectives, to reach the defining limits of phenomenology, to push them further, or to overpass them.

Outline of the Book

Within the Husserlian Framework

Unconsciousness Between Phenomenology and Psychoanalysis begins with Dermot Moran's reflections on the role of unconsciousness within Husserl's phenomenology. Following Fink, Moran argues that the starting point of any exploration of the unconscious must be a rigorous exploration of consciousness (see also A. Schnell, E. de Saint Aubert, F. Raffoul, D. Legrand). For such a project, phenomenology, and in particular Husserl's phenomenology, is the most pertinent reference. If anything, Husserl provides a fine-grained conception of consciousness where he details how the conscious ego is always bound to a horizon of non-I, including sensuous drives, undifferentiated instincts, and parcels of animality which must be idiosyncratically domesticated and owned, to therein participate to the "higher, spiritual" ego. Not unlike psychoanalysis, Husserlian phenomenology pinpoints that it is necessary to "dismantle" the natural attitude, in the aim of "uncovering" its sources; unlike psychoanalysis, however, phenomenology conceives of the latter as moments of the transcendental ego – rendering unconceivable a dynamic which could be at once mental and unconscious.

Alexander Schnell interrogates the notion of unconsciousness by embracing – rather than challenging – a phenomenological framework, that is to say, he (re)defines the notion(s) of unconsciousness by considering again the very structure of consciousness (see also D. Moran, E. de Saint Aubert). If – as phenomenology advocates – consciousness is not a given, then its very "dynamic" (a genetic and homeostatic dynamic) may be best investigated as being (the) "unconscious." In this framework, the term "unconscious" may come to qualify the "transcendental conditions" of consciousness, conditions which cannot be experienced consciously and are thus "unconscious" in this sense. The unconscious here appears as the "paradox" of consciousness, i.e., as that without which consciousness would be inoperative and as that without which consciousness would not be conscious – thus, the phenomenological unconscious ends up being that which prevents consciousness to be unconscious. What this approach to the unconscious demonstrates is that phenomenology not only can but must consider unconsciousness if its reduction to a merely descriptive approach to lived experience ought to be prevented.

From the Specific Perspective of Merleau-Ponty

Emmanuel de Saint Aubert embarks us on a journey through the evolutions of Merleau-Ponty's conceptions of unconsciousness. Doing so and relying notably on unpublished notes, he demonstrates that, rather than "the unconscious," the term "unconsciousness" better suits the phenomenological conception of unconscious dynamics vs. states. Here, it also appears clearly and explicitly that phenomenology's elaborations on unconsciousness are not only a critic or an appropriation of the psychoanalytic conception of the unconscious, but it rather grows in dialogue with but independently of psychoanalysis, within what is strictly speaking a philosophical project. Within phenomenology, in particular, Merleau-Ponty's ideas on unconsciousness evolve together with the developments of his own conceptions of consciousness (see also D. Moran, A. Schnell). What surges in this framework is not an unconscious structured via repression, but an anthropo-ontological unconsciousness as our primordial, archaic, pre-representational, pre-objective, faithful bodily consent to let Being be: "an initial yes" (see also D. Dalton). The challenge psychoanalysis is confronted with, here, is the conception of an "undivided" being (see also J. Phillips, T. Mooney).

In fact, this is a challenge for phenomenology itself, and for Merleau-Ponty's phenomenology of unconsciousness in particular, as Tim Mooney's chapter problematizes explicitly by revisiting Merleau-Ponty's key ideas under the notion of unconsciousness. The notions of body schema and motor intentionality are critical here, insofar as they allow us to consider how one's past is sedimented into one's habitual body, in turn shaping one's horizon of capacities toward future projects (see also L. Ingerslev). Although anonymous, in that one doesn't decide on them, one's bodily habits are meant to preserve one's psychic order and free one's consciousness of the burden of overplanning: it effortlessly effectuates one's adherence with one's familiar world. Moreover, one's anonymous bodily dynamics does not only impose a lack of transparency upon oneself; it also allows one's attunement with others, insofar as one shares with others a common embodiment, an anonymous intercorporeality. Altogether, one's body is a locus of integration (see also E. de Saint Aubert, J. Phillips), integration of one's past, of others, of sexuality and vitality into the whole of human's existence, integration which occurs in an admirably enabling and untroubling manner. What appears here, after such reading of Merleau-Ponty, is that unconsciousness could be conceived of as a soothing process of integration, rather than disruption and tension.

Exploring Merleau-Ponty's philosophy in yet another manner, thereby demonstrating its fertility, James Phillips elaborates upon the nonverbal unconscious. Here, what is emphasized is the unconscious as a prereflective structure of one's being in the world, generating the unity of subject and world (see also E. de Saint Aubert, T. Mooney). Such structure is a silent impulse toward meaning, the invisible armature (membrure) that supports one's visual acquaintance with the world, the reversibility and blending of the seeing/touching with the seen/touched. Together with the motive of integration or even undividedness, which is present in Merleau-Ponty's work throughout, one finds the idea that consciousness is never complete but presupposes pre-reflectivity, vision is never total but presupposes invisibility, and expression is never fully accomplished but presupposes silence. Pre-reflectivity, invisibility, silence – these are other names for unconsciousness. Throughout these different nominations, unconsciousness is structured as an unbridgeable "écart," a non-representable absence, an indefinite excess (see also E. de Saint Aubert). What surges here is nothing like an unconscious as a container of representations hidden from consciousness behind the thick wall of repression – no one really conceived of the unconscious as such, phenomenologists even less than any others – rather, unconsciousness is "in between," as the glue tying together the subject and the world he is conscious of.

At the Limit of Phenomenology

Dorothée Legrand asks whether the phenomenological framework is suitable to investigate unconsciousness and answers, after Heidegger, Merleau-Ponty, and Levinas, that the inclusion of the notion of unconsciousness into phenomenology is paradoxical. On the one hand, unconsciousness is intrinsic to the phenomenological investigation of consciousness since, as a philosophical method, phenomenology aims at clearing the modes of manifestation of what does not manifest itself spontaneously and what does not manifest itself fully as it is, i.e., what is unconscious (see also A. Schnell, F. Raffoul); on the other hand, unconsciousness pushes phenomenology beyond its defining limits by tying it irremediably to ontology and/or ethics, i.e., to the radical otherness of Being and to the radical otherness of the other subject (see also D. Dalton). Across the differences between the accounts proposed by Heidegger, Merleau-Ponty, and Levinas, each time, the phenomenological investigation of unconsciousness is revealed as involving an investigation into the modes of revelation of what cannot be possibly objectified and represented intentionally (see also J. Cohen). As such, a phenomenology of unconsciousness pushes both the conception of the phenomenon and the conception of logos to their limits, or beyond.

François Raffoul pairs Heidegger with Levinas (see also D. Legrand) to uncover how phenomenology does not and cannot dispense with unconsciousness. By employing Heidegger's account of a "phenomenology of the inapparent," Raffoul considers the different ways in which withdrawal from manifestation plays an unsubstitutable role in phenomenology, if phenomenology is conceived of as a philosophical investigation into appearing, a verb, rather than appearance, a noun. Appearing does not appear in and of itself but is veiled by what appears: within unconcealment, concealment operates; within consciousness, unconsciousness operates. Importantly, however, concealment is not a process by which something would be hidden and should be recovered (see also J. Cohen, D. Dalton); unconsciousness is the coveredness of Being which cannot possibly be recovered. Hence, phenomenology is haunted by an inner violence, a philosophical violence of interpretation, description, and nomination, which works against the non-appearing proper to Being, its manner of unceasingly throwing itself into manifested phenomena. It is one's unavoidable responsibility, however, to carry on this violent task of responding to the call of the inappropriable Being: one cannot remain indifferent to Being and to one's own being – despite its resistance to becoming conscious, a resistance one cannot overcome. It appears that the structure of Heidegger's thought, analyzed as it is here, is not foreign to the philosophy of Levinas, even though the latter recurrently, explicitly, and virulently opposed Heideggerian ontological phenomenology, placing ethics as first philosophy. What is claimed about Being becomes, with Levinas, characteristics of one's relation to others: others cannot be reduced to any object of consciousness; they constitutively escape conscious manifestations; their face does not appear as a phenomenon, but indicates their very otherness, their vulnerability to the violence of death and murder (see also D. Dalton). The other is always susceptible to withdraw radically into the unknown, and one's unsubstitutable responsibility is to respond to what can never be captured consciously: a secret.

Joseph Cohen questions the primacy of consciousness, the analysis of the unconscious into the form(ation)s it inserts into consciousness; he questions the primacy of the day, the reduction of the night to a day yet to come; he questions the primacy of the ego and of the world, the primacy of the subject-object correlation that phenomenology holds to (see also F. Raffoul). Could there be a phenomenology of the night, a night which never promises that another day will come; could there be a phenomenology of unconsciousness, an unconscious which would resist analysis; could there be a phenomenology of what is not any world for any subject, of what cannot be included within the indefinitely extensible horizon of all possible presencing? Could there be a phenomenology of what cannot possibly come to consciousness, a phenomenology of an irremediable loss (see also D. Dalton)? Such phenomenology would have to be informed by the occurrence of an event that is not present to consciousness but affects consciousness nonetheless, an event that dispossesses the subject from the possibility to respond to what occurs, an event that inhabits the subject inaccessibly, which haunts the subject fascinated by that which is both incomparably foreign and inseparable. Such event can be named the unconscious: a spectral unconscious. Is it not together with this unconscious – the specter of consciousness which irreducibly refrains phenomenalization – that phenomenology can come to think subjectivity itself (see also A. Schnell)? Is it not by realizing that an event has occurred that cannot possibly be correlated with the conscious subject, an event that cannot possibly be present, an event through which absence occurs, and is it not by realizing that death has occurred, i.e., is it not by mourning, that one may come to interrogate the birth of subjectivity?

Drew Dalton aims at reconsidering the power of the phenomenological method to access to the "thing" itself, as it would be thinkable outside of the transcendental correlation between a subject of consciousness and its intentional objects (see also J. Cohen, see also D. Trigg): what is it that may give to the human some access to the inhuman? Does unconsciousness – understood here as that which may be given to consciousness while exceeding it (see also E. de Saint Aubert, J. Phillips) – fundamentally challenge the Husserlian conception of phenomenology and of the "thing" itself? Is such notion of unconsciousness in full contradiction with phenomenological ontology? While phenomenology has been challenged, since Frege up to contemporary speculative realism, by critics firstly aiming at countering psychologism, the "inhuman" has been called upon, to rescue phenomenology from the risk of falling into idealism, reducing the world to what is subjectively accessible. The inhuman would be the absolute completely independent from the structure of consciousness – an inhuman, asubjective unconsciousness (see also D. Legrand). It may be thought that such inhuman unconsciousness may be humanly and consciously accessed through the attestation of prehuman and/or post-human "things." But more than the death of humanity, the death of a human would here provide the paradigm of what imposes itself to human subjectivity while being neither human nor subjective (see also J. Cohen). The dead body manifests itself as that which entertains no links with the one experiencing it. The corpse traumatically confronts us to the unavoidable: the recognition of something which appears to consciousness without being constrained within its structures.

With Phenomenology and Beyond

Dylan Trigg folds the study of unconsciousness into the experience that "I am not me," not fully me, not me in any unified manner, not a "me" which a linear narrative could encompass neatly. He takes up this experience through the idea of hypnagogic states – transitional states between wakefulness and sleep that are best characterized as liminal states between consciousness and unconsciousness, between self and nonself. On the one hand, hypnagogic states require from the subject a receptivity, an openness toward an ambivalent state of consciousness where one is both at once present and absent (see also J. Cohen). On the other hand, anxiety may emerge when a sense of loosening the ego surges uncontrollably. As seen in this way, anxiety imposes upon the subject the sense of an unbearable disjunction between one's subjective presence and one's disappearance from the subjective field. Here, a series of tensions form. Hypnagogia opens the subject to the marvels of ambiguous states of consciousness that exist independently of the ego (see also D. Dalton). At the same time, anxiety violates the subject's sense of being one, through the passage of time, and rises as a defense against any ambiguity between self and nonself. In both cases, what is revealed is a possible de-centering of the ego – be it in a relaxing or terrifying experience. Whereas anxiety would deploy an existential distrust and intolerance toward what does not belong to the conscious ego, hypnagogia would allow loosening the barriers of consciousness against unconsciousness.

Thamy Ayouch does not explore the phenomenological unconscious through a frontal confrontation with the term "unconscious" as used in phenomenology. Rather, he explores key phenomenological notions to bring forth a phenomenological unconscious, the latter being then put to work beyond phenomenology, to discuss with psychoanalysis and feminism about gender. With the nonrepresentational framework proper to phenomenology, which intermingles subject and object; the notion of intercorporeality which bridges the gap between self and others (see also T. Mooney); the notion of institution, blurring the boundaries of the present, carrying the traces of a sedimented past and the call for a unachievable future; the Merleau-Pontian conception of language, tying together repetition and subversion; the circularity between nature and culture, what emerges is a notion of an unconscious that is not exclusively verbal but also affective (see also J. Phillips, N. Depraz). The unconscious is not the product of a culturally loaded repression of natural drives, but an instituted affectivity in quest for figurability: just like an affect detached from its primary objects may be secondarily attached to another figure, as it often occurs in dreams, a given gender assignment may be the figuration found by the affect disconnected from one's originary gender multiplicity. This conception of the unconscious, it is argued, avoids imposing categories stretching beyond history and culture and that could be applied universally (see also A. Lingis); in particular, it allows considering, in a non-pathologizing manner, processes of non-binary gender configurations and polymorphous sexuality.

Dieter Lohmar argues in favor of a nonlinguistic mode of thinking which, investigated from a perspective that is rooted into Husserlian phenomenology, creates the space for reevaluating phenomena which psychoanalysis takes as its (conceptual and therapeutic) target: how can we both know and not know something; how does neurotic displacement operate? What is at stake here is a phenomenological study of the effectiveness of unconsciousness. Scenic phantasma are short-term visual states akin to daydreams which may not be accessible to verbal consciousness, but which nonetheless shape our present actions, our plans for the future, and our recollection of past experiences (see also T. Mooney, L. Ingerslev). Through this nonverbal process (see also J. Phillips), one may play out possible life scenarios; one may repeat an activity while slightly and progressively modifying the role one really played in it, allowing for better planning and problem-solving; one may retain a central lesson of a previous experience, avoiding further mistakes and building new habits on that basis. This nonlinguistic process is akin to a sort of knowledge insofar as it preserves experiences into types, hence transforming a unique experience into a source of reproducible knowledge; and it is akin to an unconscious process insofar as it remains opaque to the conscious report a subject may give about himself, his choices, his actions. Such unconscious knowledge is nonpublic, it is solitary: its aim is not communication, nor the search for a truth that could be shared with others; pragmatically oriented, this thought process rather aims at guiding one's life, off-line first, before plunging into the "real" world.

Line Ryberg Ingerslev engages with an overlooked topic: our everyday life. How does unconsciousness infiltrate our mode of being in the world, through the way habits restlessly shape our actions and our familiarity with the world? Because we are habitual bodies, our actions – those very actions which we feel ownership for and which we are responsible for – always originate before we can become conscious of them; they are always ahead of ourselves, and in this sense, we are always behind ourselves: we always started already, from elsewhere than our conscious will. Thus, habits prevent any self-familiarity, any self-unity: we never experience ourselves as fully unified autonomous agents; self-possession is broken, constitutively, i.e., unbrokeness has never been and will never be. Cutting out any nostalgia or promise of wholeness, this view contrasts with the consideration of habits as only smoothening the world as familiar (see also T. Mooney, D. Lohmar) and poses a challenge to the notion of agency classically tied to the conception of a subject capable of accounting for her action – meaningfully or even rationally. What's left, then, of the agentive subject? The subject, in this view, is responsive: he responds, and most importantly, he has to respond to the habit he always already finds himself caught into: if habits arise despite myself, they do not occur without me. Experiencing one's body is experiencing the urge, the necessity, the constraint to surrender to one's habitual body, thereby responding to the actions which habits always already started before me. Rather than negating the dimensions of our everyday actions which repeat themselves without being graspable consciously, responding to our habits is dealing with one's self-brokenness and assuming self-alienation without reducing our action to mere reaction about which we could decline responsibility.

Beyond Phenomenology

Natalie Depraz pushes the investigation of unconsciousness beyond classical phenomenology. She specifically investigates the "heart unconscious" which presents a twofold structure: organic (the heart is a muscle) and lived (the heart is the intuitive and sensitive location of one's affectivity). Bypassing the "hard problem" of correlating third-personal (neuronal, behavioral) modes of accessing nonconscious processes, together with first-personal modes of accessing conscious states, "cardiophenomenology" evolves from neurophenomenology and ambitions to integrate measures of emotions which are both at once objective (the modulation of one's heartbeats according to one's emotional states) and subjective (the lived experience of the rhythm of one's heartbeats, which nonetheless runs without one's control over it). In particular, it is argued that the emotion of surprise (see also F. Raffoul) provides a measurable revelator of the unconscious, together with symptoms or slips of the tongue: one's experience of surprise would be one's micro-experience of disruptions occurring along the ongoing flow of one's conscious life. As cardiophenomenology makes it accessible through the fine-grained measurement of surprise, the heart unconscious is revealed as a dynamic, multi-phased, temporally extended process.

Alphonso Lingis contrasts the psychoanalytic unconscious with the surrealist unconscious. By doing this, he puts into question the appropriation of the unconscious by psychoanalysis, by pointing out that this particular conception of the unconscious relies upon and reinforces "metaphysical subjectivism." The psychoanalytic unconscious is anthropomorphic, subjective; it is also ethnocentric. Psychoanalysis – thus understood – operates a reduction of unconscious forces to what is psychoanalytically theorized or, more generally, to what is humanly meaningful. Certainly, a very different – more charitable – light can be cast upon psychoanalysis, as a theory and as a method, but what is more important is that, in an appropriation of the phenomenological method, Lingis asks whether the formations of the unconscious would appear differently if psychoanalytical interpretations were suspended. Without prejudicing who holds the "proper" conception of the unconscious, what stands out here is the importance of thinking again what is presupposed under this notion. Is the unconscious meaningful or meaningless? Is it human? Is it organized or a chaotic field of random forces? Is it a causal force or is it deprived of any causal power? Can it be fully integrated to one's conscious field or is it an irreducible alterity? Can it be fully analyzed or is it a place of inexhaustible abundance? Can one's relation to unconscious forces be nurtured at will? Can and should one domesticate unconscious forces? Is it the uncovering of unconscious forces which may have a therapeutic impact? Can the uncovering of unconscious forces be exploited at will in a creative performance? Is uncovering unconscious forces an act of liberation from cultural, social, religious, moral, and rational constraints? Is the unconscious subjective? Singular? Are there collective unconscious forces? Universal ones? Is the human's unconscious inhuman? Are unconscious forces a source of sufferance or a site of marvels?

Introduction xvii

Needless to say, to all these questions, none of the authors writing in this book provide any definitive answer, but we hope that, by posing them polyphonically, we provide some material to better understand them and further work on them.

Acknowledgments

In closing, we wish to take this opportunity to thank all of the contributors to this volume. It is only through their generosity that this volume exists in its current form, as a collection of diverse but interconnected chapters. In addition, we wish to thank those individuals and funding bodies that supported the conference, which led up to this book. In particular, our thanks go to Dermot Moran for providing funding assistance together with the usage of the Newman House, University College Dublin. Our thanks also go to Hadrien Laroche, the cultural attaché at the French Embassy in Dublin for providing financial support for the conference. Our thanks also go to Dominique Pradelle, director of the Husserl Archives, Ecole Normale Supérieure, Paris, for participating to the founding of the conference. Additional thanks to Helen Kennedy (UCD), Margaret Brady (UCD), and Karima Argentin (ENS) for the administrative support leading up to and beyond the conference. Thanks also to Audrey Petit-Trigg for her translation work, both during the conference and for the present volume. Dylan Trigg's work on this collection was supported by a Marie Curie grant (FP7-PEOPLE-2013-IOF 624968), which is herein gratefully acknowledged. Dylan Trigg would like to also thank Dorothée Legrand for her friendship and intellectual camaraderie, both during the preparation of this volume and beyond, and Dorothée Legrand would like to flip this sentence around to thank Dylan Trigg.

Paris, France Dorothée Legrand
Dublin, Ireland Dylan Trigg

Part I
Within the Husserlian Framework

Chapter 1
Husserl's Layered Concept of the Human Person: Conscious and Unconscious

Dermot Moran

Abstract Husserl's mature phenomenology offers a complex and multi-layered account of the constitution of the human person through a developmental analysis of different stages of *constitution*, from the constitution and integration of the lived body upward to the full, free, rational functioning of the mature human person. The mature human person is, for Husserl, in the fullest sense, a self-reflective Cartesian *cogito*, a self-conscious rational agent exercising conscious "position-takings", judgings, desirings, and willings. At the same time, a person is an intersubjective social being, a member of a family, a group, a community, a nation, a participant in empathic interpersonal relations with others in the context of a social world, an environment, and a life-world, what Husserl calls *socius*. But, for Husserl, the self is also necessarily rooted in nature, and lives through its sensations, drives and tendencies, affections, feelings, emotions and motor capacities and especially through its voluntary movements and decisions (Husserl's "I can"). The ego has moments of wakeful alertness but can also be sunk in sleep or dreaming. It has dispositions, habits, a *hexis* or *habitus*, which gives it a network of habitual actions, stances and motivations. Husserl's account is an extraordinarily rich phenomenological account of the person that contains analyses comparable to psychoanalytic explorations of the unconscious, with which Husserl was barely familiar. In this paper I shall chart Husserl's conception of the person and explore some tensions in it especially between its unconscious and conscious dimensions.

Keywords Husserl • Phenomenology • Consciousness • Freud • Unconsciousness • Memory • Passivity

> I must lie down where all the ladders start
> In the foul rag and bone shop of the heart.
> William Butler Yeats, *The Circus Animals Desertion*

D. Moran (✉)
School of Philosophy, University College Dublin, Dublin, Ireland
e-mail: dermot.moran@ucd.ie

© Springer International Publishing AG 2017
D. Legrand, D. Trigg (eds.), *Unconsciousness Between Phenomenology and Psychoanalysis*, Contributions To Phenomenology 88,
DOI 10.1007/978-3-319-55518-8_1

Edmund Husserl (1859–1938) and Sigmund Freud (1856–1939) were almost exact contemporaries, both attended Franz Brentano's lectures in Vienna,[1] and both were involved in the understanding of subjective life and its meaning. As a result, various efforts have been made over the years to explore the relations between Husserlian phenomenology and Freudian psychoanalysis, between the descriptive phenomenological exploration of experienced, conscious life, in all its modalities (including memory, fantasy, emotion, habitual action), and the analytic uncovering of unconscious processes (repression, sublimation) and their effects.[2]

For many years, the standard view has been that Husserl's phenomenology deals only with the conscious self-reflective ego (what Husserl calls, following Descartes, *cogito*) and its 'lived experiences' (*Erlebnisse*) that can be accessed in conscious reflection (or at best through some kind of reflective reconstruction), whereas Freudian psychoanalysis identifies unconscious processes, forces and energies, acts of repression and recurrences, that are not immediately (and may never become) available to the conscious subject, but rather must be identified through the mediation of the psychoanalytic engagement with an analyst working through hints, traces, slips, ruptures, resistances, and absences, that point to these underlying forces at work.[3] For Freud, the psychology of the unconscious was a 'depth psychology' that entails a whole vision of human nature that portrayed humans as struggling to balance instinctual drives (the pleasure principle, the death instinct) as ways of coping with sex and aggression, albeit that Freud also had a generally Enlightenment view of humans as capable of rationality, freedom and love.[4]

---

[1] Freud attended Brentano's lectures in Vienna as a young student from 1874 to 1876, whereas Husserl attended Brentano's lectures 10 years later from 1884 to 1886. See Philip Merlan, 'Brentano and Freud', *Journal of the History of Ideas* vol. 6, no. 3 (Jun., 1945), pp. 375–377. The lectures appeared to have no lasting impression on the founder of psychoanalysis, but see Raymond E. Fancher, 'Brentano's *Psychology from an Empirical Standpoint* and Freud's Early Metapsychology', *Journal of the History of the Behavioral Sciences*, vol. 13 no. 3 (July 1977), pp. 207–227, who discusses some comparisons in their approaches.

[2] For a thorough, recent discussion of the literature on the relations between phenomenology and psychoanalysis, see Nicholas Smith, *Towards a Phenomenology of Repression – A Husserlian Reply to the Freudian Challenge*, Stockholm Studies in Philosophy 34 (Stockholm: Stockholm University, 2010), especially pp. 10–38. See also Gunnar Karlsson, 'Phenomenology and Psychoanalysis', in his *Psychoanalysis in a New Light* (New York: Cambridge University Press, 2010), pp. 1–20. See also Evelyne Grossmann, 'Inconscient freudien, inconsient phénoménologique', *Rue Descartes* vol. 4 no. 4 (2010), pp. 106–112.

[3] For an important discussion of psychoanalysis in relation to phenomenology, see Herbert Spiegelberg, *Phenomenology in Psychology and Psychiatry. A Historical Introduction* (Evanston: Northwestern University Press, 1972), especially pp. 127ff. See also the work of Alphonse de Waelhens, especially his, 'Sur l'inconscient et la pensée philosophique', in *L' Inconscient* (Paris, Desclée de Brouwer, 1966) and his 'Réflections sur une problématique husserlienne de l'inconscient, Husserl et Hegel', in H. L. Van Breda and J. Taminiaux, eds, *Edmund Husserl 1859–1959. Recueil commemoratif publié à l'occasion de centenaire de la naissance du philosophe* (The Hague: Nijhoff, 1959). See also Herman Drüe, 'Psychoanalysis', in Lester Embree, ed., *Encyclopedia of Phenomenology* (Dordrecht: Kluwer, 1997), pp. 568–572.

[4] See Philip Rieff, *Freud. The Mind of a Moralist* (Chicago: University of Chicago Press, 1977), p. 187.

In attempting to discuss the parallels between Husserl and Freud it is important to recall that Husserl had a particularly narrow and limited view of Freud's contribution. Similarly, as I argue, Husserl's thought is more complex than traditionally conceived (in part the blame lay in Husserl's explicit espousal of Cartesianism); and so too is Freud's but Freud – certainly in the early part of the twentieth century – was conceived more narrowly (primarily on the basis of *The Interpretation of Dreams*) and pessimistically than he is now viewed.[5] Karl Jaspers, for instance, was perhaps the most explicit philosophical critic of psychoanalysis in the 1920 revision of his *General Psychopathology*.[6] Ironically, both phenomenology and psychoanalysis were denounced by the National Socialists in Germany after 1933 as "Jewish" sciences. It was in fact, Eugen Fink who seemed to be particularly interested in the relations between phenomenology and various forms of 'depth psychology'. The Frankfurt School, on the other hand, especially through the work of Horkheimer, Adorno and Marcuse seemed to embrace Freud and psychoanalysis.[7]

Husserl's exhaustively detailed exploration of the intentional structures and syntheses of the flow of experiential consciousness (*Buwusstseinsstrom*, *Erlebnisstrom*), through disciplined methodological reflection, operating under the 'bracketing' (*einklammern*) and 'suspension' (*epoché*) of assumptions of actuality or 'belief in being' (*Seinsglaube*), and deliberately cast in the language of Cartesian solipsism (especially in Husserl's *Ideas* I and *Cartesian Meditations*), seems at first glance to rule out the positing of an inaccessible, unconscious domain and to be in principle incapable of tracking unconscious states.

In addition, the mature Husserl's explication of all 'sense and being' (*Sinn und Sein*) of the entire world of experience as the intentional 'achievement' (*Leistung*) of the transcendental ego seems, moreover, to bring all experience within the purview of the ego and be at least in principle, available for conscious inspection.

Furthermore, it is often pointed out that what Husserl occasionally alludes to as the 'unconscious' (*das Unbewusste*) is in fact what Freud would have called the

---

[5] See Hannah S. Decker, "The Reception of Psychoanalysis in Germany," *Comparative Studies in Society and History* 24 no. 4 (1982), pp. 589–602; and her *Freud in Germany: Revolution and Reaction in Science 1893–1907* (New York: International Universities Press, 1977).

[6] See Karl Jaspers, *General Psychopathology*, trans. J. Hoenig and Marian W. Hamilton (Baltimore, MD: Johns Hopkins University Press, 1997); and his *Die geistige Situation der Zeit* (1931), trans. as *Man in the Modern Age* (New York: Anchor Books, 1957). Jaspers is increasingly critical of psychoanalysis, see Matthias Bormuth, *Life Conduct in Modern Times: Karl Jaspers and Psychoanalysis* (Dordrecht: Springer, 2006), and his "Karl Jaspers as a Critic of Psychoanalysis A Short Sketch of a Long Story," *Existenz. International Journal in Philosophy, Religion, Politics, and the Arts*, Vol. 10, No. 2 (Fall 2015), pp. 1–10.

[7] See Martin Jay, *The Dialectical Imagination: A History of the Frankfurt School and the Institute of Social Research, 1923–50 m*(Boston: Little, Brown and Co., 1973) and Rolf Wiggershaus, *The Frankfurt School. Its History, Theories, and Political Significance* (London and Cambridge: Polity/ The MIT Press, 1994). See also Joel Whitebook, Joel, "Fantasy and critique: some thoughts on Freud and the Frankfurt School," in David M. Rasmussen (ed.), *Handbook of Critical Theory*. (Oxford: Blackwell Publishers, 1996), pp. 287–304.

'pre-conscious',[8] and, in reverse, standardly, phenomenologists tend to regard Husserl's transcendental approach as incompatible with what they regarded as Freud's mechanistic naturalism of the hidden 'forces' of the 'id' and their effects. Finally, Husserl's interest in the syntheses performed by agent consciousness appears to contrast with Freud's account of the primacy of repression as an unconscious process.

Paul Ricoeur was one of the first phenomenologically trained thinkers, in his 1965 ground-breaking and comprehensive hermeneutical study of the whole of Freud's corpus, to explore in some detail the relations between Freud's explorations of the terrain of the unconscious and Husserl's phenomenology (Merleau-Ponty earlier also made some explorations in this regard). Ricoeur, in particular, links Husserl's passive synthesis and his concept of association with the Freudian unconscious.[9] He remarks that no other philosophy of reflection has come as close as Husserl did to Freud's concept of the unconscious.[10] Others, too, have seen the close proximity between Husserl's and Freud's investigations. Thus, the mathematician and logician Kurt Gödel once remarked that 'both Husserl and Freud considered – in different ways – subconscious thinking'.[11] Husserl does see the stream of consciousness as broadly divided into 'waking' and 'sleeping' states, and waking states as built around perception. Indeed, his most careful analyses focus on embodied perception as that which provides our most basic, primitive and enduring contact with others and with the world.

Typically, the best way to approach Husserl on the unconscious has been, following Ricoeur's suggestion, to explore his analyses of passive synthesis.[12] Another interesting way of approach, proposed by the phenomenologist and psychoanalyst Rudolf Bernet, is to examine the complex relations that Husserl finds between the experience of the living present and memory and fantasy.[13] In a powerful and

---

[8] This was indeed the view of Elmar Holenstein in his *Husserls Phänomenologie der Assoziation. Zu Struktur und Funktion eines Grundprinzips der passive Genesis bei Edmund Husserl* (The Hague: Nijhoff, 1972), see especially p. 322.

[9] See Paul Ricoeur, *De l'interprétation. Essai sur Sigmund Freud* (Paris: LeSeuil, 1965), trans. D. Savage *Freud and Philosophy. An Essay on Interpretation* (New Haven: Yale University, 1970), especially pp. 380 ff.

[10] Ricoeur, *Freud and Philosophy*, op. cit., p. 376. Ricoeur is particular is referring to Freud's 1915 paper on 'The Unconscious'.

[11] See Hao Wang, *A Logical Journey: From Gödel to Philosophy* (Cambridge, MA: MIT Press, 1996), p. 167.

[12] See Edmund Husserl, *Analysen zur passiven Synthesis. Aus Vorlesungs- und Forschungsmanuskripten, 1918–1926*, Husserliana (hereafter 'Hua') XI, ed. M. Fleischer ((The Hague: Martinus Nijhoff, 1962); trans. Anthony J. Steinbock, as *Analyses Concerning Passive and Active Synthesis* (Boston: Kluwer Academic Publishers, 2001).

[13] For a reading of Husserl's phenomenology in relation to Freud, see Rudolf Bernet, 'Le freudisme de Husserl: une phénoménologie de la pulsion et des émotions', in Jocelyt Benoist, ed., *Husserl* (Paris: Cerf « Les cahiers d'histoire de la philosophie », 2008), pp. 125–147. See also Natalie Depraz, 'Pulsion, instinct, désir. Que. signifie Trieb cehz Husserl? À l'épreuve des perspectives de Freud, Merleau-Ponty, Jonas et Scheler', *Alter* 9 (2001), pp. 113–125; and Francesco S. Trincia,

illuminating discussion, Rudolf Bernet locates Husserl's discussion of the unconscious primarily in his account of 'presentification' or 'presentation' (*Vergegenwärtigung*), a kind of representational or 'making present' consciousness found in different forms in memory, fantasy, looking at photographs and pictures, and also in empathic experiences of other people (present, past, real or fictional). Already in his early writings on perception, imagination and image consciousness from around 1905, Husserl produced very careful accounts of fantasy, dream, and other representational states, and indeed, had discussed how for instance real wishes (e.g. the desire to have a holiday) can emerge within flights of daydream fantasy or in a dream.[14]

A present consciousness such as a perception, Bernet says, can comport itself towards a non-present consciousness such as a fantasy.[15] Indeed, perception and fantasy are usually found intertwined. Fantasy depends or is founded on perception, according to Husserl, but floats free in a specific way by not insisting on the present givenness of the fantasized object. Bernet criticizes Husserl for the limitations in his characterization of fantasy as such: Husserl always sees it as somehow grounded in or based on perceptions or memories and is surrounded by a consciousness of the world although not directly connected to it.[16] Fantasy, for him, always amounts to a diminished quasi-perception. Husserl, according to Bernet, had to make fantasy-experiences dependent on the experience of a *contrast* with present experienced events. Bernet argues that the concept of the unconscious must be grounded in the notion of presentification as a non-positing experience (in contrast to memory) that may deal with events that may never have been actual.[17] Fantasies in this sense can have their own objects and trajectory without being anchored to actuality. Fantasy, for Husserl, can enfold *real* feelings and wishes as well as fantasy feelings and wishes (e.g. I may identify with a film characters desire to kill someone in a movie but do not exit the movie theatre with a real desire to murder in my heart).

Husserl himself only very rarely refers to psychoanalysis in his work. In *Ideas II*,[18] Husserl discusses the domains of passivity, habituality and 'sedimentation',

---

'Some Observations on Husserl and Freud', in D. Lohmar and J. Brudzínska, eds, *Founding Psychoanalysis Phenomenologically*, Phaenomenologica 199 (Dordrecht: Springer, 2012), pp. 235–242.

[14] See E. Husserl, *Phantasy, Image Consciousness and Memory (1895–1925)*, trans. John Brough, Husserl Collected Works vol. XI (Dordrecht: Springer, 2005), pp. 251–52.

[15] Rudolf Bernet, 'Unconscious Consciousness in Husserl and Freud', *Phenomenology and the Cognitive Sciences* (2002), pp. 327–351; reprinted in Donn Welton, ed., *The New Husserl. A Critical Reader* (Bloomington, IN: Indiana U. P. 2003), pp. 199–222, especially, p. 201.

[16] Bernet, 'Unconscious Consciousness in Husserl and Freud', *The New Husserl. A Critical Reader*, op. cit., p. 204.

[17] See also Nicolas de Warren, 'Time and the Double-Life of Subjectivity', *Journal of the British Society for Phenomenology* vol. 40 no. 2 (2009), pp. 155–169. De Warren sees Husserl as recognizing the complex ways that consciousness can be split and doubled.

[18] E. Husserl, *Ideen zu einer reinen Phänomenologie und phänomenologischen Philosophie. Zweites Buch: Phänomenologische Untersuchungen zur Konstitution.* Hrsg. Marly Biemel, Husserliana IV (The Hague: Nijhoff, 1952); trans. R. Rojcewicz and A. Schuwer, *Ideas pertaining to a Pure Phenomenology and to a Phenomenological Philosophy, Second Book.* Husserl Collected Works III (Dordrecht: Kluwer, 1989). Hereafter "*Ideas* II'.

experiences where the ego simply finds itself and does not quite know how it got there. Thus, in *Ideas* II § 56 (b), he speaks about the domain of unnoticed or unacknowledged motivations that 'psychoanalysis' (*Psychoanalyse, Ideas* II, p. 235: Hua IV 222) might investigate further. Despite its focus on the unconscious, there are just two brief references to Freud and psychoanalysis in the recently published Husserliana volume of notes that the editors have entitled *Limit Problems of Phenomenology. Analyses of the Unconscious and of Instincts* (2014).[19]

In Walter Biemel's critical Husserliana edition of Husserl's *Crisis of the European Sciences* (1954),[20] there is a reference to 'depth psychology' (*Tiefenpsychologie, Crisis* p. 386; VI 473), by which presumably is meant Freudian psychoanalysis (although possibly including Freud and Adler). This reference occurs in an Appendix Husserl's then assistant Eugen Fink, added to Husserl's *Crisis* in 1936.[21] This Appendix stresses that the exploration of the unconscious must begin from a thorough study of 'being conscious' (*Bewusstheit*). Furthermore, Fink acknowledges that one should not automatically assume that the 'unconscious' is equivalent to all sorts of obscure awareness, after-effects of conscious states that can subsequently be re-awakened, since the practitioners of depth psychology actually claim the reverse, namely, that all conscious life is founded on the unconscious which is prior. Fink claims that depth psychology itself takes unconscious phenomena as self-evident in their own way:

> For the unconscious, too, as well as for consciousness, there exists the *illusion* of everyday, given immediacy: we are all familiar, after all, with the phenomena of sleep, of fainting, of being overtaken by obscure driving forces, creative states, and the like. (*Crisis*, p. 387; VI 474)

Fink rejects as "naïve" and "dogmatic" certain theoretical constructions (he means Freud) that have been built on the recognition of the unconscious, e.g. those that invoke the 'naturalistic mechanism of the "libido"' (*Crisis*, p. 386; VI 474) or some kind of "dynamics" of instincts and drives. Fink claims that these discussions begin from the naïve assumption that conscious life is immediately given and, as it were, transparent, whereas in fact Husserlian intentional analysis has shown that conscious life is a very complex and multilayered structure. Only when 'wakeful' consciousness as such is clarified can a proper discussion of the unconscious as such be undertaken.[22] Presumably Husserl and Fink discussed the problem of the Freudian

---

[19] See E. Husserl, *Grenzprobleme der Phänomenologie, Analysen des Unbewusstseins und der Instinkte. Metaphysik. Späte Ethik. Texte aus dem Nachlass 1908–1937*, ed. Rochus Sowa and Thomas Vongehr, Husserliana XLII (Dordrecht: Springer, 2014), especially pp. 113 and 126.

[20] E. Husserl, *Die Krisis der europäischen Wissenschaften und die transzendentale Phänomenologie. Eine Einleitung in die phänomenologische Philosophie*, ed. Walter Biemel, Husserliana Vol. VI (The Hague: Nijhoff, 1954), substantially translated by David Carr as *The Crisis of European Sciences and Transcendental Phenomenology. An Introduction to Phenomenological Philosophy* (Evanston, IL: Northwestern U.P., 1970), with some supplements omitted. Hereafter *Crisis*, followed by page number of English translation and Husserliana volume and page number.

[21] Eugen Fink's discussion of the unconscious was included by Walter Biemel as an Appendix in his edition of the *Crisis*, pp. 385–87; Hua VI 473–75.

[22] Husserl sometimes comment on the fact that the wakeful ego is punctuated by periods of sleep and has to actively join itself to earlier states through acts of synthesis. Husserl leaves it an open question as to whether there is ever pure 'unconsciousness' in the sense of there being no flicker of

unconscious on one or more of their daily walks in the hills above Freiburg and it is undoubtedly the case that some of Husserl's own students were interested in psychoanalysis. The mature Husserl regularly distinguishes between the 'awake' or 'wakeful ego' (*das wache Ich*) and the ego sunk in sleep or dream or other altered states (e.g. intoxication). In *Ideas* II, for instance, he speaks of the 'sleeping ego' (*das schlafende Ich*) as sunk in what he calls 'ego-matter' (*Ichmaterie, Ideas* II § 58, p. 264 IV 253) or *hyle*. In this state the ego is undifferentiated, it is 'ego sunkenness' (*Ichversunkenheit*). But Husserl was not clear on the best way of approaching these 'dull' (*dumpf*) conscious states (*Ideas* II § 26).

Aside from Eugen Fink's remarks, it is accurate to state that Husserl's phenomenology in Freiburg continued to develop more or less in parallel to Freudian psychoanalysis, without direct contact between the two disciplines (Freud himself never refers by name to Husserl and indeed there are only a couple of generic references to 'psychological phenomenology' in Freud's works). In Husserl's circle in Göttingen, Max Scheler, who came to deliver public lectures, had a deep interest in and critical understanding of Freud[23] and discussed him in his *The Essence of Sympathy*[24] and elsewhere. Generally, speaking Scheler is critical of Freud's naturalism and his lack of appreciation that human beings can discriminate and choose between values.[25] But Scheler does find that Freud's (albeit mistaken) views must be discussed in any serious phenomenological exploration of the emotions, and especially the nature of sexual love and shame (where Scheler is critical of Freud's postulations).[26]

Maurice Merleau-Ponty (especially in his unfinished *Working Notes* written in 1959 and 1960 and published posthumously in *The Visible and the Invisible*, 1964),[27] does take Freudian psychoanalysis more seriously and indeed thinks that Freud's suspicion towards the lived experience as it presents itself is pre-eminently 'philosophical' (VI, p. 181; 233). In fact, Merleau-Ponty is explicating a phenomenological conception of the unconscious that is, I believe, close to that which Husserl would have developed and which we can piece together from his scattered remarks.

---

consciousness at all. See Hanne Jacobs, 'Towards a Phenomenological Account of Personal Identity', in Carlo Ierna, Hanne Jacobs, Filip Mattens, eds, *Philosophy, Phenomenology, Sciences. Essays in Commemoration of Edmund Husserl* (Dordrecht: Springer, 2010), pp. 333–362.

[23] For a discussion of Max Scheler's relation with Sigmund Freud, see Lou Andreas-Salome's reflections in her *In der Schule bei Freud. Tagebuch eines Jahres 1912–1913* (Zurich: Max Niehans, 1958), pp. 197–203, trans. Stanley Leavey as *The Freud Journal of Lou Andreas-Salome* (New York: Basic Books, 1964).

[24] See Max Scheler, *The Nature of Sympathy*, trans. Peter Heath (London: Routledge and Kegal Paul, 1954), especially pp. 22–26 (on the nature of pathological identification in a discussion of Freud's *Group Psychology and the Analysis of the Ego*); pp. 115–117 (for the critique of Freud's view of sexual love); and pp. 177–79 (for a discussion of the difference between libido and sexual drive and the nature of repression and sublimation).

[25] Scheler, *The Nature of Sympathy*, op. cit., p. 115.

[26] See Max Scheler, 'Shame and Feelings of Modesty' [1913], in M. Scheler, *Person and Self-Value. Three Essays*, trans. Manfred S. Frings (The Hague: Nijhoff, 1987), especially pp. 31 ff.

[27] M. Merleau-Ponty, *Le Visible et l'invisible,* texte établi par Claude Lefort (Paris: Gallimard, 1964), trans. A. Lingis, *The Visible and the Invisible* (Evanston: Northwestern U.P., 1968). Hereafter 'VI' followed by the page number of the English translation and the French original.

Dreams and other phenomena must be scrutinized critically in their apparent givenness, but, the late Merleau-Ponty thinks, the ambiguous existential structures and processes in which we live in the world are not somehow 'behind' the phenomena (as in Freud) but *between* them (VI, p. 232; 281). The flow of experiences that Husserl described does not unfold solely in the present but in a landscape that is a 'field of being' (*champ d'être*, VI, p. 240; 289). As Merleau-Ponty puts it: 'The "associations" of psychoanalysis are in reality "rays" of time and of the world' (VI, p. 240; 289). In his view the phenomenon of temporality – and the peculiar indefinite pastness of the time of the unconscious – needs to be revisited (VI, p. 243; 291–92).

Following Merleau-Ponty, the phenomenologist and psychiatrist Thomas Fuchs suggests that, if the unconscious is considered more as a horizon of conscious life rather than as a depth below it, then the concept of the unconscious can be successfully accommodated within Husserlian phenomenology. In fact, Fuchs speaks of the unconscious as a '*horizontal* dimension of the lived body, lived space and intercorporeality'.[28] This seems to be consistent with Husserl's own approach. In fact, Husserl considers his discovery of 'horizon-intentionality' to be one of his most original contributions to consciousness studies.

In contrast to the writings of Husserl, Martin Heidegger's work did directly stimulate a vigorous encounter between hermeneutical phenomenology and psychoanalysis, both in terms of the existential phenomenological psychology as well as in terms of the Lacanian approach which is heavily dependent on Heidegger's conception of language. Inspired by Martin Heidegger's *Being and Time* in 1927, a new existential phenomenological analysis – *Daseinsanalyse* – was developed by Ludwig Binswanger (a life-long friend of Freud),[29] Medard Boss,[30] and others, which emphasised human spatial and temporal locatedness, mood and attunement (*Stimmung*) as part of an overall structure of 'being-in-the-world' (*In-der-Welt-Sein*). This form of analysis involved detailed exploration of phenomena such as dream, anxiety, depression (melancholia), trauma, and so on, but within the context of the person's overall modality of existing in the world (including, crucially, the manner in which the person experienced temporality).[31] Ironically, Heidegger himself, much later, in his Zollikon seminars with Boss, criticized this *Daseinsanalyse*

---

[28] Thomas Fuchs, 'Body Memory and the Unconscious', in Dieter Lohmar and Jagna Brudzínska, eds, *Founding Psychoanalysis Phenomenologically*, Phaenomenologica 199 (Dordrecht: Springer, 2012), pp. 69–82.

[29] See Ludwig Binswanger, *Die Bedeutung der Daseinsanalytik Martin Heideggers für das Selbstverständnis der Psychiatrie*, in Carlos Estrada et al., eds, *Martin Heideggers Einfluss auf die Wissenschaften* (Berne, 1949), pp. 58–72.

[30] See Medard Boss, *Psychoanalysis and Daseinsanalysis*, trans. Ludwig Lefebre (New York: Basic Books, 1982).

[31] See Ludwig Binswanger, *Melancholie und Manie: Phänomenologische Studien* (Pfullingen: Neske, 1960). See also Stefano Micali, *Überschüsse der Erfahrung, Grenzdimensionen des Ich nach Husserl* (Dordrecht: Springer, 2008).

for focusing solely on being-in-the-world and ignoring the larger issue of the 'understanding of Being' (*Seinsverständnis*).[32]

In these seminars, Heidegger maintained a distance from the Freudian concept of the unconscious and maintained that human concealment (the parallel of Freud's repression) is actually a form of manifestation and dwelling in the 'clearing' (*die Lichtung*).[33] In this regard, Heidegger's position is not that different from Husserl's (and Fink's). Heidegger, for instance, points out that although a child and an old person may both live in the same present, their 'presencing' of that temporal present is not the same. The child is more forward-facing and futural, whereas the old person dwells in 'having-been-ness'.[34] These temporal differences are not immediately obvious but can be disclosed. As Merleau-Ponty had also pointed out, the designation of events in the unconscious as somehow in a 'past' that was never present is exceptionally problematic and needs careful reframing in terms of the 'ecstatic' character of human existence.

In post-war France, furthermore, the existential phenomenological descriptions of human existence found in the writings of Jean-Paul Sartre[35] brought phenomenology into dialogical confrontation with classical Freudian psychoanalysis Sartre rejected the Freudian conception of the 'id', the 'censor' and what he regarded as the mechanistic languages of hidden drives and affirmed human capacity for freedom. Sartre thought, however, that a new kind of existential psychoanalysis could be developed that was based not on early sexual experiences and traumas but on original choices ('project') made by individuals.[36]

Soon after, Jacques Lacan (1901–1981) integrated phenomenological insights concerning the nature of language from the late Heidegger (and also Merleau-Ponty) into his revision of Freudian psychoanalysis (his *retour à Freud*) with his famous pronouncement that the unconscious is structured like a language.[37] In these

---

[32] M. Heidegger, *Zollikon Seminars. Protocols–Conversations–Letters*, ed. Medard Boss, trans. Fritz Mayr and Richard Askay (Evanston, IL: Northwestern University Press, 2001), pp. 188–195.

[33] M. Heidegger, *Zollikon Seminars*, op. cit., pp. 182–83.

[34] Heidegger, *Zollikon Seminars*, op. cit., p. 183.

[35] Jean-Paul Sartre criticizes Freud's conception of the censor and his mechanistic way of treating self-deception or 'bad faith' (*mauvaise foi*) in *L'être et le néant. Essai d'ontologie phénoménologique* (Paris: Gallimard, 1943), trans. Hazel Barnes, *Being and Nothingness. An Essay on Phenomenological Ontology* (London: Routledge, 1995), see especially, p. 53. For Sartre, the Freudian accounts involving the unconscious masks the genuine double-sidedness of consciousness in bad faith. See Jerome Neu, 'Divided Minds: Sartre's "Bad Faith" Critique of Freud', *The Review of Metaphysics* Vol. 42, No. 1 (Sept., 1988), pp. 79–101 and Ivan Soll, 'Sartre's Rejection of the Freudian Unconscious', in *The Philosophy of Jean-Paul Sartre*, ed. Paul Arthur Schilpp (La Salle, IL: Open Court, The Library of Living Philosophers, 1981), and Jonathan Webber, 'Bad Faith and the Unconscious', *The International Encyclopaedia of Ethics*, ed. Hugh LaFolette, John Diegh, and Sarah Stroud (Wiley-Blackwell, 2012).

[36] See Jean-Paul Sartre, *Existential Psychoanalysis,* trans. Hazel E. Barnes (New York: Philosophical Library, 1953).

[37] For Merleau-Ponty's relation to Jacques Lacan, see James Phillips, 'Lacan and Merleau-Ponty: The Confrontation of Psychoanalysis and Phenomenology', in David Pettigrew and François Raffoul, eds, *Disseminating Lacan* (Albany, NY: SUNY Press, 1996), pp. 69–106. For the

rich post-war explorations, the work of Edmund Husserl (apart from the scattered musings in the late Merleau-Ponty's unfinished *Notes de cours* that we have already discussed), as opposed to Heidegger, was largely ignored.[38]

Of course, in classical Freudian psychoanalysis, as Eugen Fink had recognized, the unconscious as such is not accessible in itself through conscious reflection, it is 'latent' in Freud's term,[39] and it is detected only as it manifests itself in its irruptions *in* consciousness, in dreams, obsessions, repetitive actions, fixed attitudes, associations, neuroses, and so on. This led Freud to focus on phenomena in conscious life, such as slips of the tongue, dreams, delusions, random associations, and regressive phenomena, that somehow are revelatory of deeply buried suppressed trauma and drives.[40] It is true that the concept of anxiety (*Angst*) as explored in Heidegger's phenomenology – and the developments by Binswanger, Boss, and others – are more usually associated with psychoanalytic explorations than with Husserlian phenomenology. But there is plenty of scope within Husserl also for exploring the region of the 'unconscious' (*das Unbewusste*) understood in part as encompassing the horizons around the waking, conscious ego, as we shall now explore.

Consistent with Freud, Husserl sees life as involving a more or less unconscious, instinctive 'striving' (*Leben ist Streben* is a familiar Husserlian refrain, cf. Hua XV 408)[41] towards goals and the fulfilment of intentions. Both have a conception of human life as the harmonization or balancing of conflicting forces. In agreement with nineteenth-century biology, Husserl thinks that the most basic drive of consciousness is towards living itself: 'being is self-preservation' (*Sein ist*

Heidegger/Lacan relation, see William Richardson, 'Psychoanalysis and the Being-Question', in *Interpreting Lacan*, ed. Joseph H. Smith and William Kerrigan (New Haven: Yale University Press, 1983). For the relation between Husserl and Lacan, see 'Edmund Husserl and Jacques Lacan: An Ethical Difference in Epistemology?' in D. Lohmar and J. Brudzínska, eds, *Founding Psychoanalysis Phenomenologically*, Phaenomenologica 199 (Dordrecht: Springer, 2012), pp. 133–147.

[38] The focus has largely been on the relation between Merleau-Ponty and Lacan, see David Michael Levin, 'A Responsive Voice: Language without the Modern Subject' *Chiasmi International* vol. 1 (1999), pp. 65–102, and Rudolf Bernet, 'The Phenomenon of the Gaze in Merleau-Ponty and Lacan', *Chiasmi International* vol. 1 (1999), pp. 105–118.

[39] See in particular, Sigmund Freud, 'The Unconscious' (1915), in *Complete Psychological Works of Sigmund Freud*. Vol 14. *On the History of the Psycho-Analytic Movement, Papers on Metapsychology and Other Works* (1914–1916), trans. James Strachey (London: Penguin, 2001), pp. 159–216. In this essay Freud discusses whether an unconscious presentation (*Vorstellung*) can again become conscious under a new 'registration' from a conscious act, employing much the same terminology (presentations, acts) as the school of Brentano.

[40] Rudolf Bernet, 'Unconscious Consciousness in Husserl and Freud', *Phenomenology and the Cognitive Sciences* (2002), pp. 327–351; reprinted in D. Welton, ed., *The New Husserl. A Critical Reader*, op. cit, and idem, 'The Unconscious Between Representation and Drive: Freud, Husserl, and Schopenhauer', in: John J. Drummond and James G. Hart, eds, *The Truthful and the Good. Essays in Honor of Robert Sokolowski,* Contributions to Phenomenology 23 (Dordrecht: Kluwer Academic Publishers, 1996), pp. 81–95.

[41] E. Husserl, *Zur Phänomenologie der Intersubjektivität. Texte aus dem Nachlass. Dritter Teil. 1929–1935*, ed. Iso Kern, Husserliana XV (The Hague: Nijhoff, 1973). Hereafter 'Hua XV' and page number.

Selbsterhaltung, Hua XV 367). Moreover, although this striving is endless and coincides with life itself, the *satisfaction* of drives is necessarily temporal, transitory and limited. Hunger is satisfied in the short term but it returns. Furthermore, there are drives on many different levels, and on the higher levels new goals are identified. It is possible to satisfy drives either with actual fulfilment or with fantasy fulfilment.

Husserl too talks about 'instincts' (*Instinkte*), 'drives' (*Triebe*), 'tendencies' (*Tendenzen*), and of being in the grip of moods such as anger, grief, joy, and so on, and analyses what happens in fantasy, dreaming and states of 'dark' or confused consciousness. Husserl tends to identify drives and instincts.[42] He thought of instincts as intentions that arise without the mediation of consciousness or deliberation and which form a network of habit (he even speaks of 'drive habitualities', *Triebhabitualitäten*, Hua XV 148). Husserl's own use is very broad and it is clear that he is somewhat uncomfortable with the terminology itself as he often puts the word 'drives' (*Triebe*) in quotation marks.

Indeed, the topic of instinct was commonplace late nineteenth-century German psychology and could also be found in the discussions around the evolutionary theories of Charles Darwin and other biologists, as well as in the psychology of Theodor Lipps, Max Scheler, Edith Stein, and others. The Munich philosopher and psychologist Theodor Lipps (whose work was influential on *both* Freud and Husserl), for instance, maintained that humans had a basic instinct to express themselves through their bodily actions and also to imitate others (this was the basis of empathy).[43] There is a drive towards life-expression or the communication of inner processes through bodily processes and a drive to external imitation. Lipps thought these instincts could not be further clarified; he called them 'the unclarifiable instincts (*Die "unerklärlichen Instinkte"*). Lipps gave an important lecture in August 1896 entitled "The Concept of the Unconscious in Psychology," at the Third International Congress of Psychology where he presented the problem of the unconscious as *the* central problem of psychology, a position similar to that of Freud, although it is unclear if Freud and Lipps ever met, albeit Freud credited Lipps for his insights.[44]

In his critique of Lipps, Husserl takes this postulation of instincts to be, as he puts it, a 'refuge of phenomenological ignorance' (Hua XIII 2).[45] Husserl briskly declares: 'I cannot work with unclarifiable instincts' (*Mit unerklärlichen Instinkten*

---

[42] See Nam-In Lee, *Edmund Husserls Phänomenologie des Instinkte* (Dordrecht: Kluwer, 1993). Even in Freud the terminology is confused as '*Trieb*' is translated into English as 'instinct' by James Strachey, as Lacan has noted, see Jacques Lacan, *The Four Fundamental Concepts of Psychoanalysis*, trans. Alan Sheridan (London: Penguin, 1994) p. 49.

[43] On Lipps' influence in terms of psychoanalysis, see especially Günther Gödde, "Berührungspunkte zwischen der "Philosophie" Freuds und der Phänomenologie," in Dieter Lohmar and Jagna Brudzinska, eds, *Founding Psychoanalysis Phenomenologically: Phenomenological Theory of Subjectivity and the Psychoanalytic Experience* ~(Dordrecht: Springer, 2011), pp. 105–131.

[44] See D. L. Smith, *Freud's Philosophy of the Unconscious* (Dordrecht: Springer, 2013), pp. 16–18. Freud credits Lipps for his concept of the unconscious – in letters to Fliess in 1896 and again in his *Interpretation of Dreams*.

[45] E. Husserl, *Zur Phänomenologie der Intersubjektivität. Texte aus dem Nachlass. Erster Teil. 1905–1920*, hrsg. I. Kern, Hua XIII (The Hague: Nijhoff, 1973). Hereafter 'Hua XIII'.

kann ich nicht operieren, Hua XIII 242). Husserl has a very broad concept of instinct, as is made clear in a newly published Husserliana volume,[46] that gathers a great deal of new material on the unconscious.[47] Rochus Sowa and Thomas Vongehr have written in their Editors' Introduction to this Husserliana volume:

> The word 'instinct', furthermore, is employed by Husserl, as he himself says, "in an unusually broad sense." It signifies "every drive intention, which is not originally revealed in its sense. Instincts in the narrower, "in the ordinary sense" are those drives or drive intentions that refer "to distant, originally hidden objectives' and serve the preservation of the species, or of the self-preservation of the individual. (Hua XLII xlviii)[48]

Husserl speaks frequently of the 'blindness' of instincts. There are different kinds of hunger, e.g. hunger for nourishment, hunger for sex (Husserl does not make the libidinal drive to be most basic – for him the primary drive is a drive to existence, to life).[49] But he also speaks of simple tendencies or directions of interest that are 'given' contingently – one is attracted to a particular color, taste or sound. The instincts are experienced as sensuously felt. The sensuous field is already pervaded with 'instincts or tendencies' (Hua IV 337). Husserl's favourite example of a sensuous drive is the desire to smoke (Hua IV 338), which may affect one without coming to conscious awareness. Husserl writes:

> But at best it is the Ego thought of as purely passive which is mere nature and belongs within the nexus of nature. But not the Ego of freedom.
> However mere nature is the entirety of the "mechanical I-do" [*mechanische Ich-tue*]. There arises some sensuous drive [*Trieb*] for example the urge to smoke. I reach for a cigar and light it up, whereas my attention, my Ego-activities, indeed my being affected consciously, are entirely somewhere else: thoughts are stimulating me. I am following them up. ... Here we have "unconscious" Ego-affections and reactions. (*Ideas* II, 349; Hua IV 338)

This is the level of unconscious affection and reaction for Husserl.

Husserl talks tentatively about the first stream of experiences as including certain parts that stand out and which draw the attention of the ego through what Husserl calls *Reiz*, 'affective allure', 'stimulus' (*Ideas* II, Hua IV 189) – a bright light, a sudden noise, a pattern of colour, something awakes the attention of the ego. I yield

---

[46] See E. Husserl, *Grenzprobleme der Phänomenologie, Analysen des Unbewusstseins und der Instinkte. Metaphysik. Späte Ethik. Texte aus dem Nachlass 1908–1937*, Hua XLII, op. cit.

[47] See James Mensch, 'Instincts – an Husserlian account', *Husserl Studies* 14 (1997), pp. 219–237 and Nam-In Lee, *Husserls Phänomenologie der Instinkte*, Phaenomenologica 128 (Dordrecht: Springer, 1993). See also, Nicholas Smith, 'Indirect Clarification: The Drives', in his *Towards a Phenomenology of Repression*, op. cit., pp. 253–304.

[48] Husserl: 'Das Wort „Instinkt" wird also von Husserl, wie er selbst sagt, „in ungewöhnlich weitem Sinn" gebraucht; es bezeichnet „jede Triebintention, die ursprünglich noch nicht enthüllt ist in ihrem Sinn "Instinkte im engeren, „im gewöhnlichen Sinn" sind jene Triebe oder Triebintentionen, die sich auf „auf ferne, ursprünglich verborgene Ziele "beziehen und der Erhaltung der Art bzw. der Selbsterhaltung des Individuums dienen', in Husserl, *Grenzprobleme der Phänomenologie, Analysen des Unbewusstseins und der Instinkte*, op. cit., p. xlviii.

[49] For Husserl's discussion of love, see Hua XIV 172–175.

to the allure of the object- – there is a peculiar pull of an object on the ego. This works on the level of pleasure and displeasure. I am attracted to a song on the radio; I turn away from an unpleasant smell; I shiver from the cold, I bask in the sunshine. In this case, there is a great zone than is shared with similar kinds of animality.

The stream of experience, for Husserl, is given to conscious awareness as already self-organised, unified and 'harmonious'. One sees (without conscious effort) the organised *pattern* on the carpet, the regularity of tiles on the wall, the patchwork of colour in the sky. One feels the *continuous, on-going and pervasive* warmth of the day. The ego, for Husserl, is 'awakened' to these stimuli or allures and responds to them (roughly in Brentanian terms) as either being attracted or repulsed. I find myself drawn to looking *admiringly* at the blue sky and can bask in this looking without further attitudinal stances supervening. Sensory experiences in themselves can be pleasant and be appreciated in and of themselves (scratching an itch) but they are also enfolded into more complex states with differing degrees of significance.

There is already at this basic level, for Husserl, – as every mother will recognise – already a high degree of idiosyncrasy in the make-up of the individual ego. One baby will like loud noises or like to be bounced up and down, another prefers to be held closely, and is timid in relation to sudden noises. These initial 'tendencies' (*Tendenzen*, Hua IV 189) or 'originary instincts' (*Urtriebe*, *Urinstinkte*) can develop and be embraced in later life. Adult sexual and other desires have their origin or at least their configuration and material contours already in this early life (Freud here talks primarily – as Scheler points out – of the manner in which these early drives get distorted). A baby will want to be cocooned, cuddled, or bounced, and each will have his or her own unique 'peculiarity' (*Eigenart*). These will be taken up, modified and transformed in adult social and sexual relations through various kinds of acculturation and sedimentation and not necessarily due to mechanisms of repression and sublimation.

It would be a fruitless exercise to try to find in Husserl analogues of all the key Freudian notions (both discuss 'instincts' and 'drives' and do not sharply distinguish between them – although instincts generally are seen to belong more to biological animal nature), and the matter is further complicated by Freud's evolving conception of drives.[50] For instance, Husserl does not have a specific concept of 'repression' as such, but he does have the concept of 'sedimentation' (*Sedimentation*, *Sedimentierung*), and of patterns of intentional behaviour that have 'sunk down', through habituation, so as to be unnoticed or 'unremarked' (*unbewusst*).[51] Thus in

---

[50] See the entry "Instinct (or Drive)," in Jean Laplanche and Jean-Bertrand Pontalis, *The Language of Psycho-analysis* (London: Karnac, 1988), pp. 214 ff.

[51] See Talia Welsh, 'The Retentional and the Repressed: Does Freud's Concept of the Unconscious Threaten Husserlian Phenomenology?' The Retentional and the Repressed: Does Freud's Concept of the Unconscious Threaten Husserlian Phenomenology? *Human Studies* Vol. 25, No. 2 (2002), pp. 165–183; and Nicholas Smith, *Towards a Phenomenology of Repression—A Husserlian Reply to the Freudian Challenge*, passim.

Experience and Judgment,[52] Husserl speaks of judgments as involving repetitions of other judgments although they do not have to be explicit 'memorial sedimentations' (*Erinnerungsniederschläge*, EU § 5, p. 23; 16). Husserl claims that sedimentations are not immediately accessible to consciousness. He writes of the necessity for a 'retrogression to a hidden subjectivity' (*Rückgang auf eine verhüllte Subjektivität*, EU § 11, p. 48; 47) through a specific kind of dismantling or 'unbuilding':

> It is necessary to dismantle [*Abbau*] everything which already pre-exists in the sedimentations of sense [*Sinnesniederschlägen*] in the world of our present experience, to interrogate [*Zurückfragen*] these sedimentations relative to the subjective sources out of which they have developed and, consequently, relative to an effective subjectivity. (Husserl, EU § 11, p. 48; 47)

This method of uncovering sedimented judgements through a backward questioning and dismantling of conscious complexes surely can be considered as something akin to the understanding of repression in Freud (without Freud's mechanistic, causal language). In general, furthermore, Husserl has little to say of trauma and pathological states since he is primarily interested in the constitution of 'normality' (*Normalität*).[53] The experience of death, however, is discussed by Husserl in terms of a constantly experienced threat of the disruption of future plans (Hua XXVII 69) against the backdrop of the continuous flow of experienced time.[54]

The mature Husserl, then, did not believe all aspects of intentional life can be brought to the forefront of consciousness as if they were illuminated by a Cartesian ray of awareness and incorporated into the ego as part of its own intentional acts. Quite the reverse: For Husserl, generally speaking, consciousness of the present is surrounded by horizons of consciousness of the past that is no longer, the projected and imagined future, the possible, the wished for, the feared. The person is made up of a conscious 'egoic centre' and what can be envisaged as a widening set of overlapping horizons that include fantasized selves and modifications of selves (dream personae and so on).

It is clear that Husserl became more interested in the 'unconscious' (in his broad sense) in the early 1930s when he began to group a number of problems under the

---

[52] E. Husserl, *Erfahrung und Urteil. Untersuchungen zur Genealogie der Logik*, ed. Ludwig Landgrebe (Prague: Academia-Verlag, 1938; 7th edition, Hamburg: Felix Meiner, 1999), trans. J.S. Churchill and K. Ameriks, *Experience and Judgment: Investigations in a Genealogy of Logic* (London: Routledge and Kegan Paul, 1973). Hereafter 'EU' followed by the pagination of English translation and then German.

[53] See Sara Heinämaa, 'Transcendental Intersubjectivity and Normality: Constitution by Mortals', in *The Phenomenology of Embodied Subjectivity*, ed. Dermot Moran and Rasmus Thybo Jensen, Contributions to Phenomenology Series (Dordrecht: Springer, 2014), pp. 83–103.

[54] Sometimes, Heidegger's account of finitude and authentic being towards one's own death is contrasted with Husserl's account that claims that the transcendental ego is immortal and that it is impossible to experience any 'final' moment in time. But the issue is more complex and Husserl acknowledges the humans can experience the possibility of death as a disruption. See Sara Heinämaa, 'Threat, Limit, Culture: Phenomenological Insights into Human Death', in *Mortality and Death: From Individual to Communal Perspective*, ed. Outi Hakola, Sara Heinämaa, and Sami Pihlström, Collegium Studies Across Disciplines in the Humanities and Social Sciences (Helsinki: Helsinki Collegium for Advanced Studies, 2015).

1 Husserl's Layered Concept of the Human Person: Conscious and Unconscious

title of what he called 'limit problems' (*Limesprobleme*) or 'marginal problems' (*Randprobleme*), among them are the challenges of understanding birth, death and the afterlife. In a text from 1930 (Hua XV 608) Husserl writes:

> The unconscious, the sedimented unground of consciousness, dreamless sleep, the form of birth of subjectivity, respectively, the problematic being of birth, death and 'life after death'.[55]

These are all phenomena that bound or border personal, 'egoic' conscious life.

The mature Husserlian phenomenology has an overall project of understanding how the unified flow of 'conscious life' (*Bewusstseinsleben*) hangs together and integrates into a seamless yet temporally streaming unity, and interweaves with other conscious 'egoic' (first-personal) streams to create intersubjective cultural life, what Husserl, following Dilthey and German Idealism, calls 'the life of spirit'. Husserl is often mistakenly characterized – largely because of his own deliberate starting point – as a Cartesian who seeks to establish all reality and other minds on the basis of the ego's own constituting activities. But Husserl also sees that the constituting ego actually functions in an open-ended plurality of other egos – past, present, future, possible – that he calls, borrowing from Leibniz, 'the community of monads' (*Monadengemeinschaft*).[56] The ego is constituted or constitutes itself as a social entity, as what Husserl calls a '*Socius*', a member of a social and cultural *Mitwelt,* which is constituted through the complex interweaving and coinciding of individual and collective intentionalities, in what Husserl calls *Ineinandersein*.[57] As Husserl elaborates:

> Just as each ego, each monad, is concretely named substance, but only in relative concreteness, it is what it is only as a citizen of a sociality, as a 'member of a community' in a total community.[58]

When Husserl speaks of the 'person' (as he does primarily in *Ideas* II, in the *Kaizo* articles[59] and in his lectures on ethics) he is primarily thinking of the mature, adult, rational self – the self that acts and is motivated by reasons and is involved with

---

[55] 'Das Unbewusste, der sedimentierte Untergrund des Bewusstseins, der traumlose Schlaf, die Geburtsgestalt der Subjektivität bzw. Das problematische Sein vor der Geburt, der Tod und das „nach dem Tode", Hua XV 608.

[56] E. Husserl, *Cartesianische Meditationen und Pariser Vorträg,* ed. Stephan Strasser, Husserliana I (The Hague: Nijhoff, 1950), trans. Dorion Cairns, *Cartesian Meditations* (The Hague: Nijhoff, 1967), § 49.

[57] See Dermot Moran, "*Ineinandersein* and *l'interlacs*: The Constitution of the Social World or 'We-World' (*Wir-Welt*) in Edmund Husserl and Maurice Merleau-Ponty," in Dermot Moran and Thomas Szanto, eds, *Discovering the We: The Phenomenology of Sociality* (London & New York: Routledge 2015).

[58] Husserl: Ebenso ist jedes *ego,* jede Monade konkret genommen Substanz, aber nur relative Konkretion, sie ist, was sie ist, nur als *socius* einer Sozialität, als „Gemeinschaftsglied" in einer Totalgemeinschaft, Hua XV 193.

[59] Husserl 1923/1924 Kaizo articles on ethical renewal (*Erneuerung*) are reprinted in E. Husserl, *Aufsätze und Vorträge 1922–1937,* ed. Thomas Nenon and Hans Rainer Sepp, Hua XXVII (Dordrecht: Kluwer, 1989), pp. 2–94.

others in cooperative social and cultural activity in a shared life-world.[60] Husserl begins from the mature adult in normal social relations, a social agent who belongs to a speech- and 'communications-community' (*Mitteilungsgemeinschaft* – Husserl's word later adapted by Jürgen Habermas).

Overall, the mature Husserl has a very complex and nuanced account of the concrete human person. The person is first and foremost a *unity*; and Husserl speaks of the 'unity of personhood' (*Einheit der Persönlichkeit*, Hua XIII 244).[61] Already in 1905 Husserl writes in notes collected in the *Intersubjectivity* volume (Husserliana XIII):

> Naturally personhood – just like the substance of a thing – is not a phenomenologically pre-given datum; it is rather a "unity in the manifold", a unity of validity, not a phenomenological moment [distinguishable part]. (Hua XIII 2).[62]

Furthermore, the person has properties in a completely different sense than a physical thing. The self has 'acts' which no physical thing has in the same sense (Hua XIII 244); it establishes itself through its specifically egoic acts – its decisions, its judgments, its stances. Husserl typically conceives of the human person in traditional Cartesian, and more specifically, in Kantian terms as a free, rational agent, defined primarily by its explicit position-takings, i.e. its judgments, decisions, willings, desires, convictions, value-takings, and other acts, which it defines as specifically personal or 'egoic' (*ichlich*) rather than merely occurring in the self as 'ego-belonging' (*ich-zuhörig*).

At the same time, there is of course an extremely important aspect of the human self that is located in nature, is embodied, subject to natural forces and has an entire psycho-physical constitution. In 1910 Husserl is clear that what he calls here the 'empirical human subject', the 'human-I' (*Menschen-Ich*) belongs to nature and his or her actions, thoughts, etc., are part of the nature. He writes

> The ego is the human ego in the nexus of nature [*im Naturzusammenhang*]. The acts are real natural events belonging to humans and psychophysically to the human lived body, real states of the human being, etc. Objective world-nature-research. Real causal networks.[63]

---

[60] The term 'person' was widely in use among phenomenologists, especially by Max Scheler and Edith Stein. Husserl associates personhood specifically with 'position-takings' (*Stellungsnahme*, see E. Husserl, *Zur Phänomenologie der Intersubjektivität. Texte aus dem Nachlass. Zweiter Teil. 1921–1928*, ed. I. Kern, Husserliana XIV (The Hague: Nijhoff, 1973), p. 196). For a broad and illuminating discussion, see James G. Hart, *The Person and the Common Life. Studies in a Husserlian Social Ethics*, Phaenomenologica 126 (Dordrecht: Kluwer, 1992), esp. pp. 52–75.

[61] I prefer to translate Husserl's *Persönlichkeit* as 'person' rather than 'personality', which is misleading in this context given the connotations from social and behavioural psychology. See Dermot Moran, 'Defending the Transcendental Attitude: Husserl's Concept of the Person and the Challenges of Naturalism', *Phenomenology and Mind* (2014), pp. 37–55.

[62] Husserl, 'Natürlich ist die Persönlichkeit, so wie die Substanz der Dinge, kein phänomenologisch vorfindliches Datum, es ist ja „Einheit in der Mannigfaltigkeit", Geltungseinheit, nicht phänomenologisches Moment' (Hua XIII 2).

[63] Husserl, 'Das Ich ist Menschen-Ich im Naturzusammenhang. Die Akte sind real zum Menschen und psychophysisch zum Menschenleib gehörige Naturvorkommnisse, reale Zustande des Menschen etc. Objektive Welt-Natur-Forschung. Real-kausale Zusammenhänge' (Hua XIII 245).

This physico-psychic dimension of the human self is shared with other animals. It is our distinctive animality, responses to heat and cold, nervousness, alertness in the face of danger, so called 'fight or flight' responses, experiences of hunger, thirst, fear, and so on. But, for Husserl, in human beings, higher self-conscious states can always reach down and modify or take a stance towards these lower 'animal' states. For Husserl, the ego is that which 'governs' or 'holds sway' (*waltet*) over our other responses. Thus the experience of hunger can be sensually or meaningfully intentionally configured in conscious experience as a desire to eat something specific such as *Italian pasta* or a *Chinese stir-fry*. Cultural predicates take up, overlay, and sublate the 'natural' tendencies so that, in the end, all experiences are culturally constituted. As we have seen, Husserl thinks of instincts as natural feelings such as hunger, desire for sex, fear (*Die instinktive Furcht*, Hua XXXIX 316), avoidance of pain, pleasure seeking, and so on. But he is insistent on the difference between an undifferentiated instinct, a desire for food, for satiety, and a more determinate 'humanised' longing that might be a longing for a particular food, for not just any drink buy a coffee, and so on. Husserl also acknowledges that humans are autonomous reasoners, motivated not just by nature but by spiritual values that motivate them:

> In original genesis, the personal Ego is constituted not only as a person determined by *drives* [*Triebe*], from the very outset and incessantly driven by *original "instincts"* and passively submitting to them, but *also as a higher autonomous, freely acting* Ego, In particular one guided by *rational motives,* and not one that is merely dragged along and unfree. (*Ideas* II §59, p. 267; IV 255)

Husserl's placing of the term 'instincts' in inverted commas suggests that he is simply invoking the then current concept of instincts and not necessarily endorsing either the Freudian or the Darwinian accounts.

Furthermore, at this level, the ego identifies what is egoic and what belongs to what Husserl calls 'the non-ego' (*das Nicht-Ich*). Experiences are experienced as intimate or less intimate, as 'near' or 'far' from the ego:

> In many cases we speak of near-the-I [*Ichnähe*] and distant-from-the-I [*Ichferne*], or the I may be encountered in the deepest depths or it can be encountered superficially, it has inner interest or only more external and the like. In each case this points to phenomenological distinctions: is the I, is the pure ego overall something identical and are the characteristics of this ego denoted in the cogito?[64]

The domain of the ego is to be contrasted with its always accompanying domain of the 'not-I' (*Ideas* II § 54; see Hua XIII 244).

For the mature Husserl, the pure ego is more than an 'I-pole' *(Ichpol)*, a purely formal principle of unity of the flow of experiences. He came to recognize that the ego *has a history*, and evolves: 'The Ego always lives in the medium of its "history"'

---

[64] Husserl, 'In manchen Fällen sprechen wir von Ichnähe und Ichferne, oder das Ich sei in der tiefsten Tiefe betroffen oder es werde nur oberflächlich betroffen, es habe inneren Anteil oder nur mehr äusserlichen und dgl. In jedem Fall weist dergleichen auf phänomenologische Unterschiede hin: Ist das Ich, ist ein reines Ich überall ein identisches, und <sind> Eigentümlichkeiten dieses Ich im *cogito* damit bezeichnet?', (Hua XIII 248).

(*Ideas* II, p. 350; Hua IV 338). It accrues abiding characteristics and a 'habitus' (*Habitus, Hexis*)[65]:

> The I as the I of personal convictions, intentions, decisions, actions, and these things as a kind of identical objectivities. Convictions that remain, etc. The personal I as its subject. Hexis and Having (Hua XIII 400).[66]

Husserl recognizes that these habits, convictions and permanent characteristics determine the ego – not in a causal sense – but in terms of giving it a style and an openness to certain kinds of motivations but not to others. The area of response to motivation is very complex and multifaceted but motivations have their own intrinsic 'sense'.

On the other hand, Husserl always insists that the 'spiritual ego' (*geistiges Ich*), as he calls it, has a priority, and a certain distance both from the physical world and from the body. In his overall mature phenomenology it is clear that Husserl really begins from the full concrete person as a mature self-conscious rational being who is a member of a community and who understands him or herself and others in what Husserl calls 'the personalistic attitude' which is foregrounded in *Ideas* II but which earlier appears as 'the subjective attitude' (*die subjective Einstellung*, Hua XIII 91). But, persons do not act in isolation from their context. They have certain 'intellectual and moral dispositions' (*Dispositionen*, XIII 119). Persons also have their individual 'peculiarities' on many levels:

> I do have *my peculiarities* [*meine Eigenart*], my way of moving, of doing things, my individual evaluations. My own way of preferring, my temptations, and my power of conquering certain kinds of temptations against which I am invulnerable. The next person is different, he has different pet motives [*Lieblingsmotive*], other temptations are dangerous for him, he has other spheres in which he exercises his individual powers of action, etc., but within the bounds of the normal [*innerhalb der Normalität*], specifically within what is normal for youth, for age. etc. Within this typicality there are of course idiosyncratic developments: conscious self-education, inner conversion [*inner Umkehr*], transformation through the setting of ethical goals, through exercise, etc. (*Ideas* II § 59, p. 226; IV 254)

This allows for conscious life to be shaped and motivated at all levels by one's individual drives, desires, willings, education, and so on. Thus, Husserl, in *Ideas* II § 61, claims that the personal ego has two 'layers' – a higher, spiritual ego which Husserl calls an *intellectus agens*, which is free and lives in its acts, and a lower self that he characterizes as 'unfree' ands 'dragged down by the sensual':

> The specifically spiritual Ego, the subject of spiritual acts, the person, finds itself dependent on an obscure underlying basis of traits of character, original and latent dispositions [*von einem dunklen Untergrunde von Charakteranlagen, ursprünglichen und verborgenen Dispositionen*], and thereby dependent on nature. (*Ideas* II § 61, p. 289; Hua IV 276)

---

[65] See Dermot Moran, "'The Ego as Substrate of Habitualities': Edmund Husserl's Phenomenology of the Habitual Self," *Phenomenology and Mind*, vol. 6 (July 2014), pp. 27–47; and idem, "Edmund Husserl's Phenomenology of Habituality and Habitus," *Journal of the British Society for Phenomenology*, Vol. 42 no. 1 (January 2011), pp. 53–77.

[66] Husserl, '*Das Ich als Ich personaler Überzeugungen, Meinungen, Entschlüsse, Handlungen, und diese selbst als eine Art identischer Gegenständlichkeiten. Bleibende Überzeugungen etc. (S. 402 fl.). Das personale Ich als ihr Subjekt. Hexis und Habe*', in E. Husserl, *Zur Phänomenologie der Intersubjektivität. Texte aus dem Nachlass. Erster Teil. 1905–1920*, hrsg. I. Kern, Hua XIII (The Hague: Nijhoff, 1973), p. 400.

The relation between the free and unfree aspects of the self is mediated by its embodiment. As Husserl writes, 'every free act has its comets tail of nature' (*jeder freie Akt hat seinen Kometenschweif Natur, Ideas* II, p. 350; IV 338).

At the higher spiritual level, the self is not restrained by its body. Husserl writes in 1910–1911:

> The I about which I judge is therefore not the lived body and it is not the I as such as it is bound to the lived body, it is not that consciousness that exists in a psychophysical connection with nature. Rather the I is this absolutely given complex [*Zusammenhang*] of perceptions, presentations of any kind, feelings, desires, and volitions, exactly as the complex is found in the direct viewing of reflection, of the perceiving reflection, as well as in the reflection in remembering and in other forms of consciousness as well (and not only this complex, but also what is given as taking shape in it, namely the I, the person). It is about this complex, this unified and in this sense "immanent" connection and stream of consciousness, that I want to judge alone and ascertain what can be said in regard to it.[67]

Husserl gives primacy to the notion of the person as a *sum cogitans* (*Ideas* II § 22) which does not primarily apprehend itself as a body – but rather thinks of itself as a free-acting ego which makes decisions, forms independent judgements, moves at will, and so on. As Husserl defines the notion of a spiritual person he sees it as

> ... the Ego that has its place precisely not in a Corporeality [*Leiblichkeit*]; e.g. I "think" (*cogito*), i.e. I perceive, I represent in whatever mode, I judge, I feel, I will, etc., and I find myself thereby as that which is one and the same in the changing of these lived experiences, as "subject" of the acts and states. (*Ideas* II § 22, p. 104; IV 97)

This is, as it were, the apex of the human being and when this ego enters into relations with others (or has always already been in relation with other ego-subjects), it fulfils itself as a spirit or a spiritual being. The spiritual self (the spiritual sphere, *Ideas* II, p. 344; Hua IV 332) and its associated spiritual intentionality are defined by activity – grasping, explicating, predicating, considering the individual under the universal, evaluating:

> All personal "intentionality" refers to activity and has its origin in activities. (*Ideas* II, Supplement XII, p. 344; Hua IV 333)

The spiritual self is a member of a family, a community, a society, a generation. In the wider context the person is embedded in a culture and has a specific historicity. It has its own time – its "generation" which it shares with others and which help to form its identity.

Husserl insists that everything conscious is clustered around an ego, and it is egoic or first-personal all the way down to the first stirrings of conscious life. The infant in the womb has, from a certain point, a stream of felt experiences and bodily movements. These are experienced as a unified stream linked by laws of association. The child's first experience of the other is the voice of its mother – already heard in the womb. For Husserl the mother-child relation is the first social relation and takes place at a very early stage although he does not specify exactly when. The infant ego already

---

[67] E. Husserl, *The Basic Problems of Phenomenology. From the Lectures, Winter Semester, 1910–1911*, trans. Ingo Farin and James Hart (Dordrecht: Springer, 2006), p. 96, translation modified: Hua XIII 82.

has the experience of I and "not-I" and this is determining for it. This structure of I and 'not-I' (*nicht-Ich*) is all pervasive and is constitutive of the very core of the ego.

Furthermore, Husserl thinks that the ego *constitutes itself* just as it constitutes everything else. The ego is constituted in time consciousness which is the ultimate form of constitution- – something must be designated as now and in so doing a 'before' and 'after' is at the same time constituted. In this regard he talks about 'self-temporalisation' (*Zeitigung*) of the ego. The self constitutes itself first by some kind of primitive association and gluing together of time experiences. Association, for Husserl, belongs to the very essence of sensibility:

> Association and reproduction (memory, synthesis, phantasy) belong to sensibility as well. ... Primal sensibility, sensation, etc., does not arise out of immanent grounds, out of psychic tendencies; it is simply there, it emerges. (*Ideas* II, p. 346; Hua IV 335)

The ego itself receives primary impressions in the form of its own flow of experiences, Husserl writes in *Ideas* II § 29 that every act is an impression, a being in inner time and is part of the constitution of inner time itself (*Ideas* II, p. 125; IV 118).

Husserl emphasizes – as Freud does – how humans saturate situations with meaning including imagined intonations and implications. I am bored – what I am doing no longer excites me, I have a feeling of just carrying on, not necessarily developing or advancing or going deeper, perhaps just going through the motions, doing the routines. Husserl emphasises the role of ego in investing these states with meaning and value and being motivated by them in one way or another. There is, undoubtedly, a certain passivity in which I find myself, a psychic energy that is different in each one of us (Edith Stein speaks of this as 'life-power, *Lebenskraft*, in part building on Lipps' notion of "psychic force", *psychische Kraft*).[68] There are feelings and movements of the psyche over which I do not have much control. As Husserl says, quite passively without intervention from the ego, one memory can trigger another (although Husserl, unlike Freud, never considers free association to have methodological import). I am more or less involuntarily drawn to relive the shocking moment – trauma means we cannot break free from this – I reactivate the emotion each time it reappears – and perhaps it can have increasing force rather than decreasing force.

In Husserl's very interesting example, if I bear a grudge against someone then when the grudge reappears I have to be aware that it is the *same* grudge rather than a new feeling of resentment (which may also be there). I have to re-identify the grudge, acknowledge it as the "[same] grudge coming again to givenness" (*Ideas* II, p. 120; IV 113). Another grudge might appear with the same content but it might be a different grudge. Each grudge and sorrow has its own peculiar time span. There is a sense of an ending – our love is over; my anger with you is gone. These grudges become lasting properties of the ego. A conviction or opinion has its 'founding' or 'instauration' (*Stiftung, Ideas* II, p. 120; Hua IV 113). A conviction can also weaken, or break down. But perhaps I restore it and it is now the old-conviction that had

---

[68] Edith Stein, *Beiträge zur philosophischen Begründung der Psychologie und der Geisteswissenschaften, Jahrbuch für Philosophie und phänomenologische Forschung* Vol. 5 (1922), pp. 1–116 esp. p. 71; trans. *Philosophy of Psychology and the Humanities* (Washington, DC: ICS Publications, 2000), especially p. 79.

broken down restored (*Ideas* II §29). Motives can arise to cancel something or amend it or renew it. A conviction can be reinforced; we can find new motives for believing it. Convictions have their "duration" (Hua IV 117). Husserl's account here is multi-faceted. Drives can be owned more or less by the subject; they can be embraced or resisted. I defend my drive to smoke; I assert it as belonging to my person. I can also struggle against it, deny it as essential to my person and seek to cancel or strike it out. For Husserl, the ego is involved with its drives in ways that are more complex that the standard Freudian model suggests.

In conclusion, Husserl's phenomenology of experiential, conscious life recognises its extremely complex textured unity. Even perceptions of objects can be interwoven with dreams, memories, fantasies, recalled fantasies and fantasized memories. These memories/fantasies wrap around the present object and the present act of experiencing. Someone looking at her lover does not see just the bare person in front of her – but the person as disclosed in emotion, love, memory, expectation, fantasy, hope. For Husserl, objective sense-making is correlated to the kinds of syntheses, motivations, harmonizations, and (subjective and intersubjective) horizontal contexts that make up the intentional of the subject. Husserl's account is an extraordinarily rich phenomenological account of the person that contains analyses comparable to psychoanalytic explorations of the unconscious but it is articulated in its own technical language and will need to be reconstituted carefully for a full dialogue between Husserlian phenomenology and Freudian psychoanalysis to be carried out.

Chapter 2
Reflections on the Phenomenological Unconscious in Generative Phenomenology

Alexander Schnell

Abstract In the present contribution, the phenomenological unconscious is approached not in the sense of the psychoanalytic unconscious but on an "infra-conscious" level, below the "given," as it were. I outline a threefold account of the "pre-conscious." The three fundamental types of the phenomenological unconscious (in the narrow sense of the word) are: the genetic phenomenological unconscious, the hypostatic phenomenological unconscious, and the reflexive phenomenological unconscious. I explore how the phenomenological unconscious intervenes in the articulation between consciousness and self-consciousness. It is the Husserlian model of an "omni-intentionality" with its "nuclei" that makes it possible to clarify the status of self-consciousness (at the level of the phenomenological unconscious). I end by highlighting the plurality of fields corresponding to different "spheres" of the phenomenological unconscious.

Keywords Alterity • Architectonic • (Transcendental) field • Genesis • Imagination • Reflexion • Self-consciousness • Sense

---

The expression "generative phenomenology" stems from the work of Anthony Steinbock. Even if there is an overlap in our terminology, there are nevertheless fundamental differences. For Steinbock, "generative" is approached in a literal sense, with a special accent on the difference between "normality" and "abnormality." In my own usage, "generative" refers to a surplus of meaning both beyond and below phenomenology's descriptive framework. In this respect, generativity clarifies our understanding of phenomenology as transcendental insofar as it attends to the genesis of meaning itself. In short, my usage of "generative phenomenology" is distinct from Steinbock in the same respect that the term "constructive phenomenology" is distinct from the thought of Fink.
Translated by Audrey Petit-Trigg

A. Schnell (✉)
University of Wuppertal, Wuppertal, Germany
e-mail: schnell@uni-wuppertal.de

2.1 Introduction

The "unconscious" is, as we know, one of the main concepts of psychoanalysis. In the present chapter, I won't be offering a reflection based on the given concepts of the unconscious, but to analyse the different occurrences and meanings of the unconscious in phenomenology, aiming at clarifying its status (both from an ontological point of view and from the point of view of its relationship to consciousness). Thus, the establishment of the rapport with psychoanalysis is justified from an important methodological point: if the unconscious (in any existing distinction) is defined by its irreducible qualitative difference towards "consciousness" or the "conscious", then the question is, of course, to know what justifies conceding a phenomenological "infra-conscious" level, and how this one behaves towards what is given and manifests itself to consciousness.

The question of the phenomenological unconscious matters in many regards. First of all, the exactitude of its status plays a decisive part in the justification of what cannot be left, precisely in phenomenology, to the sole level of what is given and what is let being described, in order to render the sense of the emerging. The difficulty that this perspective shares indeed with any other that meets the unconscious, is that the fact of declaring this unconscious as *un*conscious could hide a presupposition that we would introduce surreptitiously via exactly this *un*conscious character, and of which the patient emphasis and revelation would orientate massively the analyses. Would the unconscious then constitute a sort of phenomenological Trojan horse?

Such an objection could rely on the idea that the reference to sense singularly orientates the debate. What will be strongly defended here is the idea that this reference to sense, in its link with the unconscious, is precisely the fundamental horizon of transcendental phenomenology. Therefore, we can say that the notion of unconscious, in its phenomenological given, is not at first acquiring, nor even conquering, but rather supports any analysis. To find a direction in the complex meanderings of the phenomenological unconscious we will rely on known distinctions.

In his famous Supplement XXI to Husserl's *Krisis* (see Husserl 1976), Eugen Fink observed that the insufficient theorisations regarding the unconscious are holding onto a profound naïveté may it be towards the unconscious or consciousness. His principal reproach is directed against the idea that consciousness (as much as the unconscious) would be something that is given.

To define more precisely the problems that are at stake here, it would be necessary, first, to remind the different distinctions of "consciousness" in phenomenology (to which, as we will see, correspond different distinctions of the "unconscious"). In the *Fifth Logical Investigation,* Husserl had made a distinction (still employing then a—Brentanien—language, stemming for a sort of descriptive psychology, whereas he actually already clearly aimed at an eidetic phenomenological analysis) between, firstly, consciousness as the whole of *"real"* phenomenological components of the empiric Self as the entanglement (*Verwebung*) of psychological lived experience in the unity of the flux of lived times; secondly, consciousness as the internal becoming aware (*Gewahrwerden*) of the own psychological lived times and, thirdly, consciousness as "psychological act" or as "intentional lived experience". The first distinction presumes the second; the third distinction constitutes a part of what the first includes.

Yet if consciousness is defined by intentionality, the unconscious can only refer, in phenomenology, to a non-intentional dimension of consciousness: this does not concern the components of consciousness that one would inhabit or would apprehend (as, for example, the sensible data), but this underlines non-intentional "participation" (of which we will have to define the status) of consciousness in its relationship to the world. Three directions are indicated here (in response to the distinction made by Husserl): (I). The phenomenological unconscious indicates a character-in-depth (it has a *Feldhaftigkeit*), non-subjective field which, in a certain way, dissociates the consciousness from any subjectivity meaning a Self or an ego. (II). The phenomenological unconscious has a reflexive character, directing consciousness in an internal manner on itself, or, at least, on something that, inside this "depth", is not qualitatively distinct from itself. (III). Finally, the phenomenological unconscious contributes to a relationship of exteriority, it participates to the ecstatic openness to an alterity that presents itself under different types. In short, it appears that the phenomenological unconscious is thus corresponding to a threefold "preconscious" dimension preceding and instituting consciousness in a way.

In what follows, I will question the status of the unconscious in phenomenology through this threefold perspective: with respects to the distinction in between the different levels of depth, with respects to the articulation of the internal consciousness and what this one is conscious of; and with respects to the different types that the unconscious reveals, to what I would call a "phenomenology without phenomenality". What will be at stake, then, is the question of the pre-intentional dimension, or furthermore non-intentional, of the intentionality itself. For reasons justified from an architectonic point of view, I won't follow the arrangement proposed by Husserl, but I will follow the reversed order.

2.2 The Different Types of the Unconscious in Phenomenology

In a general way, the first issue is to know how to access the phenomenological unconscious. In the present set of reflections, I cannot answer directly to this question—and this is due to the very nature of the inquiry. There is a hiatus between what is given in the immanence, on one side, and the unconscious, on the other side; if we could recount this passage, the unconscious would be then reduced to a modality of consciousness. At the same time, not only must there be a certain link between these two registers, or else what is at play in the phenomenological unconscious would not have any impact on consciousness. At the same time, there must also be a certain type of consciousness recognized at the level of this unconscious (and within itself), or else, it could not be accessed. And all the difficulty here is to keep the assurance—which is no other than the loyalty to the phenomena—of not introducing what is related to projections or unfounded constructions.

In which order can this link be? The two classic answers (in the transcendental tradition) are the following. First, it is either an order of "conditioning", or, second, an effect of "residue". In the first case, what is made of this unconscious is only a combination of transcendental conditions that have to be assumed (to recount the phenomena), but that cannot be experienced because they have no sort of reality themselves. In the second case, we consider consciousness like a sort of symptom from which we are going back to its primal and original activity. We will think these two solutions one through the other. The idea of the residue of a constitutive activity only makes sense if we succeed in establishing the type of necessity created there; and the transcendental conditioning can only constitute a convincing approach if we present both the ontological status of transcendental elements and the attachment of the constituted to its transcendental origins.

If consciousness is always consciousness of something, would this mean that the unconscious would be devoid of any noematic correlate? The particularity of the phenomenological unconscious resides in the fact that this correlate is not "given"— but not in the meaning in which something non-thematic could be brought to light thanks to an intentional analytic which would reveal the implicit syntheses at stake in such and such phenomena. This non given-ness refers more to another type of correlation, that is to say a non-intentional correlation. As seen in this way, it is then a matter of clarifying the possibility and the status of such correlate, questioning the irreducible character of the intentionality.

With respects to the definition (or rather the definitions) of consciousness given by Husserl in the *Logical Investigations*, many examples of a "phenomenology of the unconscious" could be quoted. I will only mention three of these here. First, the phenomenology of time of Husserl himself, particularly in the *Bernau's Manuscripts* where the father of phenomenology operates, through his analysis of the *Zeitobjekt*, a disconnection between temporality and objectivity (and therefore between the "time-object" and the objective correlates of the intentionality of action), which necessitates to place oneself beyond the immanent sphere of consciousness (and which I call, to be faithful to the Husserlian terminology, the "pre-immanent" sphere) (Schnell 2004). Second, the Levinasian analyses in *Totality and Infinity* (Levinas 1969) of an "epiphany of the face" which are centred around a manifestation of the alterity which is not a "content" (Levinas means: a sensible content bond to be apprehended by an intentional consciousness), nor an "un-intentionality" of any sort, but involving a destitution which precisely makes any phenomenology of intentionality implode (cf. Schnell 2010). Finally, the Richirian phenomenology of the "phenomenon as nothing but phenomenon" that the author of *Phénomènes, temps et êtres* (Richir 1987), developing his own understanding of transcendental phenomenology, phrases in these terms:

> The transcendental phenomenology takes roots […] in the question of the phenomenon insofar as it is not always already "interpreted" as any other phenomenon but itself (a pre-existing structure, a thing or an object to which correspond determined concepts or ideas),

as a consequence, of the phenomenon considered as *nothing but* phenomenon, where comes out and appears only the phenomenon. [...] Our consideration of the phenomenon as *nothing but* phenomenon, comes down to radicalize the Husserlian phenomenological reduction and to give it a new meaning: what is at stake here is to consider the phenomenon outside (by bracketing or disconnection) of any positivity and any determinity which is not susceptible, for us, to come to it from anywhere and by anywhere, of which it although constitutes [...] the transcendental matrix. (Richir 1987, p. 18)

Even if the terminology will evolve during the three last decades, this project aiming at installing himself in the phenomenological sphere beyond what is given and 'symbolically instituted' characterises definitely Richir's approach in his refoundation of (transcendental) phenomenology (see Schnell 2011).

The genetic phenomenological unconscious I see in these different elaborations (which are in no way exhausting the typology of the phenomenological unconscious) trace a common motive, which I will offer to generalize or, at least, to extend to what I call the "genesis of factuality" operating in a strictly phenomenological frame. One of the first distinctions of the phenomenological unconscious is notified where we transgress or leave the sphere of an "immanent" given. But what is motivating precisely this descent beyond the immanent sphere? Two aspects are decisive here: "objectively" the encounter of originating "facts" that the phenomenologist has to "geneticise" if he or she doesn't want to remain "blocked" in the descriptive analysis; "subjectively", the search for a mode of comprehension and appropriation preventing from the mistake of the "idealistic" and the "realistic," these are phenomena that are not the result of a constitutive consciousness but that we do not yet have to consider as a simple pre-supposed state (and therefore an irreducible fact).

We know that the intentional analysis in Husserl aims at revealing the whole of operations or effectuations of the "transcendental subjectivity" (mainly this is here a matter of syntheses (may they be active and/or passive) that are at play in any consciously rapport. Insofar as these "*fungierende Leistungen*" are not explicitly conscious, but demanding to take on of the phenomenological attitude (consisting of a reflexive attitude, buried, in a way, when we are directing ourselves directly towards an object), does it mean then that it would be here a first modality of the phenomenological unconscious? The answer is negative, because the phenomenological attitude implies a method which reveals these effectuations in an intuitive evidence. These effectuations (including the "intentionality of horizon") are therefore not unconscious, but require a specific stance, allowing descriptions that are re-effectible by everyone.

But this "intuitive evidence" is not expandable to infinity: when we are apprehending "limit situations" of phenomenological description, it can happen to be leading to some impasses. For example, on the level of the constitution of the intimate consciousness of time, evidence doesn't give the legitimating resources to clarify the status of "original constitutive phenomena" and of the immanent temporality. The requirement which is then imposed, to descend beyond the immanent sphere of consciousness opens on a "pre-immanent" field which constitutes a first type of phenomenological unconscious (which is not down to refuse conceding to consciousness the possibility of "appropriating" itself its object, but rather opens on a new type of "appropriation" and "comprehension").

The particularity, which is at the same time a difficulty, cannot rely on anything that is given, but exclusively drawn from a certain negative dimension of the phenomenal content (for example: the originary temporality is *not* subjective, because this would lead to a regression to infinity, *nor* objective, because this would come down to a petition of principle). This "negativity" doesn't give room to a "nothing", but establishes exactly a link between (immanent) "consciousness" and what is possible to draw "beyond" it—and constitutes there precisely the fundamental characteristic of this first type of phenomenological unconscious (which I call the "genetic phenomenological unconscious"[1]).

2.3 The Hypostatic Phenomenological Unconscious

The "genetic phenomenological unconscious" is not submitted to a universal regulation; it discovers its legality in the genesis itself (which is different each time, depending on the considered objects) and therefore has a fundamental tendency towards mobility, diversity, and change. It reveals the share of fluctuation and of fleetness beyond the stability of objective reality. Yet there is a second type of phenomenological unconscious which goes towards fixity and immobility. The world is permanently genesis as much as hypostasis. Our relationship to it is mediated both by the genetic phenomenological unconscious and by the hypostatic phenomenological unconscious. To speak the Richirian language, we would say that the architectonic transposition (which occurs everywhere and every time) of the phantasia in imagination (and perception) precisely supposes a hypostatic fixation of what has been first moved by the genesis.

It is important to underline that the hypostasis is not first, nor exclusively, the fact of language—even if the latter is a sort of first "mark". The hypostasis (that we understand here in a different meaning than the Levinasian use) "occurs" already within the thinking and inside of it. Any reflexive consciousness carries it out; without it, we would not be conscious of space, nor of a certain aspect of time, even if, of course, time in its "flux" is precisely opposed to space insofar as it is fundamentally characterized by hypostasis. The hypostatic phenomenological unconscious is the first stabiliser of any activity of the intellect.

In a certain manner, we could relate the "genesis" and the "hypostasis" with what Freud had identified in terms of "life drive" and "death drive". With the fundamental difference, though, that the hypostasis, as Blumenberg had seen it in his way, is condition of life, an organisational principle allowing it to orientate and impose itself. Without mentioning the fact that genesis and hypostasis do not belong to an

---

[1] In the sense of a "transcendental genesis" (which is to say, I insist on a "constructive phenomenology").

individual nor to a particular psyche, but are constitutive of a transcendental dimension of the meaning waiting to happen.

What justifies here to speak about two different "types" of the phenomenological unconscious? The genetic phenomenological unconscious and the hypostatic phenomenological unconscious are already distinct by the fact that the first is by right variable to infinity (according to the "*facta*" to geneticise) whereas the second always generates one same aspect of the phenomenon (that is to say its "stability" and its "fixity").

But their difference lies in another aspect: the hypostatic phenomenological unconscious has a fundamental rapport to the *real* (to the "factuality of the 'real' world") whereas the genetic phenomenological unconscious rather concerns the clarification of a certain modality of the knowledge of phenomenon. This difference refers then to the one between an *ontological* level and an *epistemological* level, even if, of course, one is not drawing here the idea of an opposition between the ontology and the theory of knowledge. As we will see for the third type of phenomenological unconscious, we are dealing here with a perspective situated beyond this distinction. The "stabilisation" as I just indicated it, is the fact of *imagination* (in the strict meaning of the term[2]). The "act of imaging" characteristic of imagination constitutes precisely this fixation in question here.

2.4 The Reflexible Phenomenological Unconscious

A third type of phenomenological unconscious is not concerned by phenomena (to "geneticise" or to "stabilize") but by the legitimisation of the conditioning (and constitutive) quality of the phenomenological discourse itself. As I have argued elsewhere (Schnell 2015), we could make a distinction between three "sorts" of phenomenological constructions. Whereas the phenomenological construction of the first sort is strictly commended by the "facta" to geneticise, the phenomenological constructions of the second and third sorts "are feeding" themselves (in a way) from an unconscious "process" or a "operation", that the speculative transcendentalism aims at unveiling. These "operations" are no other than the ones of an *imaging* process.[3]

We must first note that the fact of raising the question of such a "feeding" entails obviously important risks. If this one corresponded to the idea of a sort of "matrix", surreptitiously introduced, that could be used here as "funds" from which would be drawn any and every elaboration of a generative phenomenology, then this would evidently have no phenomenological value and would, at the very most, be of use in

---

[2] In distinction to "phantasy" and "reflexibility" (cf. the next note).

[3] Let us note, however, that this "imaging process" must be understood as having three meanings. First, phantasy operates at the level of a genetic phenomenological unconscious; second, the imagination operates at the level of a hypostatic phenomenological unconscious; finally, reflexibility operates as that of a reflexive phenomenological unconscious.

the case of a certain "metaphysic", faced with which we would have, furthermore, every reason to be suspicious.

What is then the phenomenological meaning of the recourse to this imaging process? Here, we aim at analysing what is "founding" the "imaginary constitution" of the real. To demand the justification—all the more in the domain of the unconscious—of such a process is probably a vain request and shall never find any satisfying answer. Here, and on this aspect Hegel will always be right, only the *realisation* of such a project can act as a legitimising "guarantor". Nonetheless, all we can say is that the specificity of this third type of phenomenological unconscious is to "reflect" every other in an implicit way (that is to say, the two others and itself)—meaning that not only does it reflect *on* them but also it unveils their legality (that is to say what makes the reflexion *possible*).

Thus the reflexible unconscious is characterized by a sort of "doubling"—giving it a "possible" quality—which leads it to act on the totality of the sphere of the phenomenological unconscious. What can we understand by this? We have seen that on the level of the "hypostatic phenomenological unconscious", imagination acted as a "stabilising" factor of the real. At the level of the "reflexible phenomenological unconscious", by contrast, the imagination is developing all its constitutive and reflexive quality (notably concerning the "self-reflecting law" of reflexion). The unconscious is structured as an imaging ability—including, I insist, the genetic dimension as well as the hypostatic dimension of the two first types of phenomenological unconscious.

2.5 The Question of the "Self-Consciousness"

Up until now, the concept of a "phenomenological unconscious" was analysed with regard to the articulation of the possible articulation between an epistemological perspective and an ontological perspective. This problematic concerns the rapport to the "object" and questions the manner in which the phenomenological method contaminates, if we can say it this way, the *Being*. Yet the phenomenological unconscious also intervenes on another level: that of the articulation between the consciousness and the consciousness of "self" (naturally in the "non-subjective" sense, characterizing this "pre-conscious" field).

Fink righteously insisted on the fact (that we have already referred to), that all the problematization of the unconscious generally suffers from a lack with respects to the comprehension and clarification of the consciousness. The consciousness is not a "bone": it is not of any kind of given objectivity and, in particular, it is not an instrument or a tool that one could "apply" to something (to its "object"). The paradox of consciousness, and most particularly of the self-consciousness, is that it is precisely played and at play at the level of the unconscious (or at least in the phenomenological sense of the term).

The fundamental argument is that self-consciousness, and same for any consciousness of the object, cannot be explained through the means of reflexion, but by implementing an immediate rapport precisely stemmed from the unconscious. In the history of philosophy, and particularly in the history of phenomenology, different explanatory models of self-consciousness were offered. The most known is first the *reflexive* model (which can be traced back to Classical English Philosophy): according to this model, not only is self-consciousness a specific type of consciousness of the object (where the object is nothing else but the conscious subject itself) but (and this is a perspective that belongs to classical German philosophers) this self-consciousness is even considered as a *condition* for the object-consciousness.

For Brentano, the difficulties linked to this conception (making then impossible, in particular, the instantaneous prehension of the "*present*" consciousness) pushed him to acknowledge a "internal consciousness" which Sartre will then take on through the idea of "non-thetical self-consciousness" within any thetical consciousness of the object. But these two models are not without difficulties because they leave in the dark the status of this "internal" consciousness or of this "non-thetical" consciousness (of self).

The critiques have often repeated that the constitution of the consciousness of time in Husserl, if it prolonged the path first opened by Brentano, still nonetheless fell into difficulties marking the reflexive model (I am relying in this context on the famous Supplement IX of the *Zeitvorlesungen* published in 1928). In reality, Husserl had elaborated, since 1917/1918, in the *Bernau Manuscripts*, a strong alternative to this reflexive model, which was not really noticed (or at least did not capture the attention of the critiques). This alternative was that of an "omni-intentional" model.

I have explored this model elsewhere (Schnell 2004), showing, in particular, that Husserl was looking to give an account of the constitution of the immanent temporality using a phenomenological construction of the "original process" which was substituted to the phenomenological description of the "absolute flux of consciousness" delivered in his previous manuscripts (and reproduced in the *Zeitvorlesungen*).

This original process is constituted of phases, more precisely: of "cores" through and through intentional—hence, therefore, the idea of an "omni-intentionality". But one difficulty persists (of which we can ask ourselves if it is more due to a moment of hesitation in Husserlian analyses or to the lack of interpretative tools brought by the commentator). Is there, strictly speaking, a phenomenological testimonial of this "omni-intentionality" or is it only a matter of a somewhat epistemological system related to the phenomenological construction?

The explicative reflexive model of self-consciousness raises a fundamental issue. How can the "self (-subject)" acknowledge, in the *return* of the self to the self, that the "self (-object)" of the consciousness is *identical* to this "self (-subject)"? So that there would not be here a simple comparison between two particular "objects"— supposedly meant to be identical, each time, to the "subject"—the self(-subject) has to be, prior to this, somewhat "in acquaintance" vis-à-vis itself. This forces us to admit, if consciousness is still "consciousness of something", that is to say a subject *in scission* with its object, an *un*conscious dimension of consciousness which precisely assures the consciousness of the *self*. But this "un-consciousness" is nothing like a "phenomenological construction"—hence why we are distancing it from the three types of phenomenological unconscious exposed above. What Husserl looked to approach with his concept of "core", of "phase" of the "original process", is precisely a type of "consciousness", a *"lived experience"*, allowing the self-consciousness to appear in a pre-intentional transparency.

It is indeed the only way to give a comprehensible meaning to the "omni-intentionality", precisely because the intentionality always presupposes a level of non-intentionality (for example: the apprehension supposes an apprehension content which is not, in its turn, intentional)—which means, going backwards, that what is *omni*-intentional is not *stricto sensu* intentional, but actually *pre*-intentional. The concept of "core" is employed to clarify the dimension concerning the *self*-consciousness of any consciousness. I would characterize it (as I provisionally did above) as "pre-reflexive", if this did not suppose the *telos* of reflection. Yet the "reflection" is located in a superior level (*höherstufig*) or inferior—superior, when it is erected on an already operating consciousness; inferior, when it concerns a phenomenological construction. How are the previously analysed "constructive" dimension and the dimension of the "lived experience" articulated one to another?

2.6 The Plurality of Fields

One of the enigmas met by generative phenomenology concerns the revealing of different "spheres" or different phenomenological "fields". Two points must be made out here. On the one hand, the "transcendental subjectivity" opens on several fields or spheres. On another hand, it is fundamentally itself a field—and therefore not a subject, an ego, a consciousness of an individuality of any nature. Let us clarify the first point. One of the greatest difficulties in attempting to clarify the phenomenological unconscious concerns the determination of the different "spheres" of consciousness, notably when it comes to the difference between the "immanent" sphere and the "pre-immanent" sphere.

Fink had already warned us against the tendency (Husserlian in his opinion) to "compartmentalize" the different levels of consciousness (and notably the objective reality, the immanent consciousness and the absolute flux of consciousness). On one side, the distinction between the three types of the phenomenological unconscious already presupposes the difference between these two spheres (none of these three types is conceivable without acknowledging a *pre-immanent* sphere); on the other side, the irreducible "attachment to the real" forbids us to venture in metaphysical speculations for which we would not be able to provide a concrete testimonial.

Here operates, still anew, a "generative zigzag" not only between the (phenomenological) construction and what is to be constructed, but also between different forms of transcendental "projects", "projections", on one side, and a testimonial in the "lived experiences" on another side, of which the "cores" of the "original process" are only an illustration from the simple level of the problematic of the status of self-consciousness. Thus the rapport between the immanent sphere and the pre-immanent sphere must be conceived outside any spatial coordinate. Notably, here a tension is developed, or rather *fields* of tension which characterize the phenomenological transcendental (and its unconscious dimension) in its fleetness.

This very last aspect fundamentally contaminates the very status of "subject" and "subjectivity". The "subject" is not a "starting point" (which doesn't mean we would or should make an economy of it). What is presented at the beginning, if there is one is the production as enigmatic as ceaseless of "sense". If the expression of a "non-subjective" phenomenology can have any meaning, it is at this level that, without a doubt, it has to apply. The difficulty is not so much to know how an isolated subject comes to the world, to the exteriority, to the real, but, on the contrary, how the "*Sinnbildung*" is crystallised in a Self.

2.7 The Architectonic

Relying on a concept originated in Kant, Richir often refers to the notion that I will appropriate myself here: that of the "architectonic". The author of the "transcendental doctrine of the method" (in the first *Critique*) saw in it the internal systematic of philosophy in general, and of reason in particular. By this, I mean (following Richir) the *quasi* organic (alive, even) network of the "functions", of the "effectuations" and also (in places) of the "concepts" holding together "the thought" and making it *coherent* (presenting itself, in the Finkian language, as an "open system"). I am saying "*the* thought" even though, *stricto sensu*, it is *plural* (of an indefinite plurality); and I am saying "the *thought*" (and not the "reason") because it is not at all an "ability" attributable to a "subject". There is an "architectonic", in that sense, in any place and anytime coherence expends (complex and sometimes difficult to explore and analyse) from the "*Sinnbildung*".

Yet, if the different architectonics characterizing the "systematic" elaborations of philosophers, even the most important ones, are different each time (may it be only sensibly), it is because here, it is not the "subjectivity" that is at play, but the "singularity" (this term is from Richir as well) of the philosopher. Hence the importance to consider this term in the context of a reflection on the phenomenological unconscious: the meaning happening in an anonymous genesis is not the result of a "subject", but it is not either (and in no case) a kind of absolute and neutral structure, delivered, at the very most, to a purely conceptual, even grammatical, analysis.

Thus the phenomenology of the un-conscious must necessarily (and nevertheless) treat with the rapport to the singular consciousness, which is not amount to the simple individual and empirical consciousness, but of which Heidegger had maybe glimpsed on, by insisting on the "*Jemeinigkeit* (ownness)" of *Dasein* in *Sein und Zeit*. This "singularity" is assisting the effectuation of the "*Sinnbildung*" as much as it is assisting it. The "architectonic" is then the name given to the characterization of the thinking insofar as it puts at stake both a "generative" dimension and a "lived experience" dimension; and it refers both to the "non-subjective" dimension of the "*Sinnbildung*" and to the "subjective" dimension of the "singularity" of the "thinker" (insofar as he is on "the first line"[4] and can only "be fed", faced with "the thing itself" to be thought, from what is announced by far as a coherence to come and as a confirmation of what has been left within and in virtue of the thought to be).

2.8 Conclusion

One major point we shall remember from what precedes is the dynamic character of the phenomenological unconscious (a lesson which will of course not teach anything to the psychoanalyst that he does not already know of). What appeared was that the question of knowing what is the phenomenological unconscious turned rather into this other question which is to know how it operates and how it is effectuated. Let us recapitulate the essential results which we came to. The dynamic character of the phenomenological unconscious is inseparable from its "pre-donation" dimension. Following the order stated at the beginning (orientated with regards to a pre-intentional, non-intentional even, dimension of the transcendental consciousness), we can note three dimensions of the phenomenological unconscious:

1. Three different types of phenomenological unconscious (from the point of view of the "objective" side): the genetic unconscious, the hypostatic unconscious and the reflexible unconscious.
2. The unconscious dimension of the self-consciousness.
3. The "field" dimension characterizing this phenomenological unconscious.

But another order was crystallised in the previous elaborations, which is insisting in particular on the importance of the "imaging process" of any sense ("*Sinnbildung*") and the status of "self": indeed, we have, on one side, three ways in which the imagination (in the broad sense) operates beyond the immanent consciousness (the genesis of immanent *facta*, the hypostasis constituting the imaginal part of the factuality of the real world and the reflexibility concerning the auto-legitimisation of the phenomenological discourse); and we have, on the other side, three ways in which the unconscious participates to the clarification of the status of "self" (more precisely: of the self-consciousness, of the field character of the transcendental consciousness and of the architectonic). Thus, the phenomenological unconscious is strongly contaminated by the problematic of the image, and it raises again from a renewed perspective the question of the status of the self.

I will end with a note on the position defended here *vis-à-vis* the one defended by Levinas. One of the examples I took from the beginning to illustrate the perspective of a phenomenological unconscious was indeed that of the *face* in its Levinasian apprehension. Yet if we come back to the analyses previously developed, with respect to this unconscious in phenomenology, we could argue that the transcendental(ist) perspective adopted here is completely missing out on the project

---
[4] This expression is by P. Loraux.

exposed in *Totality and Infinity*—may it be only because this unconscious is thematized in a (transcendental, precisely) field located beyond the one of alterity, towards which Levinas had, as we know, directed the first philosophy understood as "ethical". How can we get out of such an appearing contradiction?

Levinas had considered that one approach of the "alterity" (as he had understood it) was impossible in the frame of a philosophy—and in particular of a phenomenology—of knowledge. One of the aims of the present elaborations is to "save" an "epistemological" perspective without falling again in the perspective criticized by Levinas—that is to say falling again into the position which assimilates knowledge with a sort of "identification" and which points out the priority of the objectifying consciousness. The fact to put imagination at the foreground is thus another way of attempting at giving alterity a central role in any knowledge—"alterity" which is indeed not the face of the other, but which is not either the "neutral sameness" turning knowledge into a simple instrument at the service of any "will for knowledge" or "will for power".

References

Husserl, Edmund. 1976. *Die Krisis der europäischen Wissenschaften und die transzendentale Phänomenologie. Eine Einleitung in die phänomenologische Philosophie*. Haag: M. Nijhoff.
Levinas, Emmanuel. 1969. *Totality and infinity*. Haag: M. Nijhoff.
Richir, Marc. 1987. *Phénomènes, temps et êtres. Ontologie et phénoménologie*. Paris: J. Millon.
Schnell, Alexander. 2004. *Temps et phénomène. La phénoménologie husserlienne du temps (1893–1918)*. Hildesheim: Olms.
———. 2010. *En face de l'extériorité. Levinas et la question de la subjectivité*. Paris: Vrin.
———. 2011. *Le sens se faisant. Marc Richir et la refondation de la phénoménologie transcendantale*. Bruxelles: Ousia.
———. 2015. *La déhiscence du sens*. Paris: Hermann.

Part II
From the Specific Perspective of Merleau-Ponty

Chapter 3
Merleau-Ponty's Conception of the Unconscious in the Late Manuscripts

Emmanuel de Saint Aubert

Abstract Original and daring, the late Merleau-Ponty's conception of the unconscious marks a culmination of his phenomenological project. Inseparable from his primacy of perception and his philosophy of the flesh, this conception involves essential dimensions of his anthropology as well as his ontology. I explore this thematic in a dynamic development, following the philosopher's evolution, first in a negative approach – the critique of consciousness, but also of our mistaken conceptions of the unconscious –, which gradually gives way to a positive description. Merleau-Ponty's reflection on the unconscious goes far beyond his reception of psychoanalysis: supported by his philosophical intention, rooted in his (anti) Cartesian scenario, it leads to his final answer to the *Cogito*. In its development, it involves his phenomenology of perception, his late work on imaginary and expression, and raises the delicate question of the relationship between flesh and being. In Merleau-Ponty's late manuscripts, consciousness becomes autistic, blind, while the unconscious holds the most positive if not the most expressive, the most opened if not the most fertile dimension of our being-in-the-world. It participates at the same time to the most archaic and the most refined aspects of our relationship to the world, to the other, to being. The collection of unpublished manuscripts constituted by the *Notes on the body* proves to be a major document apropos this subject.

Keywords Merleau-Ponty • Body • Unconsciousness • Cogito • Ontology

---

Translated by Audrey Petit-Trigg

E. de Saint Aubert (✉)
Archives Husserl, CNRS, Ecole Normale Supérieure, Paris Sciences et Lettres Research University, Paris, France
e-mail: e.dsta@free.fr

3.1 Introduction

Original and daring, the late Merleau-Ponty's conception of the unconscious marks a culmination of his phenomenological project, and involves essential dimensions of his anthropological work as well as his ontology. Inseparable from his primacy of perception, but also from his philosophy of the flesh – an expressive and desiring flesh – , this conception leads us to the core of Merleau-Ponty's comprehension of our being-in-the-world. The collection of late unpublished manuscripts constituted by the *Notes on the body* proves to be a major document apropos this subject.

I will explore this thematic in a dynamic development, following the philosopher's evolution, first in a negative approach (the critique of absolutists attributes of consciousness, but also of our mistaken conceptions of the unconscious) which will gradually give way to a positive description. Merleau-Ponty's approach of the unconscious goes far beyond his reception of psychoanalysis,[1] because it is supported by an expression of his philosophical intention, which lies under his relation with psychoanalysis and therefore induces a partial reception and a free interpretation of it. This intention is rooted in what I called the (anti) Cartesian scenario of Merleau-Ponty (cf. Saint Aubert 2005). In its development, it involves his phenomenology of perception, his late work on imaginary and expression, and raises the delicate question of the relationship between flesh and being.

In common representations, we are inclined to think of the unconscious like a container, the container of a content, the reservoir of a reserved, in other words, something more or less enclosed, restrained, shut out from the outside. And that an external authority (consciousness) could, under certain conditions, penetrate and explore, allowing the inside to reach the outside. Admittedly, the unconscious is also represented as expressing itself (going from the inside to the outside), but this expression remains wild and uncontrolled, even destructive – in other words, it doesn't construct our being-in-the-world as it is, nor a true bond to the other. Merleau-Ponty blows over this global representation, this staging of the unconscious (which is rather a staging of consciousness faced with unconscious). In his late manuscripts, to say it simply, consciousness becomes autistic, blind, while the unconscious holds the most positive if not the most expressive, the most opened if not the most fertile dimension of our being-in-the-world. It participates at the same time to the most archaic and the most refined aspects of our relationship to the world, to the other, to being. This unconscious, taken from the foundation of our bodily institution and the inter-corporeality that is constitutive of its structure, is not anonymous, but personal and inter-personal.

---

[1] About this reception, cf. Saint Aubert (2013).

3.2 The Merleau-Pontian Reforms of Consciousness

Merleau-Ponty's famous "primacy of *perception*" is inseparable from a never-ending debate with the notion of *consciousness*, through which he attempted to elaborate a positive conception of this notion, without ever being able to stabilize his position. These unfortunate adventures of consciousness – and notably the perceptual consciousness – finally give way, in the late manuscripts, to a radical and irrevocable opposition, in which Merleau-Ponty seems to forget the very idea that consciousness is not a monolithic phenomenon. How did Merleau-Ponty go from the positive attempt of *Phenomenology of Perception* – which aimed at re-thinking consciousness outside representation (cf. e.g. PhP,[2] p. 163/525[3]) – to the massive condemnation first sketched, at the other side of his work, in a well-known note dated from May 1960 – describing a blind consciousness, incapable of seeing its "tie to Being (…) its corporeity (…) the flesh", a consciousness which "in principle (…) disregards Being and prefers the object to it, that is, a Being with which it has broken" (NT,[4] pp. 301–302/248, in a note entitled "Blindness (*punctum cæcum*) of the 'consciousness'")? I won't narrate here all the meanderings of these adventures of consciousness. I will rather quickly draw the fertile philosophical gesture which traverses and goes beyond those, as it carries out the progressing emergence of the notion of unconscious. Indeed, the Merleau-Pontian reforms of consciousness operate like a preparation, if not anticipation of his future conception of the unconscious.

3.2.1 "The Root of the Ingenuous Affirmation"

We are reminded of this wording from *Phenomenology of Perception*: "consciousness is being toward the thing through the intermediary of the body" (PhP, p. 161/140). The last Merleau-Ponty could use the same formulation, only that it would be attributed, not to consciousness anymore, but to the unconscious. "Being toward the thing through the intermediary of the body" refers to a whole phenomenological program. But it is rooted, beforehand, in what the first thesis project of 1933 called, without any reference to Husserl nor to phenomenology, "the recent

---

[2] PhP: *Phénoménologie de la perception*. 1945. Paris: Gallimard. 2012. *Phenomenology of Perception*. Trans. Donald A. Landes. London and New York: Routledge.

[3] After each passage cited from Merleau-Ponty, we indicate the pagination of the French edition, followed, when possible, by the pagination of the corresponding publication in English. In our reference to unpublished manuscripts stored at the Bibliothèque Nationale de France, we specify the classification numbering established by the B.N.F. in square brackets, followed, when it exists, by Merleau-Ponty's manuscript pagination in round brackets. The letter "v" following the classification number of a folio page indicates that it refers to the verso of this page.

[4] NT: working notes edited by Claude Lefort. 1964. *Le visible et l'invisible*. Paris: Gallimard. 1968. *The Visible and the Invisible*. Trans. Alphonso Lingis. Evanston: Northwestern University Press.

literature of the 'perception of one's own body'" (Proj,[5] p. 13). As it is, Merleau-Ponty points out to the *Metaphysical Journal* published by Gabriel Marcel in 1927, and more precisely to his famous "I am my body" (cf. Saint Aubert 2005, chap. III). Merleau-Ponty re-appropriates this expression in an article dedicated in 1936 to Gabriel Marcel's *Being and Having*. The expression "I am my body" is then opposed, of course, to "I think therefore I am", and young Merleau-Ponty comments: "The *Cogito* is far from being the primal truth, the condition of any valid certainty. The root of the ingenuous affirmation is rather the consciousness of my body, which maybe sustains any affirmation of existence related to things" (EtAv,[6] pp. 37–38).

From "I am my body", consciousness of my body which supports every judgement of existence involving the things (1936) to consciousness as "being toward the thing through the intermediary of the body" (1945), there is already a step ahead. "The ingenuous affirmation" is not as much "I am my body" than "this is", but a "this is" inseparable from my bodily openness to the world, an expression that merges with the bodily expression itself. When Merleau-Ponty, as we will see, will talk in his last manuscripts, not about consciousness, but about the unconscious as a "yes" and "initial yes", it will be his final reformulation of the "ingenuous affirmation". And his final answer to the *Cogito*.

3.2.2 An Essential Inattention Margin

Throughout time, what will be of interest for Merleau-Ponty will be less what consciousness brings, what it gives, but rather what it misses out on and what it lacks. A native incompleteness, essential to its functioning, a self-blindness,[7] an inattention margin necessary to the production of something else but consciousness and which it cannot give. According to the lesson entitled "Senses and Unconscious", given in 1947–1948, this "inattention margin, which is not an addition, but an essential element" is "what Freud calls incorrectly the unconscious" (UAC,[8] p. 117).What Merleau-Ponty says of the unconscious here, influenced by *Gestalttheorie*, is typical of a recurrent formulation which will progressively fade in the fifties. Such an approach considerably weakens the Freudian conception: it appends more or less the unconscious to perceptual consciousness, and assimilates it to an imperception phenomenon.

---

[5] Proj: "Projet de travail sur la nature de la Perception" (April 1933), handwritten text presented for obtaining a grant from the Caisse nationale des Sciences. 1989. In *Le primat de la perception et ses conséquences philosophiques*, 11–13. Grenoble: Cynara. Reprinted. 1996. Lagrasse: Verdier.

[6] EtAv: "Être et Avoir". Review of Gabriel Marcel's *Être et Avoir*. 1936. In *La Vie intellectuelle*, 8ᵉ year, new series, volume XLV: 98–109. Reprinted. 1997. In *Parcours 1935–1951*, 35–44. Lagrasse: Verdier.

[7] "Any given consciousness is by principle something else than what it claims to be", "only thematizes something by leaving a whole implicit residue" (MSME, p. 175). MSME: preparatory notes for the 1953 course at the Collège de France on "Le monde sensible et le monde de l'expression". B.N.F., volume X. 2011. *Le monde sensible et le monde de l'expression*. Genève: MétisPresses.

[8] UAC: *L'union de l'âme et du corps chez Malebranche, Biran et Bergson*. 1978. New French edition, revised and augmented with a new unpublished fragment. Paris: Vrin.

3.2.3 *The Sensible World and the World of Expression*

We have to mention one major last step in the Merleau-Pontian reforms of consciousness and what it anticipates of his conception of the unconscious: the first lecture at the Collège de France, *The sensible world and the world of expression* (1953). I will just make a few remarks here – for further details, see the introduction I wrote for the publication of these lectures (MSME, pp. 7–38).

The overall course adopts as explicit horizon a *reform of the notion of consciousness* which oscillates between the claim for a "renewal" and the claim for "relinquishment". Merleau-Ponty denunciates the disembodied and static aspects of classical approaches of consciousness. A consciousness that contemplates its objects, possesses them by aiming at them, but that also thinks itself as object, possessing itself as such in the reflection. This consciousness is in an ambivalent relationship towards things; it misses the bond with these (by excess of distance *and* excess of proximity) and is only in a (fusional) relationship with itself. It is, quite the opposite, a matter of finding again consciousness as *openness* and as *relationship* – effective openness and relationship that will be later the very attributes of the unconscious.

In that perspective, 1953's lecture aims at coming back to the *perceptual* consciousness and approaches it as an *expressive* relation, engaging in a reciprocal relationship, a relationship of being and not anymore a simple unilateral relation of possession, of having. Merleau-Ponty approaches as well these questions based on a thorough reflection on the *body schema*, "existential layer" supporting our openness to the world and orientating it as inter-corporeality and coexistence. Yet, the body schema is not really conscious of itself, it "is not perceived" and its understanding demands a "revision of our notion of consciousness" (MSME, p. 143). "Less *object* of perception than a mean towards action" (MSME, p. 131), the body perceives itself to the scale of his motor and desiring projects. "Consciousness of our body closely depends on what we *do*" (*ibid.*), so that this consciousness only possesses itself in an expression through which it loses itself, never reaching the perfect closure of reflexivity since it is extracted from itself by the very modality of its appearance. Overall, the lecture of 1953 describes a consciousness filled with imperception phenomenon, born from the expressive relation between the body and the world, only existing in this event and evading its own self as soon as it leaves it. Merleau-Ponty then emphasises the illusory character of the possessions of consciousness, what resists its possessivity (of things) same as what prevents it from possessing itself – as many *dispossessions* which prepare the later description of the unconscious.

3.3 What the Unconscious Is Not

3.3.1 Three Conceptual Mistakes

Let's get now to what Merleau-Ponty says of the unconscious, not indirectly through his attempts at reforming the notion of consciousness anymore – which are bringing it closer to the notion of unconscious while fading behind it – , but directly and explicitly. And to do so, let's begin with the easiest: what the unconscious is not. Merleau-Ponty regularly denunciates three mistaken conceptions of the unconscious.

(a) First, this term is badly constructed: the unconscious is not un-conscious, it is not the not-conscious (cf. e.g. N-Corps[9] [87]v(8)). More broadly, it is not negation, it is not "is not". It is not the negative form of consciousness, a pure unknown, nor what I deny of myself (*ibid.*). In particular, it is not reduced to a reactive secondary formation, to the repressed unconscious.[10]

(b) And this leads us already to the second mistake: the unconscious is not a reservoir of content, such as a bin for the repressed. It is not reducible to a result, product of an accumulation and recipient of, *residue* of (what could have or should have reached or should have remained in) consciousness. In a certain way, it would have to be imagined like an ability rather than a product. But this is not suitable either, because it would expose it to the third mistake, and because the unconscious is larger than a simple ability: it is a co-extension to our being-in-the-world.

(c) Finally, the last false conception, criticized through and through by Merleau-Ponty: the unconscious is not a second "I think", *a second consciousness*, that would know what we ignore about ourselves. A second consciousness which would then complete consciousness as a parallel instance, such as "someone who would think clearly in the depths of me what I confusedly live" (Natu3,[11] p. 351/283), or which would realise what consciousness should (but yet is not able to) realise.

To sum-up, the unconscious in not a negation (of consciousness), nor a residue (of consciousness), nor a second version (of consciousness). We tend to associate it with consciousness or rather with a false conception of such consciousness. This

---

[9] N-Corps: "Notes sur le corps" (1956–1960, and especially 1960), unpublished. B.N.F., volume XVII.

[10] Cf. N-Corps [84](1), [86](5), [91]v, [92], Natu3 351/283, RC60 179/198–199. Merleau-Ponty relies on Freud himself at times. "Everything that is repressed must remain unconscious; but let us state at the very outset that the repressed does not cover everything that is unconscious. The unconscious has a wider compass: the repressed is a part of the unconscious", Freud (1915), p. 166.

[11] Natu3: preparatory notes for the 1960 course at the Collège de France on the concept of Nature, "Nature et Logos: le corps humain". B.N.F., volume XVII. 1995. *La Nature. Notes, cours du Collège de France*. Paris: Seuil. 2003. *Nature: Course Notes from the Collège de France*. Trans. Robert Vallier. Evanston: Northwestern University Press.

triple mistake lies itself on another mistake, which Merleau-Ponty calls regularly the "madness of consciousness" which is rather a "mad" conception we have of it. Which beats everything, since it is, on the contrary, a case of renouncing this madness, these delirious attributes (of consciousness), and discover and admit everything else in our relationship to the world.

3.3.2 From the Prosaic to the Oneiric, from Representation to Being

Merleau-Ponty finds one of the variants of these mistaken conceptions in the idea of "unconscious representations" (cf. e.g. N-Corps [91]v and Natu3, p. 352/284). Beyond the critic of Freud, here is engaged the Merleau-Pontian conception of our being-in-the-world, understood as taking place beyond *representation*, which is reduced to an "internal board facing a consciousness"; a being-in-the-world developed by *perception* and by what is unavoidably coming with it: an *oneiric* relation with things (cf. e.g. N-Corps [86]v(6)-[87](7), [91]v). In the late 1940s, Merleau-Ponty becomes attentive to Bachelard's psychological and metaphysical approach to the imaginary. Contra the early Sartre, he discovers the extent to which perception is not free of the imaginary; he intends to name the depth shared by reality and the imaginary as "*oneiric being*." While the imaginary is a deepening of the perceived, perception itself is strengthened by the oneiric experience that envelops it, contributing towards its success.[12]

Merleau-Ponty thus doesn't rely on the classical schema – intolerable representations, therefore repressed, therefore unconscious – a schema reducing the unconscious to a rebus part and reject of ourselves, reject (secondary formation) and rebus (bond to be deciphered). As a philosopher, he first raises the question of meaning and truth. As a phenomenologist, he raises these questions as they take place in our relationship to the world, beginning in the perceptual life and the desiring-imaginary dimensions that always come alongside of it. Yet, meaning and truth are not reducible to what Merleau-Ponty calls the "prosaic" of representation (literally), they are overlapping in a "full meaning" that is to say a *figurative meaning*, carrying oneiric dimensions (cf. N-Corps [88](9)-[88]v(10), [96]-[96]v). These analogic dimensions can be repressed, but they can be unconscious in a more fundamental way, in virtue of their anthropological situation: because they inhabit the heart of our animation. So that they express a primordial unconscious, behind the unconscious of the repressed.

---

[12] On this subject, cf. Saint Aubert (2004), section B.

3.4 The Excessive Unconscious

3.4.1 *The Excess of the Perceptual and the Excess of the Oneiric*

Merleau-Ponty thus adopts a more phenomenological schema, centred on our carnal openness to the world, unconscious by position. An openness with multiple folds (sensor-motor, imaginary-desiring, confident-interrogative) but that the philosopher aims to take over based on the perceptual foundations of intelligence. "The unconscious is not a proliferation of thoughts, hidden mechanisms, but the functioning of perceptual links" (PbPassiv,[13] p. 245/188), as he states in the lecture on passivity in 1955. And symmetrically, "perception is the true unconscious" (EM3[14] [247](32)). "The unconscious: excess of the perceptual over the notional" (PbPassiv, p. 247/246). If the unconscious is involved in the excess of the perceptual over the notional, it also entails the excess of the oneiric over the perceptual: it is also "the pre-objective, oneiric background of all perception" (PbPassiv, p. 244/187).

This "oneiric background of every perception" is to be directly understood in regards with the inspiration that Merleau-Ponty finds since 1948 in Bachelard's "psychoanalysis" of the elements. And this excess of the oneiric over the perceptual doesn't refer to a true "side" of the perception, as the sensible is already rich of this same excess. Any sensible appeals to what Merleau-Ponty calls, since *Phenomenology of Perception*, our "system of equivalences", analogic functioning of the body schema. Any sensible, in its way, is susceptible to make "analogic circumstances", that is to say to revive in ourselves a transversal dimension of our being-in-the-world.

Any sensible is for us *expressive*, calling for a hallmark of our relationship to the world, a *manner of being*, our style: our flesh, if we are remembering what is said about it in *The visible and the invisible*. By this "expressive relation" and "the carnal intercourse" it engages with us, every sensible seeks a *testimonial* into us, and not only, not even first, a representation – on this subject we refer to the beautiful pages of *The prose of the world* where Merleau-Ponty opposes expression to representation (cf. PM,[15] pp. 207–211/147–152). Like painting or drawing, the sensible "will revive in us the profound arrangement which has settled us into our body and through it, into the world" (PM, pp. 208–209/150), "test the pact of coexistence that we sealed with the world through our whole body" (PM, p. 211/152). This "profound arrangement", this "pact of coexistence" is the very unconscious.

---

[13] PbPassiv: preparatory notes for the 1955 course at the Collège de France on "Le problème de la passivité: le sommeil, l'inconscient, la mémoire". B.N.F., volume XIII. 2003. *L'institution. La passivité. Notes de cours au Collège de France (1954–1955)*. Paris: Belin. 2010. *Institution and Passivity: Course Notes from the Collège de France (1954–1955)*. Trans. Leonard Lawlor and Heath Massey. Evanston: Northwestern University Press.

[14] EM3: "Être et Monde", unpublished. B.N.F., volume VI, mainly April to May 1960, some rewritings in October 1960.

[15] PM: "La prose du monde" (1950–1951, especially summer 1951; some rewritings much later). B.N.F., volume III. 1969. *La prose du monde*. Paris: Gallimard. 1973. *The Prose of the World*. Trans. John O'Neill. Evanston: Northwestern University Press.

3.4.2 *The Surrection, or the Excesses of the Body and Desire*

Excess of the perceptual, excess of the oneiric, one going along with the other, the unconscious takes part in what *Eye and Mind* will call "the imaginary texture of the real" (OE,[16] p. 24/165). And it also plays a full role, as we would suspect, in the excesses of the body and the excesses of desire. The unconscious at stake is in no way confined in the immanence of cut-off daydreams. On the contrary, Merleau-Ponty insists on strongly articulating the oneiric to the organic, the unconscious to the effective transcendence of the perceived being, which mobilises the very foundations of our bodily institution.

The lecture on the problem of passivity (1955) is traversed by a new schema in Merleau-Ponty's writings, inaugurated in a reflection on "the fecundity of desire" in the oneirism and the unconscious: the *surrection* (upheaval). Join figure of birth and freedom, the surrection hold within itself an existential dimension, taken from its most bodily rooting. "Surrection or insurrection or resurrection (…) this fecundity or productivity" (PbPassiv [182](48), not published), writes Merleau-Ponty, "is the power of what we have desired (…). The unconscious = modality of corporeality (…). Surrection of the unconscious and erection of the body" (PbPassiv, pp. 230–231/176).

Surrection of the unconscious and erection of the body in the insurrection of desire: these audacious formulations of an intimate articulation between unconscious, corporeality and desire are engraved in Merleau-Ponty's continuous work on the perceptual logic, constituting a fruit, if not an endpoint. This fruit tends to reverse the previous assimilation of the unconscious to a "perceptual consciousness" poorly defined.

3.4.3 "The Unconscious of State, Holding onto Our Embodiment"

After the lectures on passivity, the last writings prove even more radical: the unconscious, as underlined in the *Notes on the body* (1956–1960, above all 1960), is on to "searching behind sensoriality", as "a more fundamental involvement" (N-Corps [84](1)). Since several years, and in 1960 more than ever, this more fundamental involvement which is behind sensoriality while supporting it, this "universal dimensionality" which is "primordial symbolisation" and which expresses itself through the "topology of the body schema and its 'equivalences'" (*ibid.*), this involvement has a name: *desire*.

---

[16] OE: "L'Œil et l'Esprit" (July–August 1960). 1964. *L'Œil et l'Esprit*. Paris: Gallimard. Reprinted. 1985. Paris: Gallimard, "Folio essais". 1964. "Eye and Mind." Trans. Carleton Dallery. In *The Primacy of Perception*. Evanston: Northwestern University Press.

Merleau-Ponty ends up giving a radical anthropological status to the unconscious, turning it into "the fundamental structure of the psychological apparatus" (N-Corps [86]v(6)) and our "primordial relationship to the world" (N-Corps [87](7)). It is what he calls the "unconscious of state" (N-Corps [86](5), [86]v(6), Natu3 351/283, RC60[17] 179/198), "the unconscious of state, holding on to our embodiment" (N-Corps [86](5)). This unconscious constitutes no less than "the tissue of life" (N-Corps [85]v(4)-[86](5)) of the "undivided being as human corporeality" (N-Corps [85]v(4)) that we are. And knowing that Merleau-Ponty, following Schilder, characterizes our animation as desire, this tissue of our life is itself weaving of desire, this human corporeality that we are is, beyond the very "esthesiologic body", understood as "libidinal body". We could not be closer to the heart of Merleau-Pontian *anthropology*. But this statement is immediately doubled with another: we are also at the threshold of the essential dimensions of Merleau-Ponty's *ontology*.

3.5 "A Relationship of Being": The Body and the Unconscious

3.5.1 Body Schema, Incorporation and Inter-corporeality

At the core of the *Notes on the body*, Merleau-Ponty uses one of his very idiosyncratic expressions shaped as a definition, as enigmatic as it is dazzling: "The *unconscious*: it is this dimensional relationship of being, with the other" (N-Corps [91]v). This affirmation combines precisely anthropology with ontology. How can we understand it? The entire leaf from which this proposition emanates is amazingly rich, and proves to be synthetic of the approach of the unconscious across the *Notes on the body*. What Merleau-Ponty says on the unconscious in it can be completely understood only if one reads carefully what is said of the body schema and of the incorporation as a "relationship of being". This necessity is true, more broadly, for his overall conception of the unconscious: we cannot apprehend this one without coming back to his understanding of the animating and animated body, of the flesh, which owes so much itself to his work on the *body schema* (notably from Paul Schilder). We cannot grasp the Merleau-Pontian conception of the unconscious without coming back to his understanding of *inter-corporeality* which owes so much itself to his overdetermination of the psychoanalytical notion of *incorporation* (notably from Melanie Klein). Body schema, incorporation, inter-corporeality: so many work orientations that, in Merleau-Ponty, are nourishing his conception of *flesh* (cf. Saint Aubert 2013).

How can we understand the incorporation, wonders Merleau-Ponty? Certainly not as a process of consciousness, but more as a "participation", as a "relationship

---

[17] RC: *Résumés de cours. Collège de France, 1952–1960*. 1968. Paris: Gallimard. RC60: *Husserl aux limites de la phénoménologie / Nature et Logos: le corps humain*. 1988. "Themes from the Lectures at the Collège de France 1952–1960". Trans. John O'Neill. In *In Praise of Philosophy and Other Essays*. Evanston: Northwestern University Press.

of *Einfühlung*" or "relationship of being". The same leaf affirms resolutely that the body "is" incorporation. "At the level of sensoriality", indeed, but also "far beyond". It is "relation to the world", and "total" relationship. It is relation with the other bodies, and there too, total relation: "it is a relationship of being with the other body schemas". The sensorial incorporation would then be a particular case of a more fundamental incorporation: "before the 'sensoriality'", there is the libido, which is a "relationship of incorporation to the other and [incorporation] of the other". This fundamental layer slips from the articulation of language, while being already a "primordial symbolisation" (N-Corps [91], for all these quotes).

Merleau-Ponty remarks, however, that the unconscious is precisely this relationship of being; to say it otherwise, it is itself incorporation, effective relation to the world. The unconscious, introduced as a "relationship of being", is closely associated with "the body schema as *In der Welt Sein*". And its functioning, described by Merleau-Ponty in classic Freudian terms ("condensation and shifting") would be "based on the topology of the body schema" (N-Corps [91]v).

If these *Notes on the body*, as well as the overall documents dealing with the body schema since 1953, are marked by the work of Paul Schilder on the "body image" ("body image" that Merleau-Ponty systematically translates as "schéma corporel"), they over determinate this work in orientations that are foreign to him. Schilder, even more than Henry Head, locates the essential of the functioning of the body schema in the margin, at the limits or below the consciousness, but without yet thematizing as such a new conception of the unconscious. Moreover, if Schilder himself has a radical conception of the inter-corporeality, it is under the influence of Melanie Klein that Merleau-Ponty gives such importance to the process of "incorporation". Finally, if Schilder develops a subtle description of the spatiality of one's own body, he doesn't appeal to topology – that Merleau-Ponty will take over from Piaget's work on the structuration of the infant space. And if Schilder, among his many talents, worked closely on phenomenology, he doesn't yet approach the body schema "as *In der Welt Sein*" and even less as a "relationship of being".

What remains then is the Lacanian nuance of these Merleau-Ponty's late texts, reinforced by a few borrowed patent materials – essentially the answer made by Lacan to Jean Hyppolite's essay on denegation ("A Spoken Commentary on Freud's *Verneinung*"). I say "nuance" because topology, as I demonstrated it elsewhere (cf. Saint Aubert 2006), is not at all borrowed from Lacan, and because Merleau-Ponty, philosopher and phenomenologist, doesn't need Lacan (and his very free relationship to Heidegger) to talk about an "*In der Welt Sein*" or a "relationship of being". By contrast, the friendly dialogue between the two men may have confirmed them, for one as for the other, in their respective approaches. Another dialogue may have managed to discretely support Merleau-Ponty's reflection: with Françoise Dolto, which clinic and oral as much as written contributions were already preparing his future texts on the "unconscious body image" (cf. Saint Aubert 2013, section A).

3.5.2 At the Crossroads of Body and Being: The Desiring Unconscious

It is starting with the lecture on *The sensible world and the world of expression* (1953) that Merleau-Ponty works on the *princeps* book of Schilder (*The Image and Appearance of the Human Body*, 1935), and tackles for the first time the fundamentally desiring and relational structuration of the body schema: what the late manuscripts will call the "libidinal body" (cf. MSME, pp. 158–160). This structuration is not an isolated factor, but an integral dimension that affects inevitably, and straightaway, our relationship to the world. The body schema engages the originary formation of the psychological life. But as it also sustains, indissociably, the originary formation of our relationship to the world and to the other, it is at the basis of what Merleau-Ponty calls, more broadly, our relationship to being. The primordial unconscious that it implies manifests itself through "the body as mediator of being" (PbPassiv, p. 243/186). Phenomenologically speaking, the unconscious attached then to the body schema is openness to "the things themselves". These are the daring directions that Merleau-Ponty will follow up in many later passages (1959–1960), notably in a major passage of *Notes on the body*, which relies on an analogy between the esthesiological body and the libidinal body:

> To demonstrate that, the same way esthesiological sensing is in reality in relationship with *the thing itself* through my body as the *flesh*, the erotic body is in relationship with the other body schemas by indivision. (…)
> To demonstrate that the libidinal body is openness to the others themselves (intercorporeality) the same way the esthesiological body is openness to the things and not to the representations of things. (N-Corps [99]v)

These programmatic lines are typical of a fundamental Merleau-Pontian critical gesture which relies on an implicit double opposition: between *being* and *representation*, between *body* and *representation*. A crossed double opposition, which betrays an even more implicit and yet essential association: between *body* and *being*. And the *unconscious* dwells in this very crossroads, this secret and somewhat mysterious collusion of body and being. Merleau-Ponty wants to hold together the *bodily* identity, the *unconscious* dimension, and the *ontological* radicalism of the donation in flesh: the unconscious-flesh as openness to being. It is difficult not to think about Binswanger, yet completely absent from Merleau-Ponty's writings after *Phenomenology of Perception*.[18]

In the critical and rather univocal meaning that Merleau-Ponty has of it, the *representation* is incapable of reaching "the things themselves". Indissociable from the author's anti-Cartesian scenario – from denunciation of the perverse effects of the self-reliance of *cognitive* reflexivity – , this critique has its equivalent in a certain critique of the *affective*: Merleau-Ponty reads the desire as a "relationship of being",

---

[18] Except for a furtive occurrence, of little interest, in Sorb(SHP), p. 399/318 (1951–1952). Sorb: *Merleau-Ponty à la Sorbonne, résumé de cours 1949–1952*. 1988. Grenoble: Cynara. Sorb(SHP): *Les sciences de l'homme et la phénoménologie* (1951–1952). 2010. *Child Psychology and Pedagogy: The Sorbonne Lectures 1949–1952*. Trans. Talia Welsh. Evanston: Northwestern University Press.

and not as a simple affective *state*, the affective state acting as a projective screen between me and the other (projective of me) the same way the representation acts as a projective screen between me and the things. Left with the bolting of their respective circularity, the affect, as the representation, are missing the "thing itself". But it must also be immediately understood – and it is crucial – that, acting as such, they betray the body. In other words, the type of surpassing of representation and affect to which Merleau-Ponty invites us, is nothing like a surpassing of the body, but rather, quite opposed, the accomplishment of its dynamism and the liberation of its expressivity.

In the late manuscripts, Merleau-Ponty comes back several times to the analogy between the "esthesiological body" and the "libidinal body" (cf. e.g. N-Corps [97] et [102]). The perceiving body, as Merleau-Ponty explains, is not only *also* a desiring body: the perception implies the desire, it is already a "mode of desire".[19] As the philosopher will write in the last published text of his lifetime, the perception "sketches out what is accomplished by desire" (S(Préf),[20] p. 24/17). Nor representation, nor simple emotion, nor pure cognitive state, nor pure affective state, desire is not reducible to a psychological *state*, because it is a disposition of the body schema, a fundamental behavior of the flesh. A manner of *being*, in the verbal meaning of the term. And perception is all the more a favoured gate of a philosophy of desire since it places itself in the junction of the cognitive and the affective, and aside from their differentiation: in the unconscious foundations of our openness to the world, where the desiring life is always already in action, immediately sustained by the relational and existential stakes which will still be animating our voluntary and intellectual superstructures. At the crossroads of body and being, at the core of the "body as mediator of being", perception and desire are the essential modalities of the *unconscious* in action, of the unconscious as an *act*.

3.6 "An Unconscious of Ek-stasis"

3.6.1 The Unconscious is Sensing Itself. Merleau-Ponty Critique of Freud

The *Notes on the body* tell us more about the "relationship of being" thus engaged by the bodily and desiring unconscious. The unconscious, says Merleau-Ponty, is "this primordial openness to an existing world and to the others" (N-Corps [87] v(8)). It is an "unconscious of ek-stasis" (N-Corps [87](7)), an "unconscious which is not far, which is unconscious by simple ek-stasis, and nonetheless is unconscious" (N-Corps [91]v). We already know that this ecstasy is, for Merleau-Ponty, oneiric-perceptual and bodily-desiring – which by the way implies that the eventual Heideggerian nuance of the "ek-stasis" in question runs the risk of not surpassing

---

[19] "The esthesiological structure of the human body is thus a libidinal structure, the perception is a mode of desire, a relation of being and not of knowledge." (Natu3, p. 272/210).
[20] S: *Signes*. 1960. Paris: Gallimard. S(Préf): "Préface" (February and September 1960). 1964. *Signs*. Trans. Richard C. McCleary. Evanston: Northwestern University Press.

the superficial degree of a simple nuance. The summary of 1960's lecture at the Collège de France sheds some light on the modality of this openness which would characterize the unconscious:

> A philosophy of the flesh finds itself in opposition to any interpretation of the unconscious in terms of "unconscious representations", a tribute paid by Freud to the psychology of his day. The unconscious is sensing itself, since sensing is not the intellectual possession of "what" is sensed, but a dispossession of ourselves in favor of it, an opening toward that which we do not have to think in order that we may recognize it. (RC60, pp. 178–179/198)

Merleau-Ponty was always opposed to the idea that perception and desire would be, by themselves and as if by definition, conscious. He disagrees in this way with many philosophers, starting with Sartre. But the *Notes on the body* are explicitly opposed to Freud, and more precisely to the text on "The Unconscious", written in 1915 for *Metapsychology*. Freud tends to reduce the feeling and the affect to an energetic process of discharge, which is inevitably perceived by the subject (cf. Freud 1915, pp. 177–178). Merleau-Ponty, under the precocious influence of Max Scheler, does not admit the reduction of affectivity to the "affective states", reduction that erases the intentional dimensions which sustain and cross over it (cf. ChRe,[21] 1935), and betrays the very movement of affectivity by crushing its essential openness in the possession of the feeling felt.

If the "Freudian conceptualisation" is maybe, indeed, "criticisable" (N-Corps [86]v(6), cf. also Natu3, p. 352/284), the second take made by Merleau-Ponty is as well and on many levels. (1) Approaching "representation as an internal board facing a consciousness" (N-Corps [86]v(6)) resolves the problem before even raising it, since it would not be unconscious. (2) But there is more: these notes operate a surprising shift, and unjustified, of the *feeling* [sentiment] to *sensing* [sentir],[22] a "sensing" which, at least in the late manuscripts, turns out to be vertiginously close to "perceive" [percevoir]. Yet, Freud doesn't aim at speaking about perception for itself, but actually about feelings and affects. This is not an isolated mistake from Merleau-Ponty: other passages perform the same shift:

> Freud himself reserves the unconscious to the representations, saying that there are no unconscious feelings (…).
> In reality, it is *representation* that must be excluded. Archaic "perception" is ek-stasis. Is at its core unconsciousness since the signification is not possessed, extracted, since it *is here*, figured. (N-Corps [91]v)

From the feeling to sensing and perceive: the shift is typical, Merleau-Ponty not being able to think the affectivity as an overall that we could isolate, and coming back always from the affectivity to perception. These different passages converge towards the same turnaround of the Freudian position. Freud excluded the feeling from the unconscious to place representation in it (and that of the object of the feeling). Merleau-Ponty, on his side, excludes firmly the representation from the uncon-

---

[21] ChRe: "Christianisme et ressentiment". Review of French translation of Max Scheler's *L'Homme du ressentiment*. 1935. In *La Vie intellectuelle*, 7ᵉ year, new series, volume XXXVI: 278–306. Reprinted. 1997. In *Parcours 1935–1951*, 9–33. Lagrasse: Verdier.

[22] Merleau-Ponty takes advantage of translations processes, French language introducing here different nuances that are less obvious in German.

scious, and injects it with, not the feeling, but the perception, sensing, or at least their archaic dimension, the fundamental gesture that supports them.

What lies "inside" the unconscious, explains Merleau-Ponty, is not "internal boards" (representations), but nor "traces" either, the latter referring to the idea of something that is preserved and *possessed*, as remainders. They are not either "memories" in the classic meaning of the term, as they are not available, and are not contained in *states* (cognitive or affective). They rely on an active disposition, a manner of being, a mimic of the body: a figuration (cf. N-Corps [91]v).

For the affect and the feeling, Freud talks about "discharge"; Merleau-Ponty, on his side, going from the feeling to sensing, talks about "dispossession". In Freud, the *discharge* contributes to highlight that any affect is inevitably partly conscious; in Merleau-Ponty, the *dispossession* contributes to prove the reverse ("the very sensing as it is not thought of sensing (possession) but dispossession, *ek-stasis*", Natu3, p. 351/283).

3.6.2 From Dispossession to the Initial Yes

Let us proceed deeper into the meaning of this ecstasy, understood as "dispossession". In Merleau-Ponty's texts, the dispossession (1) is clearly opposed to a *possession* heard as an "intellectual possession of 'what is' sensed", a "thought of sensing", "I think that…" – with an implicit assimilation of this possession to the *consciousness* of sensing. (2) But we shall not yet believe that dispossession is a simple negation of this possession, that it only consists in terminating it. Because it implies a part of *renouncement*, something to let go of, to release and to give; and this renouncement itself implies a form of self-dispossession. Merleau-Ponty begins this more positive characterization: this dispossession is (a) "a dispossession *of ourselves*" (RC60, p. 179/198, we stress), "everything can affirm its being only by dispossessing me of mine" already stated the philosopher in 1945 (SNS(roman),[23] p. N50/G38/29). And this dispossession is (b) "a dispossession of ourselves *in favor of it*" (RC60, p. 179/198, we stress), to the benefit of "'what is' sensed", but which, precisely as we are sensing it, is not a *what is*: is not simply facing, as a confined data, but is haunting me, dwelling in me, animates and possesses me. The positive characterization goes even further. It is not enough not to (possess), it is not enough to renounce. Yet again we have to *consent* to that what *is* and consent to let it be, yet again do we have to say "yes": which Merleau-Ponty names the "initial yes", very act of the "primordial unconscious" (*ibid.*).

When we read these expressions, two references are emerging immediately: the let-be of Heidegger,[24] and even more the *Bejahung* that Lacan takes over from

---

[23] SNS: *Sens et non-sens*. 1948, 1958. Paris: Nagel. 1996. Paris: Gallimard. SNS(roman): *Le roman et la métaphysique* (March–April 1945). 1992. *Sense and Non-Sense*. Trans. Patricia and Hubert Dreyfus. Evanston: Northwestern University Press.

[24] In the first writing phase of *The Visible and the Invisible*, echoes an Heideggerian hint, imprint of the reading of texts on science and technique (in *Vorträge und Aufsätze*) recently translated in French by A. Préau and J. Beaufret (1958). Furthermore, we have found a copy of *Gelassenheit* (1959) in Merleau-Ponty's library, but without any reading marks.

Freud.[25] Anyhow, if we explore the manuscripts as the library of Merleau-Ponty, it looks as though this one is appropriating (too) quickly some expressions that suit him because they express correctly an idea, a philosophical gesture that belongs to him and that he has been practising for a long time. A late terminological encounter then, without having substantially released Merleau-Ponty's ideas. This phenomenon is rather representative of his late relationship to Heidegger (cf. Saint Aubert 2006) – more precisely here, in the textual and notional context we are questioning, it is more a Heidegger transmitted by Lacan.

In Merleau-Ponty, the "initial yes" is explicitly *pre-linguistic*, whilst participating in the "infrastructure of language" (N-Corps [90](13)). Less linked to judgement of attribution than to a form of proto-judgement of existence preceding any attribution, it is disposed by the *flesh*; by the human being "insofar as he has a body" (*ibid.*). It engages what Merleau-Ponty calls the "primordial symbolism" (N-Corps [84](1), [91]-[91]v, [102]), "natural symbolism" (Natu3 274/211, 282/219, 289/226, RC60 180/199) or "mute symbolism" (N-Corps [86](5)-[86]v(6), [90](13)) of the body: this "*symbolism without negation, language of the body* as sensing" (N-Corps [90](13)) is instituted by the body schema. This "effective symbolisation, in action" (N-Corps [86]v(6)), "does not need language and is primarily resisting it, because it is already a symbolisation without words: by centration of the whole body schema" (N-Corps [86](5)). Symbolisation without words, but supposed by the register of the meaning and the infrastructure of the speech, which are as if initiated by this "yes".

The borrowing to Lacan then immediately shifts to an annexation to a personal anthropology, distancing and even opposed with this one. Merleau-Ponty elaborates his own non Freudian "return to Freud", according to a double accentuation of *body* and *being*: "consciousness and unconscious redefined in terms of body" (N-Corps [97]), a body understood as "a general-topological being" (*ibid.*), in the frame of an anthropology of desire with an ontological scope. The entirety of his philosophy of the flesh, far from orientating him towards an unconscious structured like a language,[26] leads him to conceive the unconscious as instituted by the "body schema as speech of the body" (N-Corps [91]v), and to evoke "language as corporeality" (N-Corps [97]), "speech as corporeality" (N-Corps [102]).

3.6.3 Unconscious and Perceptual Faith

This "yes" pronounced without words by the carnal unconscious initiates for Merleau-Ponty our relationship to being. The "initial *Bejahung*" or "primal *Bejahung*" is initial "let-be" (N-Corps [90](13)) and "let-be of Being" (N-Corps [101]v). It is consent to be and consent to being, one going with the other. Aside

---

[25] Merleau-Ponty probably comes across the *Bejahung* – literally "affirmation", the act of saying "yes"–, in Lacan's "Response to Jean Hyppolite's Commentary on Freud's *Verneinung*".

[26] As we know, Merleau-Ponty clearly expressed his opposition to Lacan on this matter in the famous conference on the unconscious in Bonneval, a few months before he passed.

from any project and any decision, underlines *Being and World* (EM2[27] [225](2), June 1959), there is already the inauguration of a *yes* through the perceptual life. And what Merleau-Ponty asks here is "not to consider the *yes* as a negation of the no. The yes is *consent*, let-be" (*ibid.*).

Merleau-Ponty follows his lifelong gesture – the one we were mentioning at the beginning, and that finds its final development in the notion of *perceptual faith*. The perceptual faith is consent and abandon to the depth of being, but in an active passivity, which solicits our body and our intelligence – Merleau-Ponty speaks, in places, of "animal faith", and associates strongly perceptual faith with "interrogative thought". This active passivity, without being possession or catch, without immobilising and determining the being, nonetheless effectuates on it a sort of pressure inherent to the interrogative posture itself. Carried by a perceptual *and* interrogative faith, the "let-be" mentioned by Merleau-Ponty is then *also* probation and interrogation of being. This non-contradictory conjunction is major, and essential to a right comprehension of his approach of the unconscious, which is not regressive, nor spiritualist. Merleau-Ponty maintains up to his ontology the existentialist tonality of an anthropology which considers the human being in a desiring-aggressive relationship with the depth of the world and the other.

Merleau-Ponty is sensitive to the permanence of certain fundamentals of our being-in-the-world. His conception of the unconscious is particularly marked by this concern and this sensibility. The relationship to perceptual *depth* is one of these main continuity lines.[28] A relationship made of abandon and penetration, of consent and interrogation. Perceptual depth, depth of the world (that is to say, in a late terminology, "the flesh of the world" or better, *being*) solicits us so that we abandon ourselves to it, that we orientate ourselves inside it while at the same time letting it configure us "in depth". In doing so, perceptual depth de-objectifies and dispossesses us.

Same goes, at the highest point, in the abandonment to the gaze of the other, depth par excellence where the dimension of desire is fully played out. We know the importance of the seeing-seen in Merleau-Ponty. The seeing-seen, explains the phenomenologist, is an "open circuit" which goes through the other, circuit forever wounded by the *rapt* of the other's gaze, by the depth of (gaze of) the other, far from the immanence of a simple auto-affection (cf. Saint Aubert 2013, Chap. III). In this rapt, is again, and more than ever, played a form of dispossession. The unconscious, as Merleau-Ponty conceives it (an "unconscious of *ecstasy*" precisely), is traversed by this rapt – far, really, from any approach that would make it a reservoir of immanent contents shut from our relationship to the world.

---

[27] EM2: "Être et Monde", unpublished. B.N.F., volume VI, various pieces of work from 1959.

[28] This question is explored by Merleau-Ponty from the most sensorimotor of its components, while still assuming the amplitude of the symbolic and the imaginary that are associated with it, up to "this research of depth that lasts an entire lifetime" (OntoCart, p. 167) – research which becomes in last writings an emblem of human desire, at the same time the most archaic, the most constant and the most achieved. (OntoCart: preparatory notes for the 1961 course at the Collège de France on "L'ontologie cartésienne et l'ontologie d'aujourd'hui". B.N.F., volume XIX. 1996. *Notes de cours 1959–1961*. Paris: Gallimard.)

3.7 Conclusion

From the "being toward the thing through the intermediary of the body" to the unconscious as an "initial yes", Merleau-Ponty then pursued and deepened one same gesture. The "root of the ingenuous affirmation" – to repeat this early expression – is a being-body to the thing which relies itself on a "let-be" the thing, and even more radically, on a "let-be" of *being*. A let-be which would be a fundamental and founding act of the *flesh*, of which the very "subject" (if we can yet still speak of "subject" or to speak about it in a completely different meaning) would be the *unconscious*. The unconscious is thus at the "root of the ingenuous affirmation".

The "this is" relies on a "let-be" which is merged with the *perceptual faith*. This joint act of the *let-be* and the *perceptual faith* (because it is indeed an act and not an affective state) engages what Merleau-Ponty names the "primordial symbolism of the body", and – and it's all one – the primal root of intelligence. The "initial yes", *infra*-linguistic, is not less of a foundation of *speech* itself: it is all the register of *meaning*, the infrastructure of the speech itself, which can be apprehended as relying on this initial yes, as rooted within it.

This joint act of the *let-be* and the *perceptual faith* is not desire as such, and operates in a certain way beneath desire, there too as sustaining its possible emergence or resurgence – its possible "surrection" (upheaval) or "resurrection", to repeat the terminology of some late manuscripts. What is expressed in the "initial yes", beneath the desire itself, is a dimension of faith in the bearing of being, of dispossession and deposition of the self which only itself can open ourselves to its openness. At the core of the flesh, is played a primordial amazement faced with the existence of things and the depth of being, as well as a primordial adherence to the existence of things and the depth of being, which would be (the act of) the primordial unconscious itself.[29] Here is at least the horizon towards which Merleau-Ponty is heading and orientates us, in this continual gesture that is his, and which thus leads to his final answer to the Cartesian *Cogito*.

References

Freud, Sigmund. 1915, 2002. *The Metapsychological Papers*. Trans. James Strachey. London: Hoghart Press.
Heidegger, Martin. 1958. *Essais et conférences*. Trans. A. Préau and J. Beaufret. Paris: Gallimard.
———. 1959. *Gelassenheit*. Pfullingen: Günther Neske.
Hyppolite, Jean. 1988. A spoken commentary on Freud's *Verneinung*. In *The seminar of Jacques Lacan*, Book I: *Freud's papers on technique*. Cambridge: Cambridge University Press.
Lacan, Jacques. 1988. Response to Jean Hyppolite's commentary on Freud's *Verneinung*. In *The seminar of Jacques Lacan*, Book I: *Freud's papers on technique*. Cambridge: Cambridge University Press.

---

[29] For further discussion on these points, see Saint Aubert (2015, 2016).

Merleau-Ponty, Maurice. 1933. "Projet de travail sur la nature de la Perception", handwritten text presented for obtaining a grant from the Caisse nationale des Sciences. 1989. In *Le primat de la perception et ses conséquences philosophiques*, 11–13. Grenoble: Cynara. Reprinted. 1996. Lagrasse: Verdier.

———. 1935. "Christianisme et ressentiment". Review of French translation of Max Scheler's *L'Homme du ressentiment*. In *La Vie intellectuelle*, 7 year, new series, volume XXXVI: 278–306. Reprinted. 1997. In Parcours 1935–1951, 9–33. Lagrasse: Verdier.

———. 1936. "Être et Avoir". Review of Gabriel Marcel's *Être et Avoir*. In *La Vie intellectuelle*, 8 year, new series, volume XLV: 98–109. Reprinted. 1997. In Parcours 1935–1951, 35–44. Lagrasse: Verdier.

———. 1945. *Phénoménologie de la perception*. Paris: Gallimard. 2012. *Phenomenology of Perception*. Trans. Donald A. Landes. London and New York: Routledge.

———. 1948, 1958. *Sens et non-sens*. Paris: Nagel. 1996. Paris: Gallimard. 1992. *Sense and Non-Sense*. Trans. Patricia and Hubert Dreyfus. Evanston: Northwestern University Press.

———. 1958–1960. *Être et Monde*. Unpublished. B.N.F., volume VI.

———. 1960a. *Notes sur le corps*. Unpublished. B.N.F., volume XVII.

———. 1960b. *Signes*. Paris: Gallimard. 1964. Signs. Trans. Richard C. McCleary. Evanston: Northwestern University Press.

———. 1964a. *L'OEil et l'Esprit*. Paris: Gallimard. Reprinted. 1985. Paris: Gallimard, "Folio essais". 1964. "Eye and Mind." Trans. Carleton Dallery. In *The Primacy of Perception*. Evanston: Northwestern University Press.

———. 1964b. *Le visible et l'invisible*. Paris: Gallimard. 1968. *The Visible and the Invisible*. Trans. Alphonso Lingis. Evanston: Northwestern University Press.

———. 1968. *Résumés de cours. Collège de France, 1952–1960*. Paris: Gallimard. 1988. "Themes from the Lectures at the Collège de France 1952–1960". Trans. John O'Neill. In *In Praise of Philosophy and Other Essays*. Evanston: Northwestern University Press.

———. 1969. *La prose du monde*. Paris: Gallimard. 1973. *The Prose of the World*. Trans. John O'Neill. Evanston: Northwestern University Press.

———. 1978. *L'union de l'âme et du corps chez Malebranche, Biran et Bergson*. New French edition, revised and augmented with a new unpublished fragment. Paris: Vrin.

———. 1988. *Merleau-Ponty à la Sorbonne, résumé de cours 1949–1952*. Grenoble: Cynara. 2010. Child Psychology and Pedagogy: The Sorbonne Lectures 1949–1952. Trans. Talia Welsh. Evanston: Northwestern University Press.

———. 1995. *La Nature. Notes, cours du Collège de France*. Paris: Seuil. 2003. *Nature: Course Notes from the Collège de France*. Trans. Robert Vallier. Evanston: Northwestern University Press.

———. 1996. *Notes de cours 1959–1961*. Paris: Gallimard.

———. 2003. *L'institution. La passivité. Notes de cours au Collège de France (1954–1955)*. Paris: Belin. 2010. *Institution and Passivity: Course Notes from the Collège de France (1954–1955)*. Trans. Leonard Lawlor and Heath Massey. Evanston: Northwestern University Press.

———. 2011. *Le monde sensible et le monde de l'expression*. Genève: MétisPresses.

Saint Aubert, Emmanuel de. 2004. *Du lien des êtres aux éléments de l'être. Merleau-Ponty au tournant des années 1945–1951*. Paris: Vrin.

———. 2005. *Le scénario cartésien. Recherches sur la formation et la cohérence de l'intention philosophique de Merleau-Ponty*. Paris: Vrin.

———. 2006. *Vers une ontologie indirecte. Sources et enjeux critiques de l'appel à l'ontologie chez Merleau-Ponty*. Paris: Vrin.

———. 2013. *Être et chair I. Du corps au désir: l'habilitation ontologique de la chair*. Paris: Vrin.

———. 2015. La chair ouverte à la portance de l'être. *Alter* 23: 165–182.

———. 2016. Introduction à la notion de portance. *Archives de Philosophie* 79 (2): 317–343. http://www.cairn.info/revue-archives-de-philosophie-2016-2-page-317.htm.

Schilder, Paul. 1935. *The image and appearance of the human body: Studies in the constructive energies of the psyche*. Londres: K. Paul, Trench, Trübner.

———. 1950. *The image and appearance of the human body: Studies in the constructive energies of the psyche*. New York: International Universities Press.

Chapter 4
Repression and Operative Unconsciousness in *Phenomenology of Perception*

Timothy Mooney

Abstract The notion of repression as active forgetfulness already found in Nietzsche and systematised by Freud and his successors is employed in a distinctive manner by Merleau-Ponty in *Phenomenology of Perception*. By showing how we appropriate our environment towards outcomes and respond to other people, he contends, we can unearth hidden modes of operative intentionality. Two such modes are the motor intentional projection of action and the anonymous intercorporeality that includes touching and being touched. Each of these is an aspect of a past that was never a present. Merleau-Ponty does have something to say about pasts that were once present and that linger on in human life. Yet he shows little interest in the unconsciousness of psychoanalysis for its own sake. Psychoanalytic accounts of repression are assimilated into his theory of the body itself, serving merely as means for illustrating the latter. I suggest that this move follows on a conception of an integrated existent whose past acquisitions are remarkably enabling and untroubling.

Keywords Merleau-Ponty • Body • Unconscious • Past • Time

4.1 Introduction

In *The Genealogy of Morals*, Nietzsche tells us that forgetting is no *vis inertiae* as the superficial imagine. Rather it is an active and positive faculty of repression. It is responsible for the fact that, while we are digesting it, what we experience enters our consciousness as little as the thousandfold process involved in physical nourishment. To close the doors and windows of consciousness for a time; to remain undisturbed by our underworld of utility organs working with and against one another; to gain a little quietness for consciousness to make room for new things, is the purpose

---

T. Mooney (✉)
School of Philosophy, University College Dublin, Dublin, Ireland
e-mail: tim.mooney@ucd.ie

© Springer International Publishing AG 2017
D. Legrand, D. Trigg (eds.), *Unconsciousness Between Phenomenology and Psychoanalysis*, Contributions To Phenomenology 88,
DOI 10.1007/978-3-319-55518-8_4

of active forgetfulness. Allowing for regulation, foresight and premeditation, it is like a doorkeeper, the preserver of psychic order and repose. Without it there could be no hope or pride or present. The person in whom positive repression is damaged or destroyed cannot 'have done' with anything (Nietzsche 1967, pp. 57–58). All of this will be taken up and systematised by Freud and his successors.

In Merleau-Ponty's *Phenomenology of Perception*, the body itself enables active forgetfulness by virtue of active remembering, a sub-reflective being aware in the world. As an operative unconsciousness it is beyond phenomenal experience, but not phenomenological investigation. We can show how we appropriate our environment towards outcomes and respond to other people, and on foot of this unearth hidden modes of operative intentionality or directed awareness. Two such modes are the motor intentional projection of action and the anonymous intercorporeality that precedes somatic self-identification. Merleau-Ponty's account of these achievements warrants his claim that the body itself is better informed about the world than we are at the accessible level of act intentionality.

In the first part of this essay I set out how Merleau-Ponty works towards and justifies his theory of motor intentionality with the help of pathological cases, which can better foreground the intentional achievements that lie behind our ordinary comportment. In the second section, I proceed to his account of the experience of the other, which is founded on the anonymous intercorporeality of touching and being touched that leaves its traces in later experience. These are aspects of a past that was never a present. I conclude by claiming that Merleau-Ponty does have something to say about pasts that were once present and that linger on in human life, while showing little interest in the unconsciousness of psychoanalysis for its own sake. Psychoanalytic accounts of repression are assimilated into his theory of the body itself. I suggest that Merleau-Ponty's move follows on a conception of an integrated existent whose past acquisitions are remarkably enabling and untroubling.

4.2 The Body Schema and Motor Intentionality

Merleau-Ponty's employment of pathological cases owes much to Husserl's procedure of bracketing and reduction and Heidegger's account of unreadiness-to-hand. The natural attitude of unhesitant action is best revealed when its absence is obtrusive. In this vein, the normal performances of the body – and hence its character as an intentional system of action – quickly become explicit when we see them in mutated form or as missing altogether (Merleau-Ponty 2012, p. 105). Such cases help us get the normal performances right descriptively, identify what is essential to them, and work back to their hidden conditions of possibility. These conditions make up what Merleau-Ponty calls *le corps propre*, 'the body itself.' This bridges Husserl's *Körper* and *Leib* (Husserl 1989, pp. 151–153) lying between the body as objectified and as lived. The body itself is my anonymous, sub-representational, and sub-conscious system of action projection and ensuing action execution.

Merleau-Ponty begins to explicate the body itself by looking at certain phantom limb phenomena. Most recent amputees attempt to use missing limbs, but a small minority of patients experience use-phantom limbs in the long term. In one case reported by Jean Lhermitte, for example, a patient keeps trying to walk with his use-phantom leg and is not discouraged by repeated failure. Such a patient needs intact nerves from the brain – and today we would add mapping from the somatosensory cortex – to maintain the use-phantom. But what most impresses both Lhermitte and Merleau-Ponty is that use-phantom cases do not articulate their missing limbs in themselves, for they are moments of integrated wholes. Thus the patient's use-phantom leg is experienced in harmony with a body that is taken as an overall and undivided power of movement. The leg is felt in the right place within a holistic awareness of position and orientation. Were it not, he could not assume over and again that he is able to walk (Lhermitte 1998, pp. 66, 68, 85–86; Merleau-Ponty 2012, p. 83).

Merleau-Ponty contends that in undamaged cases the body must enjoy a postural schema, a proprioceptive and non-representational awareness of limb position and of overall orientation. This is not enough to keep it unobtrusive, for a past is also needed in which the living body acquired certain skills or ways of achieving outcomes. When these become habitual they allow for further skill acquisition. These skills inform the present body and orient it towards the world in ever more ways. The habitual body constitutes the present body's horizon of capacities towards one's projects, and by the same token, a horizon for so-called external objects. By virtue of our informed bodies, certain things in the environment invite us into situations. We are solicited to co-intend them as means towards ends. On this account, the habitual body as the skill body schema is one's integrally unified system of motor capacities as it practically reveals the world (Merleau-Ponty 2012, p. 84).

Skills that are properly acquired are immediately available. These ingrained habits do not intrude on me, as I take them for granted. When I was little I encountered a tap as 'manipulatable eventually.' With difficulty and with help, I could turn it. The objectification and imaginative representation of my body and of the thing were doing work at this time. Eventually I learned how to turn it myself, and it became 'manipulatable for me.' The skill became habitual when I could do this immediately, with objectification and representation disappearing. As the body at my disposal became effectively anonymous, I began to apprehend the tap as 'manipulatable in itself.' It is 'ready-to-hand' to let me quench my thirst or wash my face or the dishes. It appears as a solicitation and an affordance: it unobtrusively affords drinking and washing. Hence there is an upsetting experience if a habitual expectation is suddenly frustrated, as happens to some long-term as well as recent amputees. The projective body and correlative field are revealed in being split apart (Merleau-Ponty 2012, pp. 84–85). For Merleau-Ponty, every perceived affordance has been a solicitation to action, but not every solicitation can be an affordance, since actual affordances presuppose live somatic capacities.

In developed life I embark on many skilled actions from a variety of starting positions. I reach to pick up my desk telephone from sitting forward, from slouching back, or from standing up. But position and orientation awareness is needed to move straight into the action from all these starting points. To readily activate the skill schema is to presuppose the postural schema, and this postural schema is also needed over the course of the action. I do not forget what my attitude is or where my limbs are half way through it – the where awareness is needed through the entire deployment of the how awareness. And in moving into and through the action, the where awareness is itself marked historically by the how awareness. There is thus a continuing and evolving interrelation of the two schemas. From early infancy, what I am posturally aware of has itself been built up and shaped by the evolution of my skilled habitual body (Merleau-Ponty 2012, pp. 148–150).

In the overall body schema, according to Merleau-Ponty, we discover 'organic repression' in a sense other than that of Freud, who associates the diminution of the olfactory sense and growth of shame with the assumption of the upright posture (Freud 1985, pp. 288–289n1). The body itself is an inborn complex serving the future. Psychoanalysis has also shown that a certain complex can come from a traumatic event that was abnormally repressed into the unconscious. What was once a personal and datable event lives on in a hidden form and continues to affect present experience (Freud 1984, pp. 288–291). In an analogous way some conscious bodily doings are 'sedimented' in my habitual body, becoming anonymous and motivational as well as available. There is a ceaseless sublimation of the personal and cultural into the biological, though nothing is purely natural, since we cannot find in humans a lower layer of behaviour underpinning a cultural world. The enabling body is for all that opaque – what lets us centre our existence prevents us from centering it completely. The anonymity of the body is both freedom and servitude (Merleau-Ponty 2012, pp. 87, 195).

The story of a somatic skill unconscious is developed further with the notion of motor intentionality, and the Schneider case is used to silhouette it. Injured as a front line soldier, Johann Schneider has to laboriously convert his imaginative picture of an abstract movement into the actual movement, finding a gap between the representation and its execution. For the undamaged person, by contrast, abstract as well as concrete movements are immediate possibilities. Through motor intentionality or motor projection, a movement that does not yet exist actually for him or her already exists virtually. He or she reckons with the possible. In motor-projection, sub-personal awareness of a situation plots out specific deployments of the body and its extremities to achieve a result. These comprise an action solution for and route to realisation of a certain goal. Motor projection also marks out a spatial path, since it articulates the environment into vectors and lines of force (Merleau-Ponty 2012, pp. 111–115).

The terminology of a 'schema' can help place the notion of motor-intentionality. In Kant each schematism of the understanding serves to mediate conceptual generality and empirical particularity and to produce something that contains both. A schema is a rule-governed process within a judgement whereby the productive imagination applies a concept to sensory intuitions in its generation of an image. Put another way, it is a formula by which imagination fills out intuitions in accordance with the concept, giving it an empirical application (Kant 1933, pp. 180–183, 220–221). The overall image is triggered by the sensory intuitions, and remains anchored in them. Yet in filling them out imaginatively it extends well beyond them. Thus a plopping beneath my window is imaged and judged via the schema of causation as drops from a leaking gutter. This schema of objective succession does not generate the image by itself, for I must already know what gutters and leaks and drops are. But it does structure that image in a certain order. I picture and judge that drops are forming at a leak point in the gutter before they fall and hit the ground with these actually heard plops.

For Merleau-Ponty, motor intentional prefiguration is an art hidden in the body itself, the other side of that art hidden in the depths of the soul. *What* I understand conceptually, representationally and reportably outside habitual situations is a function of act intentionality. *How* I apprehend it – as immediately realisable – is a function of motor intentionality. It informs the postural schema that is itself requisite by anticipating a result, comprising a context-sensitive skill projection, a schematising action solution. Motor intentionality is the skill schema schematising before being realised. It is the body's programme of how some of its skills will be put to work to appropriate this particular environment. It is the plan of the way the skills will be deployed in this context, the virtual precursor of an actual action situation. My embodied horizon of action is not one of bare motility, but of a power of motion towards an outcome (Merleau-Ponty 2012, pp. 139–140). Husserl showed the need for such a thesis when he posited the 'I can' as intrinsic to thoughts of action co-intended as immediate practical possibilities (Husserl 1989, pp. 270–271).

It might be thought that sub-conscious motor intentionality follows on from the conscious imaging of an action, on a Cartesian model of representation and implementation. The whole direction of Merleau-Ponty's account, however, is to deny that motor projection is a servant of consciousness, transporting the body to that point of which one has formed a representation beforehand (Merleau-Ponty 2012, p. 140). When the body gears into an actual movement, it does not follow a pictorial formula, since motor intentionality is the other side of act intentionality. More than this, the skill schema has shaped the very contours of the representation. In my perceptual and hence imaginative dealings with a situation, I explicitly pick out certain obstacles and ways around them, but only on foot of motor predelineation:

> We must in effect distinguish between my explicit intentions, such as the plan I form today to climb these mountains, and the general intentions that invest my surroundings with some value in a virtual way…my projects as a thinking being are clearly constructed upon these valuations…Insofar as I have hands, feet, a body and a world, I sustain intentions around myself that are not decided upon and that affect my surroundings in ways I do not choose… freedom makes use of the gaze along with its spontaneous valuations. Without these spontaneous valuations…we would not be in the world, ourselves implicated in the spectacle and, so to speak, intermingled with things…There is an autochthonous sense of the world that is constituted in the exchange between the world and our embodied existence and that forms the ground of every deliberate *Sinngebung*. (Merleau-Ponty 2012, pp. 464–466)

These absolute valuations are not fixed once and for all, since the skill schema is constantly reworked through life. What is sedimented in the depths of consciousness evolves in its commerce with freshly learnt skills. But it always runs ahead of me as a dark precursor, invisibly shaping whatever it is that I should see or express or report. Every perception has something anonymous in it, so that the 'I think' takes advantage of work already done. In perception we merge into the body itself, which is better informed than we are about the world and the means available (Merleau-Ponty 2012, pp. 131, 148, 248).

In this active and non-representational remembering and pre-figuring, the body itself is a doorkeeper of consciousness. There is the aforementioned organic repression *by* the skilled (and schematising) body *of* the objective body that is present to me, the anonymity of the former supplanting the objectifications it has made redundant. Using Nietzsche's words, we might say that the body itself is a preserver of psychic order and repose, and a core condition of foresight and premeditation. I am not swallowed up by practical tasks because I have the skills to cope with them unthinkingly, and hence to go beyond them. I can imaginatively create and plan because the familiar tasks of the present and the near future do not flood my awareness. My skill schema frees my consciousness from my environment so as to see it at a distance with theoretical understanding. I can see things under several aspects, and plan towards outcomes at several removes, since the successive means to reach them are unproblematic. For the most integrated existence, states Merleau-Ponty, 'that it provides itself with a habitual body is an internal necessity' (Merleau-Ponty 2012, p. 89).

Beneath my involvement with constituted objects, in conclusion, is my body as a skilled and sensori-motor system of anonymous functions. My unconscious adherence to the world bears the trace of sub-reflective as well as pre-reflective life, with sense giving by the body already shaping reportable skill acquisition in addition to more theoretical recognition and articulation. The body informs developed perceptions, which are the resumptions of a pre-personal tradition, of a communication 'more ancient than thought' that is impenetrable to reflection.' As stated above, what centres our experience stops us centering it completely. An archaeology of perceptual experience can at best unearth the communication of a finite subject with a structurally 'opaque being' from which it has emerged and with which it remains engaged. To grasp the significance of reflection is to refer 'to the pre-reflective fund it presupposes, upon which it draws, and that constitutes for it, like an original past, a past that has never been present' (Merleau-Ponty 2012, pp. 228, 252, 265).

4.3 From Expression to Anonymous Intercorporeality

Merleau-Ponty will integrate the foregoing into a wider phenomenology that explicates the intercorporeal contribution to conscious life. He begins by noting that the body itself is always already a body for others, a moment of a being-with. Even my world of objects is intrinsically public, more determinate when I go through the rooms of an abandoned house, less determinate when it is a footprint in the sand. Someone used these things and left these marks. And those others that are present to me never appear as objects exhibiting movements that require me to infer governing psyches within them, as putatively ethereal insides of mechanical outsides. If the body were just a physico-chemical structure it could have no internal relationship to significance and intentionality, and the Cartesians would be correct. But each of us is confronted by the expressive instrument we call a face, which carries a whole existence in and through it. He or she is the theatre of a certain process of elaboration and of a certain view of the world (Merleau-Ponty 2012, pp. 363–369).

Merleau-Ponty will never fail to see our bodies as processes of expressive elaboration. Just as in a painting or a melody the meaning is inseparable from the swirls of colours or the tones, so too the meanings that we express in our gestures cannot be sundered from our modes of expression, from our own unique styles. There is no kernel of meaning to be extracted from some indifferent husk that carries it. Hence the living body can best be compared with a work of art (Merleau-Ponty 2012, pp. 152–153). If I could paint someone in his or her expressivity, remarks Merleau-Ponty in a subsequent essay, what I would transmit to canvas would be more than a corporeal contour, and more again than a sensual value. It would be the emblem of a singular way of inhabiting the world, of handling and interpreting it 'by a face as by clothing, by agility of gesture as by inertia of body – in short, the emblem of a certain relationship to being' (Merleau-Ponty 1964, p. 54).

Unique ways of behaving are modulations of common ones. Studies of early childhood have shown that at 15 months a baby is already familiar with the sense of common patterns of comportment. If I pretend to bite the finger of a baby at this age, he or she reacts by opening his or her mouth. What biting looks like has an immediate, intercorporeal significance – from the inside, the baby feels its own jaw and teeth as an apparatus to bite with, and my jaw and teeth from the outside as an apparatus beginning to execute this operation. Thus the baby perceives my intention in my body (of biting), its own intention in its body (of stopping the bite with its jaw), and hence my own putative intention in its body (Merleau-Ponty 2012, p. 368). And no methodology can get behind such experience:

> When I turn toward my perception itself and when I pass from direct perception to the thought about this perception, I re-enact it, I uncover a thought older than I am at work in my perceptual organs and of which these organs are merely the trace. I understand others in the same way. Here again I have but the trace of a consciousness that escapes me in its actuality…There is, between my consciousness and my body such as I live it, and between this phenomenal body and the other person's phenomenal body such as I see it from the outside, an internal relation that makes the other person appear as the completion of the system. Others can be evident because I am not transparent to myself, and because my subjectivity draws its body along behind itself…this perspective itself has no definite limits, because it spontaneously slips into the other's perspective, and because they are gathered together in a single world in which we all participate as anonymous subjects of perception. (Merleau-Ponty 2012, pp. 367–369)

Merleau-Ponty's contention is that the earliest consciousness of expressive significance cannot be unearthed because it comprises an internal relation that is both prior to and beyond the reach of reflection. Crucial to the irreducible correlation of my body with the other's body is the fact that it preceded my identification of myself and of the other, for as a baby I had as yet no comprehension of the own and the alien. We were anonymous beings of which my present body is continuously the trace (Merleau-Ponty 2012, p. 370). This is why the immediate evidence of the other in later life is part of my lack of transparency to myself. It is grounded in this irreducible opacity of common bodily existence in babyhood.

It would be wrong to conclude that Merleau-Ponty lays too much weight on vision. In this early work he is already attentive to touch. This faculty is radically different to all the other senses in that it involves a double sensation. For Husserl, this double sensation constitutes my living body's permanent presence with me, and is also essential to recognise my outer body as mine. If I touch my left hand with my right, I touch on something that is soft and hard and smooth and warm. These qualities are tacitly taken as belonging to the left hand, and can quite correctly be objectified as properties of the body as *Körper*. Yet they are caught or felt by way of the right and active hand. In this touching hand, there is a localised correspondence between what is felt and the feeling of it. Through all of this, the left hand also has localised sensations. These are of being touched or felt. It is experienced as the living flesh or *Leib* being impinged upon. But this double sensation and double relationship is reversible. I can alternate the roles so that the left hand becomes the active touching one, and the right hand the passive one being touched (Husserl 1989, pp. 152–153).

Just as remarkably, such reversibility extends to the entire body. In tacit terms, I know what it feels like for every part of my body to be touched by some other part, and what it feels like to do the touching. Through touch, my body is constituted as both an exterior and as an interior. It is felt on from the outside, and felt in from the inside. Yet I do not even have to touch one of my body part with another. If I move one of my hands over an exterior thing, I feel its outer qualities in my hand, from within me. There are not two experiences, rather two aspects of one experience. Together they comprise a peculiar bodily reflexivity that is the feeling of feeling, of being touched in touching. Touching is the living body's self-appearance in its perceiving of things. On this account it is *Körper* and *Leib* together, a sensitive and extended living flesh. Because I feel myself from within I can recognise the body seen from outside as mine. It is only apprehended as belonging to me because it is simultaneously being felt from the inside (Husserl 1989, pp. 153, 158–159, 1960, p. 97).

On foot of this aesthetic unity of touch, claims Husserl, one can come to recognise another body as the living body of the Other and on this basis empathise with him or her, without having to engage in inferences or reasoning by analogy. The hand of the other that is touching me or touching something is appresented as also a feeling from the inside (Husserl 1989, pp. 172–174). Merleau-Ponty discovers an ambiguity or lack of coincidence in the experience, since one cannot explicitly register the reversible touching and being touched in one blow. One can only alternate between its aspects, giving one or the other my attention. I am always too late to catch the overall experience, which is structurally in the background of awareness towards the world (Merleau-Ponty 2012, p. 95). But he agrees that it founds the apprehension of the other. Just as one hand is present at the advent of being touched, so the other's body is animate when I shake his hand or look at it. He appears through an extension of my own non-coincident bodily reflexivity, each of us participating in an anonymous intercorporeality (Merleau-Ponty 1964, p. 168).

Emmanuel Levinas has contended that this aesthetic community founding empathy, intersubjectivity and intellectual communication is not directly given, only being produced by reconstruction. This is not taken as a deficiency in one's perception of others, but as a positive characteristic of that perception. Anterior to our interdependent thoughts, Merleau-Ponty is discerning – with the help of Husserl – a relation to others that depends on the carnal structure of sensibility. We find an originary articulation of the inner and the outer that is prior and irreducible to the noetic and noematic structure of intentional, cognitive awareness (Levinas 1993, pp. 98–100; Merleau-Ponty 1964, p. 159). Reversible flesh in the sense of the explicitly recognised sensitive body of oneself and of the other turns out to be constituted by conscious capacities that are already indebted to the body of sensibility. As Levinas expresses it, recognitive consciousness 'turns out to have already called upon what it is supposed to be constituting' (Levinas 1993, p. 97).

For the early Merleau-Ponty, this account of anonymous intercorporeality picks out just one founding condition of the eventual apprehension of the other as other, that is to say, one condition of the level of explicit, conceptual and hence reportable recognition. And he is adamant that what we know of each other takes place at the level of transcendental intersubjectivity. Yet as soon as a human existent commits itself to a new line of conduct, he or she falls beneath the level of perception to date. In a similar way, when I say that I know someone and like him, I aim at an inexhaustible ground that may 1 day shatter the image I had formed of him. This is the price of there being other people for me, not as the result of some illusion, but through a violent act that is perception itself. Not all the difficulties inherent in perceiving others stem from objective thought, and not all are removed by discovering the significance of expressive behaviour (Merleau-Ponty 2012, pp. 373, 379).

4.4 Repression and Pasts Once Present

Having encountered active forgetting as it has issued in the active and sub-reflective remembering of the body itself, one may still point to the diversity of contents that disappear from conscious view. For Nietzsche's forgetting refers not just to learned skills sedimented beneath an active and engaged life at the conscious and reflective level, not just to pasts that were enabling when one was aware of them. It refers also to pasts that were unhappy when they were present, to personal and datable experiences that were repressed so as not to become the gravediggers of any present oriented creatively towards a future (Nietzsche 1967, p. 58, 1997, p. 62). It can be retorted that Merleau-Ponty does not restrict the work of repression to positive and self-directed episodes of conscious awareness, nor regard this work as always successful. No impulse in the living body is entirely fortuitous in relation to psychic intentions, and no thought fails to find its germ in physiological dispositions. But if I am not a pure psyche with a pure organism, I am a movement between acts that are chiefly somatic or intellectual and chiefly enabling or frustrating, all of them moments of my intercorporeal and intersubjective being-with (Merleau-Ponty 2012, pp. 90, 366–369).

In his chapter on the body and sexuality, Merleau-Ponty discusses some pathologies that are corporeal in the main. It is because of sensori-motor damage, for example, that Schneider's range of motor projection has narrowed drastically. He can no longer extricate his body from a practical situation and live it in the realm of imagination. This too is why his sexual acts are local and perfunctory – his erotic fantasies are truncated along with his motility (Merleau-Ponty 2012, pp. 107, 158–159). However Merleau-Ponty is careful to remark that the bodily existence running through me and without my complicity 'is but the sketch of a genuine presence in the world,' even if it allows for it by establishing 'our primary pact with the world' (Merleau-Ponty 2012, p. 168). Thus he will employ ideas from psychoanalysis that are irreducible to sensori-motor deficiencies, referring with Freud to someone who embarks on a conscious course of action like a love affair or career. The person encounters an obstacle that cannot be surmounted, and since there is neither the strength to surmount it nor to abandon the enterprise, he or she remains imprisoned in the attempt by repeatedly renewing it. The subject remains committed to the same impossible future. Through abnormal repression and repetition-compulsion, one present gains an exceptional value and deprives others of their authenticity (Freud 1984, pp. 291–293; Merleau-Ponty 2012, p. 85).

According to Merleau-Ponty, one cannot get rid of psychoanalysis by impugning 'reductionist' and causal thought in the name of a descriptive and phenomenological method. But psychoanalysis can be stared in a different language (Merleau-Ponty 2012, pp. 174–175). The lasting contribution of this discipline is not to rest everything on a sexual substructure, but to discover in sexuality relations and attitudes that were previously held to reside in consciousness. Merleau-Ponty contends that Freud in his concrete analyses abandons purely causal thought, and that it is a mistake to imagine that his approach rules out the description of psychological motives, or is opposed to the phenomenological method. Albeit unwittingly, psychoanalysis has helped to develop phenomenology by claiming that every human action and every symptom has a meaning, and that the meaning is overdetermined. That is why it is not a question of knowing how much of human life rests or does not rest on sexuality, as of knowing what in the generality of life is to be understood in and through it (Merleau-Ponty 2012, pp. 160–161, 528n5).

The foregoing interpretation of Freud squares with Merleau-Ponty's sympathy for the existential psychoanalysis of Ludwig Binswanger. In Binswanger's 'Daseinsanalysis,' what is important is not merely to uncover hidden traumas, but to take seriously the patient's overall Being-in-the-world. One case concerns a young woman forbidden to meet her lover, and who then loses the power of speech and easy swallowing. Having lost her voice in childhood after frights, there is now no sign of its return. She is diagnosed with aphonia, a condition having no discernible physiological basis. One approach would posit the oral stage of development as the primary explanation of her difficulties. When she was frightened, or closed off from the activities of caressing and kissing the loved one, she relapsed into the passive oral phase. For Binswanger, such an explanation gives too much primacy to physiology and early experience. He notes that the mouth is also the organ par excellence of communal existence. The patient's future of co-existence was threatened in childhood. Later on happy co-existence was invested in the loved one. But once this tie is broken, familial co-existence appears pale and formulaic. She refuses a life that she now regards as far inferior, and this is symbolised by her loss of speech. She also refuses to assimilate the prohibition, as symbolised by her difficulty with swallowing. Her current existence is rejected (Binswanger 1935, p. 113 ff.).

Merleau-Ponty sees Binswanger's interpretation as the better one, though it leans too far towards intellectualism. Existential psychoanalysis should not serve as the pretext to revive a mentalistic philosophy in which everything important lies in freedom and decision. For Merleau-Ponty, the girl's current aphonia is not the outer indication of an inner state. It does not consist of a sign that merely conveys significance externally, like a chevron an army rank or a street number a house. Instead it is filled with the significance it conveys – what is expressed cannot be sundered from its bodily expression. Her behaviour is not the deliberate mime of a drama occurring inside consciousness. It is not like that of a politician who poses with a train driver during canvassing, or a friend who is insulted and stops speaking to me. She is not choosing to keep silence – only someone who can speak can do this (Merleau-Ponty 2012, pp. 163–164). But why then is she currently unable to speak?

Merleau-Ponty's suggestion is that there may have been an original choice that became to all effect a fate. The woman may have cast herself into a situation like that of an aphonic. There could have been a deliberate mime at the outset. We see this in everyday life when we go to bed. We put ourselves into the position of the sleeper, perhaps turning on our sides, pulling up our knees and breathing slowly. We mime the sleeper. But when sleep comes over us, then voluntary consciousness fades away. We are taken over by sleep, and the mime becomes the reality. In similar manner there might have been a conscious refusal to speak that initiated or hastened the onset of aphonia. But once it commenced, the young woman's choice became irrelevant – she could not will herself out of it. She was absorbed into the life that was presented outwardly, so it was no longer kept at a distance as possible to abandon. And choice may not have got her out of her narrowed world. She only regained speech when allowed to see her lover again – there was a conversion of her being, and regions may have been reactivated when reassigned meaning (Merleau-Ponty 2012, pp. 164–166).

The more orthodox Freudian might respond that all this departs too far from causal thinking, in spite of the criticism of mentalism. Elsewhere in his book, Merleau-Ponty is at pains to advert to the importance of causal knowledge in defending those doctors who rejected intellectualist hypotheses alone in dealing with pathologies. They were right to fell back on causal explanations, which themselves can take into account what is peculiar to illnesses. Contemporary pathology shows that there is no strictly elective disturbance, and that a structure of signification cannot be separated from the materials in which it is realised (Merleau-Ponty 2012, p. 127). On this line of thinking, the allowance for electively founded aphonia can only be a tentative one. The initial failures to speak were after all induced by frights, and the strictures set out elsewhere do not always find their way into the chapter on the body and sexuality.

When he considers language, moreover, Merleau-Ponty does not distinguish between expressive relations with immanent significations and linguistic relations, which involve differences between signifiers. It is difficult to contest Jean-Bertrand Pontalis' conclusion that a philosophy founded on the primacy of signification will lead to admitting the unconscious only if it can be integrated into a theory of the sentient body, of expression, and of the subjective activity which articulates a meaning (Pontalis 1993, pp. 85–86). And integration is one of Merleau-Ponty's master words. We will recall that it is an internal necessity for the most integrated existence to provide itself with a habitual body. We will recall too that between my consciousness and my body as experienced and that of another, there exists an internal relation that causes the other to appear as the completion of the system. Both are brought together in the one world in which we participate as anonymous subjects of perception. And finally, the significance of psychoanalysis is to reintegrate sexuality into whole of human existence (Merleau-Ponty 2012, p. 160).

We are warned that sexuality is not just an epiphenomenon that is lost in existence, despite its internal links with the rest of active and cognitive living. But for all that it is cast as another form of operative intentionality that brings into view the vital origins of perception, motility and representation (Merleau-Ponty 2012, pp. 160–162). When Merleau-Ponty considers concepts and cases from Freudian and existential psychoanalysis, it is striking how these invariably give way to his main interest in the body itself. Abnormal repression and repetition are used to illustrate that other form of organic repression in which a skill becomes sedimented in the body schema. The young woman lacking in the power of speech is a means of illustrating the impermanence of certain motor habits. If I choose to abandon a practical project the relevant skills will wither away, and any decision to renew it will increasingly become a remote rather than a proximate possibility. Even a friend's death is used to illustrate an attempted skill deployment. I do not feel his absence until I wish to ask him something. In a like manner the missing limb of the use-phantom amputee is only noticed when things go wrong for him or her (Merleau-Ponty 2012, pp. 82–83, 165–166).

Given an embodied subject whose choices and act intentionalities are well supported by their anonymous counterparts, the running presumption appears to be that the life of that subject will be more or less unproblematic. Fragile though the body is of itself, an ordinary level of happiness will be enjoyed, as against the ordinary, manageable level of unhappiness that Freud sought for his patients (Freud and Breuer 1956, p. 305). In *Phenomenology of Perception* the healthy subject makes it through most obstacles and difficulties with little or no cost, and the past of naïve as well as somatic acquisitions is for the most part enabling:

> Theoretical and practical decisions in my personal life can certainly grasp my past and my future from a distance; they can give my past, along with all of its accidents, a definite sense by following it up with a certain future…But there is always something artificial to this order. I currently understand my first twenty-five years as a prolonged childhood that had to be followed by a difficult weaning process in order to finally arrive at autonomy. If I think back to those years such as I lived them and such as I now carry them with me, their happiness refuses to be explained by the protected atmosphere of the parental milieu – the world itself was more beautiful, things were more fascinating – and I can never be certain of understanding my past better than it understood itself while I lived it, nor can I ever silence its protests. My current interpretation is tied to my confidence in psychoanalysis; tomorrow, with more maturity and more insight, I will perhaps understand my past differently and I will accordingly construct it differently. (Merleau-Ponty 2012, pp. 361–362)

Painful as the break may be, it leads to independence. We read in another place that the event of one's birth leads to a new situation, and to the fresh possibility of situations. One is not cast into the world as a new perspective, for one is not limited to any particular one and can change one's point of view (Merleau-Ponty 2012, p. 429). And were Merleau-Ponty to effect a different reconstruction of his past, it is likely that the world would remain beautiful and things fascinating. Still elsewhere, he tells us that he may be overcome with grief and given wholly over to sorrow. Yet his gaze will wander out before him and become interested in some bright object, and thus resume its autonomous existence. Personal existence is intermittent, a tide that recedes, and pre-personal time will carry away, if not a resolution, at least the heartfelt emotions that sustained it (Merleau-Ponty 2012, p. 86).

But this is scarcely faithful to the life uncovered by the psychoanalyst. Nietzsche already points us to pasts that were presents burdening us down. In their repression they persist as imperfect tenses. With some people there are solitary events that cannot be forgotten at all, destroying them like the person who bleeds to death from a single scratch. There are others who can feel tolerably well amidst or after the most dreadful disasters, but only some (Nietzsche 1997, p. 62). And it looks wrong to propose that the gaze of someone in sorrow will be attracted by something bright and go off on its own. This is hardly the story of a traumatised adult, but of a child pulled out of its momentary misery to take up some joyful if tear-stained investigation. For the adult the colour and vivacity of the world and of others may go forever. An unfinished and buried grief may leave in its wake a Sisyphean struggle to endure. Drawing on Jules de Gaultier, Merleau-Ponty does refer movingly to lingering experiences of unrequited love in which real life is imagined as taking place elsewhere (de Gaultier 1902, p. 216 ff.; Merleau-Ponty 2012, pp. 299, 373). Like certain buried traumas, such conscious states cannot be read off from the body itself. Yet they do not disturb the dominant narrative of skilfully sustained progress. Though I may be outrun by my acts and submerged in generality, he continues, with my first perception there was launched an insatiable being who appropriates everything in its path. I have inherited *my* share of the world, and I carry in myself the plan of every possible being (Merleau-Ponty 2012, p. 374).

The somatically healthy man or woman is described in a pervasive tone – and proceeds in a pervasive mood – of dynamic serenity. Pretty much everything remains interesting and enjoyable in a peacetime world that does not overwhelm, like a controlled drama that has its ups and downs whilst delivering without disappointment, and more especially without tragedy. Everything is geared towards smoothness and synchronisation, not merely as ideal but as actuality. Little is left that is out of joint, as though a crooked and splintered timber did not subtend every human life. As reported the more salutary deliverances of Freudian and existential psychoanalysis on repression are integrated into the body itself, pressed into its service without notably throwing it off track. They are assimilated means for something else. This is why the descriptions in question do not respect them adequately. As an explication of anonymous motor projection and intercorporeality, Merleau-Ponty's account stands in the first rank. No other philosophy has added so much to ideo-motor theory and to enactivism. In his peculiar employment of what is troubling and irruptive from repressed life, however, he does not quite convey the jagged and fractured character of a genuine human presence in the world, even one that is ordinarily unhappy.

References

Binswanger, Ludwig. 1935. Über Psychotherapie. *Nervenarzt* 8: 113–121.
de Gaultier, Jules. 1902. *Le Bovarysme, essai sur le pouvoir d'imaginer*. Paris: Société du Mercure de France.
Freud, Sigmund. 1984. Beyond the Pleasure Principle. Trans. James Strachey, et al. In *On Metapsychology: The Theory of Psychoanalysis*, ed. Albert Dickson, 269–338. Harmondsworth: Penguin.
———. 1985. Civilization and its Discontents. Trans. James Strachey, et al. In *Civilization, Society and Religion*, ed. Albert Dickson, 251–340. Harmondsworth: Penguin.
Freud, Sigmund, and Josef Breuer. 1956. *Studies on Hysteria*. Trans. James and Alix Strachey. London: The Hogarth Press.
Husserl, Edmund. 1960. *Cartesian Meditations*. Trans. Dorian Cairns. The Hague: Nijhoff.
———. 1989. *Ideas, Second Book*. Trans. Richard Rojcewicz, and André Schuwer. Dordrecht: Kluwer.
Kant, Immanuel. 1933. *Critique of Pure Reason*. Trans. Norman Kemp Smith. London: Macmillan.
Levinas, Emmanuel. 1993. *Outside the Subject*. Trans. Michael B. Smith. London: Athlone Press.
Lhermitte, Jean. 1998. *L'Image de notre corps*. Paris: Éditions L'Harmattan.
Merleau-Ponty, Maurice. 1964. *Signs*. Trans. Richard McCleary. Evanston: Northwestern University Press.
———. 2012. *Phenomenology of Perception*. Trans. Donald G. Landes. London/New York: Routledge.
Nietzsche, Friedrich. 1967. *On the Genealogy of Morals*. Trans. Walter Kaufmann, and R.J. Hollingdale. New York: Random House.
———. 1997. On the Uses and Disadvantages of History for Life. Trans. R.J. Hollingdale. In *Untimely Meditations*, ed. Daniel Breazeale, 59–123. Cambridge: Cambridge University Press.
Pontalis, J.B. 1993. The Problem of the Unconscious in Merleau-Ponty's Thought. Trans. Wilfried Ver Eecke, and Michael Greer. In *Merleau-Ponty and Psychology*, ed. Keith Hoeller, 83–96. Atlantic Highlands: Humanities Press.

Chapter 5
Merleau-Ponty's Nonverbal Unconscious

James Phillips

Abstract Maurice Merleau-Ponty has long been recognized as one of the phenomenologists who took a direct interest in the psychoanalytic unconscious. His interest began early and coursed through his entire career. At each stage he developed his understanding of the unconscious further, always resistant to a literalist reading of the Freudian unconscious. With the *Phenomenology of Perception* he argued that the Freudian unconscious could be understood in terms of an expanded notion of consciousness in which the ambiguities and unattended aspects of pre-reflective life could cover the ground targeted by Freud's unconscious. Further development occurred in Merleau-Ponty's courses at the Sorbonne, from 1949 to 1952, in which he carried out an intensive reading of the psychoanalytic literature. From his reading of Melanie Klein he took the notion of a primary symbolism in which the infant's mental mechanisms and defences are at the same time mental and physical. Merleau-Ponty continued his study of psychoanalysis and the unconscious in his lectures at the Collège de France from 1952 to 1060, introducing the notion of oneiric consciousness, in which again, what we call the unconscious is present in the primary process, sleep-like dimension of ordinary conscious life. Finally, he brought all these together, and developed them further, in his final, posthumous *The Visible and the Invisible*. The unconscious remains non-verbal, silent, invisible – hiding in the crevices of ordinary thought, and providing its hidden framework (*membrure*).

Keywords Unconscious • Unconscious and Merleau-Ponty • Unconscious and phenomenology • Phenomenology and psychoanalysis

---

J. Phillips (✉)
Department of Psychiatry, Yale School of Medicine,
New Haven, CT, USA
e-mail: james.phillips@yale.edu

© Springer International Publishing AG 2017
D. Legrand, D. Trigg (eds.), *Unconsciousness Between Phenomenology and Psychoanalysis*, Contributions To Phenomenology 88,
DOI 10.1007/978-3-319-55518-8_5

5.1 Introduction

Maurice Merleau-Ponty has long been recognized as one of the phenomenologists who took a direct interest in the psychoanalytic unconscious. His interest began early and coursed through his entire career. To introduce this chapter I will invoke a text written shortly before his sudden, unexpected death in 1961, the preface to a textbook on psychoanalysis by a French psychoanalyst, Angelo Hesnard (1960). The Preface provides Merleau-Ponty's summary of (and introduction to) his confrontation of phenomenology and psychoanalysis. It also provides an introduction to this chapter, which is devoted to the role of language and non-verbal experience in Merleau-Ponty's understanding of the unconscious. If Freud is ambivalent about the question of whether the unconscious contains verbal content, for Merleau-Ponty the unconscious remains, in increasingly complex ways, silent and unverbalized.

In the Preface Merleau-Ponty imagines the average reader's first experience with Freudian texts, certainly reflecting his personal experience:

> Every reader of Freud, I imagine, remembers his first impression: an incredible bias in favor of the least probable interpretations; a maniacal penchant for the sexual; and above all a distortion, through the use of archaic forms, of significations, language, and action in the interest of derisive puns. Then, to the extent that one read, that one related oneself to oneself, and that the years passed, a sort of evidence for psychoanalysis was inexplicably established and one came to live in peace with the pitiless hermeneutic. (PRE,[1] p. 67).

Merleau-Ponty adds quickly, however, that the psychoanalysis one once rejected is not the psychoanalysis one now accepts, the latter a psychoanalysis stripped of empiricism, biologism, and psychologism. In describing the relationship of phenomenology and psychoanalysis in the Preface, Merleau-Ponty writes that phenomenology offers psychoanalysis philosophically suitable concepts for expressing its insights: "…the Freudian unconscious as an archaic or primordial consciousness, the repressed as a zone of experience that we have not integrated, the body as a sort of natural or innate complex, and communication as a relation between beings of the sort who are well or badly integrated" (PRE, p. 67). For its part, psychoanalysis offers phenomenology suggestions for getting to a depth not reached in the notion of a pure transparency between noesis and noema. In referring to the hints of this in Husserl's later writings, Merleau-Ponty writes: "All consciousness is consciousness of something or of the world, but this *something*, this *world*, is no longer, as 'phenomenological positivism' appeared to teach, an object that is what it is, exactly adjusted to acts of consciousness. Consciousness is now the 'soul of Heraclitus', and Being, which is around it rather than in front of it, is a Being of dreams, by definition hidden. Husserl sometimes uses the term 'pre-being'" (PRE, p. 70). Merleau-Ponty concludes the Preface in writing that phenomenology and psychoanalysis are less at odds than working in the same direction: "Phenomenology and psychoanalysis are not parallel; much better, they are both aiming toward the same latency" (PRE, p. 71).

---

[1] Preface to Hesnard's *L'Oeuvre de Freud*.

5.2 Early Work

We witness Merleau-Ponty's first reading of Freud in *The Structure of Behavior* (1963). Merleau-Ponty states the theme of that book on the first page: "Our goal is to understand the relations of consciousness and nature: organic, psychological or even social" (SB, p.3). He argues for a major distinction between the organic and the human, and in that context he invokes Freud as an example of the attempt to reduce the human to the organic. The pathological complex with which the analyst deals is not, as in Freud, a matter of repressed biological impulses; it is rather a segment of unintegrated behavior, a persisting infantile attitude that has not been surpassed and integrated into the adult personality. In describing the patient as suffering from a fragmented consciousness, Merleau-Ponty offers his first formulation of the Freudian unconscious: "…the pretended unconsciousness of the complex is reduced to the ambivalence of immediate consciousness" (SB, p. 179).

In *Phenomenology of Perception* (1962) that followed *The Structure of Behavior*, Merleau-Ponty transformed the immediate consciousness of *The Structure of Behavior* into perceptual consciousness, an embodied consciousness that will serve him for his study of psychoanalysis in that work and what will follow. While *The Structure of Behavior* describes behavior as observed, the *Phenomenology of Perception* examines it as lived. In studying lived perceptual consciousness phenomenologically, Merleau-Ponty does not discover a transcendent consciousness that constitutes the world but rather an embodied consciousness bound to the world.

In the *Phenomenology of Perception* he uses a variety of expressions to capture this unity of perceptual consciousness and world: lived body, presence, being-in-the-world, unreflective or prereflective life, operative intentionality, and existence. All attempt to convey the prereflective unity of subject and world. In Merleau-Ponty's words, "This world is inseparable from the subject, but from a subject which is nothing but a project of the world, and the subject is inseparable from the world, but from a world which it projects itself. The subject is a being-in-the-world, and the world remains subjective since its texture and articulations are indicated by the subject's movement of transcendence" (PP,[2] p. 430).

Merleau-Ponty doesn't focus a lot on the unconscious in *Phenomenology of Perception*, but on the other hand the unconscious is everywhere, since it is coterminous with the perceptual consciousness. Throughout the text Merleau-Ponty attempts to show that the territory covered by the Freudian unconscious is covered by a perceptual consciousness that is ambiguous, unclear, and opaque, and that leaves most experiences with unnoticed and unclear aspects. As Merleau-Ponty writes: "the lived is never entirely comprehensible, what I understand never quite tallies with my living experience, in short, I am never quite at one with myself" (PP, p. 347). In *The Structure of Behavior* the fragmented consciousness was a phenomenon of pathologic conditions. Now in the *Phenomenology of Perception*, perceptual consciousness involves all experience.

---

[2] *Phenomenology of Perception.*

What comes first is lived, unreflective experience. What follows in reflection is the attempt to recover and articulate that lived experience. But the recovery is never transparent and never complete. The lived experience remains ambiguous, with dimensions not captured in the reflection. Such is the phenomenological account of the unconscious, the unconscious as unreflective life itself. It is on-going life or operative intention as lived and not focused on.

Merleau-Ponty illustrates the phenomenon of unreflective or prereflective experience with the example of falling in love. In the early stages of falling in love, I am not aware that I am "falling in love." It is only later when I am clearly in love that I reflect that, at those early moments, I was indeed already 'falling in love'. "The love which worked out its dialectic through me, and of which I have just become aware, was not, from the start, a thing hidden in my unconscious, nor was it an object before my consciousness, but the impulse carrying me toward someone, the transmutation of my thoughts and behavior – I was not unaware of it since it was I who endured the hours of boredom preceding a meeting, and who felt elation when she approached – it was lived, not known, from start to finish" (PP, p. 381).

Bringing this analysis to the area of psychopathology, Merleau-Ponty addresses the condition of hysteria, highlighted by Freud in the founding of psychoanalysis. For Freud the source, or cause, of hysteria is a repressed memory that forces itself into the patient's conscious life in the form of hysterical symptoms, and that once brought to consciousness, leads to a recovery from the hysterical symptoms. Merleau-Ponty rejects this effort to explain hysteria in the categories of an empirical, causal analysis that is reliant on representational thinking (the causal factor as a repressed thought/representation). In contrast, he describes the patient as in a state of self-deception regarding her bodily states, keeping a distance from them so that they are not felt like real bodily pain. Citing a case of Binswanger, Merleau-Ponty foresees successful treatment not as the exposure of a causal, unconscious memory, but rather through a less cognitive process that will affect the patient at a level at which the dissociated bodily states are experienced. "Neither symptom nor cure is worked out at the level of objective and positing consciousness, but below that level" (PP, p. 168).

In the effort to revision the psychoanalytic unconscious in terms of perceptual consciousness, the area that draws Merleau-Ponty's attention most strongly in *Phenomenology of Perception* is sexuality. This topic implicitly involves the role of sexuality in neurosis. As before, he rejects the Freudian unconscious as a trove of formed mental representations in favor of the ambiguous intentionalities of lived, bodily experience. For Merleau-Ponty sexuality opens onto the larger area of affective experience and its dramatic exposition of the bond of consciousness, body, and world – a consciousness that Merleau-Ponty will later describe as "not so much knowledge or representation as investment" (PRE, p. 68). Sexuality is simply the most striking example of the affective bond. Merleau-Ponty rejects any physiological explanation of sexuality in terms of sexual instinct and stimulating objects. He points out that the other person only arouses one if perceived with erotic significance. He argues further that sexuality is not a separate region of experience but rather follows the general trend of the individual's existence. "It has internal links with the whole active and cognitive being, these three sectors of behavior displaying one typical structure and standing in a relationship to each other of reciprocal expression" (PP, p. 157). His challenge is to recognize both the uniqueness of sexual feeling and at the same time its role as dramatic expression of the general themes of the subject's life. In a kind of anticipation of the criticism he will receive, he writes that "there can be no question of allowing sexuality to become lost in existence, as if it were no more than an epiphenomenon" (PP, p. 159).

Having discussed Merleau-Ponty's interpretation of the Freudian unconscious in the *Phenomenology of Perception* as perceptual consciousness, we now must address the chapter of this book that is Merleau-Ponty's earliest sustained examination of speech and language, "The Body as Expression and Speech." He begins with an assault on representational thinking, the notion that the mind contains developed, preverbal, meaningful thoughts that speech or writing brings to outward expression. He argues that there are no such pre-articulated thoughts; there is only a vague, inchoate pressure toward meaning that is fulfilled with the spoken or written word. Otherwise, he writes, "we could not understand why thought tends towards expression as towards its completion, why the most familiar thing appears indeterminate as long as we have not recalled its name, why the thinking subject himself is in a kind of ignorance of his thoughts so long as he has not formulated them for himself, or even spoken and written them, as is shown by the example of so many writers who begin a book without knowing exactly what they are going to put into it"(PP, p. 177). A little further on he states this quite simply, "Thus speech, in the speaker, does not translate ready-made thought, but accomplishes it" (PP, p. 178). The speaker's thoughts do not precede his speech; rather, his speech *is* his thought. Merleau-Ponty then asks, if speech does not express thoughts, what does it express? He responds that "It presents or rather it *is* the subject's taking up of a position in the world of his meanings" (PP, p. 193).

Merleau-Ponty adds to this discussion that what creates the impression of preformed thoughts is the fact that we all rely on a vast store of already formulated speech, sedimented speech or language, as he calls it. At some point every verbalized meaning was expressed for the first time, and it is of course the job of the poet, writer, or orator to originate such speech acts. Once sedimented into the language of one's culture, such language can be called upon by anyone in his or her thinking or speaking, and can create the impression that such speech is in fact expressing preverbal thoughts.

In moving this train of thought into the area of communication with others, Merleau-Ponty notes that speech always includes a gestural dimension that the other picks up directly, "a *gestural meaning*, which is immanent in speech" (PP, p. 179). If the argument that meaning is carried by the word is Merleau-Ponty's first major idea in this chapter, the second is his understanding of gesture. Speech, as the activity of an incarnated person, always begins in gesture, and even as fully verbalized retains its status as expressive action of a lived body. "The spoken word is a genuine gesture, and it contains its meaning in the same way as the gesture contains it" (PP, p. 183). For a brief example Merleau-Ponty states: "The gesture *does not make me think* of anger, it is anger itself" (PP, p. 184). What is striking in this analysis is that Merleau-Ponty does not say that the earliest expression of meaning is gesture, and that that more advanced, verbal expression leaves gesture behind and moves on to speech. He says rather that speech remains gesture. Presumably, to say otherwise would imply that the speaker has left his embodied status and become like an unembodied mind[3] (Castoriadis 1971).

What does all this have to do with the relation of the unconscious to language, the question of this chapter? Another phrase from the Merleau-Ponty's chapter on "The Body as Expression and Speech" helps us with the answer. "Our view of man will remain superficial so long as we fail to go back to that origin, so long as we fail to find, beneath the chatter of words, the primordial silence, and as long as we do not describe the action which breaks this silence. The spoken word is a gesture, and its meaning a world" (PP, p. 184). The key phrase is "primordial silence." The primary theme of *Phenomenology of Perception* is perceptual consciousness, and the unconscious has been explained in terms of the ambiguities of perceptual consciousness, the 'unconscious' quality of unreflective life. With this chapter of the *Phenomenology of Perception* on gesture and language, the focus turns to expression and its relations to ongoing unreflective life. If the ambiguities of perceptual consciousness represent the phenomenological unconscious, so also does the silent, preverbal quality of unreflective living. As in the example stated above, in my early moments of falling in love, I do not use those words because there are in fact no corresponding, pre-existing thoughts in my head just waiting to be expressed. Such inchoate pre-thoughts only find verbal expression with the later reflection. We have now learned that speech emerges out of a primordial silence, the silence of pre-thought, or thought that is only an impulse toward meaning until it is articulated in the word. Primordial silence is then the quality of 'unconscious', unreflective life. The unconscious of perceptual consciousness is silent.

Before concluding this review of *Phenomenology of Perception*, we should recognize that Merleau-Ponty's interpretation of the unconscious in terms of the ambiguities of perceptual consciousness provoked a strong reaction on the part of some French psychoanalysts. Their challenge was that Merleau-Ponty, in his formulation of the unconscious in terms of prereflective life and the ambiguities of perceptual consciousness, did not reach the Freudian unconscious. Indeed, Merleau-Ponty wrote in *Phenomenology of Perception* that "The lived is certainly lived by me, nor am I ignorant of the feelings which I repress, and in this sense there is no unconscious." (PP, p. 296). From the perspective of his critics, every experience that Merleau-Ponty labels unconscious fits Freud's description of the preconscious, rather than that of his unconscious.[4] Psychoanalyst André Green wrote that "The

---

[3] "Speech of the sort I have been considering remains within the domain of verbal language; this speech produces words, sounds, and utterances. However another dimension of this phenomenal field in which language is proper to the body, in which the body is appropriate to language, is gesture. Gestures describe the action which breaks this silence. The spoken word is a gesture, and its meaning, a world" (PP, p. 184).

[4] "The unconscious of phenomenology is the preconscious of psychoanalysis, that is to say, an unconscious that is descriptive and not yet topographic" (Ricoeur 1970, p. 392).

Phenomenology of Perception reflected an existential position, and the unconscious as well as sexuality were stripped of the specificity Freud gave them in order to be dissolved in all too general significations, especially close to those of existential analysis" (1964, p. 1032). And psychoanalyst J.B.Pontalis distinguished the Freudian unconscious and Merleau-Ponty's prereflective life as "the other scene" versus "the other side" (1982–1983, 85), and he argued that the phenomenological "other side" is the psychoanalytic preconscious" (1971, p. 62.)[5] Philosopher Paul Ricoeur defended the critique in focusing on the distinction between phenomenology and the clinical situation, arguing that the latter required something like Freud's system unconscious (1974).

5.3 Later Thought

In moving beyond the *Phenomenology of Perception* we first must address three areas before reaching Merleau-Ponty's final ontology. The first is his encounter with the work of Ferdinand de Saussure, the second his intense study of psychoanalysis while teaching at the Sorbonne from 1949 to 1952, and the third his lectures at the Collège de France. Merleau-Ponty first read Saussure in 1947, and the impact was of great significance in his further work. Saussure offered Merleau-Ponty support for both his critique of the representational theory language and his insistence that the word carries meaning. Further, Saussure's differential or diacritical theory of linguistic meaning – that the meaning of the word or sign is defined in terms of its difference (*écart*) from other word meanings – provided Merleau-Ponty with a new language to express his growing thought on the emergence of meaning. The huge space of difference opened in the world of possible meanings involves another approach to what we just encountered as the primordial silence of pre-thought. Indeed, in the post-Saussure period Merleau-Ponty's writing is saturated with the application of Saussure's linguistics to his own thought (reviewed in Silverman 1980).

The primary text in this discussion is "Indirect Language and the Voices of Silence," published in *Signs* in 1960 (the Preface to *Signs* is an important accompaniment to the chapter on "Indirect Language." In this chapter Merleau-Ponty begins with Saussure, addressing the puzzling phenomenon that the meanings of linguistic

---

[5] DeWaelhens (1966) and Lanteri-Laura (1966) both assume more of a middle position, emphasizing that the Freudian unconscious required not so much a second system as a profound limitation of the capacity of self-reflection. Lanteri-Laura wrote: "The unconscious, we can say, is the entire part of non-thetic consciousness that man is not able to recover through reflection alone and that he apprehends only through singular noematic qualities of objects. If man is essentially a movement of transcendence toward that which he is not, he apprehends himself in totality through the noematic qualities of objects and of others, without knowing it specifically. But he only regains himself only in part through reflection, and it is this hiatus that, in phenomenology, renders possible the very notion of an unconscious (1966, p. 399).

signs are all based on their differences from other signs. About language he writes that it is

> The lateral relation of one sign to another which makes each of them significant, so that meaning appears only at the intersection of and as it were in the interval between words. There is thus an opaqueness of language. Nowhere does it stop and leave a place for pure meaning: it is always limited only by more language, and meaning appears within it only set in a context of words. Like a charade, language is understood only through the interaction of signs, each of which, taken separately, is equivocal or banal, and makes sense only by being combined with others." (SI,[6] p. 42).

Merleau-Ponty describes the way in which thought and meaning track along with the flow of words, in the same manner that thought and meaning will follow the movement of a gesture. Merleau-Ponty continues that if we abandon the notion of language as translation of a hidden text of pre-existing thoughts, we will realize that "the idea of *complete* expression is nonsensical, and that all language is indirect or allusive – that it is, if you wish, silence" (SI, p. 43). He illustrates this silence with a little example from Saussure: that the English "the man I love" conveys the same sense as the French "*l'homme que j'aime*," the relative pronoun being expressed in English by a blank, an absence.

In this discussion Merleau-Ponty reverts back to the distinction between sedimented language and expressive language (*le language parlé et le language parlant*), the effort to say something for the first time. Describing how such meaning emerges from the oblique unfolding of words, Merleau-Ponty compares the writer to a weaver working on the wrong side of the material, the meaning emerging mysteriously from that texture of words.

Finally, Merleau-Ponty compares the writer to the painter, from whose small strokes and blank spaces a world of meaning appears. For both there is not a preexisting idea but rather a "significative intention" that longs for expression, in words or as a painted surface. To appreciate the expressive act we can imagine how well other expressions might have done in bringing birth to the significative intention, whether they demonstrate or not that only the chosen expression accomplishes the task. In reflecting on that world of possibilities, Merleau-Ponty writes: "In short, we must consider speech before it is spoken, the background of silence which does not cease to surround it and without which it would say nothing" (SI, p. 46).

In the texts dealing with the influence of Saussure on his theory of expression, Merleau-Ponty does not invoke the unconscious. It is there, however, in the diacritical notion that meaning is defined by difference, by the way in which the signified, or the meaning of a sign, is defined by its difference from other signifieds. Merleau-Ponty broadens Saussure's language to say that meaning emerges not just from the words but also from what is *not* in the text or the spoken words, and from the silence that surrounds and undergirds speech and writing. "…language is expressive as much through what is *between* the words themselves, and through what it does not say as much as what is says…" PR,[7] p. 43). This is not simply a restatement of the

---

[6] *Signs*.
[7] *The Prose of the World*.

argument of the *Phenomenology of Perception*: the unconscious as the ambiguity of perceptual consciousness, or as the primordial silence of pre-verbalized thought. The emphasis now is no longer on the unnoticed of pre-reflective life or the silence of pre-verbalized thought, but rather on what *is* there, in the speaking or text, not unnoticed but rather there as an absence or silence between the words.

The second area for discussion following the *Phenomenology of Perception* is Merleau-Ponty's treatment of psychoanalysis in the Sorbonne lectures (1988), delivered during his 3-year tenure (1949–1952) as Professor of Child Psychology (reviewed in Phillips 1999 and Beaulieux 2009). These lectures represent both a recapitulation of his treatment of psychoanalysis in *The Structure of Behavior* and the *Phenomenology of Perception*, as well as a newer perspective on it that will influence his later thought. In the recapitulation he focuses on the Gestalt psychology metaphor of the unconscious that he had introduced in the *Phenomenology of Perception*. In this reading, the unconscious represents a failure of the subject to distinguish figure from ground, and the unconscious, put simply, is the unnoticed ground. Of course this terminology allows for a shifting experience of what is figure and what is ground, and thus a shifting experience of what belongs to the unconscious. Such shifting is quite consistent with the ambiguities of perceptual consciousness or the unnoticed motivation in unreflective experience. In language reminiscent of the *Phenomenology of Perception*, Merleau-Ponty writes: "We do not know the ground although it is lived by us. We are our own ground" (MPS,[8] p. 474). It is not difficult to associate this new metaphor with other descriptions of the unconscious in *Phenomenology of Perception* – as, for instance, the ambiguity of perceptual consciousness or the unnoticed motivation in unreflective experience. Merleau-Ponty also recognizes that shifting between figure and ground may not be easy, and that recognizing the ground may require the intervention of another person.

In the newer perspectives of the Sorbonne lectures Merleau-Ponty pursues other themes of psychoanalysis such as the diffuse ambiguity of childhood sexuality and the exchange of roles in the Oedipus complex, the child identifying now with one parent and then with the other. He offers a valuable phenomenological reading of all these Freudian concepts. He then takes up Freud's followers and shows a keen interest in Melanie Klein, who developed a theory of very early development and its influence on adult pathology. According to Klein the infant's fantasies of incorporation and expulsion are experienced in a manner in which the physical and the psychological are not distinguished. These later become the psychological mechanisms of introjection and projection, which retain their early, embodied roots. As Merleau-Ponty writes: "The psychological mechanisms of introduction and projection, instead of appearing as mental operations, should be understood as the very modalities of the activity of the body. The phenomenal body is the vehicle of the infant's relations with the outside" (MPS, p. 359).

In addition to providing a lived-body understanding of some basic psychoanalytic concepts, Klein also provided a revised understanding of symbolism in the

---

[8] *Merleau-Ponty à la Sorbonne: résumé de cours 1949–1952.*

infant. "Between an image, a fantasy, the meaning of an experience, an introjection, an internalized object, the superego, there is no longer any great difference. The totality of the infant's activity appears simplified, and owing to that Melanie Klein makes of it an activity that is corporeal as much as psychical." (MPS, p. 367–8).

In summarizing this section on the Sorbonne lectures, we may take the following points: a dramatic interchange of roles as the infant alters his identifications from one parent to the other; an understanding of Freudian mechanisms as embodied experiences; and a perspective on infantile expression and symbolism that reflects the first two phenomena. These ideas will all play a role in Merleau-Ponty's final thought on the silent unconscious.

In 1952 Merleau-Ponty was appointed professor at the Collège de France, where he taught until his death. Many of the above themes recur in these courses (1970/1968), and in two of them he directly took up psychoanalytic themes. In "The Problem of Passivity: Sleep, the Unconscious, Memory," a course from 1954 to 1955, he introduces a new dimension of the unconscious. Discussing the nature of dreams, he challenges the conventional objections to the reified Freudian unconscious, including that of Sartre, who viewed the unconscious as a phenomenon of bad faith. Pointing toward Sartre he writes: "Such a view loses sight of what was Freud's most interesting sight – not the idea of a second "I think" which could know what we do not know about ourselves – but the idea of a symbolism which is primordial, originary, the idea of a "non-conventional thought" (Politzer) enclosed in a "world for us," which is the source of dreams and more generally of the elaboration of our life" (TFL,[9] p. 49).

Merleau-Ponty calls the 'unconscious' life of dreams "oneiric consciousness" and says of it: "What these descriptions mean is that the unconscious is a perceiving consciousness and that it operates as such through a logic of implication or promiscuity, follows closer and closer a path whose slope it cannot see clearly, and envisages objects and creatures through the negative that it withholds, which suffices to regulate its steps without enabling it to name them 'by their name'" (TLF, p. 50). He adds that "our waking relations with objects and others especially have an oneiric character as a matter of principle: others are present to us in the way that dreams are, the way myths are, and this is enough to question the cleavage between the real and the imaginary" (TLF, p. 48). Merleau-Ponty doesn't mention that his oneiric consciousness is a restatement of Freud's primary process thought, brought into the conscious life of the subject. What these citations suggest is a concurrence in oneiric consciousness of Freudian primary process thinking and Saussurian diacritical linguistics, as suggested in another citation:

> Freud's contribution is not to have revealed quite another reality beneath appearances, but that the analysis of a given behavior always discovers several layers of signification, each with its own truth, and that the plurality of possible interpretations is the discursive expression of a mixed life in which every choice always has several meanings, it being impossible to say which of them is the only true one. (TLF, p. 50)

---

[9] *Themes from the Lectures at the Collège de France 1952–1960.*

In his last recorded Collège de France course from 1959 to 1960, "Nature and Logos: The Human Body," Merleau-Ponty moves closer to the themes of his final thought – flesh, reversibility, and the invisible – and brings psychoanalytic concepts, especially those of Melanie Klein, into this discussion. He again takes up the theme of oneiric consciousness and develops it into his concept of the flesh, developed preliminarily in this course and to play a great part in his final ontology.

Oneiric consciousness begins to break down the separation of self and other, as well as that of embodied consciousness and world. In shifting from embodied self to flesh, Merleau-Ponty addresses the way in which a global embodiedness splits into the sensing and the sensed – the body in its reflexivity, the body as seeing-seen, as touching-touched, the "idea of corporeality as an entity with two faces or two 'sides'" (TLF, p. 129). In *Eye and Mind*, Merleau-Ponty's last published work, he writes: "There is a human body when, between the seeing and the seen, between touching and the touched, between one eye and the other, between hand and hand, a blending of some sort takes place – when the spark is lit between sensing and sensible, lighting the fire that will not stop burning until some accident of the body will undo what no accident would have sufficed to do" (EM).[10]

In the context of global embodiedness, Merleau-Ponty recalls Melanie Klein's corrective sense of corporeality as an interchange of the internal and the external, again described as "a global and universal power of incorporation." With her analysis of the psychologically primitive process of the infant's effort to "incorporate" the mother, she provides a productive correction of Freudian thinking with her concept (as understood by Merleau-Ponty) of a "global and universal power of incorporation" (TLF, pp. 129–130). Reflecting Merleau-Ponty's interpretation of oneiric consciousness as the unconscious, Klein points to the idea of the human body as a natural symbolism, a "tacit symbolism of undividedness" that underlies conventional symbolism, a "logos of the sensible world? (TLF, p. 131).

When the distinction between consciousness and nature breaks down in the global unity of flesh, what happens to the concept of the unconscious? Merleau-Ponty poses this question to himself and again rejects any interpretation of the unconscious as unconscious representations – "a tribute paid by Freud to the psychology of his day" (TLF, p. 130). He describes the unconscious as "feeling itself, since feeling is not the intellectual possession of 'what' is felt, but a dispossession of ourselves in favor of it, an opening toward that which we do not have to think in order that we may recognize it" (TLF, p. 130).

In describing repression he describes two sides of consciousness, that of ordinary, adult experience, and another side, the repressed "unconscious' that drifts back into pregenital life but is also "a permissive being, the initial yes, the undividedness of feeling" (TLF, p. 131). He ends by describing the latter in terms of a natural, bodily, tacit symbolism of undividedness. With regard to the question of a silent unconscious, this Collège de France lecture again reflects silence, that of Kleinian undividedness rather than that of Saussurian difference. The lecture also looks forward to what will be Merleau-Ponty's final thought on this matter.

---

[10] *Eye and Mind*.

5.4 Final Thought

At this point in his trajectory of the unconscious, Merleau-Ponty has taken us from the ambiguous consciousness of *Phenomenology of Perception* to the unconscious as unseen ground, and finally to the unconscious as oneiric consciousness, reciprocal sensing, and the primordial symbolism of an embodied consciousness. Intertwined with this development of the unconscious are the notions of speech as non-representational thought and Saussure's understanding of diacritical linguistics, in which meaning emerges from what is unthought and silent.

We have had hints of his final ideas of the flesh, invisibility, and reversibility. Now we have to see how these ideas all come together in his final works, especially the posthumous text and working notes of *The Visible and the Invisible*, to give us a sense of a non-verbal unconscious.

Regarding the role of psychoanalysis and the unconscious in the final thought, we can see that Merleau-Ponty's understanding changed over time; and as Green remarked, his changing view of the unconscious was not simply a reflection of his changing philosophy but may have been one of the fermenting elements in that change (Green 1964). To use one of Merleau-Ponty's favourite phrases, the relations of psychoanalysis and philosophy are those of mutual encroachment. On the one hand psychoanalytic terminology has infiltrated philosophic description. Polymorphism and promiscuity are no longer simply attributes of infantile sexuality but of Being itself. We hear of "the vertical or carnal universe and its polymorphic matrix" (VI,[11] p. 221), and that "the world, Being, are polymorphism, mystery and nowise a layer of flat entities or of the in itself" (VI, p. 252).

On the other hand, we also see philosophy encroaching on psychoanalysis. Merleau-Ponty writes that "the philosophy of Freud is not a philosophy of the body but of the flesh" (VI, p. 269), and that "the in-itself-for itself integration takes place not in the absolute consciousness, but in the Being of promiscuity" (VI, p. 253).

In discussing the major categories of Merleau-Ponty's final thought – flesh, reversibility, invisibility – we quickly see that they overlap to a degree that it is difficult to treat them separately. The category of flesh dominates Merleau-Ponty's late writings. Flesh of course takes over the role of the body, emphasizing the carnal nature of all experience, but it is more and different from the early presentation of bodily experience. Merleau-Ponty begins with a vision of a unified world of flesh that "dehisces" or "cleaves" into a multiplicity of beings, some of them sentient/sensible (ourselves), others only sensible or not even sensible.[12] Regarding sentient/sensible beings, Merleau-Ponty writes that "my body is made of the same flesh as the world (it is a perceived), and moreover that this flesh of my body is shared by the world, the world *reflects* it, it encroaches upon it and it encroaches upon the world (the felt [*senti*] at the same time the culmination of subjectivity and the culmination of materiality), they are in a relation of transgression or of overlapping"

---

[11] *The Visible and the Invisible*.

[12] Unlike in *The Structure of Behavior*, animal life doesn't get much attention here.

(VI, p. 248). To capture these overlapping qualities of flesh, Merleau-Ponty, as noted above, uses the psychoanalytic language of polymorphism and promiscuity (VI, p. 221), and well as Melanie Klein's "global and universal power of incorporation." He also introduces a new set of terms – chiasm, dimensions, levels, pivots, hinges – to hint at ways in which beings of flesh interact with one another. The Husserlian noema, perceived through perspectives or *Abschattungen*, is now expanded to Being and beings.

To develop the notion of flesh further, we need to move to the concept of reversibility. In describing the human being as both sentient and sensible, Merleau-Ponty uses the examples of touching and seeing. I feel myself touching, and I see myself seeing. The embodied I who touches another person or thing is aware of itself touching the other, and is aware of itself as touchable *by* the other. And of course when the toucher touches himself, he is in a dramatic way both toucher *and* touched. The point for Merleau-Ponty is that these roles of toucher and touched are immediately reversible. As he writes "…because my eyes which see, my hands which touch, can also be seen and touched, because, therefore, in this sense they see and touch the visible, the tangible, from within, because our flesh lines and even envelops all the visible and tangible things with which nevertheless it is surrounded, the world and I are within one another, and there is no anteriority of the *percipere* to the *percipi*, there is simultaneity or even retardation" (VI, p. 123).

We see the concepts of reversibility and flesh dramatically at play in the area of interpersonal relations. Recall that the parties are both flesh, and in some manner belong to that global flesh that defines the world. How do they relate and communicate with one another? In a combination of Hegelian, Sartrean and psychoanalytic language, Merleau-Ponty writes: "There is not the For Itself and the For the Other. They are each the other side of the other. This is why they incorporate one another: projection-introjection – There is that line, that frontier surface at some distance before me, where occurs the veering I-Other Other-I" (VI, p. 263). Merleau-Ponty means that, in a conversation, for instance, it is not simply that each party experiences herself at one moment as the speaker and at another as the spoken-to, but rather that, in a fully engaged conversation, each party experiences herself as both speaker and listener, regardless of whoever is, in fact, speaking.

Merleau-Ponty's final thought culminates in the concept of the invisible. In his TLF lecture on nature he connects the invisible with the concepts of flesh and reversibility, describing the body as sensing and sensible, and concluding that "[t]he body proper embraces a philosophy of the flesh as the visibility of the invisible" (TLF, p. 129). And in the area of interpersonal relations he makes the same connection: "There is here no problem of the *alter ego* because it is not *I* who sees, not *he* who sees, because an anonymous visibility inhabits both of us, a vision in general, in virtue of that primordial property that belongs to the flesh, being here and now, of radiation everywhere and forever, being an individual, of being also a dimension and a universal" (VI, p. 142).

The invisible certainly includes what is literally not visible. It is thought and meaning, it is the space between visible things. But for Merleau-Ponty this "absence" has formative power. It somehow structures the visible. The visibles are "centered on a nucleus of absence" (VI, p. 229). In a longer description Merleau-Ponty writes:

> Meaning is *invisible*, but the invisible is not the contradictory of the visible: the visible itself has an invisible inner framework (*membrure*), and the in-visible is the secret counterpart of the visible, it appears only within it, it is the *Nichturpräsentierbar* which is present to me as such with the world – one cannot see it there and every effort to *see it there* makes it disappear, but it is *in the line* of the visible, it is its virtual focus, it is inscribed within it (in filigree) (VI, p. 215).

Of the final categories, invisibility is the one that seems closest to the concept of the unconscious. As we have seen, the unconscious is everywhere in Merleau-Ponty's final thought. Whatever else invisibility means, it includes the 'unconscious' of unnoticed prereflective consciousness and the 'unconscious' unseen of the Gestalt metaphor. But it is much more than that. In an important note Merleau-Ponty writes: "The unconscious is to be sought not at the bottom of ourselves, behind the back of our 'consciousness', but in front of us, as articulations of our field. It is 'unconscious' by the fact that it is not an *object*, but it is that through which objects are possible, it is the constellation wherein our future is read – It is between them as the interval of the trees between the trees, or as their common level" (VI, p. 180). In this citation, in each use of the word 'unconscious' Merleau-Ponty could have written 'invisible'. Speaking of either the invisible or the unconscious Merleau-Ponty uses variety of terms to convey an invisible, unexpressed structure that holds the visible world together. He cautions us against using terms like 'undergirding', 'support', or 'foundation' because they convey a sense of 'behind the scene' or 'supporting from below', all of which suggest one physical structure, e.g. a plinth, supporting something above, e.g. the column or statue. He faults Freud for that kind of reification of the unconscious. Merleau-Ponty's invisible (or unconscious) is not behind or under; it is *between*.

Merleau-Ponty uses one more expression to capture this sense of the invisible and the unconscious, namely the 'existentials'… Of them he writes: "It is these existentials that make up the (substitutable) *meaning* of what we say and of what we understand. They are the armature (*membrure*) of that 'invisible world' which, with speech, begins to impregnate all the things we see …" (VI, p. 280). He directly brings in the unconscious when he writes: "Criticize Freud's unconscious in this manner…the overdetermination, the ambiguity of the motivations must be understood by rediscovering our quasi-perceptual relationship with the human world through quite simple and nowise hidden existentials: only they are, like all structures, *between* our acts and our aims and not behind them…" VI, p. 232).

And returning now to our theme of a non-verbal unconscious, just as the unconscious/invisible is not the trees but between the trees, so also is it not in the words but between the words. It is what makes expressive speech possible as its silent structure. When Merleau-Ponty writes that the unconscious is not in back of consciousness but rather "in front of us, as articulations of our field," he is describing it as the silent, unheard, unexpressed structure that makes expression, whether speech or painting or any other form of expression, possible (VI, p. 214).

To capture this sense of the unconscious/invisible in its relation to expression, we can reintroduce the notion of *écart*, which Merleau-Ponty invokes frequently in his last writings. Stemming from Saussure's argument that meaning emerges through difference and absence, Merleau-Ponty aligns it with his sense of the invisible. Écart involves any difference that is not opposition, e.g. that between perceiver and perceived, or that between significative intention and expressed speech.

5.5 Discussion and Conclusion

In tracking the trajectory of Merleau-Ponty's argument for a non-verbal unconscious, we should not conclude the discussion without addressing his main contemporary opponent, Jacques Lacan, the French psychoanalyst who famously argued for a linguistic unconscious – one of his shibboleths being that the unconscious is structured like a language. I have reviewed their confrontations in another publication (Phillips 1996; see also Duportail 2005). Here I will focus on the one that occurred in 1960, shortly before Merleau-Ponty's death. The occasion was the colloquium in Bonneval, France in1960, organized by psychiatrist Henri Ey on the topic of the Freudian unconscious (Ey 1966). The colloquium was attended by many psychoanalysts and philosophers, including Jacques Lacan and Merleau-Ponty. As Roudinesco writes: "For Lacan, what was at stake at Bonneval was considerable. It was a question of demonstrating in France, in the teeth of the IPA [International Psychoanalytic Association], that Freudianism as revised and corrected by linguistics had the full status of a science. If philosophy wanted to escape its rut, it would have to interrogate psychoanalysis and admit that the Freudian unconscious placed the certitudes of consciousness in jeopardy" (1990, p. 308). Merleau-Ponty gave a presentation at the conference but died before writing a review of his remarks. The psychoanalyst, Jean-Bertrand Pontalis, however, published a review of Merleau-Ponty's remarks based on his own notes at the conference. He paraphrases Merleau-Ponty's remarks, including this remark with reference to the notion of a primordial symbolism:

> Only, this primordial symbolism, must we not seek it, rather than in language as such – 'It makes me uneasy to see the category of language occupy the entire field' – in a certain perceptual articulation, in a relation between the visible and the invisible that Mr. Merleau-Ponty designates by the name of latency, in the sense that Heidegger gives to that word (*Verborgenheit*), and not in order to specify a being that would conceal itself behind the appearances. Perception, on condition of not conceiving it as an operation, as a mode of representation, but as the double of an imperceptions, can serve as a model, and even the simple fact of seeing: 'to see, this is to have no need to form a thought.' Mr. Merleau-Ponty recalls that in his view, the opening to being is not linguistic: it is in perception that he sees the birthplace of the word. (Ey 1966, p. 143)

In this citation it is important to understand that in the last line, "it is in perception that he sees the birthplace of the word," Merleau-Ponty is returning to his original notion of perception as unreflected life, life as immediately experienced, before being thought about in verbal reflection. As he had written much earlier, "It is true that we discover the unreflected. But the unreflected we go back to is not that which is prior to philosophy or prior to reflection. It is the unreflected that is understood and conquered by reflection" (PRI,[13] p. 19).

In his further remarks at Bonneval, Merleau-Ponty rejects both Freud's mechanistic, cause-driven unconscious as well any phenomenological effort to understand it in terms of clear, transparent consciousness. In a probable reference to Lacan, he also rejects an understanding of the unconscious as the reverse (*l'envers*) of consciousness. In language that points to his final, mostly posthumous, thought, he rejects any sharp opposition between the conscious and the unconscious, arguing that each contains the other, just as the visible and invisible, rather than being in simple opposition, are present together in a relationship in which each involves the other.

Although asserting his differences from Lacan, Merleau-Ponty always remains tentative, suggesting that phenomenology and psychoanalysis are equal partners, each struggling in its own way toward a barely understood depth in human experience. That is the thrust of Merleau-Ponty's remarks in the Preface that "psychoanalysis converges with other efforts" and that "they are both aiming toward the same *latency*." (As is apparent in the above quotation, Pontalis' had introduced that word at Bonneval.) It is also the thrust of a remark Merleau-Ponty made in an interview toward the end of his life:

> Does psychoanalysis render the human individual transparent? Does it allow us to dispense with philosophy? On the contrary, the questions that psychoanalysis now asks, even more energetically than ever before, are questions that one cannot begin to answer without philosophy: How can the human being be at once wholly spiritual and wholly corporeal? The psychoanalyst's techniques contribute in conjunction with many other investigations in resolving this question, and philosophy is again at their crossroads (Merleau-Ponty 1992, p. 6.).

For his part Lacan will have nothing to do with the partnership suggested by Merleau-Ponty. He insists that phenomenology and indeed Western philosophy have been dominated by a philosophy of consciousness that has been upended by Freud's discovery of the unconscious. For him phenomenology and philosophy are at a dead end until they recognize that their analyses have been largely vitiated by their failure to bring the unconscious into the heart of philosophy.

In attempting to sort out the differences between Lacan and Merleau-Ponty, we need to recall the very different circumstances of their respective interpretations of the unconscious: on the one hand, the clinician dealing with the unconscious in the context of symptoms and treatment, on the other hand the philosopher recognizing that the unconscious brings an unknown depth to phenomenology and trying to grasp it philosophically. In his presentation at Bonneval, Ricoeur addressed this difference. While agreeing with Merleau-Ponty in rejecting a naïve-realistic notion of the unconscious as a thing in the world, he also recognizes a certain reality to the unconscious required by the clinical situation. In understanding that reality he finds

---

[13] *The Primacy of Perception* Merleau-Ponty (1973/1969).

phenomenology quite helpless and proposes a Kantian understanding that combines transcendental idealism and empirical realism. "A critique of Freudian realism must be epistemological in the sense of a 'transcendental deduction' whose task is to justify the use of a concept through its ability to organize a new field of objectivity and intelligibility" (1974, p. 103). In this sense the unconscious has no meaning outside its clinical, organizing function. "We can say, therefore, that the unconscious is an object in the sense that it is 'constituted' by the totality of hermeneutic procedures by which it is deciphered. Its being is not absolute but only relative to hermeneutics as method and dialogue" (107). In rejecting the naïve-realistic view of the unconscious, Ricoeur credits Freud for never attributing developed thought to the unconscious. "Freud himself *never* makes the unconscious think, and in this respect the discovery of the term *Es* or id was a stroke of genius. Unc. is the id and nothing but the id. Freudian realism is a realism of the id in its ideational representations and not a naïve realism of unconscious meaning" (108). Citing Ricoeur, Merleau-Ponty might retort to Lacan that he (Lacan) does make the id think, and think in language. Around this point it could be argued that Freud comes down on the side of Merleau-Ponty. In his essay on the unconscious Freud writes:

> We now seem to know all at once what the difference is between a conscious and an unconscious presentation (*Vorstellung*). The two are not, as we supposed, different registrations of the same content in different psychical localities, nor yet different...states of cathexis in the same locality; but the conscious presentation comprises the presentation of the thing plus the presentation of the word belonging to it (*Sachvorstellung plus der zugehörigen Wortvorstellung*), while the unconscious presentation is the presentation of the thing alone (*die unbewußte ist die Sachvorstellung allein*). (Freud 1915/1957, p. 201)

For Freud himself, then, should we conclude that, *pace* Lacan, the unconscious is not verbal?[14]

References

Beaulieu, Alain. 2009. Les démêlês de Merleau-Ponty avec Freud: des pulsions à une psychoanalyse de la Nature. *French Studies* 63 (3): 295–307.
Castoriadis, Cornelius. 1971. Le dicible et l'indicible. *L'Arc* 46: 67–79.
de Waelhens, Alphonse. 1966. Sur l'inconscient et la pensee philosophique. In *L'Inconscient, VI^eColloque de Bonneval*, ed. H. Ey, 371–385. Paris: Desclee de Brouer.
Duportail, Guy-Felix. 2005. Le chiasme d'une amitié: Lacan et Merleau-Ponty. *Chiasmi International* 6: 345–365.

---

[14] In fact there are two sides to Freud. After reviewing Lacan's and Freud's linguistic unconscious, Antoine Vergote writes: "The unconscious is then never structured simply as a language. All of Freud's theoretical effort aims to conceive at the same time the similarity and dissimilarity of, on the one hand, unconscious content and functioning, and on the other hand, language. Thus his opposing texts. The metaphors of translation or of a rebus speak to the similarity. The more theoretical texts insist on the cleavage. Thus for Freud language defines the structure of the preconscious, in contrast to the unconscious. The latter is said to be lacking in everything that characterized language: time, chain of causality, intention to communicate (Vergote 1982).

Ey, Henri. ed. 1966. *L'Inconscient, VIe Colloque de Bonneval*. Paris: Desclee de Brouer.
Freud, Sigmund. 1915/1957. *The unconscious. Standard Edition*. Vol. 14, 159–209. London: Hogarth Press.
Green, André. 1964. Du comportment à la chair: itinéraire de Merleau-Ponty. *Critique* 221: 1017–1046.
Hesnard, Angelo. 1960. *L'Oeuvre de Freud et son Importance pour le Monde Moderne*. Paris: Payot.
James, Phillips. 1999. *From the unseen to the invisible: Merleau-Ponty's sorbonne lectures as preparation for his later thought*, 69–90. Albany: University of New York Press.
Lanteri-Laura, Georges. 1966. Les problemes de l'inconscient et la pensee phenomenologique. In *L'Inconscient, VIeColloque de Bonneval*, ed. H. Ey, 399. Paris: Desclee de Brouer.
Merleau-Ponty, Maurice. 1962. *Phenomenology of prception*. London: Routledge and Kegan Paul.
———. 1963. *The structure of behavior*. Boston: Beacon Press.
———. 1973/1969. *The prose of the world*. Evanston: Northwestern University Press.
———. 1982–1983. Phenomenology and psychoanalysis: Preface to Hesnard's L'Oeuvre de Freud. Review of Existential Psychology and Psychiatry. XVIII, 1, 2, & 3, pp. 67–81.
———. 1988. *Merleau-Ponty à la Sorbonne: résumé de cours 1949–1952*. Paris: Cynara.
———. 1992/1960. Merleau-Ponty in person, an interview with Madeleine Chapsal. In *Maurice Merleau-Ponty, texts and dialogues*, ed. H. Silverman and J. Barry. New Jersey: Humanities Press.
———. 1996. Lacan and Merleau-Ponty: The confrontation of psychoanalysis and phenomenology. In *Disseminating Lacan*, ed. D. Pettigrew and F. Raffoul, 69–108. Albany: SUNY Press.
Phillips, James. 1996. Lacan and Merleau-Ponty: The confrontation of psychoanalysis and phenomenology. In *Disseminating Lacan*, ed. David Pettigrew and François Raffoul, 69–108. New York: State University of New York Press.
Pontalis, Jean-Bertrand. 1971. Presence, entre les signes, absence. *L'Arc* 46: 56–66.
———. 1982–1983. The problem of the unconscious in Merleau-Ponty's thought. *Review of Existential Psychology and Psychiatry* 18: 83–96.
Ricoeur, Paul. 1970. *Freud and philosophy*. New Haven: Yale University Press.
———. 1974. Consciousness and the unconscious. In *The conflict of interpretations*, ed. P. Ricoeur (D. Ihde), 99–120. Evanston: Northwestern University Press.
Roudinesco, Elisabeth. 1990. *Jacques Lacan & Co*. Trans. J. Mehlman. Chicago: University of Chicago Press.
Silverman, Hugh. 1980. Merleau-Ponty and the interrogation of language. *Research in Phenomenology* 10: 122–141.
Vergote, Antoine. 1982. De "l'autre scène "de Freud à "L'Autre" de Lacan. In *Qu'est-ce Que L'homme? Hommage à Alphonse de Waelhens (1911–1981)*. Bruxelles: Publications des Facultes Universitairs Saint-Louis.

Part III
At the Limit of Phenomenology

Chapter 6
Is There a Phenomenology of Unconsciousness? Being, Nature, Otherness in Heidegger, Merleau-Ponty, Levinas

Dorothée Legrand

Abstract Is there a phenomenology of unconsciousness? How does posing this question impact both the very conception of phenomenology as a philosophical enterprise and of unconsciousness as a concept participating to the very definition of psychoanalysis? What is unconsciousness, if it can be thought of, not only in psychoanalysis, but also in phenomenology? What is phenomenology, if there can be a phenomenology of unconsciousness? The multifaceted determinations which Heidegger, Merleau-Ponty, Levinas give to unconsciousness summon notions as crucial as consciousness, subjectivity, humanity, nature, being, and go down to redefining the very concepts of phenomenon and logos without which there could be no phenomeno-logy. Placing the notion of unconsciousness within the scope of phenomenology allows considering not only conscious but also unconscious subjectivity, and allows characterizing both asubjective and subjective modes of being unconscious. Considering this framework will help understanding the scope of the question: is there a phenomenology of unconsciousness? Yes, the investigation of unconsciousness participates to the very definition of phenomenology; No, phenomenological conceptions of unconsciousness do not leave intact the defining limits of phenomenology, but pushes them further by the mobilization of a surplus it intrinsically contains and that is revealed in its investigation of unconsciousness: ontology and ethics.

Keywords Ethics • Ontology • Phenomenon • Logos • Subjectivity • Asubjectivity

D. Legrand (✉)
Archives Husserl, CNRS, Ecole Normale Supérieure, Paris Sciences et Lettres Research University, Paris, France
e-mail: dorothee.legrand@ens.fr

6.1 Introduction

The working hypothesis of the present incursion into a phenomenology of unconsciousness is that, just as the notion of phenomenology does not belong only to Husserl as its founding father, so the notion of unconsciousness does not belong either to Freud as the founding father of psychoanalysis; rather the starting point of this inquiry is that there is a possible and fruitful articulation between the notion of phenomenology and the notion of unconsciousness, an articulation that impacts both the very conception of phenomenology as a philosophical enterprise and unconsciousness as a concept participating to the very definition of psychoanalysis. It is this articulation that will be considered here – stated differently, what will be discussed is neither the notion of phenomenology in and of itself, nor the notion of unconsciousness in and of itself, but phenomenological considerations of unconsciousness.

What is unconsciousness, if it can be thought of, not only in psychoanalysis, but also in phenomenology? *What is phenomenology*, if there can be a phenomenology of unconsciousness? How does placing the notion of unconsciousness within the scope of phenomenology allow considering *not only conscious but also unconscious subjectivity*, and how does it allow characterizing both *asubjectiveand subjective modes of being unconscious*?

In the following, we will read Martin Heidegger, Maurice Merleau-Ponty and Emmanuel Levinas. Rather than doing justice to how their thoughts have emerged, and have been prolonged, and without neglecting the relevance and importance of such enterprise, we will try to read them again *together*, as if they could *now* be followed in parallel. Granted, these thoughts have *not* been parallel for their authors themselves and thus cannot be understood fully without considering their intersections with each other. In the scope of this paper, however, we won't retrace the history these thoughts entertain with each other, filiations which are both evident and complex. Likewise, we won't select one of these lines of thoughts, by exclusion of the others, since the aim of this paper is not to perform a genealogy of *the* phenomenological conception of *the* unconscious. Rather, what is proposed here is to shed light on what unconsciousness may be, from phenomenological perspectives (plural) which are irreducible to each other. Reading these three authors in this way demonstrates that it is *from within* a given conceptualization of consciousness that each philosopher is confronted to unconsciousness.

6.2 Heidegger: Clearance of the Inapparent

To contribute to a phenomenology of unconsciousness, a first step may be to start with the very definition of phenomenology as a method of philosophical investigation. The conceptual tool proper to the phenomenological method is the *phenomenon*. There cannot be any more trivial claim – almost tautological – but complexity haunts phenomenology, already at the level of this simple characterization. In §7 of *Being and Time*, Heidegger reminds us of this complexity as he distinguishes different modes of manifestations, within "the totality of what lies in the light of day or can be brought to the light" ([1927][1] 2001a: 51). Among these manifestations, and according to the phenomenological conception, the *phenomenon* is defined as "*that which shows itself in itself*" (*Ibid.*). Nonetheless, the material which phenomenology investigates is "something that proximally and for the most part does not show itself at all: it is something that lies *hidden* […]; but at the same time it is something that belongs to what […] shows itself, and belongs to it so essentially as to constitute its meaning and ground" (*Ibid.*: 59): the hidden and the manifest belong constitutionally to each other. This is the reason why phenomenology must be a *method* which, *as such*, is "directly opposed to the *naïveté* of a haphazard, 'immediate', and unreflective 'beholding'" (*Ibid.*: 61). What phenomenology aims at is "that which demands that it *become* a phenomenon" (*Ibid.*: 59, emphasis added). To be a phenomenologist is thus to work on that which does *not* show itself but *insists* on showing itself.

Phenomenology is thus *inevitably* a "phenomenology of the inapparent", to use here the term that Heidegger himself will use in the end of his philosophical enterprise ([1973] 2003: 79–80), thereby radicalizing the opening of the phenomenological field to that which does *not* show itself as itself. Already in *Being and Time*, Heidegger underlines that "covered-up-ness is the counter-concept to 'phenomenon'" [*Verdecktheit ist der Gegenbegriff zu "Phänomen"*] ([1927] 2001a: 60). As the uncovered phenomenon cannot be untied from its covered-up-ness, phenomenology involves a process of phenomenalization which is *unceasingly* bound to repeat itself inasmuch as what does *not* show itself *keeps* insisting on showing itself. The totalization of phenomenalization would not be the achievement of phenomenology, but its end – or rather, it would render it unconceivable as a philosophical enterprise and reduce it to a branch of scientific inquiry. Indeed, it would limit its scope to some extensive enumeration of beings, ignoring Being as what remains irreducible to any manifestation of beings, no matter how exhaustively beings are manifested: "What is it that phenomenology is to 'let us see'? […] not just this entity or that, but rather the Being of entities. […] In the phenomenological conception of "phenomenon" what one has in mind as that which shows itself is the Being of entities, its meaning, its modifications and derivatives" (*Ibid.*: 59–60). Phenomenology is thus necessarily an ontology, as our way of access to Being that irremediably withdraws from the manifestation of beings.

It here appears that consciousness, as a mode of appearance, is necessarily tied to inappearance, which could in turn be taken as a mode of unconsciousness. What

---

[1] Throughout this text, the parenthesis contains the following information. The first number, in square brackets, indicates the date at which the work referred to has first been published, or the conference referred to has been pronounced. The second number indicates the date of the edition used here, as listed in the reference list. The last number indicates the pagination as in this edition.

is the unconsciousness which such phenomenology is pregnant with? What is the mode of inappearance which phenomenology here involves?

Rather than considering consciousness and unconsciousness, Heidegger favours the notions of "clearing" and "concealment". On the one hand, "there is a relationship to clearing which need not be "conscious" and reflected on in the Freudian sense" ([1963] 2001b: 183); on the other hand, "concealment is not a hiding as is Freud's "repression" [*Verdrängung*]" (*Ibid.*). Moreover, rather than opposing unconsciousness to consciousness, Heidegger ties clearing and concealment to each other: "concealment is not the antithesis of consciousness but rather concealment belongs to the clearing. Freud simply did not see this clearing" (*Ibid.*: 182). Whereas "in Freud's repression we are dealing with hiding [*Verstecken*] a representation [*Vorstellung*]" in such a way that "the phenomenon withdraws itself from the domain of the clearing and is inaccessible – so inaccessible that this inaccessibility as such cannot be experienced anymore" (*Ibid.*: 183), for Heidegger, contrastively, the inaccessible is not "so inaccessible". Rather, "the inaccessible shows and manifests itself as such – as the inaccessible. [...] The inaccessibility is cleared [*gelichtet*]; I am aware of it" (*Ibid.*). Considering concealment as a mode of clearing, Heidegger thus withdraws from "the fatal distinction between the conscious and the unconscious" ([1960] 2001b: 254).

This view is inevitably shaped by Heidegger's conception of the human mode of being in the world. Commonly, "we are assuming that a being would be accessible by the fact that the "I" as a subject would represent an object" ([1964] 2001b: 187–8). But that is not quite so. The rapport that a human being entertains to his world is "not subject-object" ([1965] 2001b: 193): the human being, i.e. Dasein, "is not a "subject"" (*Ibid.*: 192); the world is not its object. Rather than subjectivity, Dasein is transcendence: "Dasein transcends" and "transcendence is not the "structure of subjectivity," but its *removal!*" (*Ibid.*). "Transcendence [is] not a property of the subject and of its relationship to an object as "world," but the relationship to being" (*Ibid.*: 193). Transcendence is "the clearing of being. Presencing, unconcealedness of beings" (*Ibid.*: 194). It is within this realm that the human being is: da-sein ([1964] 2001b: 188). Thus, what makes the human being distinctively human is not "an ego-subject and an ego-consciousness" but "transcendence" as clearing, unconcealing: "its main feature is always unconcealing [*entbergen*] something, which must not be represented as an event "immanent in the subject"" ([1965] 2001b: 37). The human being stands in the "openness of being, in the unconcealedness [Unverborgenheit] of what comes to presence" ([1965] 2001b: 90).

Here, Heidegger forcefully underlines: "the human being's distinctive character" is not only "receiving-perceiving" but also, and *as such* "saying" (*Ibid.*: 37). Saying here means "to make manifest" and it is because saying is "letting see" that "we as human beings have something to say" (*Ibid.*: 90). "Dasein transcends", the human being "stands [...] in the unconscealedness", and "this is the reason for the possibility, indeed the necessity, the essential necessity, of "saying," that is, the reason that the human being speaks" (*Ibid.*). This view is introduced already back in 1927, within the very definition of *phenomeno-logy*: the phenomenon is "that which demands that it become a phenomenon" ([1927] 2001a: 59) and *logos* is "a

6 Is There a Phenomenology of Unconsciousness?

letting-something-be-seen" (*Ibid.*: 56). *Logos* is here specifically important as an "apophantical discourse" (*Ibid.*: 58), i.e. as that which makes manifest that which is talked about. Logos is here defined as that which allows Dasein's transcendence to let the phenomenon show itself in itself, to let himself be hosted in the clearance of unconcealment.

Heidegger's view, rooted in the very definition of phenomenology, may be exploited here – against his own will – within the scope of an investigation of unconsciousness. If we don't enclose the notion of unconsciousness into a representationalist view of Freud's psychoanalysis, if we then enforce a (distorting) translation and allow ourselves to conceive of (un)consciousness as a mode of (un)concealment, then Heidegger's view brings to the fore the idea that

- Clearing is not separated from concealment; concealment is a moment of clearing; unconsciousness is not separated from consciousness; unconsciousness belongs to the structural dynamic of consciousness.
- (Un)concealing the inaccessible, as inaccessible, is saying that which does not show itself as itself but demands that it become a phenomenon; (un)consciousness is a specifically human process that involves apophantical language.
- (Un)concealedness is transcendence; what is (un)concealed is irreducible to an object immanent to the subject; (un)consciousness is a process of transcendence; it is not the subject's innermost psyche.
- (Un)concealing is a mode of being towards Being; it is a letting-be of Being; it is not a subjective operation; (un)concealedness is an ontology; (un)consciousness is not the structure of subjectivity, but its removal; (un)consciousness is asubjective.

It is evident that these translations are not mere reformulations; quite on the contrary, it is in and of itself subversive to translate Heidegger's logos into a language which reinserts the subject, consciousness, unconsciousness. The motivation for operating such a violent translation here is to move one step further into a phenomenology of unconsciousness, thus moving with Heidegger – since he provides an unavoidable conceptualization of phenomenology itself – and moving beyond Heidegger – since he himself disdained unconsciousness as he conceives of it after reading Freud.

6.3 Merleau-Ponty: Savage Osmosis

Inserting unconsciousness within the scope of phenomenology, this leaves unaffected neither the notion of unconsciousness as defined in psychoanalysis, nor the definition of phenomenology as a philosophical enterprise. To knit together phenomenology and unconsciousness is not to draw a comparison between phenomenological and psychoanalytic notions, as if these fields would have a fixed identity which they could keep intact independently of their articulation with each other; nor is it to build fragile bridges between these two continents of thoughts separated by wide oceans of theoretical and practical differences; rather, a phenomenology of unconsciousness can insert itself in a conceptual landscape where "phenomenology and psychoanalysis are not parallel" ([1960] 1994: 71) but intersect each other. Such is the framework which has been described by Merleau-Ponty in a text, brief and condensed, a preface which he wrote in 1960, 1 year before his death. This multifaceted description offers a culminating summary as much as the prospect of an on-going continuation of Merleau-Ponty's own venture into the phenomenological investigation of unconsciousness, an investigation which he undertook throughout his work.

Merleau-Ponty starts by considering that psychoanalysis "confirms phenomenology in its description of consciousness [...] it brings to phenomenology a wealth of concrete examples that add weight to what it has been able to say in general of the relations of man with the world and of the interhuman bound [...For the clinician] the contact with patients and with illness always brings a surplus of meaning, of weight, of density to the meagre concepts of the theory" (*Ibid.*: 67–68). Psychoanalysis would thus nourish phenomenological descriptions with clinical nutriments.

But psychoanalysis is not only a practice; it is a practice informed theoretically; thus "it cannot content itself with concepts that are simply good enough for working *in vivo*; it must formulate the treasure of experience that is hidden in psychoanalytic communication" (*Ibid.*: 68). For that, phenomenology brings to psychoanalysis "the framework of a better philosophy" (*Ibid.*: 69) by providing "certain categories, certain means of expression that it needs in order to be completely itself" (*Ibid.*: 67). Here appears a *failure* of the philosopher to recognize the capacities proper to psychoanalysis to conceptualize its own practice and practice its own conceptualization. Nonetheless, Merleau-Ponty soon departs from this dominating position and, "to express in a different way relations of phenomenology and psychoanalysis" (*Ibid.*: 69), he relies on "a philosophy that is now perhaps more mature" (*Ibid.*), as well as on "the growth of Freudian research" (*Ibid.*).

To intersect phenomenology and psychoanalysis, Merleau-Ponty pursues a reappropriation of Husserlian phenomenology and underlines that "the more one penetrates phenomenological thought [...] the better one can distinguish phenomenology from [a] new philosophy of consciousness" (*Ibid.*). "All consciousness is consciousness of something" (*Ibid.*: 70) – such is the intentional structure of consciousness, a credo untiringly repeated, progressively enriched. But this "something" is *not* an object "exactly adjusted to acts of consciousness", as some "phenomenological positivism" would have taught (*Ibid.*). What Merleau-Ponty forcefully underlines here is the necessity to design a "phenomenology which descends into its own substratum"; such is the phenomenology that can avoid both "phenomenological idealism" and "phenomenological positivism"; and such is the phenomenology which "is converging more than ever with Freudian research" (*Ibid.*). This phenomenology is an "infinite curiosity" (*Ibid.*: 69) an "ambition to *see everything*", but this ambition is unceasingly animated by an irreducible "hidden being" which it seeks to surprise (*Ibid.*: 70).

As phenomenology shall remain irreducible to a philosophy of consciousness, psychoanalysis shall refrain from becoming *"too well tolerated"*, as its concepts would then loose "their enigma and furnish the themes of a new dogmatism" (*Ibid.*). Rather, it is essential that psychoanalysis remains "a paradox and an interrogation" (*Ibid.*: 71). For that, Merleau-Ponty proposes, one must "learn to read Freud […] by understanding his words and theoretical concepts, not in their lexical and common meaning, but in the meaning they acquire from within the experience they announce" (*Ibid.*). From such reading, one may depart from one's "first impressions" when encountering Freud's "incredible bias in favor of the least probable interpretations" (*Ibid.*: 68): despite one's resistances, and "to the extent that one read[s], that one relate[s] oneself to oneself, […] a sort of evidence for psychoanalysis [is] inexplicably established" and the philosopher comes to "live in peace" with it (*Ibid.*: 68–69). A "misunderstanding […] has been lifted", a transformation operated, and "the psychoanalysis that we accept and like is not the one that we refused" when first encountering it (*Ibid.*: 69). To accept, and even like psychoanalysis, therefore, Merleau-Ponty needed to report himself to himself, not only to his own philosophy, but to his own lived experiences, including his experience of *reading psychoanalysis*. In other terms, for the phenomenologist, entering psychoanalysis is not only a conceptual venture, but an experiential one too.

Read as such, the word "unconscious" is and remains the "index of an enigma" (*Ibid.*: 71). Such is the *"latency"* at which both phenomenology and psychoanalysis aim: the unconscious – "what phenomenology implies or unveils as its limits", that which "a consciousness cannot sustain" (*Ibid.*). To reach such latency, and design a phenomenology of unconsciousness, one ought to step out of the conception of phenomenology as a philosophy of consciousness; and for this, Merleau-Ponty argues, one ought to depart from subjectivity. Indeed, if one starts by assuming subjectivity, one remains "definitively confined within the correlation of subjectivity and its objects" ([1957] 2008: 49[2]). Merleau-Ponty thus demands that we start, not with subjectivity, but with Nature (*Ibid.*: 51), conceived of "as an index of what in the things resists the operation of subjectivity" (*Ibid.*: 53). Investigating Nature, Merleau-Ponty aims at "rediscovering" the "brute or savage being which has not yet been converted into an object of vision or choice" (*Ibid.*), the being "which precedes us, circumscribes us, holds us, which holds haphazardly other men with us […] which 'holds' itself on its own" (*Ibid.*: 51).

To further specify Merleau-Ponty's "ontology of Nature" (*Ibid.*: 52), let us note that here Nature is a "primordial being" (*Ibid.*: 46), as such irreducible to man and men, uncapturable in "a chapter of anthropology" (*Ibid.*: 45), as "a detail of human history" (*Ibid.*: 46). But if philosophy of Nature is not a "philosophy of mind" (*Ibid.*: 45), not a transcendental idealism, nonetheless for Merleau-Ponty Nature is linked to humanity, uncontingently. In Merleau-Ponty's ontology, Nature "is authentically only *such* as it offers itself within a field of perception" ([1954–1955] 2010: 128[3]),

---

[2] All translations of this text are here mine.

[3] Translation modified. Note that Merleau-Ponty here talks about the body. I transfer this thought to his consideration on Nature, assuming that the body is notably, for Merleau-Ponty, a natural body, and as such, an incarnation of Nature.

but if Merleau-Ponty refuses to distinguish Nature "in itself" and Nature as it is perceived in human experience, if Nature is "exactly as it appears", it is because "*percipere* is to be surpassed... as much as to surpass" (*Ibid.*: 127[4]). Intrinsically surpassed, human perception is impregnated by the "inhuman", the "pre-human perceived" Nature (*Ibid.*: 128).

But how may inhuman nature ever be linked to man and men? To dig into this question, one may consider Merleau-Ponty's study of one's "*natural* self" ([1945] 2012: 174), i.e. one's own body. To start with, Merleau-Ponty never conflates the *lived* body with the body present or represented in one's conscious field. Rather, the lived body comes to consciousness in an indirect and evanescent manner: "I am conscious of my body through the world" and as such my body is "the unperceived term at the centre of the world toward which every object turns its face" (*Ibid.*: 84). "Regions of silence are thus marked out in the totality of my body" (*Ibid.*). Through Merleau-Ponty's words, the silence of the body resonates, a conscious silence which lets us hear the rumbling world. The body is consciously experienced prereflectively, insofar as the perception of objects "occupies and obliterates my consciousness" (*Ibid.*: 249). By its intentional structure, consciousness projects itself towards its objects, phenomena which substantialize themselves by overwriting both the act of consciousness and its subject. Yet the object, always already there, is experienced by a subject here and now, a subject who experiences himself as the author of perception and action, in a silent, prereflective manner.

But what does happen if I "repress" the prereflective consciousness I have of "my gaze as a means of knowing" and which I normally experience silently (*Ibid.*: 73)? If instead of seeing the world, I look at my retina, if I am forgetful of "the perspectivism of my experience", I then "treat my eyes as fragments of matter" and regard my body "as one of the objects of that world" (*Ibid.*); I thus represent that "I have a retina, a brain like other men and the cadavers I dissect" (*Ibid.*: 97). The "repression" of my body prereflectively *lived* as a mode of *being* in the world would thus give way to my body as *object*. What Merleau-Ponty here calls "repression" is thus a curious operation which *suspends the silence* of the body lived prereflectively; repression here abstracts the subject from the world, closes the body upon itself and thus lets it appear as some inert matter.

But there is another operation which Merleau-Ponty describes as a "repression". He describes not only repression as an *opposition* between, on the one hand, the lived body silently projected in experiential life, and on the other hand, the non-lived objectified matter which would be its abstraction. Besides, he also describes repression as an *undividable intermeshing* of the lived body with the impersonal organic functioning of my living body, which most of the time remains non conscious: "bodily existence, which streams forth through me without my complicity, [...] and establishes [my] primary pact with the world" (*Ibid.*: 168). The living body is nothing like an "integrated or rigorously unique totality" but underlies my con-

---

[4] Translation modified.

scious experience with "a margin of *almost* impersonal existence [...] to which I entrust the care of keeping me alive" (*Ibid.*: 86). This body is *common*, comparable to the body of any other man, a body, therefore, which does not singularize itself, a body which is *in-different*: "I have "sense organs", a "body", and "psychic functions" comparable to those of others" (*Ibid.*). In this sense, "the subject of perception is never an absolute subjectivity [...] Perception is always in the impersonal mode of the 'One'" (*Ibid.*: 249).

This body, living, impersonal, in-different, is most of the time non conscious, and it is precisely here that Merleau-Ponty describes an "organic suppression [*refoulement organique*]" (*Ibid.*: 80, 86). But this repression never fully divides the lived body from its living support. "Organic repression" is not the mere deletion of the organism from the field of consciousness but rather the "advent of the impersonal" (*Ibid.*: 86) as an "active nothingness" which "continually offers me some form of living" (*Ibid.*: 168), by opening my living body to the world. Thus, for Merleau-Ponty, there seems to be no divergence between the living body and the lived body, as the former unceasingly structures and sustains the latter. This undividable intermeshing of the lived body with the living body is what allows Merleau-Ponty to describe "organic repression" as the "advent of the impersonal".

Of particular interest for the design of a phenomenology of unconsciousness, Merleau-Ponty indicates that what ties together the subjectively lived body and the asubjective living body is: the *unconscious*. Indeed, "in order to account for [the] osmosis between the body's anonymous life and the person's official life [...], it [is] necessary to introduce something *between* the organism and ourselves considered as a sequence of deliberate acts and explicit understandings. This [is] Freud's *unconscious*" ([1951] 2007: 194). Here, the unconscious is the *link* between, on the one hand, the ability of being oneself a singular subject, and on the other hand, the "anonymous *adversity*" (*Ibid.*: 203) by which "our initiatives get bogged down in the paste of the body, of language, or of that world beyond measure" (*Ibid.*: 203). The unconscious would be the glue allowing the "osmosis" between different dimensions of one's being, an osmosis which would make the man "admirable": "installed in his fragile body, in a language which has already done so much speaking, and in a reeling history", this man nonetheless "gathers himself together and begins to see, to understand, and to signify" (*Ibid.*: 204).

What appears here is the conception of an *osmotic unconscious* which would come between the savage nature and the symbolic institution of the subject. Identified with neither of these realms, the osmotic unconscious would rather come in between these dimensions to link them together, preventing the man from being divided and pulled apart by antagonist forces. Unconsciousness would here be the name of a process operating one's integration with elements which one cannot control but which one cannot expel either. Unconsciousness is here the name of one's adhesion to *oneself*.

This conception of an osmotic unconsciousness is further elaborated upon when Merleau-Ponty investigates "the unconsciousness of the unconscious" as an "unknown" process "acting and organizing dream and life" ([1954–1955] 2010: 159). In dreams operates a "very special" intentionality, "not an intentionality of acts, positing objects, but an exhibition of concretions" (*Ibid.*: 156), a "subject-object solidarity" (*Ibid.*: 158): in dreams, we make "a pseudo-world where subject and object are indistinct" (*Ibid.*), "we wallow in being" (*Ibid.*), we "return to the pre-objective organization of the world" (*Ibid.*: 150). Such archaic organization is interwoven in all awaken life. This "oneirism of wakefulness" (*Ibid.*: 152) characterizes our relation to the world and to others insofar as it is irreducible to a relation to objects which a subject may observe at a distance. In particular, "one does not *observe* an interlocutor" ([1951] 2003: 194[5]) and "others are present to us as dreams" (*Ibid.*: 268) because, in an encounter between oneself and others, "the rule is [...] un-distinction, and the exception, differentiation" (*Ibid.*: 205). The unconscious is here conceived of as "the echo of others in me, of me in others" (*Ibid.*: 264) and becoming conscious is "pulling the self-other rapport out of its ambiguity" (*Ibid.*: 246–7). As a venture in unconsciousness, psychoanalysis thus involves the "revelation of intercorporeity, of the *Ego*-others montage, as it is realized by each one" (*Ibid.*: 246).

We understand here that for Merleau-Ponty, osmotic unconsciousness is "the primordial unconsciousness" defined as "the initial yes, the indivision of feeling" ([1959–1960] 1988: 179[6]). Such indivision cannot be performed as an act of a subject at an intentional distance from its object of consciousness; rather, it is a "letting-be" (*Ibid.*): "the unconscious is sensing itself, since sensing is not the intellectual possession of 'what' is sensed, but a dispossession of ourselves in favor of it, an opening toward that which we do not have to think in order that we may recognize it" (*Ibid.*[7]).

It is particularly striking to read this Résumé of the 1959–1960 course on Nature, where Merleau-Ponty thus defines *unconsciousness* as dispossession, together with a working note dated of November 1960, where he defines *philosophy*: "philosophy [...] cannot be total and active grasp, intellectual possession, since what there is to be grasped is a dispossession" ([1960] 1968: 266). In the last words of his Résumé, Merleau-Ponty links primordial unconsciousness to a "logos of the sensible world" which he demarcates from "explicit logos" ([1959–1960] 1988: 179). Thus, the parallel with the Working Note invites us to reconsider how philosophy "shows by words" ([1960] 1968: 266): if it "shows" without possessing, its "words" must not be reduced to some "explicit logos" thematizing what there is; rather, it must be recognized that a "logos of the sensible world" animates philosophical words – words which thus let the sensible world show itself thought them.

Like unconsciousness involves a pre-objective "exhibition of concretions" ([1954–1955] 2010: 156), a "subject-object solidarity" (*Ibid.*: 158), the logos of the sensible world involves a symbolism "of nondivision, of nondifferentiation, with a latent, blind meaning", to be distinguished from another symbolism, "artificial, con-

---

[5] From here to the end of this paragraph, translations of this text are mine.
[6] Translation modified.
[7] Translation modified.

ventional, with a manifest meaning" ([1956–1960] 1995: 289[8]). The "silent communication of perception" (*Ibid.:* 282) is a "natural symbolism" hosted by the human body (*Ibid.:* 381), an "incorporated meaning" (*Ibid.*: 219), the "animality" of the human subject (*Ibid.*), a "brute and savage spirit" (*Ibid.:* 274) which ought to be revealed beneath any cultural symbolism and instituted language (*Ibid.*: 274, 290).

Animated by the logos of the sensible world, as an interrogative thought akin to perception, philosophy here appears as a manner to let unconsciousness be; or to phrase it differently: unconsciousness is here the name given to what a philosophical logos may let be: one's sensible osmosis with the unknown. Such a philosophy is not "an *awakening of consciousness (prise de conscience)* […] never will the lacuna be filled in, the unknown transformed into known; the "object" of philosophy […] the thing itself […] offer themselves […] only to someone who wishes not to have them but to see them, […] to let them be and to witness their continued being – to someone who therefore limits himself to giving them the hollow, the free space they ask for in return, […] who is […] a question consonant with the porous being which it questions and from which it obtains not an *answer*, but a confirmation of its astonishment" ([1960] 1968: 101–2).

It appears here that, as with Heidegger, with Merleau-Ponty, the design of a phenomenology of unconsciousness involves reconsidering phenomenology, its logos, that which it aims at letting be. Several key features run throughout Merleau-Ponty's various characterizations of unconsciousness:

– Unconsciousness is the index of an enigma which cannot be approached outside of one's own experience; it is intermeshed with consciousness which can never be total; unconsciousness is constitutive of consciousness, both in dreams and awaken life.
– (Un)consciousness does not have the structure of intentionality, with its subject at a distance from its object; it involves a pre-objective and pre-subjective latency which can manifest itself neither as a pre-reflexive subject nor as an intentional object.
– (Un)consciousness involves a dispossession of oneself as a separated, distinguished, unique subject; it involves an osmosis with brute, savage, unknown, uncontrollable dimensions which are unceasingly participating to one's being, an immersion into the sensible world one is part of, an intercorporeity with others, whom one doesn't differ from.
– (Un)consciousness involves a sensible, corporeal, animal, mute logos, a letting-be which requires the openness of a (philosophical) faithful but interrogative perception, in which one does not possess anything but confirms one's astonishment.

---

[8] Translations of this text are here mine.

6.4 Levinas: Assigned to Be Uniquely Oneself for the Other

With both Heidegger and Merleau-Ponty, it appears that a phenomenology of unconsciousness ought to be an ontology, as it involves the letting-be of Being. In both cases, ontology is what requires phenomenology to conceive of unconsciousness; unconsciousness is what allows phenomenology to be an ontology: unconsciousness is the ontological dimension that prevents phenomenology to be equated with a philosophy of consciousness and a theory of subjectivity. To play this role, unconsciousness ought to be a mode of Being; it cannot be properly, singularly subjective. But what would a phenomenology of unconsciousness be, if unconsciousness were specifically subjective? The first move required to consider this question is not a move backwards, pulling phenomenology out of ontology but a move forward, allowing the consideration of what subjectivity would be, otherwise than Being.

Levinas defines ontology as a "comprehension of being" ([1961] 1969: 43), and phenomenology, he argues, suffers from an "ontological imperialism" (*Ibid.*: 44). Phenomenology is safeguarded from idealism by its consideration that "an existent arises upon a ground that extends beyond it" (*Ibid.*: 44–5); the Being of the existent guaranties "the non-coinciding of thought with the existent". But, Levinas criticizes, in phenomenology, "the independence and the extraneity of the existent" (*Ibid.*: 45) is converted back into an ontology, i.e. a "thematization and conceptualization" (*Ibid.*: 46) of Being by a human subject "neutralizing the existent in order to comprehend or grasp it" (*Ibid.*), notably conceiving of Being in terms of nature: "impersonal fecundity, faceless generous mother, matrix of particular beings, inexhaustible matter for things" (*Ibid.*). Thereby, the relation with Being that is enacted in ontology is not a relation with the unknown but its reduction to the known. Distortingly translated in the terms of our current investigation of a phenomenology of unconsciousness: phenomenology's ontology leaves out that which is otherwise than conscious. Thus, Levinas conceives of phenomenology's ontological guise as a movement that is constantly countering itself: a movement starting with a transcendental subject, a subject relative to who the independence of the object must be preserved, an object which then relies on asubjective Being, whose otherness is then captured again by the subject. Levinas' philosophy is diametrically opposite to this movement and, accordingly, he refrains from characterizing the unconscious in terms of an asubjective Being.

Notably, unconsciousness is neither Being nor Nature akin to some "obscure viscous ground" out of which sensations would emerge (*Ibid.*: 138). Indeed, relative to such background, "the consciousness of the sensible would already have lost its sincerity" (*Ibid.*), whereas Levinas underlines forcefully that "to sense is precisely to be sincerely content with what is sensed, […] to refuse the unconscious prolongations" (*Ibid.*: 138–9). For Levinas, consciousness as a mode of being-in-the-world "is precisely sincerity" ([1947] 2013: 50[9]), and he underlines "the fundamental and

---

[9] Translations of this text are here mine.

irreducible self-sufficiency of sensibility" ([1961] 1969: 138), which needs relying on no unconscious ground. Fully itself, i.e. fully absorbed by its world, consciousness does not host unconscious motives. But, such intentionality of consciousness, by which a subject is thrown in a given world, is precisely where Levinas inserts his questioning, underlining that "it is perhaps not necessary to maintain that intentionality is the ultimate secret of the psyche" ([1975] 2000: 18). For Levinas, if consciousness means an intentional relation between subject and object in the world, then "it is "before" the world comes about that the unconscious plays its role" ([1947] 2013: 51). Unconsciousness is neither Being nor Nature blindly sustaining the correlation of the conscious subject with its world; unconsciousness comes about "before" such correlation unfolds as one's mode of being in the world. Such "before" is not the "before" of an "after" that would unfold linearly along some chronology; what Levinas gives us to think of is the advent of a subject, its unceasing occurrence, unceasingly unaccomplished, an event which is always already passed and never finished.

If such a thought is possible for Levinas, it is because he departs not only from phenomenological ontology – since he refrains from presupposing Being – , but also from phenomenological transcendentalism – since he refrains from *pre*supposing subjectivity. His whole enterprise rather involves characterizing – showing, naming – the process of subjectivation. As such, his philosophy could be aptly seen as a phenomenology of the subject, in the objective sense of the genitive: not a phenomenology that gives itself the subject as its point of departure, and which takes as its aim to determine both the correlation and the autonomy of the object vis-à-vis the transcendental subject, but a phenomenology that investigates how the subject comes to being, how "a being, a subject, an existent, arises in impersonal Being" (*Ibid.*: 17). What Levinas reveals is how "someone exists who assumes Being, henceforth his being" (*Ibid.*: 120). Subjectivation, he argues, is a "de-neutralization of Being" (*Ibid.*: 10) which occurs as "the beginning, the origin, the birth" (*Ibid.*: 16) of a unique subject assuming the weight of his existence. "The advent of the subject" (*Ibid.*: 98), "subject of the verb *to be*" (*Ibid.*: 120), surmounts the "inhuman neutrality" of Being (*Ibid.*: 10) and as such the subject is "an ex-ception […] which can no longer be stated in terms of being" ([1974] 1991: 17).

Such subjectivity is constituted by consciousness; to be a conscious subject is to emerge as "a name, in the anonymity of the night", "to be torn away from the *there is*" ([1947] 2013: 85). By contrast with such conception of conscious subjectivity, it may seem that unconsciousness is that which "insinuates itself in the night" (*Ibid.*: 84). However, this is not quite so, and Levinas stipulates explicitly that the movement through which the subject may dissolve back into the night of anonymous Being, the "movement which will strip consciousness of its very 'subjectivity'" is not "lulling it into unconsciousness" but is rather "throwing it into *impersonal vigilance*" (*Ibid.*: 85). Here again Levinas departs from ontology and clearly demarcates unconsciousness from Being, as the latter "resists a personal form" and is characterized as general, indeterminate, anonymous, impersonal, inhuman, asubjective, yet inextinguishable (*Ibid.*: 81). What imposes itself, in the horror of a night of insomnia, is not the unconscious Ego, but "the disappearance of all things and of the I", a disappearance which "leaves what cannot disappear, the sheer fact of being in which *one* participates" (*Ibid.*: 82): universal *there is*, impersonal Being belonging to no one. The "rustling" of inhuman anonymity captures one in horror (*Ibid.*: 84) because "a subject is stripped of his subjectivity, of his power to have private existence. The subject is depersonalized" (*Ibid.*: 86). Again, Levinas is explicit: this "impersonality is the exact contrary of an unconsciousness" (*Ibid.* 97): it is an "extinction of the subject" (*Ibid.*: 98).

The idea that asubjectivity is the exact contrary of unconsciousness suggests that unconsciousness is subjective. If that is so, then it appears that:

- Unconsciousness is not asubjective Being which would ground the subject's mode of being in the world – thus unconsciousness cannot play for phenomenology the role of an ontological safeguard against idealism.
- Moreover, linking unconsciousness and subjectivity allows considering that subjectivity escapes both self-consciousness as the "knowing of oneself by oneself" ([1974] 1991: 102), and an unconscious which "preserves the structure of self-knowledge" by involving "a quest of self" where one seeks and may find oneself (*Ibid.*: 194).
- The idea that unconsciousness is subjective is linked to the idea that unconsciousness participates to the way subjectivity is given birth out of impersonal Being. As revealed by Levinas, "the advent of consciousness […is] a power to "suspend" being by […] unconsciousness" ([1947] 2013: 38): from a movement of unconsciousness relative to asubjective being, surges a subject, an I, an ego.

In the most concrete manner, the idea that unconsciousness surges as a movement of subjectivation ought to be characterized as the subject's mode of being corporeal. As irremediably corporeal, the subject suffers a sensitivity which is an exposure to that which one cannot hide away from. Such is the "absolute passivity" of "incarnation, corporeity" ([1974] 1991: 197). As sensible, the subject is an "ipseity" without will, with no consent (*Ibid.*), "a passivity beneath all passivity" (*Ibid.*: 101). One's unavoidable sensibility, i.e. the frankness of one's body involves a "subjective condition" which is imposed as an "irreversible assignation" to be oneself. Expulsed outside of Being, one ought to be oneself, "assigned without recourse" (*Ibid.*: 103). It appears here that "the subject called incarnate does not result from a materialization […] which would have been realized by a consciousness, that is, a self-consciousness"; rather, the subject is body, "subjectivity is sensibility" (*Ibid.*: 77).

For Levinas, this assignation to one's body, this sensible subjectivation is not operated by Being, since the latter is an asubjective indifference; subjectivation is not either an operation of the subject towards himself, since the latter does not preexist the process which gives him birth: subjectivation thus ought to be imposed upon the subject from elsewhere, from where he is not, where he cannot be. The movement of subjectivation has an "active source [which] does not, in any way, occur in consciousness": the source of subjectivation is exterior to the subject; the source of consciousness is unconscious. "This exteriority has to be emphasized. It is not objective or spatial, recuperable in immanence and thus falling under the orders of – and in the order of – consciousness" (*Ibid.*: 102). Birth is given to the subject by a transcendence, by another, irreducible to oneself.

Against the background of phenomenological ontology and transcendantalism, Levinas designs a movement of subjectivation that suspends the subject's egoistic pre-existence; the subject is the effect of a process of subjectivation through which it is by the other that the subject is elected as such, as "one and irreplaceable, one inasmuch as irreplaceable" (*Ibid.*: 103). In the indifference of Being, the subject is imposed as "a right to exist"; in the anonymous "*there is*", surges "the importance of that which there is" ([1948] 2011: 89); over and above the bare fact of being, "this fact of being is important for the outside" (*Ibid.*: 94), for what transcends the subject, for the other: the subject exists for the other – here in the sense that one is "justified" from the other (*Ibid.*: 96). Such is the non-indifference of the other.

Crucially for Levinas, this non-indifference *of* the other – out of which one surges as subject – is tied to the subject's non-indifference *to* the other: insofar as "subjectivity is sensibility", it is a passive exposure and more specifically, it is "an exposure to others", that is, a sensitivity to others, an exposure to others' sensitivity, from which one's sensitivity cannot withdraw. In this sense, "matter is the very locus of the for-the-other" and it is inasmuch as it is irremediably corporeal that the subject is irremediably "the-one-for-the-other" ([1974] 1991: 77). To insist: "the psyche in the subject" is the "subjectivity of a man of flesh and blood; subjectivity is "a being torn up from oneself for another in the giving to the other of the bread out of one's own mouth. This is not an anodyne formal relation, but all the gravity of the body"; subjectivity is a passive "extradition to the other" (*Ibid.*: 142). It appears here that, insofar as it occurs as a "non-indifference" to the other, subjectivation is an ethics: a "relationship of man to man ([1961] 1969: 79).

The subject is a creature ([1948] 2011: 95): he is created by the absolute other, in a "transcendence without transcendence" (*Ibid.*: 89). The transcendence of the subject is the other – from and for who he surges. The non-transcendence of this transcendence is perhaps the most difficult and the most crucial aspect of the process of subjectivation which ought to be specified here, in the unfolding of a phenomenology of unconsciousness. What ought to be understood is the paradoxical nature of the subject's relation to others: it is insofar as it is for others that the subject is forced to return to itself. Indeed, the process of subjectivation can involve others as such only if it does not involve *any* fusion between oneself and others, any reduction of oneself to others, any reduction of others to oneself. Thus, the process of subjectivation must be of a kind that preserves the radical singularity of oneself and others: created by the other, the subject is "riveted to itself" (*Ibid.*: 96). This non-detachable tie to oneself is what safeguards one's singularity together with the other's alterity: "the very difference between me and the other is non-indifference, is the-one-for-the-other" ([1974] 1991: 178).

Born from the other, the subject is irremediably thrown back to itself, in "a resignation not consented to", and which "crosses a night of unconsciousness. That is the sense of the unconscious, night in which [occurs] the reverting of the [198] ego into itself" ([1974] 1991: 197–8). "The notion of subjectivity that is proposed here […] does not amount to the inwardness of the transcendental consciousness […].

Subjectivity signifies by a passivity more passive than all passivity, more passive than matter, by its vulnerability, its sensibility, […] by the accusative of the oneself without a nominative form, by exposedness [… This passivity] confounds consciousness which remains wakeful, but is cast into a resignation in the night, in which, [despite itself] the ego reverts to the self. In a night of the unconscious, to be sure"; this is where Levinas finds "the inter-human drama and the unconscious again beyond the vigilance of transcendental idealism and classical psychology" ([1972] 1987: 147).

As often, the same word repeated by Levinas does not have twice the same meaning and what is *said* ought to be heard together with the fact that he is *saying* it – in different contexts of enunciation. The "night of unconsciousness" referred to here is not the same "night" as the one described above. The "night of unconsciousness" here is not the horror of impersonal being; it is its exact opposite: the "night of unconsciousness" here is the return of oneself to oneself, the assignment of oneself to be oneself irremediably. The night of unconsciousness, here, is not the indifference of being; it is the non-indifference to the other which ties the subject to the non-indifference of/to the other.

Assigned by the other to be uniquely "one self", the subject is forced to exist "outside of being, and thus in itself as in exile" (*Ibid.*: 103), in the night of unconsciousness. There, in the assignment to be oneself irremediably, assignment imposed by the very fact of being exposed to the other before any consent and by the very fact of being for the other before any altruistic willingness, "the ascendancy of the other is exercised upon the [movement of subjectivation] to the point of interrupting it, leaving [the subject] speechless" (*Ibid.*: 101). Subjectivation is a violence exerted upon the subject's response to the other's call: by addressing oneself to the other, one is elected by the other as "one and unique"; justified in being for the other, one is thrown back to oneself in a violence that "breaks off every justification […], every logos" (*Ibid.*: 197). Thus, subjectivation is a "reduction to silence" (*Ibid.*). Subjectivation occurs between oneself and the other, in transcendence – this requires language as what ensures an inviolable respect for the alterity of the other, i.e. a respect for his singularity; and in turn this forces one to return to one's own singularity from within the movement through which one is for the other. This "return" is the pre-ontological silence contained in speech: within the interlocution inevitably operates the unsayable Saying of what is said between subjects singularly foreign to each other. Mute is the unconsciousness of a subject constituted with logos; unsayable is the importance of being irreplaceably oneself for the other.

6.5 Is There a Phenomenology of Unconsciousness?

Together with Heidegger, Merleau-Ponty and Levinas, several key authors could and should be present even in the most introductory investigation of unconsciousness from a phenomenological perspective. But already here what appears is that considering unconsciousness within the scope of phenomenology is unavoidable since it participates to the very definition of this discipline as a philosophical method. With the philosophical investigations performed by three thinkers who fundamentally and continuously reformed the field of phenomenology, not only one must recognize that there are as many phenomenologies of unconsciousness as there are phenomenologies of consciousness; but more importantly, here in our presentation of various phenomenological conceptions of unconsciousness, it has been unavoidable to extend the defining limits of phenomenology, by the mobilization of a surplus it intrinsically contains and that is revealed in its investigation of unconsciousness: ontology and ethics, i.e. the radical alterity of Being and the radical alterity of the other – alterity from which one's singular subjectivity cannot be untied.

References

Heidegger, Martin. 2001a. *Being and Time*. Trans. J. Macquarie and E. Robinson. Oxford: Blackwell.
———. 2001b. *Zollikon Seminars. Protocols – Conversations – Letters*, ed. Medard Boss. Trans. F. Mayr and R. Askay. Evanston: Northwestern University Press.
———. 2003. Seminar in Zähringen 1973. In *Four Seminars*, ed. Curd Ochwadt, 64–81. Trans. A. Mitchell and F. Raffoul. Bloomington: Indiana University Press.
Levinas, Emmanuel. 1969. *Totality and Infinity*. Trans. A. Lingis. Pittsburgh: Duquesne University Press.
———. 1987. Humanism of the Other. In *Collected Philosophical Papers*, 141–151. Trans. A. Lingis. Dordrecht: Martinus Nijhoff Publishers.
———. 1991. *Otherwise than Being or Beyond the Essence*. Trans. A. Lingis. Dordrecht : Kluwer Academic Publishers.
———. 2000. *God, Death and Time*. Trans. B. Bergo. Stanford: Stanford University Press.
———. 2011. Parole et Silence, Conférences du Collège philosophique des 4 et 5 février 1948. In *Œuvres complètes, tome 2: Parole et silence et autres conférences inédites au Collège philosophique*, ed. Rodolphe Calin and Catherine Chalier, 69–104. Paris: Grasset-Imec.
———. 2013. *De l'existence à l'existant*. Paris: Vrin.
Merleau-Ponty, Maurice. 1968. *The Visible and the Invisible. Followed by Working Notes*. Trans. A. Lingis. Evanston: Northwestern University Press.
———. 1988. Themes from the Lecture Courses. In *In Praise of Philosophy and Other Essays*. Trans. J. O'Neill. Evanston: Northwestern University Press.
———. 1994. Phenomenology and Psychoanalysis: Preface to Hesnard's *L'œuvre de Freud*. In *Merleau-Ponty & Psychology*, ed. Keith Hoeller, 67–72. Trans. A. Fisher. New Jersey: Humanities Press.
———. 1995. *La Nature: Notes de cours du Collège de France (1956–60)*. Paris: Seuil.
———. 2003. *L'institution, la passivité: Notes de cours au Collège de France (1954–1955)*. Paris: Belin.
———. 2007. Man and adversity. In *The Merleau-Ponty reader*, ed. Ted Toadvine and Leonard Lawlor. Evanston: Northwestern University Press.
———. 2008. La Nature ou le monde du silence (pages d'introduction). In *Maurice Merleau-Ponty*, ed. Emmanuel de Saint Aubert. Paris: Hermann.
———. 2010. *Institution and Passivity: Course Notes from the Collège de France (1954–1955)*. Trans. L. Lawlor and H. Massey. Evanston: Northwestern University Press.
———. 2012. *Phenomenology of Perception*. Trans. D.A. Landes. Oxon: Routledge.

Chapter 7
Phenomenology of the Inapparent

François Raffoul

Abstract Phenomenology is traditionally considered to be a thought of presence, assigned to a phenomenon that is identified with the present being, or with an object for consciousness. In all cases, the phenomenon with which phenomenology is concerned always seems to be accessible to a conscious experience. Indeed, consciousness itself is nothing but a form of presence, i.e., a presence to self. As a thought of presence, and of presence to consciousness (itself, then, a form of presence), phenomenology would know nothing of the unconscious. However, I will suggest in the following pages that phenomenology is haunted by the presence of a certain unappearing dimension, an alterity that escapes presentation, which led Heidegger to characterize the most authentic sense of phenomenology as a "phenomenology of the inapparent." I show how the "inapparent" plays in phenomenality and in phenomenology, stressing its ethical import as this withdrawal of presence within phenomena involves a responsibility to the otherness of a secret. Ultimately, this secret is a dimension that constantly haunts phenomenology, and to which it belongs, whether it knows it or not.

Keywords Inapparent · Phenomenology · Secret · Otherness · Invisibility

7.1 Introduction

Phenomenology is traditionally considered to be a thought of presence, assigned to a phenomenon that is identified with the present being, or with an object for consciousness. The very term "phenomenon," which has its roots in the Greek verb *phainestai*, means "to appear," "to show itself." As a middle-voice construction of *phaino*, *phainestai* means to bring to light, to place in brightness, where something can become visible and manifest. The phenomena are thus the "totality of what lies

---

F. Raffoul (✉)
Louisiana State University, Baton Rouge, LA, USA
e-mail: fraffoul@yahoo.com

in the light of day or can be brought to light."[1] Now, one may immediately conclude from this that by definition the phenomenon is what appears and shows itself, and shows itself to a perceiver or to a consciousness, which would exclude any problematic of an unconscious to enter phenomenology. The phenomenon would be synonymous with presence itself, with what manifests itself in a presence that can be attested in a conscious experience. Indeed, is consciousness itself not a form of presence, i.e., a presence to self? As Jacques Derrida remarks: "But what is consciousness? What does 'consciousness' mean? Most often, in the very form of meaning, in all its modifications, consciousness offers itself to thought only as self-presence, as the perception of self in presence," which also explains why the "privilege granted to consciousness therefore signifies the privilege granted to the present."[2] As a thought of presence, and of presence to consciousness (itself, then, a form of presence), phenomenology would know nothing of the unconscious. However, I will suggest in the following pages that phenomenology is haunted by the presence of a certain unappearing dimension, a claim that was made by Heidegger in his last seminar in 1973, when he characterized the most proper sense of phenomenology as a "phenomenology of the inapparent": "Thus understood, phenomenology is a path that leads away before..., and it lets that before which it is led show itself. This phenomenology is a phenomenology of the inapparent [*Phänomenologie des Unscheinbaren*]."[3] What the term "unconscious" designates, perhaps improperly, is such an alterity escaping presentation, an alterity that frustrates any effort of presentation by a phenomenological disclosure. "Improperly," for it must be stressed from the outset that the very term "unconscious" paradoxically belongs to the metaphysical tradition of consciousness inherited from Descartes, and represents as it were its reverse or counterpart.[4] This led Heidegger to remark that the notion of the unconscious belongs to "the representation of the human as an organism and subject of consciousness," and that, paradoxically, "The consciously maneuvered interest in the unconscious is a sign of the last triumph of the conception of the human as a subject of consciousness."[5] Further, did Freud not

---

[1] Martin Heidegger, *Sein und Zeit* (Tübingen: Max Niemeyer Verlag, 1953), p. 28. I draw from both extant English translations: *Being and Time,* trans. John Macquarrie and Edward Robinson (New York: Harper, 1962), and *Being and Time*. Trans. Joan Stambaugh. Revised and with a Foreword by Dennis J. Schmidt (Albany: State University of New York Press, 2010). Hereafter cited as SZ, followed by the German pagination.

[2] Jacques Derrida, "*Différance,*" in *Margins of Philosophy*, trans. by Alan Bass (Chicago: University of Chicago Press, 1984), p. 16.

[3] Martin Heidegger. *Seminare*, ed. Curd Ochwadt (Frankfurt am Main: Klostermann, 1981), GA 15, p. 399. *Four Seminars*, trans. Andrew Mitchell and François Raffoul (Bloomington, IN: Indiana University Press, 2002), p. 80.

[4] On this belonging of the unconscious to a Cartesian philosophy of consciousness, see Michel Henry, *The Genealogy of Psychoanalysis*, trans. D. Brick (Stanford, CA: Stanford University Press, 1993).

[5] Martin Heidegger. *Feldweg-Gespräche (1944/45)*, ed. Ingrid Schüssler (Frankfurt am Main: Klostermann, 1995), GA 77, p. 183. *Country Path Conversations*, trans. Bret W. Davis (Bloomington, Indiana University Press, 2010), p. 119.

introduce (for instance in *The Ego and the Id*) the very concept of the unconscious in order to complete a rational account of psychic life, to "fill in" the blanks of consciousness, thus betraying that the unconscious is an epistemic notion in the modern scientific project as applied to the psyche? As Heidegger notes on this point, "Freud's metapsychology is the application of Neo-Kantian philosophy to the human being [*Freud's Metapsychologie ist die Übertragung der neukantianischen.*

Philosophie auf den Menschen]... For conscious, human phenomena, he [Freud] also postulates an unbroken [chain] of explanation, that is, the continuity of causal connections. Since there is no such thing 'within consciousness,' he has to invent 'the unconscious' in which there must be an unbroken [chain of] causal connections. The postulate is the complete explanation of psychical life... This postulate is not derived from the psychical phenomena themselves but is a *postulate* of modern natural science."[6] The very term "unconscious" would then remain a metaphysical designation, belonging to the Cartesian and post-Cartesian metaphysics of subjectivity and its rational project. To that extent, as Heidegger suggests, it would not be a phenomenological notion, i.e., "not derived from the psychical phenomena themselves." Nonetheless, the unconscious can be said to name, even improperly, a certain alterity that consciousness cannot encompass, and to that extent will prove central to the phenomenological approach. If it is the case, as Jacques Derrida put it, that "a certain alterity – to which Freud gives the metaphysical name of the unconscious – is definitely exempt from every process of presentation by means of which we would call upon it to show itself in person,"[7] then phenomenology must come to the fore as a privileged instance of such play of otherness in phenomenality. Focusing in particular on the phenomenologies of Heidegger and Levinas, I will first attempt to show in what sense the "inapparent" plays in phenomenality and in phenomenology; I will then envisage the question of the invisible as Levinas thematizes it in terms of the invisibility of the face, and finally, dwell on the motif of the secret bas Derrida engages it, revealing finally its ethical import. For this withdrawal of presence within phenomena involves a relation and responsibility to the otherness of a secret.

7.1.1 Inapparent Phenomenality

As just mentioned, a certain presence of the *inapparent* can be traced in Heidegger's very definition of the phenomenon, and indeed of phenomenology. This claim might seem at first paradoxical and even go against the very definition that Heidegger gives of the phenomenon in paragraph 7 of *Being and Time*: "Thus we must *keep in mind* that the expression '*phenomenon*' signifies that which shows itself in itself, the

---

[6] Martin Heidegger. *Zollikoner Seminare*, ed. Medard Boss (Frankfurt am Main: Klostermann, 2006), GA 89, p. 260. *The Zollikon Seminars,* trans. Franz Mayr and Richard Askay (Evanston, Ill.: Northwestern University Press, 2001), pp. 207–208.
[7] Jacques Derrida. "*Différance*," p. 20.

manifest" (SZ, 28). Now, we should clarify from the outset that a phenomenon for Heidegger, that is the phenomenon with which phenomenology is concerned, cannot be reduced to an empirical intuition or an ontical given, to the present being. In fact, Heidegger rejects explicitly the Kantian notion of an "empirical intuition" to designate the phenomenon with which phenomenology is concerned (SZ, 31). Why? Because the phenomenon is approached by Heidegger *in its verbal sense,* that is, as that which shows or manifests itself of itself and from itself. The phenomenon is defined as "the-showing-itself-in-itself" (*das Sich-an-ihm-selbst-zeigen*)" (SZ, 31), and not simply as the ontical given or as the entity. The term "phenomenon" thus immediately refers to the event of a self-showing, and the "given" is consequently assigned to the event of its givenness. A phenomenological approach of the phenomenon is not turned towards the ontic phenomenon, but rather towards the event of its manifestation. This is why for Heidegger phenomenology is not about beings but about the being of beings. For Heidegger, phenomenology is the very method of ontology, thus allowing him to grasp the phenomena, not in relation to a constituting consciousness, but to the *event* of being as such. Indeed, Heidegger stresses that phenomenology is concerned about the *being* of phenomena, their modes of givenness, or of happening. Unlike with his former mentor, Husserl, Heidegger defines phenomenology in relation to ontology, as giving us access to the being of beings. "With regard to its subject-matter, phenomenology is the science of the being of entities – ontology" (SZ, 37); or: phenomenology is the "way of access to the theme of ontology" (SZ, 35). In turn, and most importantly, "*Ontology is only possible as phenomenology*" (SZ, 35, modified). Phenomenology is thus rigorously approached as *ontology,* that is, concerned with being in its event.

Thus, it is worth noting here that in this ontological understanding of phenomenology (phenomenology as concerned with the being of beings), the emphasis shifts from phenomena (things) to the *being* of these phenomena (their happening or eventfulness), from phenomena to phenomenality. As Jean-Luc Marion clarifies, phenomenology consists in showing, not the appearance itself, but the *appearing in the appearance*: "If in the realm of metaphysics it is a question of proving, in the phenomenological realm it is not a question of simply showing (since in this case apparition could still be the object of a gaze, therefore a mere appearance), but rather of letting apparition show *itself* in its appearance according to its appearing."[8] Such a phenomenology would bring to light the appearing of appearances, i.e., phenomenality or manifestation. "The privilege of appearing in its appearance is also named manifestation – manifestation of the thing starting from itself and as itself, privilege of rendering *itself* manifest, of making *itself* visible, of showing *itself*" (BG, 8). Phenomenology is concerned with the self-showing of the phenomenon as such, the appearing of the appearance, and not simply the appearance, that is, the present being. Here one glimpses for the first time the possibility of the inapparent in phenomenology: the phenomenon is not the appearance but the appearing of the appearance, an appearing that therefore *does not appear.* Such appearing could

---

[8] Jean-Luc Marion. *Being Given. Toward a Phenomenology of Givenness,* tr. Jeffrey L. Kosky (Stanford, Ca: Stanford University Press, 2002), p. 8. Hereafter cited as BG.

properly be said to be invisible, although, as Merleau-Ponty shows, we are here speaking of an invisibility *of* the world, and not a metaphysical, transcendent invisibility. Merleau-Ponty wrote famously in *The Visible and the Invisible* that the invisible is "not a *de facto* invisible, like an object hidden behind another, and not an absolute invisible, which would have nothing to do with the visible. Rather it is the invisible *of* this world, that which inhabits this world, sustains it, and renders it visible, its own and interior possibility, the Being of this being".[9] The invisible is an "an idea that is not the contrary of the sensible," but rather "its lining and its depth" (VI, 149). (VI, 151). There is an invisibility of the visible, an invisibility of phenomenality itself, concealed and nonetheless sheltered in the visible.[10]

By approaching the phenomenon as an event of presence, by understanding being in distinction from beings, and by distinguishing the present being from its presence, Heidegger allows to seize being as an event, the event of presence. Now the very movement of presence, of givenness, seems to require a certain *withdrawal*. In the tradition being has been understood as presence, *Anwesenheit*. But its eventfulness has been repressed in the reference to *constant* presence (*beständige Anwesenheit*), substantiality, Heidegger speaking of how the temporal meaning of *Anwesenheit* was "repressed" [*abgedrängt*] in the tradition of substantiality.[11] In fact, the very term *Anwesenheit*, presence, reveals the withdrawal at the heart of manifestation. The *an-* in *An-wesen* or *An-wesenheit* suggests a coming into presence, a movement, a motion, from concealment to unconcealment, from withdrawal to visibility. Thus, to characterize a being as *an-wesend*, which "is to implicitly understand presence as an *event*,"[12] also shows that the preposition *an*, as Françoise Dastur notes, "indicates a movement of approach that enters in a conflict with a movement of withdrawal" (ibid), a play between unconcealment and concealment

---

[9] Maurice Merleau-Ponty. *The Visible and the Invisible*, trans. Alphonso Lingis (Evanston, IL: Northwestern U. Press, 1968), p. 151. Hereafter cited as VI.

[10] This invisibility was already named by Kant when he wrote in the first Critique of the "invisible" or "unappearing" character of time as pure form of intuition: as pure form of inner sense, time itself is not visible in the outer dimension of space. "For time cannot be a determination of outer appearances; it belongs neither to a shape or a position, etc., but on the contrary determines the relation of representations in our inner state." Immanuel Kant. *Critique of Pure Reason*, trans. and ed. by Paul Guyer and Allen W. Wood (Cambridge, UK: Cambridge University Press, 1998), B 50, p. 163. 473, Hereafter cited as CPR, followed by the A and B edition pages, and page number of the translation. Time can only be *represented* in space by way of analogy: "And just because this inner intuition yields no shape we also attempt to remedy this lack through analogies, and represent the temporal sequence through a line progressing to infinity, in which the manifold constitutes a series that is of only one dimension, and infer from the properties of this line to all the properties of time, with the sole difference that the parts of the former are simultaneous but those of the latter always exist successively." CPR, B50, p. 163.

[11] Martin Heidegger. *Vom Wesen der Wahrheit. Zu Platons Höhlengleichnis und Theätet* (1931–1932). Ed. Hermann Mörchen (Frankfurt am Main: Klostermann, 1988, 1997), GA 34, p. 144. The English translation reads: "the concept of being loses its primordial innermost meaning, i.e., presence; the *temporal* moment is completely shaken off." *The Essence of Truth: On Plato's Cave Allegory and "Theaetetus."* Trans. Ted Sadler (London: Continuum, 2002), p. 104.

[12] Françoise Dastur, "Présent, présence et événement chez Heidegger," *Heidegger, le danger et la promesse*, eds. G. Bensussan et J. Cohen (Paris: Kimé, 2006), p. 121.

already captured by the Greeks in the contrast between the prepositions *para* and *apo* in *parousia* and *apousia*. This implies, in turn, a break with the model of constant presence, that is, with a kind of "stability" that represses the temporal happening in the phenomenon of presence, including the phenomenon of withdrawal that seems to affect, each time, the event of presence. This is why Heidegger could write that the phenomenon, precisely as that which is to be made phenomenologically visible, does not *show itself*. "And just because the phenomena are proximally and for the most part *not* given, there is need for phenomenology" (SZ, 36). The very concept of phenomenology, insofar as it is defined as a "letting something be seen," necessarily implies the withdrawal of the phenomenon.

Indeed, if phenomenology is a "letting be seen" (*sehen lassen*), then the phenomenon of phenomenology cannot be that which is simply apparent or manifest; the phenomenon, precisely as that which is to be made phenomenologically visible, *does not show itself*, while nonetheless belonging to what shows itself, for Heidegger also stresses that "'behind' the phenomena of phenomenology there is essentially nothing else" (SZ, 36). What does not appear in the phenomenon is not some noumenal reality hidden behind the phenomenon, but a dimension that belongs to it. "What is it that must be called a 'phenomenon' in a distinctive sense? What is it that by its very essence is *necessarily* the theme whenever we exhibit something *explicitly*? Manifestly, it is something that proximally and for the most part does *not* show itself at all: it is something that lies *hidden*, in contrast to that which proximally and for the most part does show itself; but at the same time it is something that belongs to what thus shows itself, and it belongs to it so essentially as to constitute its meaning and its ground" (SZ, 35). Now, for Heidegger, what does not appear in what appears is its *being*: "Yet that which remains *hidden* in an egregious sense, or which relapses and gets *covered up* again, or which shows itself only '*in disguise*,' is just not this entity or that, but rather the being of entities" (SZ, 38). Phenomenology, in its very essence, is a *phenomenology of what does not appear, a phenomenology of the inapparent*.

Being, in its advent, is concealed. Indeed, the structures of the being of beings are not accessible in some kind of immediate clarity, are not presented to some pure, contemplative gaze. Already in *Being and Time*, Heidegger insisted that although Dasein was a historical being, its relation to the tradition was far from transparent. That the tradition is inscribed in Dasein's average everydayness, and penetrates every way of Being, as well as every understanding thereof and behavior belonging to Dasein, does not imply that it delivers its contents or gives "access" (SZ, 21) to what it transmits. On the contrary, the tradition presents itself as an *obstacle* (it "*blocks our access* to those primordial "sources" from which the categories and concepts handed down to us have in part been quite genuinely drawn" [SZ, 21. My emphasis]), as an *uprooting* ("*Dasein has had its historicality so thoroughly uprooted* by tradition that it confines its interests to the multiformity of possible types, directions, and standpoints of philosophical activity in the most exotic and alien of cultures; and by this very interest it seeks to veil the fact that it has no ground [*Bodenlosigkeit*] of its own to stand on" [SZ, 21. My emphasis]), and as an *obliteration* or *omission* of the origin ("Indeed [the tradition] makes us *forget* that they have had such an origin, and it makes us suppose that the necessity of going back to these sources is something which we need not even understand" (SZ, 21).

An opacity thus affects Dasein's being. Indeed, Dasein's "privilege," that is, the fact that it comes to the fore in the inquiry, the fact, above all, that *I am* this being each time, does not mean that it would be immediately and fully accessible in its *being*. On the contrary, Heidegger emphasizes a paradoxical structure by which the ontical proximity to one's own self is always accompanied by an ontological distance and obscurity. This structure can be read in all its enigmatic simplicity in this passage from paragraph 5 of *Being and Time*. "Dasein is ontically "closest" to itself and ontologically farthest; but pre-ontologically, it is surely not a stranger" (SZ, 16). Dasein is "closest" to itself because it is, itself, that entity: Dasein is the entity that I am each time and not another. This ontical proximity to one's self ("Ontically, of course, *Dasein* is not only close to us – even that which is closest: we *are* it, each of us, we ourselves" [SZ, 15]) nevertheless cannot provide an appropriate *access* to Dasein's *Being*. On the contrary, it takes place in a vague and ordinary understanding that obscures the most proper constitution of our being. This is why Heidegger adds: "In spite of this, *or rather, for just this reason*, it is ontologically that which is farthest" (SZ, 15. My emphasis). Dasein's ontological opaqueness or distance from itself must be referred to its tendency to understand itself on the basis of the simply given being, and it is *against* this tendency (but at the same time *through* it, since this tendency, *Verfallen*, is constitutive of Dasein) that its being could be elucidated.

This is indeed why there is a need for a real *phenomenological forcing*, the goal of which is essentially to elucidate, to bring to light and to uncover that which remains hidden, covered over or dissimulated. There is thus an unavoidable *violence* of thought or interpretation. The philosophical interrogation of the tradition, because of the withdrawal of the phenomenon, carries with it a constitutive violence. This necessity of a philosophical violence turned *against* the self-concealment of being is described in the early courses Heidegger gave when he was engaged in a so-called "hermeneutics of factical life." It was then a matter for Heidegger of deriving "the phenomenological interpretation out of the facticity of life itself."[13] Thinking begins in life's *expropriation* from itself. Life is indeed characterized by a constant moving-away from itself (*Abfallen*), a constant fleeing from itself. Life is "inclined" toward the world,[14] and this inclination takes the form of a "propensity" to becoming

---

[13] Martin Heidegger. *Phänomenologische Interpretationen zu Aristoteles. Einführung in die phänomenologische Forschung*, ed. Walter Bröcker and Käte Bröcker-Oltmanns (Frankfurt am Main: Klostermann, 2nd edn, 1994), GA 61, p. 87. *Phenomenological Interpretations of Aristotle: Initiation into Phenomenological Research*, trans. Richard Rojcewicz (Bloomington: Indiana University Press, 2001), p. 66. Hereafter cited as PIA.

[14] Martin Heidegger. "*Phänomenologische Interpretationen zu Aristoteles. Anzeige der hermeneutischen Situation*," *Dilthey-Jahrbuch für Philosophie und Geschichte der Geisteswissenschaften* 6 (1989), 237–74; reprinted in *Phänomenologische Interpretationen zu Aristoteles. Ausarbeitung für die Marburger und die Göttinger Fakultät (1922)* (Stuttgart: Reclam, 2003). *Phenomenological Interpretations in Connection with Aristotle: An Indication of the Hermeneutical Situation* trans. John van Buren, in Heidegger, ed. John van Buren, *Supplements: From the Earliest Essays to Being and Time and Beyond* (State University of New York Press, 2002), p. 117.

absorbed in the world, and be taken along by it; a movement that is a falling away. "This propensity of the anxious concern of life is the expression of a basic factical tendency in life toward *falling away* from itself and, as included in this, *falling into* the world and itself *falling into ruin*" (*Supplements*, 117). Heidegger speaks indeed of this falling away as "the ownmost character of movement belonging to life," and the expropriation of what he calls "ruinance" is thus the most "proper" movement of life. In this movement of falling away into ruins, life is opened to its own possibility and becomes an issue for itself in an originary self-estrangement. We recall in this respect how in the 1929–1930 lecture course, drawing from Novalis, Heidegger defined philosophy as homesickness [*Das Heimweh*], exiled as it is in the "not-at-home" of expropriated existence.[15] *Homelessness* is the origin of philosophy. Now, philosophy itself is part of this movement of life, and is a sort of *counter movement*, a response to the event of life, a counter-event to such event. That is the origin of what Heidegger would call the "counter-motion" of thought, going against life's "own" tendency to fall into expropriation. Thinking originates from the need to go counter to life's tendency to move away from itself. "Philosophy is a mode of life itself, in such a way that it authentically 'brings back,' i.e., brings life back from its downward fall into decadence, and this 'bringing back' [or re-petition, 're-seeking'], as radical re-search, is life itself" (PIA, 62). Heidegger writes of "the constant *struggle* of factical, philosophical interpretation *against its own factical ruinance*, a struggle that accompanies the process of the actualization of philosophizing" (PIA, 114). *Life: a movement fleeing itself and falling into ruins. Thought: a movement going against life's ruinance. Thought is counter-ruinance.* "Phenomenological interpretation... manifests by its very essence a 'counter-movedness'" (PIA, 99). It is a counter-violence to the originary violence of the ruinance and self-estrangement of life, indicating the essential *polemos* of philosophy. The violence of interpretation responds to the violence of the self-estrangement of life and goes against it.

In *Being and Time*, the necessity of this violence is explained by reference to Dasein's hermeneutic situation; the ontological interpretation of this being must go "against" its own tendency to conceal, and can only be "won," Heidegger explains, by "following an opposite course (*im Gegenzug*)" from the tendency that distances Dasein from its being by throwing it towards beings. "The laying-bare of Dasein's primordial being must rather be *wrested* from Dasein by following the opposite course from that taken by the falling ontico-ontological tendency of interpretation" (SZ, 311). The existential analytic thus recognizes its phenomenological violence. "Dasein's *kind of Being* thus *demands* that any ontological Interpretation which sets itself the goal of exhibiting the phenomena in their primordiality (*Ursprünglichkeit*), *should capture the being of this entity, in spite of this entity's own tendency to cover*

---

[15] Martin Heidegger. *Die Grundbegriffe der Metaphysik. Welt—Endlichkeit—Einsamkeit*, ed. Friedrich- Wilhelm von Herrmann (Frankfurt am Main: Vittorio Klostermann, 3rd edn, 2004), GA 29/30, pp. 7–8. English translation *The Fundamental Concepts of Metaphysics; World, Finitude, Solitude*, trans. William McNeill and Nicholas Walker (Bloomington: Indiana University Press, 1995), pp. 5–7.

things up. Existential analysis, therefore, constantly has the character of *doing violence (Gewaltsamkeit)*, whether to the claims of the everyday interpretation, or to its complacency and its tranquilized obviousness" (SZ, 311).

The entire phenomenological problematic is thus rooted in the concealment of being, its *non-appearing*. In a passage from the essay "*Moira*," Heidegger thus speaks of how the play of the calling, brightening, expanding light "is not actually visible." That play, he writes, "shines imperceptibly [*scheint so unscheinbar*], like morning light upon the quiet splendor of lilies in a field or roses in a garden."[16] Being withdraws to only let the being appear. As Heidegger puts it in a crucial passage from "Anaximander Saying" (repeating that statement twice in the essay), stating a veritable law of the givenness of being: "By revealing itself in the being, being withdraws" [*Das Sein entzieht sich, indem es sich in das Seiende entbirgt*]."[17] In the essay "Nietzsche's Word: 'God is Dead'," Heidegger also clarifies: "Being does not come to the light of its own essence. In the appearance of beings as such, being itself stays away. The truth of being escapes us. It remains forgotten [*Das Sein kommt nicht an das Licht seines eigenen Wesens. Im Erscheinen des Seienden als solchen bleibt das Sein selbst aus. Die Wahrheit des Seins entfällt. Sie bleibt vergessen*]." (GA 5, 264/*Off the Beaten Track*, 197). Finally, Heidegger posits that being is the mystery because "Being itself withdraws [*entzieht sich*] into its truth. It saves [*birgt*] itself in its truth and conceals [*verbirgt*] itself in such shelter [*Bergen*]" (GA 5, 265/*Off the Beaten Track*, 197, slightly modified.)

This withdrawal of the phenomenon affects the very definition of phenomenology, now assigned to a secret or mystery, the renewed secret of the event of being, as Heidegger concedes in a later text, "My Way to Phenomenology" (1963): "And today? The age of phenomenological philosophy seems to be over. It is already taken as something past which is only recorded historically along with other schools of philosophy. But in what is most its own phenomenology is not a school. It is the possibility of thinking, at times changing and only thus persisting, of corresponding to the claim of what is to be thought. If phenomenology is thus experienced and retained, it can disappear as a designation in favor of the matter of thinking [*Sache des Denkens*] whose manifestations remains *a mystery* [*Geheimnis*]."[18] We see here emerge the notions of mystery or secret in the manifestation of the phenomenon of being. There is an invisibility of phenomenality itself, an invisibility to which phenomenology is assigned.

---

[16] Martin Heidegger, *Vorträge und Aufsätze* (1936–1953), ed. Friedrich-Wilhelm von Herrmann (Frankfurt am Main: Klostermann, 2000), GA 7, p. 256. *Early Greek Thinking*, trans. David F. Krell and Frank A. Capuzzi (New York: Harper & Row, 1975), p. 96.

[17] Martin Heidegger. *Holzwege*, ed. Friedrich-Wilhelm von Hermann (Frankfurt am Main: Klostermann, 1977), GA 5, p. 337. *Off The Beaten Track*, ed. and trans. Julian Young and Kenneth Haynes (New York: Cambridge University Press, 2002), pp. 253, 254.

[18] Martin Heidegger. *Zur Sache des Denkens* , ed. Friedrich-Wilhelm von Herrmann (Frankfurt am Main: Klostermann, 1962), GA 14, p. 101. *On Time and Being,* trans. Joan Staubaugh (New York: Harper & Row, 1972), p. 82, my emphasis.

7.1.2 The Invisibility of the Face

This inapparent or invisible dimension is constitutive of Levinas' ethical phenomenology, which is situated in the experience of the face to face with the other, and no longer in the relation to an impersonal power, whether being or the metaphysical idea of the Good. As Derrida explains in *The Gift of Death*, responsibility is possible on the condition "that the Good no longer be a transcendental objective, a relation between objective things, but the relation to the other, a response to the other."[19] Far from being included as one moment in being, as one existential in the analytic of Dasein for instance (being-with), far from being inscribed in the element and horizon of being, ethics is situated in the relationship to the other person, in the "inter-subjective," a relation which for Levinas takes place "beyond being." The inter-subjective relation is the original experience, i.e., is not mediated by being. Levinas insists that the origin of meaning is not Dasein's relation to being, not the understanding of being displayed by Dasein, but lies in the inter-subjective relation. Meaning, the meaningful, lies in the encounter with an otherness. "My main point in saying that [the face of the other is perhaps the very beginning of philosophy] was that the order of meaning, which seems to me primary, is precisely what comes to us from the inter-human relation, so that the face... is the beginning of intelligibility."[20] For Levinas the face to face is the irreducible form of relation to the other: the relationship with the other can only be an encounter face to face, and never a synthesis or a communion. "The irreducible and ultimate experience of relationship appears to me in fact to be... not in synthesis, but in the face to face of humans, in sociality, in its moral signification... First philosophy is an ethics."[21] The encounter with the inappropriability of the other is the original experience: before knowledge, since knowledge presupposes such an encounter and before ontology, since being as such presupposes the encounter with the specific being. Further, this encounter what cannot be totalized: it is an opening to infinity. Ethics breaks totality, opening onto an irreducible exteriority, and otherness. There is for Levinas a non-synthesizable, and that is the face to face: "The relationship between human beings is certainly the non-synthesizable par excellence" (EI, 77, slightly modified). There is no context (being, the world, or horizon) that would include the face to face with the other, as the face "originally signifies or commands outside the context of the world" (EN, 167). The originary encounter with the face of the other, with the other as "presenting" a face (although we will see that for Levinas the face is not a presentation) is of an ethical nature, rooted in the phenomenon of a responsibility for the other.

What does Levinas mean by the face (*visage*)? In one word: vulnerability. A human vulnerability, or, better, vulnerability as the very humanity of the human

---

[19] Jacques Derrida. *The Gift of Death*, trans. David Wills (Chicago and London: University of Chicago Press, 1996), p. 50. Hereafter cited as GD.

[20] Emmanuel Levinas, *Entre Nous*, trans. Michael B. Smith and Barbara Harshav (New York: Columbia University Press, 1998), p. 103. Hereafter cited as EN.

[21] Emmanuel Levinas, *Ethics and Infinity* (Pittsburgh: Duquesne University Press, 1985), p. 77. Hereafter cited as EI.

being.[22] In the encounter with the face, I am faced with the destitute and vulnerable nature of the other and called to be responsible for him or her. Now what is most striking about the face is that precisely it *does not appear*: the face is invisible because it manifests an absolute alterity. In the late interviews gathered in *Ethics and Infinity*, returning to the question of the face, Levinas insists that the face is not an object of perception, a perceptual phenomenon, indeed perhaps not even a phenomenon, if a phenomenon is what appears and becomes present. To the question posed by Philippe Nemo, "What does this phenomenology of the face, that is, the analysis of what happens when I look at the Other face to face, consist in and what is its purpose?", Levinas immediately objects: "I do not know if one can speak of a 'phenomenology' of the face, since phenomenology describes what appears" (EI, 85). Further, the access to the face might not even be the "look," if this supposes once again perception: "So, too, I wonder if one can speak of a look turned toward the face, for the look is knowledge, perception" (EI, 85). The face would then not be accessible through the perceiving of a consciousness, not appearing to a perceptual or cognitive consciousness. In *Otherwise than Being or Beyond Essence*, Levinas specifies in this respect that the face escapes presentation and representation, that it is indeed "the very collapse or defection of phenomenality,"[23] not because it would be an excessive phenomenon (as in Marion's saturated phenomenon, or "excess of givenness"[24]), but on the contrary due to its *poverty*, its weakness: the face, Levinas writes in a striking formulation, is "a non-phenomenon because 'less' than the phenomenon" (AE, 141). Phenomenology is here exceeded by default or by excess of poverty, and Levinas does state that his work exceeds the confines of appearance in being (*l'apparoir de l'être*), and therefore "ventures beyond phenomenology" (AE, 281). I would suggest here that Levinas does not so much move beyond phenomenology as point to an alterity inhabiting it. In fact, despite what some commentators have hastened to claim with respect to a theological nature of Levinas' discourse, Levinas has clearly maintained the phenomenological status of his discourse, stressing that his vocabulary, even when at times it borrows from a religious tradition, takes on a phenomenological meaning. For instance: "The terminology I use sounds religious: I speak of the uniqueness of the I on the basis of a *chosenness* that it would be difficult for it to escape, for it constitutes it; of a debt of the I, older than any loan. This way of approaching an idea by asserting the concreteness of a situation in which it originally assumes meaning seems to me essential to phenomenology. It is presupposed in everything I have said" (EN, 227). Even the absolute of which Levinas speaks, the absoluteness of the other, is for Levinas a phenomenological

---

[22] The French word *visage* immediately gives a human character to the face as thematized by Levinas, as *visage* refers exclusively to the human face, whereas for animals one speaks of a *gueule*. The humanism of Levinas' thought is thus as it were pre-inscribed linguistically in the French language.

[23] Emmanuel Levinas, *Autrement qu'être ou au-delà de l'essence* (Dordrecht: Kluwer Academic, 1996), p. 141. Hereafter cited as AE.

[24] Jean-Luc Marion. *In Excess: Studies of Saturated Phenomena,* trans. Robyn Horner and Vincent Berraud (New York: Fordham University Press, 2002), p. 51.

notion: "The absolute – an abusive word – could probably take place concretely and *have meaning only* in the phenomenology, or in the rupture of the phenomenology, to which the face of the other gives rise" (EN, 167, my emphasis). The face, as manifesting such absolute alterity, is the interruption of phenomenology (interrupted by its "other"), an interruption that phenomenology undergoes.

Interrupted by the in-visibility of the face, phenomenology itself is transformed from a phenomenology of the present being, of perception, to a phenomenology assigned to the givenness of the otherness of the other in the face. It is in this sense that Levinas states: "one can say that the face is not 'seen'" (EI, 86), not the object of a thematic gaze. The face, he continues, "is what cannot become a content, which your thought would embrace; it is uncontainable, it leads you beyond" (EI, 86–87). The face takes us beyond being, beyond the adequation with knowledge, because vision "is a search for adequation" and "is what par excellence absorbs being." This break with perception appears clearly when Levinas states that the best way of encountering the face "is not even to notice the color of his eyes!" (EI, 85). Indeed, that would reduce the face to an object, an object of perception: "you turn yourself towards the Other as toward an object when you see a nose, eyes, a forehead, a chin, and you can describe them" (EI, 85). Certainly, it is always possible to apprehend the face as a present phenomenon that one can describe objectively; but when one does that, "one is not in social relationship with the Other" (EI, 85). It is an unethical manner of apprehending the other person. "The relation with the face can surely be dominated by perception, but what is specifically the face is what cannot be reduced to that" (EI, 85–86). In fact, this way of looking at the face would be a kind of defacement, and the face seen in this perceptual way would then be "defaced," as in the French *dévisager*. To *dé-visager* someone is tantamount to a de-facing. This is why Levinas specifies that "Defacement occurs also as a way of looking, a way of knowing, for example, what color your eyes are. No, the face is not this."[25]

The face does not *present* a countenance or a form but exposes a nakedness and a passivity: "The disclosure of the face is nudity – non-form – abandon of oneself, aging, dying; more naked than nakedness: poverty, wrinkled skin" (AE, 141). The face expresses a poverty and a vulnerability. To this extent, the access to the face is not perceptual but *ethical*. "I think rather that access to the face is straightaway ethical" (EI, 85). Indeed, the face displays a kind of uprightness or straightfulness, a *droiture*, which in French designates not only the physical characteristic of being straight or upright but also a moral feature: someone who is *droit* is someone who is direct, honest. This straightfulness or frankness is also the naked exposure of a vulnerability, an exposure without defense; "there is first the very uprightness of the face, its upright exposure, without defense" (EI, 86). Levinas describes further this aspect in his analysis of the poverty of the skin (*la peau*) as opposed to the flesh (*la*

---

[25] Emmanuel Levinas, *Is It Righteous to Be?* Ed. Jill Robbins (Stanford, Calif.: Stanford University Press, 2001), pp. 144–145.

chair). The skin of the face, he tells us, "is the most naked" (EI, 86), a nakedness that is described in its moral dimension. "There is first the very uprightness of the face, its upright exposure, without defense. The skin of the face is the most naked, though with a decent nudity" (EI, 86). The skin is thought of in terms of the exposure and poverty of the face, its nakedness. It is not pornographic or obscene, but is a *moral nakedness*, that is an exposure of poverty and vulnerability. In *Otherwise than Being or Beyond Essence*, Levinas develops such phenomenological analysis of the skin, the "contact of a skin," emphasizing its thinness (*minceur*), thin surface, "almost transparent," barely appearing, already pointing to the face's poverty and lack of substantiality. Levinas speaks of the "poverty" of the face, as "there is an essential poverty in the face" (EI, 86). It is *only* what it is, it has no riches, a (non)phenomenon, a poverty emphasized by our attempts to cover or disguise it, or simply by our attempts to *present* a face. It is as if the face was by itself not presentable, not providing a form; one then puts on make-up, makes a face or takes a countenance, *to give it a presence*, attempting to adorn the essential poverty of the face, to make up for its poverty. That poverty, that nakedness, that exposure to death of the face is an invitation. It is an invitation to violence, specifies Levinas, who is very clear on this point: "The face is exposed, menaced, as if inviting us to an act of violence" (EI, 86). That negation of the other which is violence is thus in a sense inscribed in the face itself. Levinas writes that there is in the face of the other "always the death of the other and thus, in some way, an incitement to murder, the temptation to go to the extreme, to completely neglect the other" (EN, 104). The face is upright because exposed, and vulnerable because exposed. This radical exposure of the face is radically stripped of protection, defenseless: the face is defencelessness itself, Levinas stating that the rectitude of the face indicates a movement forward, "as if it were exposed to some threat at point blank range, as if it presented itself wholly delivered up to death" (*Is it Righteous?*, 126–127). Extreme exposure, beyond or before all human intending, "as to a shot at 'point blank'," *à bout portant*! (EN, 145).

The face is described as exposure, and exposure to injury, that is, already, to death. The face is exposure to death, that is, to a *secret*, Levinas speaking of the exposure of the face to "an invisible death and mysterious forsaking" (EN, 145). What is laid bare in the face? Death. The face *expresses* the death of the other, behind all the masks and defences: "Face of the other – *underlying* all the particular forms of expression in which he or she, already right 'in character,' plays a role – is no less *pure expression*, extradition with neither defense nor cover, precisely the extreme rectitude of a *facing*, which in this nakedness *is an exposure unto death*: nakedness, destitution, passivity, and pure vulnerability. *Face as the very mortality of the human being*" (EN, 167, my emphasis). Such exposure to the secret of death, to the non-appearing of death, takes on an ethical signification: I become responsible for the death of the other.

7.1.3 The Secret

As we saw, Levinas distinguishes the face from the domain of vision and perception, refuses "the notion of vision to describe the authentic relationship to the Other" (EI, 87–88). The authentic relationship to the other lies in language, in discourse, which is for Levinas a response, and already a *responsibility*. Ethical responsibility arises out of the vulnerability of the other, who calls me insofar as "the face speaks" (EI, 87). The face is above all a language. It speaks to us, it is a saying (as opposed to a said, following Levinas' distinction between saying and said, *le dire* and *le dit*) to which I must respond. Discourse is an *address*. Whereas understanding only names things, gives them designations, original language as saying is an "instituting sociality" (EN, 7). Such original language lies in the fact that "before the face I do not simply remain there contemplating it, I respond to it" (EI, 88). This saying "is prior to the statements of propositions communicating information and narrative" (EN, 166). The face speaks, and is a discourse to which we respond, a response that is straightaway a responsibility, an originary responsibility: "it is discourse and, more exactly, response or responsibility which is the authentic relationship" (EI, 88). In the words of Jean-Luc Marion, "The face does not appear; it manifests itself by the responsibility that it inspires in me" (*In Excess*, 78). Such responsibility to the other, however, proves to be to a secret if it is the case, as Jacques Derrida put it, that "the other is secret insofar as it is other."[26]

Derrida addresses the secret in his essay "Passions," following the thread of the leitmotif repetition of the expression: "*Il y a là un secret*," or *il y a là du secret*," "*there* is something secret" (literally: there is there a secret or some secret). This expression seeks to emphasize that it is first a matter of recalling, not "what" the secret would be, but rather *that there is* a secret at all; it is as if, through this shift from the "what" to the "that," it was a matter of remembering, or removing from its necessary oblivion, the presence of a secret in experience. *Il y a* a secret, there is a secret, and its being a secret precisely means that we do not know and cannot know *what* it is. If we could, it would no longer be a secret, but a temporarily withdrawn presence or content that in right could always become disclosed. It is a matter then of affirming the *irreducible* existence of a secret, the fact that the secret, precisely in order to be a secret, must remain secret; it is a matter of recognizing the being-there (*il y a*) of the secret, leaving it, as it were, to its secrecy, to its eventfulness as a secret: "We testify [*témoignons*] to a secret *that is without content*, without a content separable from its performative experience, from its performative tracing."[27]

There is a secret in the event for instance: an event can never be included in a horizon of expectation, I cannot *see* it come: an event never arrives "horizontally," it does not appear or *present itself* on the horizon from where I may be able to

---

[26] Jacques Derrida. "Autrui est secret parce qu'il est autre" [*Autrui* is secret because it is another], interview by Antoine Spire, *Le Monde de l'Education* (July–August 2001), www.lemonde.fr/mde/ete2001/derrida.html.

[27] Jacques Derrida. "Passions," in *On the Name* (Stanford, CA: Stanford U. Press, 1995), p. 24, my emphasis. Hereafter cited as P.

fore-see it, anticipate it: rather, an event falls upon me, comes from above, vertically, from a (non-theological) height and is an absolute surprise. The event falls upon me from up high (in French: *me tombe dessus,* even at times: *me tombe sur la tête*): "In the arrival of the *arrivant,* it is the absolute other who falls on me. I insist on the verticality of this coming, because surprise can only come from on high. When Levinas or Blanchot speak of the "Très Haut," the Most High, it is not simply religious terminology. It means that the event as event, as absolute surprise, must fall on me. Why? Because if it doesn't fall on me, it means that I see it coming, that there's a horizon of expectation. Horizontally, I see it coming, I fore-see it, I fore-say it, and the event is that which can be said [*dit*] but never predicted [*prédit*]. A predicted event is not an event. The event falls on me *because I don't see it coming.*"[28] The surprise of an event that happens vertically, but also "by coming from behind me, or from underneath me, from the basement of my past, in such a way that I can never see it come, having to content myself at times to feel it or hear it, barely."[29] Coming by surprise, an event suspends understanding, comprehension through the invisibility of its arrival.

The secret makes the "I" "tremble." A secret "always *makes* you tremble. Not simply quiver or shiver, which also happens sometimes, but tremble" (GD, 53). The secret makes the self "tremble," the whole self, as "when one trembles all over… unsettling everything," as in the case of a *tremblement de terre* (earthquake, literally: earth trembling), adds Derrida. The self trembles before the secret event of itself, as before "a future that cannot be anticipated; anticipated but unpredictable; *apprehended,* but, and this is why there is a future, apprehended precisely *as* unforeseeable, unpredictable; approached *as* unapproachable" (GD, 54). The self trembles before the im-possible happening of the future: "Even if one thinks one knows what is going to happen, the new instant of that happening remains untouched, still inaccessible, in fact unlivable" (GD, 54, modified). We tremble from not knowing, from being exposed to what I can neither see nor foresee (the secret "undoes" seeing, foreseeing, and knowing). "In the repetition of what still remains unpredictable, we tremble first of all because we don't know from which direction the shock came, whence it was given (whether a good surprise or a bad shock, sometimes a surprise received as a shock); and we tremble from not knowing, in the form of a double secret, whether it is going to continue, start again, insist, be repeated: whether it will, how it will, where, when; and why *this* shock. Hence I tremble because I am still afraid of what already makes me afraid, of what I can neither see nor foresee" (GD, 54). One "doesn't know *why one trembles,*" writes Derrida, a symptomatology, he adds, which is "*as enigmatic as tears*" (GD, 54), and rebellious to causes. We tremble before the secret, before the secret of the event, always beyond knowledge. "Most often we neither know what is coming upon us nor see its origin; it therefore remains a secret" (GD, 54). The secret is what exceeds knowing, understanding, an excess within the self that is felt by the self, in trembling: I tremble "at

---

[28] Jacques Derrida. "A Certain Impossible Possibility of Saying the Event," in *Critical Inquiry,* Vol. 33, No. 2 (Winter 2007), p. 451.
[29] Jacques Derrida et Elisabeth Roudinesco. *De quoi demain…* (Paris: Fayard/Galilée, 2001), p. 91.

what exceeds my seeing and my knowing [*mon voir et mon savoir*] although it concerns the innermost parts of me, right down to my soul, down to my bone, as we say" (GD, 54). The secret is in me but without me, it is in me but I have no access to it, am separated from it: "It is," Derrida continues, "a secret that I carry, if one can say, *in* me but which is not me, which is thus greater than I and to which I have no access myself." The secret designates a separation, a spacing, that is, an otherness. The secret is an alterity within myself, "*within myself other than myself*" [en moi autre que moi]" (GD, 49). Derrida describes this otherness of the self to itself towards the end of *The Gift of Death* as having within myself "a witness that others cannot see, and who is therefore *at the same time other than me and more intimate with me than myself*" (GD, 109). This secret of the self is not *my* secret (as the secret belongs to no-one). One might perhaps say instead that one belongs to the secret, in the sense in which, as one says in French, one would be "*au secret*" (locked out if not locked up – as one of the senses of *au secret* is to be imprisoned in solitary confinement without possibility of communication with others – kept apart): There is a secret of the self because the self is *au secret*, separated and locked out from itself, other than itself. "Others are secret because they are other. I am secret, I am *in secret,* like any other. A singularity is of its nature in secret."[30] And one belongs to oneself only to the extent that one belongs to such secret, for the secret is in the play in the constitution of the self. Derrida explains how Patočka was right in speaking of a "mystery or secrecy in the constitution of a *psyche* or of an individual and responsible self." The self is constituted (and divided) in the relationship to an absolute secret and invisibility: "For it is thus that the soul separates itself in recalling itself to itself, and so it becomes individualized, interiorized, becomes its very invisibility" (GD, 15).

This invisibility of the secret cannot be an invisible visible, as when something now invisible is visible in another aspect, or can become visible at any instant. The invisible secret is not "a visible that conceals itself, for example, my hand under the table – my hand is visible as such but I can render it invisible" (GD, 89). The invisibility of the secret is *absolute*, i.e., not derivative of the visible: "the absolute sense of invisibility resides rather in the idea of that which has no structure of visibility," writes Derrida (GD, 89). Derrida thus distinguishes two different senses of the invisible: there is, on the one hand, the "in-visible," the "visible in-visible," that is, the invisible as a visible that I can "keep in secret by keeping it out of sight"; in this sense, the invisible is a visible kept hidden. It is therefore not truly invisible but remains of the order of the visible: "whatever one conceals in this way becomes invisible but remains within the order of visibility; it remains constitutively visible" (GD, 90). For instance, the organs in my body may be invisible, but they clearly remain of the order of visibility; their invisibility – interiority really – is only provisional. On the other hand, there is another invisibility, which Derrida calls an "absolute invisibility" (GD, 90), an absolutely non-visible, not the invisible as concealed visible, but the invisible as "that which is other than visible," which is not of the order of the visible, that "falls outside of the register of sight." That is the absolute

---

[30] Jacques Derrida. *Paper Machine* (Stanford, CA: Stanford U. Press, 2005), p. 162.

invisibility of the secret, the absolute secret to which we belong and to which we are responsible. The respect for the secret, for that invisibility, must thus be unconditional, absolute, because the secret is absolute, like the other.

7.2 Conclusion: The Ethics of the Secret

There is no knowledge of the secret, but there is, one might say, an *ethics* of the secret, a respect and a responsibility for the secret. Indeed, the demand for the revealing of a secret, the demand that the other confesses, that he or she explains him/herself and reveals their secret, may be the greatest violence. "Is there any worse violence than that which consists in calling for the response, demanding that one *give an account of* everything, and preferably *thematically?*" (P, 25). In fact, the secret is non-thematizable, "not phenomenalizable." The secret is not a phenomenon, in the sense of what can become present, although its inappearance does not mean that it belongs to some noumenal realm. Not locatable, not presentable, not knowable, it is the object of *respect*: one must respect the secret, not do violence to its withdrawal, its non-appearing. "Nowadays, there is perhaps an ethical and political duty to respect the secret, a certain kind of right to a certain kind of secret," writes Derrida. The lack of respect for the secret is a quest for total transparency (and thus for control), the sign of any totalitarianism, which can also *use* and instrumentalise the secret: "The totalitarian vocation is manifested as soon as this respect is lost. All the same – and this is where the difficulty comes in – there are also forms of abuse in relation to the secret, political exploitations of the 'state secret,' like the exploitations of 'reasons of state,' and police or other archives" (PM, 162). The respect for the secret cannot simply be conditional, i.e., a secret that can be shared, always capable of being disclosed, "undone or opened" (GD, 88). As we saw, a secret "worthy of the name" is not a knowledge that is provisionally withheld. Further, to share a secret, *as secret*, precisely does not mean to reveal its content in the light of day: "To share a secret is not to know or to reveal the secret, it is to share we know not what: nothing that can be determined" (GD, 78). Sharing the secret thus means sharing a not-knowing, a sharing in which the secret *remains a secret*. There is a respect and a responsibility due to the secret, to the secret as an alterity to which we are exposed.

This responsibility to a secret is developed in Heidegger's thought, which, it is perhaps not stressed enough, entails a major thought of responsibility, as I have tried to argue elsewhere.[31] Being is an event for which each Dasein is responsible, responding and corresponding to its call. Responsibility designates no less than the co-belonging of being and Dasein, a co-belonging that is *the* question and the very heart of Heidegger's thought. Yet, such co-belonging remains affected by a certain *expropriation*, as the correspondence to the event of being always implies withdrawal

[31] On this point, I take the liberty of referring to my *The Origins of Responsibility* (Bloomington, IN: Indiana U. Press, 2010).

and expropriation. For what must be stressed is that the response to a call, whether the call of conscience in *Being and Time* or the address of being in later writings, is always a response to what remains *inappropriable* in such calls. Indeed, as Heidegger explains in *What is Called Thinking*, it is from a certain withdrawal of being that Dasein finds itself called. "Whatever withdraws, refuses arrival. But withdrawing is not nothing. Withdrawal is an event. In fact, what withdraws may even concern and claim man more essentially than anything present that strikes and touches him [*Was sich entzieht, versagt die Ankunft. Allein – das Sichentziehen ist nicht nichts. Entzug ist Ereignis. Was sich entzieht, kann sogar den Menschen wesentlicher angehen und in den Anspruch nehmen als alles Anwesende, das ihn trifft und betrifft*]" (GA 8, 10/ WCT, 9). Being happens by and in withdrawing. Being is the withdrawal, being withdraws [*Entzieht sich*] (GA 8, 10/WCT, 8), and from such a withdrawal it calls us. "What withdraws from us, draws us along by its very withdrawal, whether or not we become aware of it immediately, or at all" (GA 8, 11/WCT, 9). Heidegger speaks of the event of withdrawal [*Das Ereignis des Entzugs*] as that which is closest to us: "The event of withdrawal could be what is most present in all our present, and so infinitely exceed the actuality of everything actual" (GA 8, 11/WCT, 9). In its very eventfulness, being withdraws, is the mystery: such a withdrawal, Heidegger stresses, *calls us*. Responsibility to being would then be a responsibility to a secret and an inappropriable. When discussing moods (*Stimmungen*) in *Being and Time*, that is, thrownness and facticity, Heidegger emphasizes the element of opacity and withdrawal entailed in them. Having a mood brings Dasein to its "there," before the pure "that" of its There, which as such, Heidegger writes in a striking formulation, "stares directly at it with the inexorability of an enigma" (SZ, 136). In being-in-a-mood, the being of the There "becomes manifest as a burden [*Last*]," Heidegger then adding, "One does not *know* why." In fact, Dasein "cannot know why" (SZ, 134), to because of some weakness of our cognitive powers, but because the "that" of our being is given in such a way that "the whence and whither remain obscure" (SZ, 134). In the phenomenon of moods, there is a "remaining obscure" which is irreducible. In a 1928–1929 course, *Introduction to Philosophy* (*Einleitung in die Philosophie*), Heidegger evokes this "darkness of Dasein's origins," contrasting it with the "relative brightness of its potentiality-for Being." He then states the following: "Dasein exists always in an essential exposure to the darkness and impotence of its origin, even if only in the prevailing form of a habitual deep forgetting in the face of this essential determination of its facticity."[32] This darkness is irreducible.

And yet, it is at this juncture, at this very *aporetic* moment, that Heidegger paradoxically situates the responsibility of Dasein. As we saw, Heidegger speaks of the "burden" of the There felt in a mood. Interestingly, the very concept of weight and burden reintroduces, as it were, the problematic of responsibility. In a marginal note added to this passage, Heidegger later clarified: "'Burden': what weighs [*das Zu-tragende*]; human being is charged with the responsibility (*überantwortet*) of Dasein, appropriated by it (*übereignet*). To bear [*tragen*]: to take over something

---

[32] Martin Heidegger. *Einleitung in die Philosophie* (1928–1929), Ed. Otto Saame and Ina Saame-Speidel (Frankfurt am Main: Vittorio Klostermann, 1996), GA 27, p. 340.

from out of belonging to being itself" (SZ, 134, tr. slightly modified). The burden is "what weighs," what has to be carried. In the course *Introduction to Philosophy*, Heidegger explained that it is precisely that over which Dasein is not master that must be worked through and survived: "[What] . . . does not arise of one's own express decision, as most things for Dasein, must be in such or such a way retrievingly appropriated, even if only in the modes of putting up with or shirking something; that which for us is entirely not under the control of freedom in the narrow sense is something that is in such or such a manner taken up or rejected in the How of Dasein" (GA 27, 337). Responsibility is hence the "carrying" of the inappropriability or unpresentability – the secret – of being. This secret of being represents an unappearance that constantly haunts phenomenology, and to which it belongs, whether it knows it or not.

Chapter 8
From the Night, the Spectre

Joseph Cohen

Abstract Can there be a phenomenology of the night? Can there be a phenomenology of the "un-world", of that which so absolutely obscures the world that it leaves it, the world, void of form, of unity, dismantling and shattering all possibility of a *correlation* between thinking and being? Can there be a phenomenology of that which gives itself always and already as other than "presentation", always and already as other than according to the order of possible constitution, and thereby outside or beyond any horizon of intentionality? With these questions, we seek in the following contribution, to deploy a phenomenological analysis of the "unconscious" whereby the very idea of phenomenology will undergo a profound shift of its Husserlian orientation and require its own "deconstruction". This deconstructive shift, it is argued, with Husserl and against Husserl opens towards the singularity of an *event*, the *spectre*, which projects thinking towards that which resists its enclosure in the intentional horizon of presence.

Keywords Spectrality • Event • Night • Mourning • Temporality • Alterity

Perhaps the day will come when we will question the primacy of the day. Perhaps one day we will ask from where originated the privilege and the prestige of "presence" in the clearness of the light. Perhaps one day we will question the significance and the centrality, in and for our culture, of the "wake" and of the experience of "waking", of the insistence on always keeping our "eyes wide open", consciously attentive to all that appears, and thus of always and already conjuring, circumscribing, restricting the night, confining dreams to being only chimeric or stammering destinies. And perhaps one day we will request the day to return to the night without already transforming the night into the promise of a dawn. Perhaps one day we will abandon the prevalence and the priority of our awakened sight and confront that which cannot be thought without losing and forsaking the very possibility of constituting meaning.

J. Cohen (✉)
University College Dublin, Dublin, Ireland
e-mail: Joseph.cohen@ucd.ie

In the wake of the day, in this wake where clarity emerges from the night, our philosophical history and tradition has without doubt certainly sketched one of its fundamental events. For it is in this wake which is traced a *partition* between clarity and obscurity, between certainty and ambiguousness, between the possibility to comprehend and the vacuity of incomprehensibility – a *partition* from where can incessantly be heard the question which opened the very place of philosophical thinking: what is the meaning of appearance? What is the signification of appearing? And how does appearance constitute itself by liberating the possibility for things to appear?

The instant of this *partition* remains, to this day and perhaps for all days, unthinkable. For one can only think, write, speak, *after* it has occurred and succeeded in distinguishing, in the clearness of the waking day, discourse from silence, meaning from void, reason from irrationality, consciousness from unconsciousness. One cannot even recognize it as such, this *partition*, for the very words we mobilize, convoke or evoke to describe it, to signify it, to "pin-point" it are always drawn, can only be drawn, from the luminous presence of the day and thus from the instant when the night has been confined to its uncertainty, thereby marking thinking as that possibility which can only be engaged from this delineated disposition to enlighten the heart of darkness. Perhaps one day, however, at the height of the day, will erupt the night, not as yet another momentary negation of light promising to return in yet another wake, but as a *wholly other night*, that night of which Maupassant wrote "was of an entirely different matter. Dense, thicker than the very walls of this country house, and empty, void, so obscure, so immense, that within it you brush up against unspeakable events and things, and feel roaming and prowling around a mysterious and unthinkable horror." Perhaps one day, will surge in thinking this mysterious and unthinkable horror of the night – that "pure night" which Hegel also typified as a "horror" – firstly in the early Iena writings when he was elaborating the project of the *Real Philosophie*, and then again in the *Phenomenology of Spirit* when defining the *Terror* – that "night of the world" where all difference is undifferentiated and all identities unrecognizable, where all possibility of thought thus, and with it the very actuality of History, is emptied out in the vast bareness of an "*unconsciousness*" so devoid of meaning it only engenders indiscriminately representations without order – "here a bloody head, there a white field" – representations thus which incessantly assail both thought and action without there ever being a possibility of framing these in a "world-picture".

Can there be a phenomenology of the night? Can there be a phenomenology of the "un-world", of that which so absolutely obscures the world that it leaves it, the world, void of form, of unity, dismantling and shattering all possibility of a *correlation* between thinking and being? Can there be a phenomenology of that which gives itself always and already as other than "presentation", always and already as other than according to the order of possible constitution, and thereby outside or beyond any horizon of intentionality? We could reformulate the question of this symposium in the following manner: if the world, conceived as the universal horizon, is a field of vision where are drawn the possibilities of presence, of presentification, of appearing, of manifesting, how to explicate that which occurs to the world, not only as that which is unplanned, unpredicted, unexpected, but as that which blinds vision itself, prediction and expectation, rememoration and remission? How to explicate phenomenologically that *event other* to any form or frame, any light or recognition, any habitus or habitual experience, and which as an *event*, occurring to the self, also undermines the very possibility, for the self, of forming or framing its eventuality? How to explicate phenomenologically, quoting Husserl, the "absolute night of intentionality"?

We have just quoted Husserl. The quote is taken from the *Analysis on Passive Synthesis*. In these analyses, Husserl hesitates, or feigns hesitation, in the face of what, later, Fink and also Patocka called a certain "limit" of phenomenology. Of course, Husserl counters this threat of this "limit" by marking the *fact* that there is never any end or endpoint which could be imposed, opposed or drawn onto that which is lived. In phenomenology, for Husserl, nothing could ever, would ever, did ever or ever will, break, halt, interrupt the movement by which the transcendental constituting ego, consciousness thus, returns to always novel horizons of intentionality for novel possible experiences. And hence, inscribed within the very movement of phenomenological explication there always lies the possibility of conversion, of translation, of alteration, that is of transforming the unfamiliar into the familiar, the improper into the proper, the "un-world" into a world. And hence the accent is placed not only on the indefinitely open character of the world, but also and more importantly on the fact that its "openness" is precisely what *is* the world, which thus always re-forms itself as it is always and already presupposed as a form, and consequently as that which forms. Instead of underlying the integration of all experience in the horizon of a world, the accent will be placed, in phenomenology, on the very *possibility* for this field, this plane, this sphere to integrate, form and conform, that is on the fact that the world *is* this possibility. For to speak of the "world" is always, in phenomenology, to affirm, to mark, to situate the place, the emplacement, the "there" *from* and *in* which the subject is already involved, implicated, engaged. This involvement, implication or engagement is certainly not explicated as such in the "natural attitude" of consciousness. Indeed, this attitude is precisely said "natural" in that it leaves its own "being-within-the-world" *un-explicated*. Certainly, the "natural attitude" belongs *to* the world, lives *in* the world, is never removed or casted out from the world, but the mode of its "belonging to", "living in", "being-within" remains without explication capable of signifying its own-most relation towards the world. The "natural attitude" is always already *within* the world, but remains *without* the power to circumscribe the world *as* world. To access the world *as* world, to reveal the world as collected and gathered in its *formal unity*, means to "suspend", to "bracket", to "interrupt", and thus to "set aside" or "intercept" all thesis, judgment, assumption and belief on and about the world. And such is the work of the "phenomenological *epochè*" which, as we know, does not "negate" or "annihilate" the world, nor does it deny the "natural attitude" of consciousness. Rather, it reveals the constituting activity of a transcendental subjectivity through which appears the intentional *order* of the world. That is, it leads, at once and simultaneously, the subject to "step back" from the world whilst engaging the explication of its very intentionality. And in this sense, the *"phenomenological epochè"*, in its circumscribing the world, plays a double and antagonistic role: it reveals the world *as* world, and correlatively, it reveals the subject *as* subject. It reveals thus a *correlation* and a *co-belonging* between the subject *and* the world. And this correlation, this co-belonging, far from simply transforming the world into a subjective perception, opens to the conditions of possibility of "appearing" *as* the very *being* of the world. The "*phenomenological epochè*" opens thus to an *ontology*. An ontology not founded or grounded on empirical data, but rather which insists on the being of "appearing" *as* that which constitutes the intentionality of the world.

But the intentionality of the world must not be confounded nor be interpreted as a "*res*" or as a "substance". The intentionality of the world signifies rather the undetermined, indefinitely extensible horizon of all possible "*presencing*". Which means: the intentionality of the world is the *gathering* of possible "presencing" – whereby this "presencing" is conferred by and only by the constituting act of the transcendental ego. And thus, not simply remaining at the level of the manifest, of the present, of that which appears, the "*phenomenological epochè*" opens to the originary possibility of "seeing" the "manifesting" of the manifest, the "appearing" of "appearance", the "presence" of the "present". In other words, is opened the *place* in which are deployed the conditions of possibility of the "manifesting of the manifest", the "appearing" of that which appears, the "presencing" of that which is present. In this sense, the self *is* the condition of possibility of the "presencing" of the world, and correlatively, the world, as originary horizon, *is* the condition of possibility of the "presencing" of the self. Which means: the transcendental ego is the ordering center of a universal structure, the world, only as it is *within* this very structural explication with the world. Intentionality marks that all *objectity* is only possible if it arises from and by this structural correlation. And in this manner, all that is not *actually* an object of experience can enter and appear within the world – for the constitution of the world is always and already *correlative* to the "worldlying" of the constituting transcendental ego.

Husserl explicitly marks this correlation when is described, in the *Cartesian Meditations*, the "apperception of the self" as already belonging *in* the world. Indeed, the self reveals its own-most constituting power through its being-in-the-world for this constituting power is precisely its correlation with the world. Which means, in effect: the world – constituted by the transcendental ego – is always and already *pre-given*, *pre-donated* as the "appearing" of all that can or does appear. In this sense, the world is the *pre-given* or the *pre-donated* lived-present which occurs to the self before any or all experience. Of course, Husserl is here anticipating slightly on the analyses Heidegger will later perform in *Being and Time*. But what is important to claim at this time for Husserl is that this *pre-givenness* or *pre-donation* as "originary structure", as "*archi-*structure" (*Ur-struktur*) of intentionality marks an *otherness* of consciousness *within* consciousness. There is, in consciousness, for Husserl, an instance which does not belong to consciousness, an instance *other* than consciousness which nonetheless constitutes the "lived-present" of consciousness. This otherness within consciousness marks its passivity. And indeed, the self is always and already "re-action" to a *pre-givenness* or *pre-donation*; the self is always and already *response* to a prior provocation. This is why Husserl, retrieving the terminology of Fichte in the *Analyses on Passive Synthesis*, marks that the relation between the "self" and the "non-self" is asymmetrical, since the occurrence always, firstly, stems from the non-self. That is: the self is primordially affected, but its "being-affected" leads into an "affective reactive force that is already there at work, an affective force proceeding from the primordial impression (Husserl 1966, 1977).[1]" This is why phenomenology must never simply acquiesce the *pre-givenness* or *pre-donation* of the world – it rather must "reduce" this *pre-givenness* or *pre-donation* within the *temporalization* of a lived-present. This "reduction" marks the subject as an always and already affected subject but which in return is also awakened to *respond*, and hence awakened to effectively engage in the world. "Being-affected" by the world always and already marks the effective return of the self to the world. Which means: "being-affected" is the primary mode of being of the self, its originary or primordial impulse, so to speak, as if *before* the objectifying act of consciousness lived an *affected* consciousness which never disappears and whose vitality consists in responding, returning, to the world as *lieu* of all possible experience.

Husserl is here interrogating the *birth* of the self. And in speaking of this birth, he evokes a "beginning of experience where no constituted *ipse* is yet pre-given." In this sense, Husserl marks that to this birth as a waking, as an awakening from a primordial affection as response, lies also a self *before* any affection whatsoever. A self of the night, that is for Husserl, a "sleeping" self, or an "unconscious", a self for whom "objects have slipped into sheer night fall". (p. 244).

This quote is taken, again, from the *Analyses on Passive Synthesis*. Husserl however, and even as he investigates this "limit-case" which the unconscious represents, never envisages that the conversion, the translation, the transformation cannot operate and accomplish itself. In this sense, the question phenomenology leaves vacant, untouched, unthought is that of an *event* whose donation is un-integrable, whose "occurence" remains irreducible to any horizon and yet pierces through, occurs as that very piercing of the horizon in the horizon. What remains unapproached thus, although it is indicated by Husserl, is the *event* which, by its very "occurrence", opens not to a world, but to the "absolute night of intentionality". All seems to happens thus as if Husserl marks such a "limit-case" by also dismissing it as an impossibility in itself. But we could perhaps re-read Husserl through this question: is it not in and within this impossibility, through this un-integrable event, that lies the very possibility of thinking subjectivity itself?

How thus to think this impossible, that which occurs as the *impossible*, following Lacan's lead as he marks in the 1961–1962 Seminar entitled *L'Identification*, that the "real is the impossible"? One could certainly denounce this confrontation with the impossible. One could naturally dismiss such an *event* which occurs as the *impossible*. Or the supposition of such an *event*. In this sense, no *event* can be impossible as such – for if it were as such, it would simply never arrive to anyone anywhere. And hence all *events*, however great or small, however intense or insignificant, are always and already *possible events*, that is "objects of a possible

---
[1] Husserl, Husserliana XI, p. 174.

subjective evaluation". At the limit, the subject can judge it, the *event*, as that which *excesses* its own capacities to interiorize it and intentionalize it. But to be an *event*, it must, in some manner or other, inscribe itself in the realm of *possible events*. However, what we seek to point towards here, and that which we associate with the "unconscious", are not such *excesses* of consciousness. They are rather *events* whose very *impossibility* make up their *eventuality*, their *singularity* – that is, *events* which cannot be inscribable and thus refuse, retract and recede from judgment, deter from being judged *après coup*. Events thus which *occur as impossible*, that is, occur always without origin or already without source, and come to the world but from *outside* the world or horizon by incessantly breaking apart the form of any world or the constitution of any horizon. In these events, what is given is not and never that which leads into the experience of a *passage*, but rather that which occurs as an *irremediable loss*, a dispossession – events where what opens itself for the subject is not a future nor a past, nor the possibility to integrate these in the plasticity of rememoration and projection, but rather the *abyss* of both futurity and remission. Such would be the singularity proper to the *givennes* of the "unconscious": that which occurs in the horizon as its incessant rupture, or that which is lived in the course of lived-experience as its incessant piercing "impossibilization".

How could we think this impossible and this incessant rupture and piercing of lived experience? How could we approach this *rapport* with that which excludes itself from all rapport? How could we approach the "absolute night of intentionality"? To approach these questions, and thus to force them to comply with the very project of phenomenological reduction was Husserl's wager in the *Analyses on Passive Synthesis*. And, as we have sketched it, to approach such a "night", for Husserl, is also to respond to this "night" by always evoking, from its affection, the "free spontaneity of the self" and thus the act of its constitution. Our supposition here, however, that which marks the singularity of the "unconscious" – a singularity marked by Husserl albeit negatively – is that of an *event* which, in occurring, dispossesses the capacity to respond, presents itself by absenting its potential intentionality, and hence recuses the very pole of a spontaneous subjectivity by opening *perhaps* another mode of subjectivity. Our supposition here thus is that of an "I" which has lost the rapport with that which is given to it and yet subsists as subjected to an occurrence where all correlation or correspondence with the world in which this occurrence could be said to have been has already been dismantled.

8.1 How to Approach This *Event*?

Perhaps by invoking an occurrence which would never be either present nor absent, neither here nor there but which would at the same time, be here and there. Such an *event* could perhaps be approached as a *spectre*. That is as that which incessantly returns to the self in the *indistinction* of both presence and absence, in the evanescence of an obsession which always dispossesses the self. Perhaps the unconscious is this *spectre* neither in us nor outside of us but neither entirely removed from us, neither in presence nor in absence, but which occurs as incessantly haunting, rupturing the identifiable pole of our subjectivity by prying it open and revealing it as a wholly *differential* being.

The *spectrality* of the "unconscious" can be said to have three, at least three traits. Firstly, it is not an object: radically disseminated, the *spectrality* of the "unconscious" does not return to any center which could function as a pole or a transcendental guide. It is as such inaccessible and unseizable. Secondly, it entertains an oblique and estranged relation in its occurrence. Indeed, to be haunted by the *spectrality* of the "unconscious" is not and never can be reduced to a relation or an encounter. When haunted by the "unconscious" it is the entirety of the self which is inhabited by that which is beyond identification. And thirdly, that which haunts dispossesses entirely the self in the sense that it, the self, is entirely possessed by that which is unidentifiable in the other.

These three traits of *spectrality* allow a certain unedited modality of exposition to that which occurs – a modality irreducible to "being-confronted" to an object. For this modality of exposition blurs the very demarcation between judgment and experience by opening to the *absence that the self is – that absence that the self has become by the occurrence of the spectre.*

And it is precisely this last point which must be radicalized. For what this *spectrality* opens to is an exposed passivity which, without conversion, projects the self into *fascination*. The duality which must be analysed here is thus between *vision* and *fascination*. To *see* supposes a certain distance – and it is precisely this *distance* and thus the *separation* between "what is seen" and "the subject who sees" that allows for the encounter we call "vision". *Fascination*, on the other hand, is "contact" and thus supposes the abolition of this separation. In this sense, fascination is not thinkable as a relation or as a rapport. Its reign, where no duality is preserved, is solely the reign of the Other – an Other which never ceases to return as it is never limited by anything whatsoever. In this sense, fascination is not a vision, but rather a *blinding* where "seeing" means *ceasing to see*.

This analysis is not entirely novel. It was, in some manner, already sketched by Sartre, notably in *Being and Nothingness* where knowledge is defined metaphorically as fascination. Nevertheless, contrarily to Sartre, what fascinates in the *spectre* is precisely its unique "presence" which occurs without appearing – not in the sense that it would remain hidden or concealed, but because it would be present without being present, visible without making itself visible. The *spectre* disavows the ascent to phenomenality and occurs as that silent and blind insistence, without limit and without point of view barring all or any escape from its happening. How to speak to it? How to think it? How not speak to it? How not think it? The *spectrality* of the "unconscious" is "something" like the *event* of a presence indistinguishable from the *event* of an absence and which is, at once and simultaneously, given and not given, and provokes, in the self, a fascination which imposes itself on the self whilst suspending the self from itself. What is thus at stake is the break of the privilege and primacy of vision in phenomenality and the urgency for phenomenology to pose the following question: how to think an occurrence which is never allied to a determined source or pre-given originarity? Which is occurring from outside the rapport between visible and invisible, presence and absence, that is *within* the indifference of presence and absence.

The *spectrality* of the "unconscious" as *event*, in this sense, takes its meaning from an incontestable phenomenological given, that is the rupture of meaning which characterizes the night, but which phenomenology itself marked as impossible and consequently that this night could not manifest itself as such since the dissolution it would provoke would contradict the very conditions of phenomena. What we have attempted to show, however, is that this impossibility is only conjured – that is, that the *spectrality* of the "unconscious" does indeed occur not as a manifestation but as an undifferentiated, unconditional, indeterminable play between presence and absence. The *spectrality* of the "unconscious" would thus be this *outside within* consciousness turning consciousness outside itself and rendering any consciousness of its occurrence impossible to have.

Perhaps phenomenology ought to express a language capable of addressing the *spectrality* of the "unconscious". How is such a language possible? How can a language speak to that which does not possess a language, the *spectre*, and whose very occurrence always testifies of *our* language having "survived" the language of the Other? Perhaps phenomenology ought to express a language for "whom" is no longer addressing or speaking but whom, at the same time, incessantly "addresses" and "speaks", for "whom" no longer "appears" but whom, simultaneously, is never either "inapparent". Perhaps phenomenology ought to pose itself the question: *how do we mourn?*

References

Husserl, Edmund. 1966. Husserliana XI., ed. M. Fleischer. Den Haag: Martinus Nijhoff. In *Analyses concerning passive and active synthesis: Lectures on transcendental logic*. Trans. Steinbock, Anthony. Dordrecht: Kluwer Academic Publishers, 2001c.

———. 1977. *Cartesian mediations: An introduction to phenomenology*. Trans. Cairns, Dorion. The Hague: Martinus Nijhoff Pub.

Chapter 9
Phenomenology and the Problem of the Inhuman: Psychologism, Correlationism, and the Ethics of Absolute Materiality

Drew M. Dalton

Abstract All phenomena appear to and are circumscribed by some form of conscious life – this is *sine qua non* of phenomenological inquiry. How then is phenomenology to account for those objects which appear to conscious life precisely in their refusal to be contained by conscious life – objects which seem to testify to that which is radically outside of and other than consciousness? This is a challenge which has haunted phenomenology from its beginning, first under the guise of *psychologism* as diagnosed by Frege, but more recently under the heading of *correlationism* as addressed by Meillassoux. Whatever its name, the problem is the same: phenomenology's apparent inability to account for the radical alterity of certain manifest existents. This paper will examine the ways in which both Husserl and Heidegger failed to respond adequately to this problem. To illustrate this failure, the phenomenological status of the dead body of will be examined. The aim of this paper is to show that while classical phenomenology cannot account for the inhuman realty of such phenomena, the alternatives offered by Frege and the speculative realists fare no better, occulting in their solutions the inherent traumatic power of such phenomena. To explore this power, the work of Freud and Lacan will be drawn upon. Finally, this paper will conclude that it is only through a reappraisal and reinterpretation of the ethics of Emmanuel Levinas that the limitations of both phenomenology and its critics can finally be overcome.

Keywords Body • Corpse • Unconscious • Levinas • Lacan • Meillassoux

---

D.M. Dalton (✉)
Dominican University, River Forest, IL, USA
e-mail: drew.dalton@hotmail.com

© Springer International Publishing AG 2017
D. Legrand, D. Trigg (eds.), *Unconsciousness Between Phenomenology and Psychoanalysis*, Contributions To Phenomenology 88,
DOI 10.1007/978-3-319-55518-8_9

9.1 The Unconscious for Phenomenology

There is an unthinkable possibility forestalled from the outset by the phenomenological project – a possibility which, when systematically pursued and fully articulated, appears to threaten the very aim of "returning to things themselves." This possibility is the "naïve" and "uncritical" assumption that some-*thing*, some absolute, radically independent reality, could present itself to human perception free from and outside of the structures inherent in perception. Existence is a predicate of perception; phenomenology arises in and is maintained by this alibi. Everything which is, the phenomenologist therefore concludes, exists in and through some form of conscious life. Though there may be some reality beyond conscious life, he or she concedes, it remains fundamentally inconceivable, falling outside the structures of consciousness. It is ultimately, in other words, an *unconscious* possibility.

What is phenomenology to do, then, with those presentations which fundamentally rupture, trouble, or call into question the perceptual structures which circumscribe their appearance – those phenomena which exceed or precede the bounds of subjective meaning making? What, in other words, is phenomenology to do with that which manifests to consciousness as the refusal to be contained within the parameters of consciousness – that which is unframable by consciousness: the nonsensical, the traumatic, or the absurd? What is phenomenology to make of those appearances within conscious life which represent the upsurge of the phenomenologically unconscious, like the possibility of an absolutely independent existence? It is to these sorts of questions that this volume endeavours to attend, in part by examining those phenomena which seem to tarry on the border of phenomenality. What is at stake in an analysis of the unconscious is the very heart of the phenomenological project: the possibility of a pre-critical conception of objectivity which would threaten the very definition of phenomenological consciousness.

Following Kant's revolutionary claim that any sophisticated (read: non-dogmatic) account of the nature of phenomena must necessarily involve a concurrent analysis of the transcendental structures of subjectivity, Husserl initiated the phenomenological project as an attempt to establish a dialogical account of objects of consciousness. For Husserl, famously, objects appear at the nexus of the accretion of pure sensorial *noetic* data and preconceived shared *egoic* ideas which, as he made clear in his later work, are received in part through participation in an intersubjective life-world. The ontological structure of *noematic* thinghood emerges, claims Husserl, when the infinite miasma of *noetic material* is given a concrete and definite shape by the perceiving subject according to the ideas of intersubjective life (Husserl 1970b, p. 227). Thus, while emergent from the structures of subjectivity, Husserl maintains that the hard core of *noematic* thinghood resides in the profusion of *noetic* data received by the senses. Nevertheless, *things themselves*, he insists, are always constituted in, by, and for a perceiving subject. Independent from the structures placed upon *noetic* data by the subject, nothing at all appears. There are no beings hiding innately within the infinite *hyle* of stuff for Husserl.[1]

---

[1] For more on the ontological status of hyletic data in Husserl see Dalton (2014).

Conceived as a means of tarrying within the liminal space between empirical reality and subjective life, Husserl presented the phenomenological project as a means of escaping what he saw through the Kantian critique as the twin pitfalls of modern philosophy: empirical naturalism, on the one hand, and rational idealism, on the other. By limiting each of these trajectories with its other, Husserl believed that the phenomenological method would provide a means by which the aims of the enlightenment could finally be fulfilled, ensuring complete access to a potentially transcendental certainty.

Not everyone, of course, was convinced of the effectiveness of Husserl's method in accomplishing this task however. From the very beginning there were those who feared that Husserl's conceptions were too prohibitive, too narrow – seemingly eliminating by definition a whole panoply of possible phenomena, phenomena which fundamentally challenge the Husserlian conception of existence.

9.2 Frege and the Charge of Psychologism

As early as 1894 Gottlob Frege, in his review of Husserl's 1891 *Philosophy of Arithmetic*, suggested that despite Husserl's best efforts, Husserl's phenomenology collapsed into a sophisticated form of idealism, accomplishing at best a novel form of philosophical *psychologism*; and, at worst a wholesale return to solipsism (Frege 1972). For Frege, the heart of this problem lies in Husserl's insistence that phenomena be addressed in and through the structures of egoic perception. By beginning with the first person subjective experience, Frege suggests, Husserl's phenomenology fails to recognize the radical a-subjective status of certain phenomena; in this case, the radically independent nature of arithmetic principles. For Frege and his followers, the laws of mathematics must be conceived of existing entirely independently of human perception lest they lose their transcendental validity. Even if there were no subject to perceive it, Frege insists, two and two must still make four. By insisting that such principles, qua noematic identities, are only deduced by and for a subjective consciousness, according to the structures of egoic life, Husserl has, Frege argues, effectively undermined the universal project of mathematics as a transcendental science. By Frege's reasoning, mathematics becomes for Husserl nothing more than a singular form of human language and not, as Frege and others would have it, the absolute language of material reality itself.

For Frege then, the real problem with Husserl's project is the way in which it reduces all reality to the transcendental structures of subjective life, and does not therefore allow for the possibility of the appearance within conscious life of something which exists independently of that life. As a result, he reasons, though the phenomenological project promises to cut a path to the absolute reality of "things themselves," all it finally accomplishes, he concludes, is a more determinate account of the psychological structures of subjective experience of reality. Far from establishing a basis for transcendental science, Frege's critique suggests, phenomenology in fact undermines the possibility of a truly absolute science, rejecting, as it does, the possibility of radically a-subjective pre-existent structures and patterns.

9.3 The "Speculative Turn" and the Problem of the Inhuman in Phenomenology

This is a critique of the phenomenological project which has been renewed of late, and to great acclaim, in the so-called *speculative realism* of such thinkers as Quentin Meillassoux, Ray Brassier, Ian Hamilton Grant, Graham Harman, Levi Bryant, and a fluctuating set of other thinkers. For Meillassoux and his colleagues, phenomenology's inability to conceive of the possibility of a meaningful and absolutely independent reality is an inheritance it receives from its fealty to the Kantian critique. "[T]he price to be paid," by Kant's critique in phenomenology, they write, "is the renunciation of any knowledge beyond how things appear to us. Reality-in-itself is cordoned off at least in its cognitive aspects," (Bryant et al. 2011, p. 4). This price is, in other words, the ability to speak meaningfully about a world which precedes or exceeds human experience – precisely the realm of scientific and mathematical discourse defended by Frege. As a result, they reason, phenomenology, as the inheritor of the Kantian critique, is fundamentally incapable of treating meaningfully a whole panoply of relevant and challenging phenomena. Quentin Meillassoux has called this the "problem of *ancestrality*," in contemporary philosophy (Meillassoux 2008, p. 10). For Meillassoux, by grounding reality in the structures of a knowing subject, Kant and his phenomenological children abnegate the possibility of making sense of any "scientific statements bearing explicitly upon a manifestation of the world that is posited as anterior to the emergence of thought and even of life – *posited, that is, as anterior to every form of human relation to the world*," (Meillassoux 2008, pp. 9–10).

For Meillassoux, the existence of the kind of ancestral "fossil-matter" treated by the contemporary material sciences testifies not merely to "the traces of past life," but to "the existence of an ancestral reality or event; one that is anterior to terrestrial life," (Meillassoux 2008, p. 10). What the existence of such *arche-fossils* signify for him, is the possibility of a reality that is radically and absolutely independent from human meaning making – a reality which appears entirely free from the structures of subjective constitution – a reality which was constituted by and testifies to a world without consciousness. What is manifest in the arche-fossil for Meillassoux, in other words, is the appearance of a material reality which ruptures what he calls the *correlationism* inherent in Kant and the phenomenological tradition: "the idea according to which we only ever have access to the correlation between thinking and being, and never to either term considered apart from the other," (Meillassoux 2008, p. 5). What appears in the ancestral object, according to Meillassoux, is a challenge to the fundamental assumptions of correlationism: a being which does not need consciousness to take structure and form or signify a meaning. What appears therein, in other words, is something fundamentally literally *unconscious* and *unthinkable* to phenomenology: a material reality which precedes and exceeds the structures of consciousness, which though apparent to consciousness, exceeds the structures and bounds of consciousness.[2]

What we find in Meillassoux's critique of the *correlationism* of post-Kantian philosophy is in many ways a revitalization of the charge of psychologism against phenomenology. What is at stake in Meillassoux's analysis then, is something not dissimilar to what was at stake for Frege: the appearance of what is fundamentally unconscious for phenomenology, what Jean-Francois Lyotard called the *inhuman*: the possibility of a reality devoid of human meaning-making (Lyotard 1991, p. 10). Where for Frege the *inhuman* object was exemplified in the absolute independence of mathematical principles (the *a-human*, as it were), and for Meillassoux it manifests in the existence of ancestral objects which testify to "events anterior to the advent of life," "the date of the origin of the universe," for example (what we could call the *pre-human*) (Meillassoux 2008, p. 9); for Lyotard the reality of *inhuman* is best testified to in the imminent appearance of the *post-human*: the universe which remains after the explosion of the sun and the complete erasure of all human artefacts (Lyotard 1991, p. 8).

The goal for contemporary philosophy, according to Meillassoux and his contemporaries, in parallel with Lyotard and Frege, must be to forge a system of thought which could make sense of such *inhuman* realities – to make room within thought of that which exists independently from it – to make room, in other words, for that which is apparently *unconscious* for and *unthinkable* by phenomenology. This can only be accomplished, they all seem to agree, to a greater or lesser extent, in opposition to the phenomenological project: by postulating a new ground for the nature of thinghood – by discovering, in other words, a non-subjective absolute that is radically independent from the structures of human consciousness (cf. Meillassoux 2008, pp. 34 and 51).

For Frege, of course, the absolute inhuman ground for the presentation of phenomena must be grounded in the laws of mathematics (Frege 1980). For Lyotard, by contrast, the ultimate absolute is to be found in the "inert mass" and "stupidity" of pure matter, which represents for him the ultimate "failure of thought," (Lyotard 1991, p. 38). However it is conceived, thinks Meillassoux and his colleagues, it is only by "speculating once more about the nature of reality independently of thought and of humanity more generally," – i.e. by "recuperate[ing] the pre-critical sense of 'speculation' as a concern with the Absolute, while also taking into account the undeniable progress that is due to the labour of [Kant's] critique," that philosophy will be able to make sense of hard core of phenomena (Bryant et al. 2011, p. 3). In order to "construct a transcendental naturalism capable of providing an ontological foundation for science," they thus conclude, the project of correlationism in general, and phenomenology more specifically, must be abandoned (Bryant et al. p. 7).[3]

---

[2] How such a phenomena is actually a manifestation of the unconscious will become clear later through a reading of Lacan, in whom, famously the unconscious, as for Freud, is linked inexorably to a manifestation of the material ground of conscious life.

[3] For more on the relationship of phenomenology to the "speculative turn" see Sparrow (2014).

9.4 Questioning the Power of the Phenomenological Reduction

For Husserl, of course, precisely the opposite is true. By returning to a pre-critical (read: pre-Kantian) conception of objectivity, Husserl believes that philosophy necessarily falls into a kind of naïve naturalism. It is in fact precisely naturalisms of this kind that Husserl identifies as the source of the "crisis" threatening the European sciences (Husserl 1970b, pp. 43–57). Thus the whole phenomenological project is, in many ways, initiated to correct the kind of pre-critical naturalistic speculations sought by his critics. And yet, Husserl was not-immune to the counter charge of psychologism. Indeed, it was a challenge with which he was very nearly obsessed, returned consistently throughout his work in apologia of the phenomenological project against the charge of psychologism. Indeed, an overview of Husserl's work shows him dedicating more time to the defense of the phenomenological project against the charge of psychologism than to the critique of the empirical sciences for their pre-critical naturalism. From volume I of the *Logical Investigations*, published in 1900, where we find the most extended defense of the phenomenological method against the critique of psychologism (Husserl 1970a), to section B of Part II of the *Crisis*, written near the end of Husserl's life, where the transcendental status of phenomenological philosophy is asserted almost dogmatically (Husserl 1970b, p. 202), Husserl appears incapable of launching even the most cursory survey of the phenomenological method without taking at least some time to shore it up against the possible critique of psychologism.

This seems to indicate that Husserl recognized the fundamental risk the phenomenological project ran, occupying, as it did, a liminal space between empirical science and psychologistic idealism, of collapsing into either errancy. What protects it from giving way to this risk, Husserl insists, is the methodological constraints demanded by proper phenomenological research. In other words, for Husserl the success of the phenomenological project hinges on the success of the *reduction*. First intimated by Husserl in the *Logical Investigations*, but most fully articulated in *Ideas I*, the phenomenological reduction is the only guarantor, thinks Husserl, that phenomenological research can fulfil its aims and achieve the status of a rigorous science (Husserl1998, pp. 131 ff.). Thusly, he concludes, the reduction is what ensures that "nothing at all stands in the way of accomplishing a transcendental [...] science of lived experiences," through phenomenological research (Husserl 2006, p. 62). By ensuring a properly phenomenological attitude, free from the vicissitudes of naturalistic assumptions and commonplace judgments, Husserl argues that the reduction grants the subject immediate access to precisely the kind of "immanent," "absolute," and "empirical" "givenness" (read: *inhuman* reality) sought by the empirical sciences (Husserl 2006, pp. 53 ff.). For Husserl then, it is only by way of the reduction that some absolutely pure and immediately given "*This*" can be encountered without falling into naturalism. Only in and through the phenomenological reduction, Husserl maintains, can some pre-critical *inhuman* ground be attained non-dogmatically.

But Husserl's sensitivity to the charge of psychologism belies an internal suspicion that the even his reduction was not enough to protect the phenomenological project. What's more, this is a suspicion which seems to have been shared by even the greatest champions of the phenomenological project: Husserl's own students. Take Edith Stein, for example, perhaps Husserl's most faithful student entrusted with editing the *Ideas* manuscript into a manageable and publishable piece. For Stein, the fundamental problem of the reduction, as she makes clear in the *Problem of Empathy*, is that while it functions to bracket the intellectual *content* of subjective judgment, it does nothing to ground the subject in a *structure* beyond itself. Instead, she argues, it only serves to re-entrench the subject within its own being, only now at the transcendental level (Stein 1989, pp. 3–6). As a result, she concludes, a strict adherence to the Husserlian method would, in fact, accomplish nothing more than what Levinas calls a kind of ego-ology – a comprehensive study of conscious life and nothing more. In this regard, Stein seems to concede to those critics who see the seeds of psychologism in phenomenology.

For Stein, the only way to ensure that phenomenological research escapes the lure of psychologism is by grounding the structures of phenomenal consciousness in a more primordial intersubjective life. By re-establishing the grounds of subjective apprehension in a shared life-world, argues Stein, the transcendental status of phenomenological research can be ensured. The guarantor of the scientific legitimacy of the phenomenological project thus becomes for Stein not eidetic reduction, but *empathy* – an empathy forged through an understanding of the nature of the lived body, a position Merleau-Ponty would later develop to arguably even greater ends (Stein 1989, pp. 41–65; Merleau-Ponty 1962).

As is well known, and has been extensively documented elsewhere, Stein's solution to the charge of psychologism in phenomenology seems to have influenced Husserl profoundly later in his career, as is particularly evident is his last works, most obviously *Ideas II*, edited by Stein, and the *Crisis*. There, Husserl re-frames the reduction as a path towards the other and the shared life world of the immediately corporeally given (Husserl 1999, pp. 117–140). By re-envisioning the reduction as a means of accessing the shard life-world, Husserl positioned the phenomenological project as a way in which the subject could access its own intersubjectivity and move from its home-world, into the foreign world of both the other human and the inhuman ground of both worlds.[4]

This turn towards the other and the lived body was not enough, however, to convince many of Husserl's greatest critics that the risk of psychologism had been fully mitigated, and that phenomenology now posed a viable path to a rigorous accounting to the absolute transcendent nature of reality. Most famously it did not convince Martin Heidegger, arguably Husserl's greatest student. Indeed, in many ways, the initial impetus behind Heidegger's break with Husserl was his distrust of the value of the phenomenological method. For Heidegger, the only way to ensure that phenomenological research escaped the dangers of psychologism was by abandoning

---

[4] For more on the possibility of envisioning the foreign in Husserl see Steinbock (1995, pp. 173–186).

the project of phenomenological subjectivity entirely – by grounding philosophical thought on the absolute existence of the being of beings.

9.5 Heidegger and the Abandonment of Phenomenological Subjectivity

Heidegger's most extensive analysis of the shortcomings of the Husserlian reduction appear in his 1923–1924 winter semester lecture course on phenomenological research (Heidegger 2005). Heidegger goes to great lengths there to distinguish Husserl's method from other philosophical programs which, he agrees with Husserl, inevitably collapse into various forms of psychologism. Heidegger begins there by acknowledging the accomplishments of Husserl's project. Through Husserl's "discovery of intentionality [by way of the reduction]," he writes, "for the first time in the entire history of philosophy, the way is explicitly given for a radical ontological research," (Heidegger 2005, p. 205). Nevertheless, Heidegger continues, Husserl did not initiate that research himself. Thus while his work made great strides, Heidegger contends, it ultimately failed to achieve its final aim. What inhibited this accomplishment, Heidegger claims, was Husserl's faithfulness to the Cartesian/Kantian conception of subjectivity. According to Heidegger, "in spite of Husserl's accomplishment, the *cogitosum* and its *certitudo* are in fact at work in a much more fundamental sense in him," ensuring that even with the reduction, Husserl never fully escapes the lure of psychologism (Heidegger 2005, p. 208).

In order to escape psychologism entirely and carry the phenomenological insights of Husserl to their logical conclusion, Heidegger insists that the concept of the modern subject must be abandoned entirely. It is with this conviction that Heidegger sought to revolutionize the phenomenological project by re-grounding it in a "fundamental ontology": an analysis of the foundational being of beings (Heidegger 1999, pp. 1–3). "For Husserl," Heidegger writes, "phenomenological reduction [...] is the method of leading phenomenological vision from the natural attitude of the human being [...] back to the transcendental life of consciousness," (Heidegger 1982, p. 21). By contrast, he writes, the "phenomenological reduction [should mean] leading phenomenological vision back from the apprehension of a being [...], to the understanding of the being of this being," (Heidegger 1982, p. 21). In other words, for Heidegger the only way to escape the dangers of psychologism in phenomenology, and thereby ensure access to an inhuman absolute transcendent reality, is to ground phenomenological research in the primordial structures of being itself; and not the structures of subjectivity, nor even intersubjectivity.

Heidegger's first systematic attempt to accomplish this task is of course *Being and Time* (Heidegger 1962). There Heidegger attempts to circumvent the risk of psychologism by grounding phenomenological research in an analysis of *Dasein*, qua being-in-the-world. Re-envisioned as a mode of *being-in-the-world*, Heidegger thinks, Dasein is not bared from the factical inhuman reality of existence. Thusly, the objectivity of existence is not for him, as it was for Husserl, something to which consciousness must gain access through a comprehensive method. Instead, Heidegger insists, Dasein's way of being, qua being-in-the-world, is "always 'outside' alongside entities which it encounters and which belong to a world already discovered," (Heidegger 1962, p. 89). Dasein's access to a transcendent absolute is therefore guaranteed, he argues, by virtue of its very facticity – it is an integral part of its being-in-the-world (Heidegger 1962, p. 174). Dasein's existence is thus for Heidegger its transcendence in-the-world (Heidegger 1962, pp. 165–170). Dasein is its own access point to that which is ontologically absolute.

As a result, Heidegger insists, the way in which Dasein moves beyond its mode of *being-in-the-world* into the inhuman worldhood of a world as such, is not some intentional/active project. Instead, it is a kind of ontological passivity. It occurs when Dasein finds the primordially of its being-in-the-world interrupted by the world it is given over to by its very being. The ontologically absolute is thus not attained *by* Dasein, instead it is apparent *in* Dasein when the world fails to conform to Dasein's projects – when it refuses to give itself over to Dasein's interests and use (Heidegger 1962, p. 103). In other words, for Heidegger, the being of the world does not become manifest as the result of some activity by Dasein, but results from an interruption of Dasein's active projection in-the-world. In this way Heidegger grounds access to the absolute phenomenality of the world in something not only beyond subjectivity, but beyond the first person experience entirely: namely the "obtrusiveness" and "obstinacy" of Being-in-itself (Heidegger 1962, pp. 103 and 106).

Nowhere is Heidegger's reformulation of the phenomenological reduction qua passivity and interruption more apparent than in his analysis of death, an event in being which functions for him as the ultimate guarantor of Dasein's access to the absolute. Death, as "that possibility which is one's ownmost, which is non-relational, and which is not to be outstripped," opens the ultimate channel by which Dasein can ground itself in being as radically absolute – free from the structures of subjective life (Heidegger 1962, p. 294). By being-towards-death as the "possibility of the absolute impossibility of Dasein," Heidegger discovers a form of phenomenological reduction which could never collapse into psychologism (Heidegger 1962, p. 294). As such, being-towards-death opens for Heidegger a path towards certainty which exceeds any Husserl could hope to achieve through "the immediate givenness of Experiences, of the 'I' or of consciousness," (Heidegger 1962, p. 310). The anticipatory anxiety opened up in an authentic being-towards-death, he thinks, is thus the phenomenological attitude *par excellence*: the ultimate projection of Dasein's transcendence: "Being held out into the nothing – as Dasein is – on the ground of concealed anxiety is its surpassing of beings as a whole. It is transcendence," (Heidegger 1998, p. 93).

For Heidegger, an authentic being-towards the absolute transcendence of death is the ultimate way to overcome the risk of psychologism in phenomenological research (Heidegger 1998, pp. 96–97). Strangely, however, it is precisely here, in his analysis of Dasein's death qua absolute transcendence that even Heidegger's project appears to falter, reasserting precisely the kind of *correlationism* he at first seems to overcome. This failure is most apparent in his analysis of Dasein's experience of the dead body of another in section 47 of *Being and Time*.

9.6 The Problem of the Dead Body of the Other

"In the dying of the Other," Heidegger writes there, "we can experience that remarkable phenomenon of Being which may be defined as the change-over (*Umschalg*) of an entity from Dasein's kind of being (or life) to no-longer-Dasein," (or death) (Heidegger 1962, p. 281). For Heidegger, what one observes in the death of another, is a kind of existential alchemy: the transformation of one mode of being, namely living-Dasein (*Leib*), into another mode of being, the "Being-just-present-at-hand-and-no-more (*Nur-noch-vorhandenseins*) of a corporeal Thing (*Körperdinges*) which we encounter," like a rock or a tool (Heidegger 1962, p. 281). This latter comparison is made explicit by Heidegger who writes that once a body has passed from life into death (from being as a *Leib* to being as a *Körper*) it loses its interest for us as another Dasein with whom we may dwell, and is thus no longer the subject of a Being-with (*Mitsein*), nor is it part of an intersubjective life-world. Instead, he suggests, it appears solely as an *object* of possible reflection, like a tool/thing (*Zeug*), retaining interest only to "the student of pathological anatomy," who may address it as the cobbler does the shoe or the butcher a slab of meat (Heidegger 1962, p. 282). The only possible interest the dead body of the other holds for Dasein, Heidegger contends, comes from the way in which the living Dasein may project itself, qua mineness (*Jemeinigkeit*), onto the corpse of the other, treating it as a clearing wherein the possibility of its own death may appear. The only real significance the body of another has is its status for the proximal Dasein, Heidegger reasons, is as "something *unalive* (*Unlebendinges*);" something "which has lost its life," as opposed to something which has never been alive (Heidegger 1962, p. 282).

As something *unalive*, the dead body of another bears the potentiality of signalling (*vertreten*) for Heidegger the possibility of Dasein's own death (Heidegger 1962, p. 283). It is only this potentiality to operate as a placeholder for a living Dasein's own-most ultimate possibility, thinks Heidegger, which separates the dead body of the other any special ontological significance distinct from tool/things one encounters in one's being-in-the-world.[5] The corpse is, for him, little more than a kind of *memento mori*. In other words, according to Heidegger, Dasein's interest in the dead body of another grows from nothing more than its own self-care and being-towards-death (Heidegger 1962, p. 283). The ontological nature the corpse is therefore not emergent from something singular or absolute in its own nature, reasons Heidegger. Instead, he suggests, it belongs entirely to the perceiving Dasein.

What we find here, precisely where we expect to see it finally overcome, is yet another iteration of the kind of correlationist loop identified by Meillassoux and his colleagues – little more than a species relative of Husserlian psychologism. What is exposed in Heidegger's account of the dead body of the other is the correlationist assumptions which are concealed in his analytic of death qua absolute transcendence for Dasein. By attempting to establish a route to that which lies beyond

---

[5] Heidegger openly confesses that he is not interested in "asking about the way in which the deceased has Dasein-with or is still-a-Dasein [*Nochdaseins*] with those who are left behind," but exclusively interested in how the presence of the deceased opens living Dasein up to an encounter with its own potentiality (Heidegger 1962, p. 283).

Dasein through Dasein's appropriation of its ownmost possibility, whether presented in contemplative anxiety before the nothingness of one's own being or apparent concretely in the object of the dead body of another, Heidegger simply further entrenches his understanding of being in the structure of Dasein's care. Nothing, it seems for Heidegger, can appear to Dasein that does not exceed nor outstrip its relation and care for its own being. So it is that we can conclude with Meillassoux that even here, in his most radical attempt at a fundamental ontology, Heidegger "remains faithful to the correlationist exigency inherited from Kant and continued in Husserlian phenomenology," (Meillassoux 2008, p. 8).

By reducing the appearance of the dead other to nothing more than an event within Dasein's attempt to appropriate of its own-most possibility, Heidegger misses the radical inhuman alterity of the dead body. In doing so, Heidegger misses the traumatic core of one's experience of a corpse: its power to possess and obsess the onlooker – to usurp his or her attention and refuse to relinquish it without the aid of another person, and/or symbolic rituals. In this way the copse is nothing like other simple tool/object at-hand; for, unlike the desk at which I sit, or the pen with which I write, the dead body of the other possess the power of transcending my projects, looming as a sort of absolute object within the perceptual field. Unlike these simple tool-beings, the corpse appears to possess a kind of ontological power which bends the phenomenal field around itself – something like an ontological black-hole, capable of drawing all that appears within its horizon of appearance into itself, transforming and transmuting their nature through its immanence. The bed upon which the dead body lies, is no longer just a bed. It radiates with the ontological power of the dead, appearing as a kind of sacred object which can never be slept upon again without invoking the memory of the corpse upon it. The rings upon the fingers of the dead are no longer symbols of wealth or status; they become relics of the deceased, or perhaps funerary objects to be laid to rest alongside them. This power of the corpse to transform all that comes into contact cannot be accounted for within the psychologistic or correlationist assumptions of classical phenomenology.[6] To the contrary, it demands a rethinking of the nature of thinghood entirely. In this regard, the corpse is in many ways the inhuman object *par excellence*: something which appears to consciousness without being constrained within the structures of its apperception – the ultimate manifestation within conscious apperception of something which challenges it: a kind of object of unconsciousness, what Freud terms *the uncanny*.

9.7 The Uncanniness of the Corpse

The *uncanny* for Freud signifies "that species of the frightening that goes back to what was once well known and long been familiar," (Freud 2003, p. 124). It is, he thinks, the human response to the reassertion or re-appearance of something that is

---

[6] For more on the special status of the corpse as an object of phenomenological research see: Dalton (2012).

typically taken for granted, something which typically operates silently in the background of all that we do and think. Thus, quoting Schelling, Freud defines the uncanny as that which "was intended to remain secret, hidden away, [but] has come into the open," (Freud 2003, p. 132).

As something we typically experience within the horizon of life, the body rarely appears to us in its own ontological singularity. Instead, it nearly always appears alongside of and concurrent with other expressions of life – expressions behind which it retreats: gesture, speech, mood, movement, etc. In the dead body of another, however, what we are presented with is a body stripped of all these typically foregrounded features. What we perceive is the body exposed in its full, raw, mute materiality – an object it is horrifying nudity. What takes center stage in the appearance of the corpse is the inhuman ground of life, typically hidden behind the finery of our living projects and interests. For Freud, it is this ability to foreground something typically operating relatively unseen in the background of our interactions with others which grants the corpse its special ontological status "belong[ing] to the real of the frightening, of what evokes fear and dread," (Freud 2003, p. 123). For these reasons, Freud identifies the dead body of the other as the "acme of the uncanny" (Freud 2003, p. 148).

It is this power of the corpse qua uncanny identified by Freud to unsettle us – to present us with something which no longer relates to us – that Heidegger misses in his analysis of the dead and signals the limits of fundamental otology to escape psychologism and correlationism. Interestingly, it is precisely this possibility of being confronted with an inhuman object, one capable of rupturing the powers of consciousness, traumatizing it with the presentation of a reality which exceeds its structural capacities that Jacques Lacan, unquestionably the most influential inheritor of the Freudian tradition, attempts to highlight in his analysis of the objectivity of objects qua *Ding*.[7]

9.8 Lacan on the Traumatic Core of the Inhuman

Lacan was of course deeply influenced by Heidegger as well, even going so far as to travel to Freiburg in 1955 to meet *Herr Professor* to request permission to translate an article of his on the concept of *logos* for the French journal *La Psychanalyse*.[8] And yet, his account of the possibility of something appearing uncannily outside of, and indeed counter to, the structures of lived experience, appears to break with Heidegger. Indeed, what Lacan identifies in his analysis of what he called *das Ding* (the *Thing*) in his 1959–1960 seminar on *The Ethics of Psychoanalysis* is the possibility latent within certain objects to exceed the structures of Dasein's self-care. For Lacan, the *Thing* expresses the possibility of an object which "only presents itself to the extent that it becomes word," like any other object, and yet nevertheless

---

[7] This reading of the dead body qua Lacanian *Thing* is also suggested by Zizek (2006, pp. 43–47).

[8] For more on Lacan's relation to Heidegger see: Roudinesco (1997, pp. 219–231).

manifests somehow "beyond-the-signified," of language expressing the "dumb reality" of a material world that does not speak and refuses to be contained by the meaning of our words or the structures of consciousness (Lacan 1992, pp. 55 and 54, respectively). As such, the *Thing* represents for Lacan the possibility of an aperture within experience through which one catches a glimpse of the inhuman ground of experience: an object through which the unconscious bedrock of conscious experience appears – something not unlike Freud's *uncanny*. What the *Thing* presents for Lacan is the manifestation within consciousness of the hard core of all experience – that kernel around which consciousness life organizes itself in representation, but which remains, nevertheless, excluded from consciousness (Lacan 1992, p. 71).

Following the insights of phenomenology and the Freudian conception of ego, Lacan sees conscious life as operating at the level of representation (*Vorsteullung*). Consciousness, he asserts in full compliance with the Kantian critique, only has access to reality via the symbolic order which it filters, structures, and organizes. In this regard, Lacan is perfectly in line with what Meillassoux identifies as the correlationism dominant in the history of modern philosophy and the phenomenological project. Nevertheless, Lacan thinks, it is possible that something appears within that symbolic field which pierces its structure, and opens a whole within it to that which lies beyond it – something which can create an aperture onto the raw inhuman material ground of the symbolic order, what Lacan calls the *Real*. Such objects, such *Things*, for Lacan, reveal in symbolic form a reality which refuses to be reduced it the symbolic – a reality which, though only experienced in and through language, refuses to conform to the contours of language. The experience of such a *Thing* is perfectly exemplified in a story Lacan shares in seminar XI on *The Four Fundamental Concepts of Psychoanalysis* of an exchange he had in his early 20s with "an individual known as Petit-Jean," (Lacan 1998, pp. 95–96).

According to Lacan, one day, while sharing a small fishing boat "[Petit-Jean] pointed out to me something floating on the surface of the waves. It was a small can, a sardine can [...] It flittered in the sun. And Petit-Jean said to me – *You see that can? Do you see it? Well, it doesn't see you!*" (Lacan 1998, p. 95). For Lacan, there was something traumatic in this exchange, a recognition in the can that he, like the can, somehow did not belong where it appeared. "I, at that moment – as I appeared to those fellows who were earning their livings with great difficulty, in the struggle with what for them was a pitiless nature – looked like nothing on earth. In short," Lacan concludes, "I was rather out of place in the picture," (Lacan 1998, p. 96). For Lacan, the traumatic core of his perception of the can was his recognition through it of his fundamental alienation from the scene. But, I think we glimpse more in this story than even Lacan recognized at the time.

In the can, Lacan was forced to perceive a mute materiality which did not conform to his expectations – an object which, while he could see and structure according to his symbolic system, refused to see him back or conform to that system. What appears in the can, for Lacan, is a sort of a splinter in perceptual reality – a tear in lived experience through which one can see beyond it to the dumb inhuman reality upon which the entirety of the symbolic order appears as little more than refuse, flotsam and jetsam upon the sea of the real. In a word, what Lacan perceived in the can was the traumatic power of the *Thing*.

This is what Heidegger seems to miss in the corpse: the traumatic alterity of objects. The possibility which lies in things to refuse to be confined by or circumscribed within the strictures of human care, meaning making, or conscious apperception. The usefulness of the dead body of the other as a phenomenological object is that through it we begin to glimpse the latent potential which exists in all objects to exceed their presentation, and to manifest as a *Thing* – an open passageway to that which stands forever beyond human consciousness: the inhuman reality of material ground. The heart of such an "encounter with the real," as Lacan notes, is the traumatic force of things (Lacan 1998, pp. 53–54). In order for phenomenology to overcome the charge of psychologism, it must find a way to do justice to this excessive plenitude present in within material reality: its capacity to exceed and even challenge conscious life.[9]

9.9 Speculative Realism and the Language of the Inhuman

After all, it is precisely to such a task that the speculative realists hope to attend. In order to overcome the correlationism seemingly inherent in phenomenological research, and give proper deference to absolute independence of materiality, speculative realism aims to chart a way towards what Graham Harman has called an "object-oriented ontology," (cf. Harman 2002). This is a goal which they hope to achieve, as we have already seen in part, by speculating a new absolute ground for thinghood in materiality itself, thereby clearing a path towards an ontology of the inhuman object, the *Thing*. But the problem still remains for them how to talk meaningfully about such inhuman objects without reducing them through discourse to structures of human conception, and thereby falling back into the correlationist loop. The problem is, in other words, how to formulate the nature of the inhuman in a philosophical language capable of doing its alterity justice – one capable of maintaining its inhumanity in its discourse.

In response to this charge Alain Badiou has renewed Frege's project, calling for an effort to frame ontology in the language of mathematics (Badiou 2008, pp. 110–112). According to Badiou, "[p]ure presentation as such, abstracting all reference to 'that which' – which is to say, then, being-as-being, being as pure multiplicity – can be thought only through mathematics," (Badiou 2001, p. 127). This is a suggestion which Meillassoux, for his part, seems to second, praising "mathematics' ability to discourse about the great outdoors, to discourse about a past where both humanity and life are absent," (Meillassoux 2008, p. 26). In mathematics, Badiou and Meillassoux discover a language in which to speak about the inhumanity of material reality – a language to capture the reality of the ancestral-object.

---

[9] One of the richest and most intriguing recent accounts of the phenomenological power of the Thing can be found in Trigg (2014).

The problem with mathematics, however, is that it seems to occult the traumatic core of the phenomena identified by Lacan – the horror and uncanniness of the dead body. While mathematics may be the language of the mute celestial bodies in their pure and absolute nature, it fails to encompass the traumatic horror of the inhuman body: a power which it appears to possess in its own right and not merely as the result of some human project. The question still remains then of how to talk meaningfully of the inhuman without reducing it to the human, nor reducing its appearance to nothing more than a number, as Levinas puts in, "in an alien accounting system," (Levinas 1969, p. 56). Indeed it is in many ways this same dilemma which drives Emmanuel Levinas' critical revaluation of phenomenology qua ethics.

9.10 Levinas and the Ethical Approach to the Absolute

It was Levinas' goal to discover through phenomenology an ethical absolute which did not bow to "the myth of a legislative consciousness," on the one hand, nor lost itself in metaphysical abstractions, on the other (Levinas 1996, p. 14). In this regard, Levinas' project is not dissimilar to that of the speculative realists. In order to accomplish this goal, as is well known, Levinas sought to ground ethical reasoning in the concrete and determinate material appearance of the *face* of the other.

According to Levinas, the human face, though apparent in the world alongside other beings in the world, nevertheless appears *otherwise* than those beings; for the face, he argues, breaks with the continuity of the world in which it appears. Unlike other simple phenomena which appear perfectly circumscribed by the world, according to Levinas, the face exceeds the "illuminative horizon," of subjective apperception and appears, in his words, "in its own light," (Levinas 1969, p. 71). As such, he argues, the human face, though a discrete phenomenon in the world, nevertheless appears to us as if it came from *outside of* or *beyond* the world. The face of the Other is thus for him a kind of *an-archic* phenomenon: one which "disturbs," or unsettles the grounding order, or *arche*, of phenomenality – one which ruptures with the horizon of its apperception (Levinas 1998, p. 137). It is for this reason, he claims, that the face of the Other appears as an "enigma," to the perceiving subject, one situated on the "hither side of consciousness," (Levinas 1996, p. 70).

Given its anarchic nature, Levinas claims, "the relation with the Other," opened in the presentation of the face "does not immediately have the structure of intentionality. It is not opening onto…, aiming at…, which is already an opening onto being and an aiming at being. The absolutely Other [of the face] is not reflected in a consciousness; it resists the indiscretion of intentionality," (Levinas 1996, p. 16). Indeed, he argues, quite to the contrary, the enigma of the face functions to put the intentionality of the perceiving ego into question. It is this "putting into question" implied in the enigma of the face which Levinas thinks opens up the possibility of ethical consideration and responsibility. "The face resists possession, resists my powers," Levinas writes, and in doing so presents an ethical counter to my being in the world – one which reorients my perception of the world and myself (Levinas 1969, p. 197). The relation one has to the face of the Other, Levinas therefore concludes, "is not therefore ontology," but more properly something like "religion," an way of encountering something absolutely and radically other, something which transcends the limits of human experience and understanding (Levinas 1996, pp. 7–8).

As a result of its "refusal to be contained" by a perceiving subject, Levinas argues that the face of the Other "cannot be comprehended, that is, encompassed," within being (Levinas 1969, p. 194). Since, for Levinas, the face of the Other bears a special meaning and status that exceeds other existent phenomenal presentations, it appears unlike any other phenomenon. Namely, whereas other phenomena appear in and through the finitude placed upon them by the perceiving subject and its phenomenal horizon, the face of the Other, claims Levinas, presents beyond itself, *beyond being*, rupturing the consciousness of the perceiving ego and shattering the continuity of world. In other words, the face of the Other for Levinas, in presenting beyond the bounds of phenomenal reality, presents beyond finitude itself. Thus, though it appears in a concrete and seemingly finite *morphe* qua face, the face of the Other, he argues, somehow signifies *infinitely*, presenting more in its givenness than any discrete possibly phenomena can. The face of the Other thereby represents for Levinas a conceptually impossible phenomenon: an infinite presentation. "The *in* of the Infinite," here for Levinas signifies "both the *non* and the *within*" of the face in relation to subjectivity and its phenomenal world. Though the face appears *within* the realm of finite beings, according to Levinas, its refusal to be contained by that world, signifies for him "[t]he presence of a being not entering into, but overflowing, the sphere of the same," (Levinas 1969, p. 95).

Signifying as it does a presentation which cannot comprehend, the face of the Other, signals for Levinas an openness within the horizon of phenomenality – an openness within being itself. Its exceptional nature as a phenomenon, its ability to present more than it could possibly present, is what makes Levinas account of the face so essential to his project. Since the face presents a possibility that cannot be accounted for within the logic of ontology, Levinas claims, it opens a channel within being for that which lies *otherwise than* and *beyond being*, towards what he terms the *absolutely other*. Hence his description of the face as an "epiphany" and a "visitation," one which "enters into our world from an absolutely foreign sphere, that is, precisely from an absolute, which in fact is the very name for ultimate strangeness," one which can only be attended to properly, he thinks, in ethical responsibility (Levinas 1996, p. 53). Indeed, it is in pursuit of a phenomenological account of such a responsibility that Levinas pursues this aperture in being in the first place.

Interrupting as it does the power of consciousness, Levinas conceives of the face of the other as a "traumatic" presentation within consciousness – one which threatens to *obsess* consciousness, *captivate* and take it *hostage* (Levinas 1981, pp. 148 and 111–112). In this regard, the face of the other operates within Levinas' phenomenology as an analog of the Lacanian *Thing*: the possibility of a presentation within consciousness of that which could potentially overwhelm it, presenting as it does that which exceeds it as its ground. As such, we find in Levinas' phenomenology of the face a means of discussing the brute materiality of the Thing, thereby escaping the *correlationist* loop, without occulting its traumatic power, as the mathematical languages of Frege and the speculative realists appear to do. Understanding how this could be the case requires a brief survey of Levinas' account of what he terms the *il y a* of existence.

9.11 The Possibility of an Inhuman Ethics of Absolute Materiality

Of course, the face of the other is still a *human* phenomenon for Levinas. Indeed, it is for him the human phenomena *par excellence* (Levinas 1969, p. 213). In this regard, Levinas' ethics could still be seen as operating within the limitations of a kind of correlationism. Such a reading, however, would miss the real heart of the Levinasian critique. Note that in the face of the other Levinas identifies a rupture in the legislative power of consciousness – a rupture through which that which lies beyond consciousness may appear. Thus, while something like the human may appear in and through the face of the other, that human which appears in the face of the other is, what Levinas calls non-relational, nothing at all like my being. Moreover, Levinas asserts, the rupture opened in the presentation of the face allows for other others, other *inhuman* others to appear as well. Levinas identifies precisely such an inhuman other in what he terms the *il y a* of pure being, in all of its material excesses.

For Levinas, the *il y a* signifies "[t]he discovery of the materiality of being," the discovery of "its formless proliferation. Behind the luminosity of forms, by which beings already relate to our 'inside,' matter is the very fact of the *there is* [*il y a*]," (Levinas 2001, p. 51). The *il y a*, in other words, signifies for Levinas, the "impersonal" and "anonymous" force of a "being in general," (Levinas 2001, p. 52). As an "existent without existents," which does not express itself, nor even *this* or *that* being, the *il y a* presents the possibility of "absolute indetermination, […] an incessant negation, to an infinite degree, consequently an infinite limitation," (Levinas 1969, p. 281). In this regard, the *il y a* of inhuman materiality, like the human face of the other, presents an infinite power which "transcends inwardness as well as exteriority," (Levinas 2001, p. 52). But, whereas for Levinas the infinite overflowing power of the face of the other presented the possibility of a Good beyond being, the infinity signalled in the "always still more" of the *il y a* represents for Levinas the possibility of evil "in its very quiddity," (Levinas 1998, p. 180). Thus where the face of the other arrests the power of consciousness, traumatizing it with the demands of infinite responsibility, the *il y a* of inhuman material reality horrifies consciousness captivating it in an "impersonal vigilance," which Levinas equates to "insomnia," (Levinas 2001, p. 55). In this regard we find in the *il y a* an inhuman sub-dimension to the human face – equally traumatic in its presentation to consciousness of that which lies beyond it.

It is in Levinas' analysis of ethical power of the *il y a* that we discover the language by which we can talk meaningfully about the inhuman power of material reality without falling into the trap of correlationism and psychologism on the one hand, nor giving into the abstraction of a mathematics which misses the traumatic core of the inhuman, on the other. By re-envisioning the objects of phenomenological analysis a-subjectively in this way, as a metaphysical power inherent in and emergent from material reality itself, Levinas establishes a means of thinking and talking about the absolute alterity of a universe which exists both anterior to and exterior to human meaning making. In this way, he charts a route by which phenomenology can confront the challenges posed by a radical manifestation of absolute materiality and finally fulfils its project to discover a route back to *things* themselves. What this will mean for phenomenology and how such a language can be utilized requires more work, a task which I attempted elsewhere. Here, however, it is sufficient to discover through Levinas' analysis a strain of the phenomenological tradition which is capable to responding to the critique of Frege and the speculative realists and truly getting back to "things themselves" as they appear in their radical traumatic alterity, prior to and outside of the structures of consciousness.

References

Badiou, A. 2001. *Ethics: An essay on the understanding of evil*. Trans. P. Hallward. London: Verso.
———. 2008. *Conditions*. Trans. S. Corcoran. London: Continuum.
Bryant, L., et al. 2011. *The speculative turn: Continental materialism and realism*. Melbourne: Re.Press.
Dalton, D. 2012. The object of anxiety: Heidegger and Levinas on the phenomenology of the dead. *Janus Head* 12 (2): 67–82.
———. 2014. Phenomenology and the infinite: Levinas, Husserl, and the fragility of the finite. In *Levinas studies*, ed. Bloechl, vol. 9, 23–51. Pittsburgh: Duquesne University Press.
Frege, G. 1972. *Review of Dr. E. Husserl's Philosophy of Arithmetic*. Trans. Kluge, E.W. *Mind: A Quarterly Review of Philosophy and Psychology* 81(323): 321–337.
———. 1980. *The Foundations of Arithmetic: A Logico-Mathematical Enquiry into the Concept of Number*. Trans. J.L. Austin. Evanston: Northwestern University Press.
Freud, S. 2003. *The Uncanny*. Trans. D. McLintock. New York: Penguin Books.
Harman, G. 2002. *Tool-being: Heidegger and the metaphysics of objects*. Chicago: Open Court Publishing.
Heidegger, M. 1962. *Being and Time*. Trans. Macquarrie and Robinson. New York: Harper and Row Publishers.
———. 1982. *The Basic Problems of Phenomenology*. Trans. A. Hofstadter. Bloomington: Indiana University Press.
———. 1998. *What is metaphysics*. In: *Pathmarks*. Trans. D.F. Krell, ed. McNeill. Cambridge: Cambridge University Press.
———. 1999 *Ontology: The Hermeneutics of Facticity*. Trans. J. van Buren. Bloomington: Indiana University Press.
———. 2005. *Introduction to Phenomenological Research*. Trans. D. Dahlstrom. Bloomington: Indiana University Press.
Husserl, E. 1970a. *Logical investigations: Volume I*. Trans. J.N. Findlay. London: Routledge.
———. 1970b. *The Crisis of the European Sciences and Transcendental Phenomenology*. Trans. D. Carr. Evanston: Northwestern University Press.

---. 1998. *Ideas Pertaining to a Pure Phenomenology and to a Phenomenological Philosophy: First book: General Introduction to a Pure Phenomenology*. Trans. F. Kersten. Dordrecht: Springer.

---. 1999. *The Cartesian Meditations*. Trans. D. Cairns. Dordrecht: Springer.

---. 2006. *The Basic Problems of Phenomenology*. Trans. I. Farin, J.G. Hart. Dordrecht: Springer.

Lacan, J. 1992. *The Ethics of Psychoanalysis: 1959–1960 Seminar of Jacques Lacan*. Trans. D. Porter. London: Routledge.

---. 1998. *The Four Fundamental Concepts of Psychoanalysis: The Seminar of Jacques Lacan Book XI*. Trans. A. Sheridan. London: W.W. Norton and Company.

Levinas, E. 1969. *Totality and Infinity: An Essay on Exteriority*. Trans. A. Lingis. Pittsburgh: Duquesne University Press.

---. 1981. *Otherwise than Being or Beyond Essence*. Trans. A. Lingis, Pittsburgh: Duquesne University Press.

---. 1996. In *Basic philosophical writings*, ed. Peperzak et al. Bloomington: Indiana University Press.

---. 1998. *Collected Philosophical Papers*. Trans. A. Lingis. Pittsburgh: Duquesne University Press.

---. 2001. *Existence and Existents*. Trans. A. Lingis. Pittsburgh: Duquesne University Press.

Lyotard, J. 1991. *The Inhuman*. Trans. G. Bennington, R. Bowlby. Stanford: Stanford University Press.

Meillassoux, Q. 2008. *After Finitude: An Essay on the Necessity of Contingency*. Trans. R. Brassier. London: Bloomsbury.

Merleau-Ponty, M. 1962. *Phenomenology of Perception*. Trans. C. Smith. London: Routledge.

Roudinesco, E. 1997. *Jacques Lacan*. Trans. B. Bray. New York: Columbia University Press.

Sparrow, T. 2014. *The end of phenomenology: Metaphysics and the new realism*. Edinburgh: Edinburgh University Press.

Stein, E. 1989. *The Problem with Empathy*. Trans. W. Stein. Washington, DC: ICS Publications.

Steinbock, A.J. 1995. *Home and beyond: Generative phenomenology after Husserl*. Evanston: Northwestern University Press.

Trigg, D. 2014. *The thing: A phenomenology of horror*. Washington, DC: Zero Books.

Zizek, S. 2006. *How to read Lacan*. New York: W. W. Norton & Co..

Part IV
With Phenomenology and Beyond

Chapter 10
Hypnagogia, Anxiety, Depersonalization: A Phenomenological Perspective

Dylan Trigg

Abstract This chapter investigates the phenomenological significance of so-called hypnagogic states of consciousness. The hypnagogic state refers to the transitional zone between wakefulness and sleep, which tends to be characterised by vivid visual phenomena. Phenomenologically rich, the hypnagogic state appears to dissolve the boundary between different levels of subjective existence. While there has been a modest amount of phenomenological research into hypnagogic visions and images, what has been overlooked is the affective relation we have to this experience. Investigating this oversight, this chapter aims to do two things. First, I provide a phenomenological account of hypnagogia. Second, I argue that that there is a close relation between hypnagogia and states of anxiety, evident in conditions such as depersonalization. My argument is that both hypnagogia and anxiety involve a loosening of the ego together with an exposure to temporal ambiguity. I demonstrate this claim through case studies detailing first, the anxious experience of hypnagogia; and second, the hypnagogic experience of anxiety. I conclude with some remarks considering the implications these findings have for our understanding of unconsciousness.

Keywords Consciousness • Anxiety • Waking • Dreaming • Self

> I'm scared like I can't tell you. Of all people, you're standing right over there…by that counter. You're in both dreams and you're scared too. I get even more frightened when I see how afraid you are and then I realize what it is. There's a man…in the back of this place. He's the one who's doing it. I can see him through the wall. I can see his face. I hope that I never see that face, ever, outside of a dream. (David Lynch, *Mulholland Drive*)

D. Trigg (✉)
School of Philosophy, University College Dublin, Dublin, Ireland

University of Memphis, Memphis, TN, USA
e-mail: dylan.trigg@ucd.ie

10.1 Introduction

This chapter investigates the phenomenological significance of so-called hypnagogic states of consciousness. The hypnagogic state refers to the interstitial zone between wakefulness and sleep, and is characterised by vivid visual phenomena. Hypnagogic phenomenon pre-empts the content and imagery of dreaming yet it is nevertheless distinct from dreaming (Mavromatis 1983). Furthermore, the hypnagogic state is phenomenologically rich insofar as it appears to unsettle the division between different aspects of the self (cf. Thompson 2015). Indeed, for Sartre (and to a lesser extent Merleau-Ponty), hypnagogia merits special attention in terms of what it reveals about the structure of subjectivity (Merleau-Ponty 2010; Sartre 2004). While there has been a modest amount of phenomenological research into hypnagogic visions and images, what has been overlooked is the affective relation we have to this experience.

Investigating this oversight, this chapter aims to do two things. First, I provide a phenomenological account of hypnagogia. Second, I argue that that there is a close relation between hypnagogia and states of anxiety, evident in conditions such as depersonalization. My basic claim is that both hypnagogia and anxiety involve a loosening of the ego. The difference between hypnagogia and anxiety is that whereas the former involves what Sartre calls a "captive consciousness," whereupon consciousness is fascinated by its porous boundaries, in the case of anxiety, we find the inverse: a consciousness that is repelled and undermined by the loss of boundaries, such that a partial fragmentation of self occurs (Sartre 2004). I demonstrate this claim through case studies detailing first, the anxious experience of hypnagogia; and second, the hypnagogic experience of anxiety giving special attention to the temporal dimension of this experience. I then conclude with some speculative remarks on the implications these claims have for our understanding of unconsciousness.

10.2 Toward a Phenomenology of Hypnagogia

To obtain a sense of the phenomenological character of hypnagogia, let us begin with a vivid example from Edgar Allan Poe. According to Poe, hypnagogic images present themselves as a "class of fancies, of exquisite delicacy, which are thoughts: they seem to me psychal rather than intellectual. They arise in the soul…only its epochs of most intense tranquillity—and at those mere points in time where the confines of the waking world blend with those of the world of dreams. I am aware of these 'fancies' only when I am on the very brink of sleep, with the consciousness that I am so" (cited in Mavromatis 1983, 13). A number of points emerge from this rich passage. First, the hypnagogic state is a liminal state, it occurs in-between dreaming and waking, such that there is an overlap between the two spheres. Alongside this delicate swaying between dreaming and waking, Poe's "fancies" gravitate toward the threshold of sleep and dream without ever falling into dreaming itself. The movement is delicate precisely because of its instability. At any point, but especially upon deliberate self-reflection, the dreamer can break the spell of the hypnagogic state, returning him to the wakeful realm from where he began his journey.

"To tell the truth," so Sartre writes, "a certain indulgence is necessary on my part. It remains in my power to shake this enchantment, to knock down these cardboard walls and to return to the wakeful world. This is why the transitory, unstable hypnagogic state is, in a sense, an artificial state" (Sartre 2004, 44). In order to maintain an attention toward this artificial state, it is necessary, so Sartre continues, to regard hypnagogic phenomena as being "on the level of quasi-observation" (37). What this means is that the image has a double-sidedness to it, whereupon it is both observable but at the same time is never accessible, as such. This balance is not only between sleepfulness and wakefulness, but also between different modes of attention, as Evan Thompson has noted in his recent book on dreaming: "Getting the images to arise requires being open and receptive, while seeing them takes a certain kind of diffuse attentiveness" (Thompson 2015, 114). The specificity of this state is a peculiar—indeed, paradoxical—one insofar as it is predicated on both passive and active dimensions, as Poe reflects upon his own collapse into sleep "with the consciousness that I am so." Throughout, consciousness manifestly remains intact, and at no point is extinguished by the onset of hypnagogia. Indeed, consciousness is not only operational but also silently self-aware of its own augmentation, as Sartre puts it: "Consciousness would be a modifying capacity, endowed with a certain efficacy, which withdraws from the game and lets the phenomena unroll in blind succession, in the case of half-sleep" (Sartre 2004, 43). What is displaced from the scene, then, is not reality as understood in an objective sense, but rather the centrality of the ego, where we take the ego as a prereflective sense of ipseity.

Notably, it is precisely this recuperation of the ego that transpires when hypnagogia morphs into dreaming. To pass from hypnagogia to dreaming is to regain a referential world, in which I myself am situated and to some extent distanced from the theatre of images that unfolds before me. As Thompson argues, whereas the hypnagogic state is characterised by the presentation of visual patterns that absorb us, in dreaming, we ourselves are at the centre of the dream world (Thompson 2015, 127). It is true that the subject who appears in a dream is a distorted and often strange version of the self we identify with in waking life. But even within this haze, what is intact in dreaming is the totality of a world, in which I become immersed (127). In contrast to the dream, the manifestation of the hypnagogic image does not emerge for me from a fixed position, whereby I still retain a contemplative distance. Rather, consciousness become absorbed with it, tied up in it, and thereby enchanted by its very presence. In his commentary on Sartre, Merleau-Ponty remarks that we "are at the mercy of (vague) suppositions, of the swarming impressions, and they are at the mercy of what we attempt to make them say" (Merleau-Ponty 2010, 143). This overlapping between form and formlessness is distinct from dreaming. What is preserved through the dream, beyond the augmentations of one's mirror image and even when perceiving oneself in the third-person, is the felt sense of mineness. It is

I who am affected by the contents of the dream, whether it be horrifying or pleasurable, and when I awake from the dream, then it is I who am reflecting upon an experience that I have just undergone.

Again, we discover that hypnagogia is both active and passive at once: active in the sense that we can partly observe and to some extent will it, yet passive in the sense that it acts upon us. The sense of hypnagogia acting upon us is evident in Sartre's depiction of the hypnagogic as being "fantastic" (Sartre 2004, 40). The image is fantastical given that it emerges abruptly without any previous knowledge. As such, we become "spellbound [by an] identification of consciousness with what it spontaneously imagines," such that it is impossible to speak of a "hypnagogic ego" (Thompson 2015, 124). In the absence of an ego gazing upon the hypnagogic image, consciousness itself undergoes a radical modification, as Sartre has it: "Hypnagogic phenomena are not 'contemplated by consciousness': they *are consciousness*" (Sartre 2004, 43).

10.3 Anxiety I: "Where Am I?"

Having provided a brief outline of the phenomenological dimensions of hypnagogia, I want now to consider in more detailed terms the affective dimension of this state. We proceed in three stages. First, I consider the anxious experience of hypnagogia. Second, I take seriously the sense of anxiety as being dreamlike through focusing on instances of anxiety in depersonalization. Finally, I reflect on the temporal dimension of both hypnagogia and anxiety, arguing in the process that the loosening of the ego involved in each state is interwoven with a temporality outside of experience. Let us in the first instance, then, consider the harmonious dimension of hypnagogia before turning to its anxious counterpart.

As contemplative in character, hypnagogia is often framed as involving a state of repose. For both Thompson and Mavromatis, the affective quality of hypnagogia is registered as a restorative if not relaxing experience (Mavromatis 1983, 106). According to Mavromatis, the hypnagogic state carries with it a feeling of "invigoration" and a decrease in anxiety, insofar as this reduction of anxiety is tied up with muscle relaxation (106). Inversely, a heightening of anxiety tends to inhibit the production of hypnagogia, given that hypnagogic images are predicated on the capacity to enter a "receptive mode" of consciousness freed from a concern with futural action, which tends to be prevalent in anxiety (106). In fact, in what follows I would like to suggest that far from precluding one another, anxiety and hypnagogia instead unfold in close relation, involving what Merleau-Ponty terms the "lowering of the barrier of the official personality" and what Mavromatis terms in a parallel way the "loosening of the ego boundaries" (Merleau-Ponty 2010, 149; Mavromatis 1983, 460). Anxiety and hypnagogia emerge together in two ways. The first relation is that of the anxious experience of hypnagogia. The second concerns the hypnagogic structure of anxiety. Let us take the first dimension initially.

If anxiety and hypnagogic are similar in that each involves a redefinition of the boundaries of selfhood, then an important difference nevertheless separates them. In non-anxious modes of hypnagogia, consciousness freely submits to the "deliriums of influence" that lead us from ourselves to an elsewhere (Sartre 2004, 41). This admission into hypnagogia is framed by a state of relaxation, in which the semi-dreamer expands his or her boundaries in a movement of exploration, knowing in advance that hypnagogia carries with it a potential "source of insight" (Thompson 2015, 124). From Poe to Proust, the experience of hypnagogia is imbued with a felicitous orientation, providing a source of inspiration for the literary imagination (112–113). Indeed, the experience of toppling between wakefulness and sleep is one of pleasure, a movement of freedom and spontaneity, in which the semi-dreamer enters a state of deep relaxation (Mavromatis 1983, 514). Sartre will also describe the hypnagogic state as involving a mood of deep relaxation. His descriptions of the moments falling into hypnagogia are incisive:

> The eyes remain convergent, the eyelids are kept closed by the voluntary contraction of the orbicular muscles. Then thought becomes more vague. At the same time, the retractors become slackened. A positive effort is now needed to open the eyes. The large oblique muscles relax and the eyes roll in their sockets. At the least resumption of our reflection, the large oblique muscles contract and the eyes resume their position. Similarly, when I hear a noise, I sense my eyes 'becoming fixed,' which is to say there is probably a double reflex of convergence and accommodation. At once the hypnagogic visions disappear and so, it seems, do the phosphenes. (Sartre 2004, 41)

As this deep state unfolds, so consciousness entertains a series of striking images, which are both illuminating and confounding at once. Merleau-Ponty speaks of the oneiric quality of perception as belonging to the fabric of everyday existence, rather than materializing as a rupture within this existence. "Our waking relations with things," so he writes, "and, above all, with others, have in principle an oneiric character: others are present to us as dreams, as myths, and that is enough to contest the cleavage between the real and the imaginary" (206). Throughout, there is an interweaving of distinctions; a life that is always exposed to the outside, a dream that infringes upon wakefulness, and a wakefulness that finds itself on the inside of a dream.

The point of departure for the anxious subject's relation to hypnagogia begins not with an affirmation of the fluidity of the self but with a self that is fortified against ambiguity and otherness. This claim will need unpacking. Accordingly, in what follows, I will briefly explicate the salient dimensions of anxiety, focusing, above all, on the temporal structure peculiar to anxiety. As we will see, each of these dimensions is untied by a joint intolerance of ambiguity.

One key way in which this intolerance presents itself is through the figure of temporality. As I have developed it elsewhere, the anxious subject is a temporally fragmented self (Trigg 2016a). What this means is that the narrative structure of the anxious subject consists of a pre-anxious self, an anxious self, and a post-anxious self. The pre-anxious self is the futurally oriented self that anticipates the emergence of anxiety. This modality of selfhood is the source of self-identification, given that it is from this more or less stable point that anxiety can be rationalized. The anxious self, the second temporal modality of the anxious subject, is the self in the grip of anxiety. This aspect involves an experience of oneself as other and foreign, given that the thematic presentation of anxiety—loss of control, disorientation, depersonalization, together with a series of bodily symptoms that constitute the overall experience of panic—is at odds with the self-identification central to the pre-anxious self. Indeed, far from identifying with anxiety's sensations and symptoms, the anxious self registers them in a movement of repulsion and rejection, as though they were acting upon the subject. Finally, I define the post-anxious self as the (fatigued) self that emerges from the onset of anxiety, reflects back upon the experience, and fails to integrate the experience into a coherent temporal whole. These three divisions in the structure of self do not form an intelligible unity, but instead divide and fragment the self into contradictory and opposing aspects.

I will return to the temporal structure of the anxious subject toward the end of this chapter, but in the meantime it is worth noting that this threefold disunity is framed by the subject's relation to intersubjective relations, spatial experience, and the perceptual experience of one's own body. Other people enter the world of the anxious subject in one of two ways. First, as sources of reinforcement for the subject. Second, as sources of threat, which undermine the construction of the subject's narrative identity (cf. Trigg 2013a). In each case, narrative identity is grounded in an intersubjective structure, such that the person I was, I am, and will be is presented before the presence of another person (Trigg 2016b). Spatiality, in addition, is not a neutral canvas, upon which the anxious subject freely inhabits. The anxious subject does not dwell in the world in a spontaneous way, expanding the boundaries of their self in an uninhibited fashion. Rather, it is a bounded and circumscribed space, delineated by points of safety and danger (Trigg 2013b). Finally, the experience of one's own body is marked by a constant vigilance, as though the body were an autonomous, anonymous, and impersonal organism responding to the world with an agency, not only of its own, but in conflict with the subject's selfhood.

The anxiety inherent in these aspects—intersubjective, spatial, and corporeal—can be consolidated under the theme of *an intolerance toward ambiguity*. We take ambiguity here as indexing the porous indivision between different aspects of bodily existence, those that are personal, impersonal, latent, explicit, subjective, intersubjective, and so forth. In non-anxious experience, we experience the differences within subjective life without any discord; different states appear and disappear, and throughout these transitions the singularity of our sense of selfhood remains intact. In cases of anxiety, the tolerance of temporal divergence and ambiguity is more restricted. What is specific about the structure of the anxious subject is the constricted and rigid sense of self, such that any deviations from this sense are either avoided (as in the case of phobic anxiety) or repressed (as in the case of rationalizing anxiety as an interruption in an otherwise non-anxious life) (Trigg and Gallagher 2016). When anxiety does emerge, then it does so not as something integral to the pre-anxious self, but instead as moments of rupture and divergence, such that these temporal variations effectively fragment the idea of the self as being non-anxious. To put it simply, the story told to oneself is ruined by the onset of anxiety.

We see that with anxiety, the boundaries of the self are intolerant of ambiguity and incapable of entertaining contradictory thoughts simultaneously. As seen in this context, hypnagogia presents an illuminating challenge to the anxious subject, given that what is at stake in hypnagogia is not an anxious loosening of the ego boundaries, but a pleasurable one. Hypnagogia takes as its point of departure the notion of the ego as a construct employed to discriminate and forge boundaries between self and other. For the present sake, we can take the ego to be equivalent to the narrative self. These boundaries entail a series of restrictions, not only between the ego and its environment, but also between "wanted" and "unwanted" information (Mavromatis 1983, 464). One source of such unwanted information is an "intolerance of ambiguity" (464). When the boundaries of the ego are loosened, either through deep relaxation or through disorders of the self, perceptual and conceptual boundaries are partly dissolved, in turn, "objects merge into one another and their meanings change, concepts lose their sharpness and expand to include other concepts remotely related to them or become identified with apparently entirely unrelated concepts" (465).

For Sartre, the non-anxious experience of hypnagogia carries with it a sense of pleasure, "it is *charmed* in the proper sense by it, which is to say it does not observe it, but *accepts* it" (Sartre 2004, 41). The spellbound consciousness is a consciousness that is in part freed of the constraints of the ego, and thus more accepting of a set of strange images otherwise denied expression. As with hypnagogic subjects, anxious subjects also experience a loosening of the ego boundary. Only their relation to this loosening of the ego—experienced as a fragmentation of selfhood—is neither desired nor willed, but instead experienced as an involuntary rupture in the temporal unity of selfhood. Let us be clear on this. As we understand it, ambiguity unfolds as a series of gradients, such that a minimal ambiguity would simply reinforce the existence of an already unified ego. When we reflect upon the fact that our heart and our breathing function of their own accord, then we are exposed to a level of existence, in which bodily life is revealed as having a double-sidedness to it. Yet for the most part, such an exposure does not undermine the integrity of selfhood; the beating of the heart and the inhalation and exhalation of the lungs reinforce rather than detract from the sense of who we are. But ambiguity is not delimited in this way. In the case of anxious subjects, we can see how a more troubling ambiguity intervenes in the structure of the subject, resulting not only in the loosening of the ego boundaries but in the very rupture of those boundaries.

One site of ambiguity that cuts through the subject concerns the division between consciousness and the ego. Indeed, a compelling dimension of hypnagogia is that it reveals a certain divergence between the ego and consciousness, and thus raises the question of who the actual subject of perception is (a question we will return to). For the anxious subject, the unbound consciousness, now freed of its domesticity to the self, is experienced as a deviant consciousness, a consciousness that betrays the sense of self as having one story, and one story alone. For this reason, the hypnagogic state is registered as an invasive and unsettling presence. The anxious self is *either* a self *or* a no-self, and there is no space for any radical ambiguity therein.

To consider this troubled relation to hypnagogic states in concrete terms, let us consult a report from 1897. The American psychologist G. Stanley Hall provides us with the following account of an anxious subject waking up:

> Children's dreams of place are very vivid and melt like dissolving views into the waking sense of the real environment. "Where am I?" is often the first problem of the morning consciousness, and there are often as strange ossifications and mosaics of two states, as in hypnagogic phenomena. Everything in the room is a lighthouse or buoy to aid them into safe harbour from the far dream voyages, and so cannot be moved without confusion. (Hall 1897, 161)

We are presented with an outline of the anxiety tied up with hypnagogic phenomena. The gap between sleepfulness and wakefulness is framed as a moment of vulnerability, in which the semi-dreamer no longer knows where he is and also what he is. In order to find his way back to the world, objects of stability must endure the night, so that they can establish a sense of temporal continuity. Hall's reference to objects in the room assuming the function of lighthouses is an exemplary way to phrase this relation. As with the lighthouse, the familiar object in the room radiates its presence through the cloud of sleep, dispatching a signal long before the dreamer has returned home. For this reason, another patient "can never have furniture moved in her bedroom, because the feeling of being turned around gives her a terrible panic" (160). To conceal the object or to position it elsewhere would be to dissolve the integrity of the room as a whole. It is thus not a question of the object as a localized entity; rather, the object acts as a waypoint—spatial and temporal—around which the patient orients himself or herself both when sleeping and then upon waking. As this orientation collapses, the residue of dreaming creeps into waking life, unnerving the distinctions between form and formlessness, self and non-self, thus producing anxiety. The relational nexus between things is dissolved, causing a fissure in both spatial and temporal orderings. Characteristically, the dream of anxiety (and the anxiety of dreaming) is a dream of immobility, of being present but unable to act in the face of impending threat. This stasis is predicated on a dispossession of space and time, each of which are seized from our control. As a result, we remain passive in the face of a world that takes place irrespective of our attitude toward it.

Clinical reports verify that the experience of waking up and falling to sleep is a crystallization of the anxiety tied up with the loss of selfhood. Thus we read of a patient who "often woke up in terror and cried loudly because she could not think where she was, even whether in bed or not" (Halls 1897, 160). Another who "sweats, feels faint and nauseated if she cannot instantly locate every door and window on waking nights" (160). Yet another who "is speechless and motionless with dread if she wakes up crossways or diagonally in bed, often thinking she has been carried elsewhere" (160).

To not know where one is; to be unable to locate the means of escape; and to wake in a position different to how one went to sleep: with each of these cases, waking (and thus sleeping) elucidates with peculiar clarity the gap between the image imposed upon the world and the opaque, anonymous, and constitutionally unfamiliar zone of existence that underpins that image. Sartre himself reinforces this anxiety in his discussion of hypnagogia, writing how, "[o]ne feels one's body very confusedly, even more vaguely the contact with the sheets and the mattress. The spatial position of the body is very poorly defined. The orientation is prone to blatant disorders. The perception of time is uncertain" (Sartre 2004, 40). The confused and anxious quality of hypnagogia finds root in these distortions of boundaries. As we will see toward the end of this chapter, the question of where I am is thus also a temporal question concerning at which point I cease to be "me."

10.4 Anxiety II: "As If Living in a Continuous Dream"

In the previous section, we considered the anxious quality of hypnagogia. Through cases of hypnagogia, we find evidence of the porous boundary between different levels of consciousness. In non-anxious modes of engagement, hypnagogia presents itself as an unfolding of consciousness, which renews the dynamism of selfhood through a process of exploration and expansion. By contrast, where anxiety is concerned, the moment between wakefulness and sleep serves to disorder the grounds of selfhood. But what happens if we reverse this anxiety; can we conceive of a hypnagogic experience of anxiety? In the present section, we will respond to this section by considering the experience of depersonalization. Depersonalization is chosen here as a case study because the condition often involves an accompanying sense of patients being in a dreamlike state (Sierra 2009; Trigg 2015). As such, it serves as rich material to investigate whether this dreamlike state is a metaphor, or whether there is a structural affinity between anxiety conditions and hypnagogic states.

The conception of what we now know as depersonalization derives from the psychologist, Ludovic Dugas, where he will describe the condition as "a state in which there is the feeling or sensation that thoughts and acts elude the self and become strange; there is an alienation of personality; in other words a depersonalization" (cited in Sierra 2009, 7–9). Contemporary research reinstates this description. Thus for scholar, Mauricio Sierra, depersonalization involves three central aspects: a feeling of disturbed bodily subjectivity; a diminishment of affective feeling; and a corresponding and overarching sense of unreality (which carries with it a sense of estrangement or alienation, be it from one's surroundings or, in the case of "anomalous subjective recall," from one's past) (Sierra 2009).

Critically, the feeling of being unreal also assumes the term "derealization," and indeed, depersonalization is often twinned with derealization, such that there is an on-going debate as to whether these terms are two sides of the same phenomena or whether they can be considered in isolation from one another (Varga 2012). In nosological terms, we align with Varga in suggesting that depersonalization and derealization present themselves not as distinct conditions, but instead as expressions of the same disturbed sense of realness (Varga 2012, 104). Indeed, the precedent for this thought is already established in Merleau-Ponty, and in particular in his analysis of existential spatiality (Merleau-Ponty 2012). Thus for Merleau-Ponty, the bodily subject does not exist in space in the way an object exists in a container. Nor is spatiality formed in terms of cognitive perceptions and beliefs. Rather, the perception of space takes form through the expression of the "total life of the subject" (296). What this means is that to perceive one's body as depersonalized is simultaneously to perceive the surrounding world as correspondingly derealized (cf. Merleau-Ponty: "External perception and the perception of one's own body vary together because they are two sides of a single act" [211]).

Typically, the experience of depersonalization involves an alienation from one's sense of self. Thus, in a report from 1847, we read of a patient occupying an interstitial space between the living and the dead, "she claimed to feel as if she were not dead or alive, as if living in a continuous dream…objects [in her environment] looked as if surrounded by a cloud; people seemed to move like shadows, and words seemed to come from a far away world" (cited in Sierra 2009, 8). Further illustrations reinforce this relationship between depersonalization and being in a dreamlike state.

> As the day unfolded, she felt she was in a dream, navigating through fog in slow motion, dazed and semi-aware of what was going on around her; time seemed eternal (Simeon and Abugel 2006, 35)
>
> To the depersonalized individual the world appears strange, peculiar, foreign, dream like. Objects appear at times strangely diminished in size, at times flat. Sounds appear to come from a distance. (cited in Sierra 2009, 25)

The result of this alienation from the self is that patients can experience a double consciousness, such that it can even result in visual observation of oneself as perceived externally. Thus we read of a patient, "with long-standing depersonalization [who] complained of intermittent out-of-body experiences during which she felt herself to be out of her body, about 1 foot above her head, from where she could see the top of her head" (cited in Sierra 2009, 30). Notably, this doubling of consciousness also plays a role in hypnagogia, Thompson writes how "we retain awareness of the outside world while watching the inner mental scene usurp its place" (Thompson 2015, 124). The double consciousness at work in depersonalization, together with its relation to dreaming and anxiety, is also reported by Merleau-Ponty. In one of several references to depersonalization in *Phenomenology of Perception*, he reflects:

> In autoscopy, prior to seeing himself, the subject always passes through a state of dreaming, musing, or anxiety, and the image of himself that appears on the outside is merely the other side of this depersonalization. The patient feels himself in his double, who is nevertheless outside of himself, just as I feel the substance of my body escaping through my head and crossing the limits of my objective body when an ascending elevator stops abruptly. (Merleau-Ponty 2012, 212)

Merleau-Ponty draws our attention here to the space in-between seeing oneself from one's own visual field and seeing oneself as a double. As a double consciousness unfolds, so a state of existence is passed through, which is characterised by a dreamy anxiety. What is at stake in autoscopy concerns the interstitial space between self and other, between personalized and depersonalized consciousness. Indeed, with the idea of the body escaping one's head in the elevator, we have an especially striking image of the porousness of the body extending itself beyond its own reach. Merleau-Ponty underscores the point that depersonalization often carries with it a disturbed sense of selfhood, such that the depersonalized self experiences him or herself outside the physical boundaries of their body. In some cases, patients suffer from visual hallucinations, as when they see themselves "as experienced from extrapersonal space" (Sierra 2009, 30).

10.5 Anxiety III: When Am I Me?

With this preliminary outline of depersonalization established, I want to return to the temporality of anxiety. Already I have presented the anxious subject as a temporally fragmented subject. More precisely, the narrative structure of the anxious self is divided between a pre-anxious self, an anxious-self, and a post-anxious self, with each aspect failing to converge into one unified whole. As we near the end of our investigation, I propose to deepen—and, indeed, widen—this temporal arc beyond the fragmentation of lived experience to an immemorial dimension that transcends subjectivity. As I will now suggest, a central facet in the dreamlike quality of the anxiety tied up with depersonalization is the experience of being outside of time. The reason for this can be formulated as follows: *The experience of oneself as being outside of time—outside of the narrative construction of who one is—is inextricably bound with the anxiety involved in depersonalization, given that the immemorial and anonymous dimension of time serves as the primordial source of rupture and anxiety for a subject whose identity and sense of selfhood is tied irreducibly to the present.*

To contextualize this claim, let us consider at the outset our prereflective grasp on the temporality of selfhood. Each of us is bound and defined by our relation in time. Our temporality, moreover, operates on complex levels, from personal memory to shared history to collective history, and so forth (Trigg 2012). These dimensions are not mutually incompatible, but instead are mutually edifying in terms of forming the felt sense of what it is to be a person. Furthermore, the narrative basis of selfhood is not static, but instead dynamic, and thus constantly unfinished, as Merleau-Ponty writes: "My hold on the past and my hold on the future are precarious and my possession of my own time is always deferred until the moment when I fully understand myself, but that moment can never arrive since it would again be a moment, bordered by the horizon of a future, and would in turn require further developments in order to be understood" (Merleau-Ponty 2012, 362). Even if we are not explicitly reflecting upon this endless stream of being a person, we nevertheless tend to implicitly operate according to the idea that our actions, thoughts, memories, and desires are in some sense intelligible within the context of our existence more broadly. Of course, within the duration of a life, our sense of self is often tested and contested. Throughout these tribulations, however, a sense of narrative order tends to remain intact, and indeed is often reinforced despite—or because—of the ambiguities and uncertainties we face.

In order to understand the other side of this integral temporal order, we will return to the anxiety tied up with depersonalization. Such a rupture in time is not only interesting in and of itself, it also discloses fundamental structures that are common to both depersonalized and non-depersonalized subjectivities. As we will now see, the case of anxiety tied up with depersonalization operates on a different temporal register. Speaking of the depersonalized subject's experience of time, the Austrian psychiatrist Paul Schilder notes,

> [T]he present is a concept which has meaning only in relation to experiencing personalities. The inanimate has no past, present or future…Cases of depersonalization, whose total experience is splintered, all have an altered perception of time. In extreme cases, time seems to them to be at a standstill, or the present seems to be like the distant past. (cited in Simeon and Abugel 2006, 35)

This altered sense of time is evident not only in an abstract fashion, but is also present in perceptual experience. Thus, in one report, we read of a patient who underscores the regressive movement of depersonalization, as "if I were seeing these things for the first time, like a child, there should be some sense of wonderment, but there isn't…I know that there's something wrong with me, and all it does is fill me with fear" (cited in Simeon and Abugel 2006, 8).

How should we understand this fearful apprehension of a disjointed temporality? In positivistic terms, the temptation would be to provide an explanatory account of such experiences, as though they were a symptomatic expression of a more pervasive breakdown in an already fragile selfhood. Against the grain of this thought, however, I would like to consider the modulation of time as it is conceived in depersonalization as an invariant structure of temporal experience more generally.

The point of departure for this claim can be sourced in Merleau-Ponty. Central to the phenomenology of depersonalization is the question of who the subject of perception is, given that the subject has been depersonalized. Indirectly, Merleau-Ponty raises this question in discussing the generality of the senses (Merleau-Ponty 2012, 223). To perceive a thing is not to take it upon myself as a personal consciousness to instate perception. Rather, "[e]very perception takes place within an atmosphere of generality and is presented to us as anonymous" (223). As Merleau-Ponty sees it, the subject of perception is a subject that perceives in and through me as the personal expression of this other side, as he says, "if I wanted to express perceptual perception with precision, I would have to say that *one* perceives in me, and not that I perceive" (223). The ambiguity of the perceiving subject is not simply a case of being both subject and object at once. Merleau-Ponty directs us in a more paradoxical direction. Now, the ambiguity at stake involves an account of the subject as personalized and depersonalized, timely and untimely at once. For this reason, the question becomes not only *who* is the subject that is doubled before me, but also who is the subject that perceives *through me*? In each case, the other side of perception and subjectivity returns us to depersonalization, Merleau-Ponty writes:

> Every sensation includes a seed of dream or depersonalization, as we experience through this sort of stupor into which it puts us when we truly live at the level of sensation…this activity unfolds on the periphery of my being; I have no more awareness of being the true subject of my sensation than I do of my birth or death. Neither my birth nor my death can appear to me as my personal experience, since if I conceive of them in this way, I must

imagine myself as preexisting or as surviving myself in order to be able to experience them (223).

With this rich and elaborate passage, we have a statement of the multiple narratives and temporalities structuring the subject of experience. Merleau-Ponty's reference to the "seed of dream" rather than dreaming itself suggests that we are not yet within the recuperated world of an ego-centric perspective that is common to dreaming and which is different from hypnagogic states. In fact, Merleau-Ponty seems to be positioning his thought precisely on this peripheral hinge between states, in which the ego is neither one thing nor another. To live truly at the level of sensation is to divest consciousness of its personal attributes, and thus to enter into the dream state that characterizes the recognition of bodily sensation being beyond possession (cf. "I never have an absolute possession of myself by myself" [250]). The "one" who perceives in and through me is not strictly me, nor is it knowable by me: "He who sees and touches is not exactly myself" (224). More than this, the "one" is not only "beneath" me, it also precedes and will survive me (224). Merleau-Ponty's enigmatic discussion of a subject both beneath and prior to me is not an appeal to Gnosticism. Rather, what he is describing is situated in the realm of phenomenology itself, as he remarks, it is "the life of my eyes, hands, and ears [where we find] so many natural selves," each of which has "already sided with the world" (224). Such claims are not abandoned by Merleau-Ponty as he thinking evolves. Indeed, so important is the formulation of the subject as structured by a primordial depersonalized mode of perception that he will return to it at the end of his life. Thus, in a working note from May 2, 1959, he writes as follows:

> I do not perceive any more than I speak. Perception has me as has language. And as it is necessary that all the same *I* be there in order to speak, *I* must be there in order to perceive. But in what sense? As *one*. What is it that, from my side, comes to animate the perceived world and language? (Merleau-Ponty 1968, 190)

The subject of depersonalization for Merleau-Ponty is subjected to an impersonal level of time, belonging neither to memory nor to calendar time, but instead to the anonymity of time, which is both everyone's and no one's at once. Against this order of time and perception, my own construction of time is always exposed to a dimension of contingency and tentativeness, as he writes:

> My voluntary and rational life thus knows itself to be entangled with another power that prevents it from being completed and that always gives it the air of a work in progress. Natural time is always there. The transcendence of moments of time at once establishes and compromises the rationality of my history: it establishes it since it opens me up to an absolutely new future in which I will be able to reflect upon what is opaque in my present; it comprises it since from the perspective of that future I will never grasp the present that I am living with apodeictic certainty, since the lived time is thus never entirely comprehensible in this way (which I understand never precisely links up with my life), and since, in short, I am never at one with myself. Such is the fate of a being who is born, that is, a being who once and once and for all was given to himself as something to be understood…This anonymous life is merely the limits of the temporal dispersion that always threatens the historical present. To catch sight of this formless existence that precedes my history and that will draw it to a close, all I had to do is see, in myself, the time that functions by itself and that my personal life makes use of without ever fully concealing (362).

In this revealing and dense passage, Merleau-Ponty suggests that "natural time"—the immemorial and anonymous time of perception enacted in depersonalization—both constitutes our sense of a personal narrative whilst also being an obstruction to that narrative. This "threat" stands before me as an order of time that can never be integrated nor appropriated as my own. Thus immemorial time is anterior to my own experience, never fully aligning with that experience, and thus rendering me an outsider to my own temporality. Never quite one with myself, in order for me to survive as a personal and unified self, it becomes necessary to accept the paradox of existing both inside and outside of time concurrently. No matter how much one's personal narrative strives to master and personalize selfhood, there exists the residue of a formless existence, which is wholly resistant to the work of personalization. Yet in turning toward this formless, impersonal life it vanishes on the exterior of my existence. Remaining a blind spot, it is only when I cease to be strictly identifiable with myself—that is, when I am depersonalized, hypnagogic, anxious—that it appears for me as a dream.

Merleau-Ponty's formulation of a depersonalized perception operating on another level of time helps us understand in part the clinical experience of depersonalization as a temporal disorder. Alienated from the personal self, the depersonalized subject loses the ability to consolidate time into a unified whole. This serves not only to fragment narrative identity as whole, but also distorts the perceptual experience of time as it is lived. Thus, we read of patients who refer back to their morning experiences, as though it took place weeks ago, whilst other patients report being "outside of time" altogether (Sierra 2009, 35). These rich experiences are not affectively neutral, but are tied up with the anxiety of losing one's sense of self. As seen in this way, what is lost in this dreamlike anxiety is not the primordial core of the selfhood, as though my first-person perspective were destroyed. A felt sense that this is *my* experience persists. Rather, what is fragmented during anxiety is the narrative construction of myself as being identifiable with the story I tell myself of who I am. In cases of depersonalization and in the anxious experience of hypnagogia, another dimension of the self is revealed. This is not a dimension that can be integrated into the order of temporal coherence, given that it exists "on the periphery of my being," constituting a constant blind spot in narrative self-interpretations.

10.6 Conclusion: "Just Beneath the Surface of All Waking Life"

As we have seen, hypnagogia and anxiety each involve a partial loosening of the boundaries of the ego. In both anxiety and hypnagogia, we open ourselves more fully to the level of impersonal and immemorial existence that is for the most part masked by the dominance of the ego-centric self. The eclipse of the ego through the awakening of the impersonal side of existence forces us to exist at the level of pure sensation, oneiric and unarticulated, silent and obscure, yet experienced from the perspective of the still intact self. If hypnagogia affords us a dizzying fusion of pleasure and strangeness, then where anxiety alone is concerned, the lowering of the ego coexists with an impending sense of collapse. Here, any such pleasure in the adventure of consciousness is augmented with a sense of being too close to the unfillable gap, which threatens to annihilate the sense of self as a self-same and knowable construct. The differences between these states are at once affective but also structural. In the case of hypnagogia, there is a dynamic rapport between the egocentric-self and the egoless-self, such that these two dimensions operate in conjunction with one another, each strengthen the bond between them. In the case of anxiety, the egocentric-self does not entirely fragment in the face of an egoless-self. Rather, the ego resists its own fragmentation as a threat to the stability of an already fragile relationship to ambiguity.

What remains to be said, finally, is how unconsciousness enters this scene. Notwithstanding the explicit absence of unconsciousness within our study, it has nevertheless been implicit from the outset. Let us think in this respect of our earlier formulation concerning an immemorial and anonymous dimension of time, which serves as the primordial source of rupture and anxiety for a subject whose existence is tied up with the delimitation of the present. Let us think more generally of the separation of the ego from consciousness, of a consciousness that pursues its own world with only a minimal intervention from the residue of an otherwise normally present ego. In such peripheral encounters, the ground might look fertile for an analysis of the unconscious as the means of production for a series of symbols, the meaning of which is concealed from waking life but is indirectly transmitted in liminal situations. Do hypnagogia and depersonalization generate access to an occult layer of meaning belonging to the unconscious? To posit such a claim would mean advocating an unconscious structured as a vertical plane of existence, the meaning of which awaits our retrieval. Such a model, which is no doubt Freudian in scope, is patently at odds with the approach we have developed in this chapter. Even in its tacit status, it is clear that anxiety, depersonalization, and hypnagogia do not signal a radical departure from non-pathological modes of selfhood; rather, they amplify and extend already existing structures of subjectivity. Accordingly, the unconscious that opens itself up in these thematic experiences is not a privileged domain accessible only in traumatic modes of existence, but is instead an unconscious that is common to subjectivity generally.

In ending, we can think in terms of phrasing the unconscious, not as a reservoir of deposited knowledge, buried beneath the surface of perception, which we encounter in the darkness, but as the oneiric ground upon which states of consciousness form and deform. The unconscious that forms an arc around our existence is not buried with a thousand repressed ciphers, but serves, in Merleau-Ponty's words, as a "principle of crystallization" that organizes dream and life into the same plane of existence (Merleau-Ponty 2010, 159). Such an elaboration of the relation between unconsciousness, hypnagogia, and anxiety would require a separate study. Such a study would follow Merleau-Ponty in situating unconsciousness as an "oneirism just beneath the surface of all waking life" (157). The figure of the unconscious in Merleau-Ponty as a horizontal rather than vertical force reappears throughout his thinking; it is an unconscious that is neither "distant" nor "behind our back" (159). Rather, it is "quite near, as ambivalence" (159). Toward the end of his life, Merleau-Ponty will expand upon these thoughts, phrasing the unconscious as that which is "in front of us, as articulations of our field" (Merleau-Ponty 1968, 180). How does a subject come into different modalities of existence, some of which unify the structure of the ego while others threaten to disperse that unity; how is meaning and sense organized in a perceptual horizon, the origin of which both precedes and outlasts us; how, finally, can consciousness enter a series of different states, some of which act upon "us" whilst in other cases, it is "we" who inaugurate those states in the first instance? To all these questions, the unconscious must serve a critical place.

As Merleau-Ponty sees it, the unconscious is not that space opened up in moments of dreaming; rather, it is "the indestructible ground from which our dreams are drawn" (207). Dreaming, for him, is not the translation of content nor is it the representation of an otherwise latent content. Nor does dreaming commence upon the transition from sleep to dream itself. Dreaming takes up a thought that was there from the outset as a "perceptual consciousness" that stems from the unconscious (208). We may say the same of hypnagogia, anxiety, and depersonalization. Each of them fashion a series of images and thoughts that are not introduced by way of a break from consciousness. Their existence belongs to a set of expressive possibilities, each of which is situated on the border upon which waking life rests without ever being reducible to that border.

References

Hall, Stanley. 1897. A study of fears. *The American Journal of Psychology* 8: 147–249.
Mavromatis, A. 1983. *Hypnagogia: The Nature and Function of the Hypnagogic State*. PhD thesis, Brunel University.
Merleau-Ponty, M. 1968. *The Visible and the Invisible*. Trans. A. Lingis. Evanston: Northwestern University Press.
———. 2010. *Institution and Passivity: Course Notes from the Collège de France (1954–1955)*. Trans. L. Lawlor, H. Massey. Evanston: Northwestern University Press.
———. 2012. *Phenomenology of Perception*. Trans. D. Landes. London: Routledge.
Sartre, J.-P. 2004. *The Imaginary: A Phenomenological Psychology of the Imagination*. Trans. J. Webber. London: Routledge.
Sierra, Mauricio. 2009. *Depersonalization: A new look at a neglected syndrome*. Cambridge: Cambridge University Press.
Simeon, Daphne, and Jeffery Abugel. 2006. *Feeling unreal: Depersonalization disorder and the loss of self*. Oxford: Oxford University Press.
Thompson, Evan. 2015. *Waking, dreaming, being: Self and consciousness in neuroscience, mediation, and philosophy*. New York: Columbia University Press.
Trigg, Dylan. 2012. *The memory of place: A phenomenology of the uncanny*. Athens: Ohio University Press.
———. 2013a. The body of the other: Intercorporeality and the phenomenology of agoraphobia. *Continental Philosophy Review* 46 (3): 413–429.

———. 2013b. Bodily moods and unhomely environments: The hermeneutics of agoraphobia. In *Interpreting nature: The emerging field of environmental hermeneutics*, ed. Forrest Clingerman et al. New York: Fordham University Press.

———. 2015. On the role of depersonalization in Merleau-Ponty. *Phenomenology and the Cognitive Sciences*. doi:10.1007/s11097-015-9451-x.

———. 2016a. *Topophobia: A phenomenology of anxiety*. London: Bloomsbury.

———. 2016b. Agoraphobia, Sartre, and the spatiality of the other's look. In *Forthcoming: Body/self/other: Phenomenology of social encounters*, ed. Luna Dolezal and Danielle Petherbridge. New York: SUNY Press.

Trigg, Dylan, and Shaun Gallagher. 2016. Agency and anxiety: Delusions of control and loss of control in schizophrenia and agoraphobia. *Frontiers in Human Neuroscience* 10: 459.

Varga, S. 2012. Depersonalization and the sense of realness. *Philosophy, Psychiatry, and Psychology* 19 (2): 103–113.

Chapter 11
Merleau-Ponty's Non-Exclusively-Verbal Unconscious: Affect Figurability and Gender

Thamy Ayouch

Abstract In the name of psychoanalysis, for more than one century, various theories have been produced about non-binary gender and sexualities, evaluated with respect to their conformity to the Oedipus complex, the castration complex, or the formulas of sexuation and the phallus. Most of these analyses refer to the Symbolic, a Lacanian or Lacan-inspired register of transcendental, universal rules that determine subjectivity and the "normal" processes of subjectivation. This raises the question of the effect of a structuralist conception of the Unconscious on human lives, and on the constitution of "lives worth living". For many psychoanalysts, Merleau-Ponty's conception of the Unconscious proves misconstrued insofar as he leaves aside its linguistic dimension. Hence, to which extent may a non-language-based conception of the Unconscious avoid imposing universal subjectivation categories that stretch beyond history and culture? The aim of this article is to show how Merleau-Ponty's non-exclusively-verbal Unconscious is concerned with affect, a perspective that entails a different, not exclusively linguistic conception of the Symbolic. For that purpose, I argue that Merleau-Ponty's phenomenology, differently from Husserl's, is a phenomenology of affectivity. Expatiating on the centrality of the lived body, it moves away from constitution to institution, in a way that places affectivity, and not language at the core of the Unconscious. This conception results in two consequences: the Unconscious is not, or not entirely verbal, which implies the possibility of a non-binary reading of gender and sexuality. This non-exclusively-verbal Unconscious may lay the ground for a feminist analysis of gender.

Keywords Non-verbal unconscious • Merleau-Ponty • Gender • Symbolic

T. Ayouch (✉)
Université Lille 3, Villeneuve-d'Ascq, France

Université Paris 7, Paris, France

Universidade de São Paulo, São Paulo, Brazil
e-mail: thamy.ayouch@gmail.com

11.1 Introduction

In the name of psychoanalysis, for more than one century, various theories have been produced about non-binary gender and sexualities, evaluated with respect to their conformity to the Oedipus complex, the castration complex, or the formulas of sexuation and the phallus. Same-gender, sado-masochist, multiple-partner or non-genital sexualities have often been deemed perverse, for their denial of the other's sexual identity (Pirlot and Pedinelli 2009), their "ferocious offensive and defensive denial of the female sex" (Bergeret 1996), their repudiation of castration and challenge of the Law (Aulagnier and Al. 1967) or their "non-renunciation to the Phallic mother" to avoid "the Real of sexual difference" (Dor 1987).[1] Similarly, transidentities have been considered as "narcissism disorders" that expel all elaboration out in the body or in acts (Chiland 2005). In Lacanian analyses, they are said to mistake the organ – the penis – for the function – the phallus – (Lacan 2011; Czermak 1982; Frignet 2000; Morel 2004), which constitutes them as the "paradigm of the sexual identity pathology that lies in every psychotic organisation" (Czermak 1996, p. 15).[2]

Most of these analyses refer to the Symbolic, a Lacanian or Lacan-inspired register of transcendental, universal rules that determine subjectivity and the "normal" processes of subjectivation. An intertwining of multiple chains of signifiers, this "Realm of the Law", is a language-mediated order: it relies on the conception of a verbal Unconscious. Although Lacan moved away from the primacy of the Symbolic in the 1970s, part of his legacy, for both Lacanian and non-Lacanian psychoanalysts, remained linked to these "Symbols [that] in fact envelop the life of man in a network so total that they join together (…), so total that they bring to his birth … the shape of destiny" (Lacan1966). This determination of subjective destinies has often been the criterion used by various psychoanalysts to evaluate and condemn non-intelligible gender and sexuality configurations. This perspective raises the question of the effect of a structuralist conception of the Unconscious on human lives, and on the constitution of "lives worth living" (Butler 2014, p. 62).

For many psychoanalysts, because he fails to capture the linguistic dimension of the Unconscious, Merleau-Ponty develops a misconstrued phenomenological version of the Unconscious. However, to which extent may a non-language-based conception of the Unconscious avoid imposing universal subjectivation categories that stretch beyond history and culture? The aim of this chapter is to show how Merleau-Ponty's non-exclusively-verbal Unconscious is concerned with affect, a perspective that entails a different, not exclusively linguistic conception of the Symbolic. For that purpose, I will argue that Merleau-Ponty's phenomenology, differently from Husserl's, is a phenomenology of affectivity. Expatiating on the centrality of the lived body, it moves away from constitution to institution, in a way that places affectivity, and not language, at the core of the Unconscious. This conception results in

---

[1] About psychoanalytical theories on perversion, cf. Ayouch (2014).
[2] About psychoanalytical theories on transidentities, cf. Ayouch (2015).

two consequences: first, the Unconscious is not, or not entirely verbal, which, second, implies the possibility of a non-binary reading of gender and sexuality.

I will first present how Merleau-Ponty's philosophy is what I call a "phenomenology of affectivity", which renders it more likely to account for an affective Unconscious. This perspective brings about much psychoanalytical criticism, which may be addressed if we consider that Merleau-Ponty's research is not so much interested in the Unconscious as in the affect and what I call affect quest for figurability. This poses the question whether this Unconscious is non-verbal, and how it relates to language and the Symbolic. I will then try and show how this non-exclusively-verbal Unconscious may lay the ground for a feminist analysis of gender, through the categories of expression and institution that bear a particular relation to language.

11.2 Rereading Reduction and Constitution

Unlike a phenomenology based on cognitive act-intentionality, Merleau-Ponty's reinterpretation of Husserl gives high priority to affective intentionality. While Merleau-Ponty takes over Husserl's interest for intersubjectivity, he moves away from the Husserlian eidetic method, points out the limitations of reflexive attitude, criticizes the necessity of an absolute rationality and stresses the importance of the originary doxa, and pre-predicative intentionality. This results in a rereading of both Husserlian reduction and constitution. Although Merleau-Ponty maintains the notion of intentionality, he nonetheless parts away from its idealistic implications, and conceives of his work as a development of the "latest" Husserl, whose notions of facticial essences, passive syntheses, and Lebenswelt he chooses to prolong. My purpose is to show that through the reinterpretation of Husserl's reduction and constitution, Merleau-Ponty launches a phenomenology of affectivity that allows conceiving the Unconscious as an affect search for figurability.

11.2.1 From Reduction to Affect Figurability

11.2.1.1 A Reduction to Affectivity

My hypothesis is that Merleau-Ponty's existential reading of transcendental reduction presents it as a reduction to affectivity. The "Foreword" of *Phenomenology of Perception* stresses that reduction is always incomplete[3]: radical reflection always depends on an un-reflexive, initial life (Merleau-Ponty 1945, p. ix). The transcendental level proves inseparable from a being-in-the-world level, as Merleau-Ponty

---

[3] "Le plus grand enseignement de la réduction est l'impossibilité d'une réduction complète" (Merleau-Ponty 1945, p. viii).

does not oppose reflection and perception, phenomenological analysis and naïve attitude in a binary way.

Consequently, reduction sets forth the affective value of the elements it describes: returning to the Lebenswelt, it stresses out an affective perception. *Phenomenology of Perception* targets what is excluded from empiricism: the sad or happy dimension of a landscape, the anger or pain sensed on a face, and the style of a building that prefigures the essence of a city (Merleau-Ponty 1945, p. 32). Giving priority to the Schelerian conception of object as a "unity of value" (ibid., p. 371), Merleau-Ponty underlines the way I may, when a picture was removed from a room, feel the room's transformation without thematizing it, the same way I may feel the presence of a storm or the respect and friendship of other humans as an atmosphere (ibid.). Reduction highlights an affective perception that dwells in things, as the "original faith" that links us to the world: I appear related to the world, the other or to myself through an unthematised affect, feeling, or affective tonality.

In the chapter of *Phenomenology of Perception* dedicated to space, Merleau-Ponty establishes a parallel between general perception and the affective dimension of the perception of others. Objects are perceived through the affective experience of implicated perceptive moments. This experience is made similar to the perception of the other, insofar as it consists in identifying a style. Phenomenological reduction aims at seizing this affective dimension, as Merleau-Ponty points out in many passages, this "more profound life of consciousness under perception" (Merleau-Ponty 1945, p. 327). The "subjective past" and "secret act" supposed by every perception (ibid., p. 326) seem similar to a fantasmatic unconscious inscription of perception. Yet this stratum is not, *stricto sensu*, only unconscious. It is rather akin to the Freudian pre-conscious, insofar as it appears as an affective atmosphere common to both unconscious and preconscious ideas, introducing continuity between consciousness and the Unconscious.

11.2.1.2 A Problematic Conception of the Unconscious

This continuity certainly constitutes the main divergence between Merleau-Ponty's conception of the Unconscious, and that of Freudian or Lacanian psychoanalysis.[4] The Unconscious is conceived by Merleau-Ponty as a continuation of consciousness, and lodged at its heart. Throughout his work, from *Phenomenology of Perception* to *The Visible and the Invisible*, the Unconscious alternatively refers to un-reflexive intentionality, latency, imperceptions at the core of perception, blindness at the centre of consciousness, the invisible, a negative figure, simultaneous presence and absence, a hinge between the self and the world, or a background on which forms appear. For psychoanalysts, this sense of an Unconscious not separated from consciousness boils down to the pre-conscious. According to J.B. Pontalis (1961/1993), Merleau-Ponty fails to grasp the very specificity of the Unconscious when reducing it to the implicit, ambiguous, or overdetermined dimension of

---

[4] Cf. Ayouch (2012, 2009a, b).

existence. Merleau-Ponty's subject-centred philosophy of sense tries to account for the Unconscious through a theory of the sensitive body. On the contrary, structure-centred psychoanalysis would decentre the subject and give priority to anonymous processes taking place through the subject, in which linguistic and unconscious mechanisms compare in no way to perceptive ones. In this respect, a philosophy of the perceptive body, according to Pontalis, can only bring about a misconception of the Freudian theory.

Similarly, André Green (1964) stresses that for Freud, the body is originally libidinal, whereas for Merleau-Ponty it proves only secondarily related to desire. The pre-reflective, impersonal subject that Merleau-Ponty reveals does not correspond to the barred, separated subject of the Unconscious: Merleau-Ponty's phenomenology stops at the preconscious. The impersonal dimension of the body, and even the non-subject-centred perspective of the philosophy of flesh fail to render unconscious primary processes. They remain linked, though indirectly, to consciousness. The Unconscious is in no way similar to ambiguous perception, nor to imperception, it is not only the other side of perception, but defines, Green reminds, as the "other scene".

Even more severe is Lacan's critique (1961a, b), when he states that Merleau-Ponty fails to comprehend the Symbolic, and does not conceive of reality as the result of a net of signifiers. Lacan asserts that by giving priority to a presence through the body, phenomenology remains stuck to the Imaginary. And Castoriadis (1971) maintains this critique of Merleau-Ponty's failure to apprehend the Symbolic.

These four psychoanalysts agree that what Merleau-Ponty presents as the Unconscious, linked to the lived body, is no way akin to the structural, fundamentally linguistic psychoanalytical Unconscious. The continuity he maintains between the perceptive and the symbolic level is what prevents Merleau-Ponty from giving a separate, linguistic, non-phenomenal status to the Unconscious. Let us now consider how this phenomenological version of the Unconscious is more concerned with affect.

11.2.1.3 Affect Search for Figurability

If, for Merleau-Ponty, the body becomes impersonal, abandons itself to sleep or to sexual excitement, if it experiences the pathological phenomena of the phantom limb or anosognosia, if it anonymously tends towards the world in an always already made and non-thematisable synthesis, that is because it proceeds neither from a representative nor from an objective stream, but from an affective one. The generality and "depersonalization" of the body are signs of what I conceive of as a Merleau-Pontian "phenomenology of affectivity", that aims at a particular sense of the Unconscious: that of the affect.

In Freudian metapsychology (1915b), a drive has two representatives: the ideational-representative (Vorstellungsrepresentanz) and the affect. Every psychic act has a primary instinctual moment, after which the ideational-representative of the drive remains in the Unconscious. This unconscious dimension remains radically separated from consciousness, unless repression is lifted. Yet this separation between consciousness and the Unconscious applies only to ideas and not to affects. The latter, Freud argues in many texts, circulate more freely from soma to psyche and from one agency to another. Placed between the body and the ego, consciousness and the Unconscious, the affect operates a transition between psychic systems, and stretches beyond the topic, dynamic and economic opposition of consciousness and the Unconscious, or primary and secondary processe.[5] Affect is then, I believe, the metapsychological category that should make it possible to bridge the gap between a phenomenology of the body and Freudian psychoanalysis.

In other words, if the psychoanalytical critique of Merleau-Ponty's indivision conception of the Unconscious seems perfectly legitimate as far as the ideational-representatives of drives are concerned, it fails to apply to affects, both conscious and unconscious. The topic, dynamic and economic limit between the Unconscious and consciousness doesn't stop affects as it stops ideas, but rather transforms them. Merleau-Ponty's phenomenology of affectivity aims to cross this limit in order to reveal the unconscious affects sedimented in the conscious affects. It thus tackles what I call the affect search for figurability. When speaking of drives, Freud introduces the notion of "work": a measure of the demand made upon the mind in consequence to its connection with the body (Freud 1915b), a transformation of free energy into bound energy. This notion enables me to conceive of the affect movement as a search for figurability. Figurability is not a representation or idea, Vorstellung, referring to a mental image, but a direct presentation, Darstellung. This presentation corresponds to a work of figuration operated by the affect when it crosses over from the Unconscious to consciousness. In other words, non-verbal bodily affectivity strives here for symbolization. This affect search for figurability that I choose to read in Merleau-Ponty entails a different conception of constitution.

11.2.2 A Non-constituent Constitution

11.2.2.1 Incarnate Constitution

If Merleau-Ponty refutes idealism in *Phenomenology of Perception*, it is in order to detach constitution from any absolute, a-temporal and a-cosmic consciousness. Husserl opposed the absoluteness of the experience of the pure ego and the contingency of the perceived, which always presents itself in progressive sketches

---

[5] Strictly speaking, the affect cannot be unconscious. Freud mentions "unconscious affects" only in a second sens : an instinctual impulse, as he writes in "Notes on the Unconscious" (1915a), means an impulse whose ideational-representative (*Vorstellungsrepräsentanz*) is unconscious, and strictly speaking, there are no unconscious affects similar to the unconscious ideas. Yet, we could speak of unconscious affects to refer to the displacement of an affect from a repressed idea to a conscious one : the affect is felt, yet not recognised. In another context, an affect can be considered unconscious when it is transformed into a qualitatively different affect, mainly anxiety, or suppressed. The unconscious affects are those revealed to consciousness once repression is lifted. In other words, unconscious affects are never directly attested: they prove always differed.

(Husserl 1950, § 42). Merleau-Ponty, to the contrary, questions the very apodicticity of the pure ego, and refuses the conception of a constituent transcendental subject who would unify the multiple Erlebnisse. To that subject, he opposes a self-affected incarnate one, assumed by the perceiving body (Merleau-Ponty 1945, p. 247). Constitution does not refer to a constitutive act of synthetic consciousness, but rather to a pre-given bodily synthesis (Merleau-Ponty 1945, p. 275). Let us now show that this bodily constitution is essentially affective.

11.2.2.2 Operative Intentionality and Motricity

One of the specificities of Merleau-Ponty's phenomenology is to lay emphasis on operative intentionality (fungierende Intentionalität) much more than act intentionality. In the latter, every "consciousness act" – perception, imagination, remembrance, dream, – poses a perceived, imagined, remembered or dreamt object. Operative intentionality, on the contrary, does not pose any object: it frees the world, the other and the self from any analytical perspective, and is the basis of the natural and ante-predicative unity of the world with our lives. It appears in our desires, expectations or affections more clearly than in any objective knowledge (Merleau-Ponty 1945, p. xiii). The corporeal experience is the centre of such intentionality: we often inhabit our lived body without thematizing it as the perceived or reflective object of a subject. Operative intentionality extends to various acts: Merleau-Ponty applies it to language, to early childhood experiences or to intersubjective comprehension. This intentional activity links external perception to the affective psychic reality that grounds it.

Furthermore, Merleau-Ponty redefines operative intentionality as a motor intentionality: he underlines Husserl's notion of consciousness as "I can", a movement which is distinct from knowledge. The motor experience of the body is a way to relate to the world, a "praktognosis" which allows my body to apprehend the world in an affective, and not ideational way. This intentionality is, in my hypothesis, an affective movement which shapes every perception (internal or external) and whose sense remains non-thematized. It corresponds to the affect search for figurability.

11.2.2.3 From Intentionality to Affect

If, in *Phenomenology of Perception*, operative intentionality still proceeded from an – albeit non-reflexive – consciousness, in *The Visible and the Invisible*, it is conceived of as the gap (*écart*) in the sensitive being from which the sentient proceeds. Thus, in a work note, Merleau-Ponty advocates for a "reform of consciousness" in which "affectivity structures are as constituent as the others" (Merleau-Ponty 1960a, p. 292). Even more, in this reformed consciousness, "representative sensation too (…) is affection, being a presence to the world through the body and to the body through the world, being flesh" (ibid.).

This non-representative non-ideational intentionality is comparable to desire. For R. Barbaras (1999), Merleau-Ponty presents us with a non-representative, affective or volitional relation to objects, which does not reduce perception to an objectifying act submitted to knowledge categories. Barbaras interprets it as a profound movement, a tension and aspiration intentionality, an originary desire greater than any form of lack, defined as pure overflowing (Barbaras 1999, p. 136). Differently from Barbaras who metaphysically extends this desire to every living creature (ibid., p. 146), and presents it as a vital stream, I contend that desire is specific to the human drive (the Freudian Trieb). Contrary to instinct, which is cyclical, characteristic of a species, and has fixed objects, drive is untimely, individual, and its object is interchangeable.

However, is it correct to assimilate operative intentionality to non-intentional drive? If drive is a "concept on the frontier between the psychic and the somatic" (Freud1915b), its somatic part cannot be reduced to any psychic intentionality. If drives have a teleological "goal intentionality" (Benoist 2006, p. 120) which orients them towards satisfaction, they raise the question of an anonymous will, detached from any consciousness, a paradoxical intentionality with no intention, a border, blind intentionality (ibid., p. 126).

Insofar as it is motor, desire-like and a-representative, operative intentionality is a "goal intentionality" too. Yet it is distinct from the non-intentionality of drives, which cannot be reached by any phenomenological approach, because it exceeds attestation. If I say that operative intentionality is affective, it is by conceiving it as the "emerged part of the iceberg" of an affect movement which lost its significance when it transited from the Unconscious to consciousness, an affect movement which is, I would argue, in search for figurability.

As a result, when Merleau-Ponty points at a Nothingness at the core of Being (Merleau-Ponty 1960a), analyses the invisible that structures visibility, and conceives the Unconscious as the Nichtürpräsentierbar at the centre of presence (ibid, p. 308), he is designating, in my view, the non-figurable part of this desiring intentionality, and pointing out the "immerged part of the iceberg", the non-intentional dimension of drive.

Because it refutes the traditional categories of subject and object, the reversibility of flesh (ibid.) may reveal the "a-subjective subject" of the affect. What Merleau-Ponty calls invisible "lining" of the visible is, in my reading, the affect: an a-representative movement that underlies every representation or idea. Analysing the relation between Merleau-Ponty and Lacan, B. Baas (1996, 1998) draws a parallel between the reversal of sensitive into sentient and the drive reversals evoked by Freud (1915b). The similarity lies, in my opinion, only in the affect part of the drive. When "seeing" becomes "being seen", as voyeurism turns into exhibitionism, it is through a movement which is not ideational, but affective. The interchangeability of subject and object in the drive reversal is akin to the conversion of sensitive into sentient in the flesh. The "fundamental narcissism of all vision" (Merleau-Ponty 1960a, p. 183) seems to account for the middle, reflexive form of "seeing oneself", intermediate between "seeing" and "being seen". The "gap", the irreducible non-coincidence between sensitive and sentient is, in my view, the non-figurability that is at the basis of affects.

Constituent constitution, the "professional imposture of the philosopher" (ibid., p. 233), is then only an artefact constructed upon a primary affectivity. In other words, there is no primary thought but a primary perception, which is characteristic of what Merleau-Ponty calls the "sensitive cogito".

11.2.2.4 Sensitive Cogito and Language

The constituent body is a felt body that produces what Merleau-Ponty calls the "tacit cogito", an affective experience whose relation to language is particular. Reverting the Cartesian cogito, Merleau-Ponty deduces the certainty of the thoughts of loving, hating, or wanting from the effective existence of my acts of love, hatred or will (Merleau-Ponty 1945, p. 430). Sum ergo cogito, Merleau-Ponty seems to say: the thought of my existence is derived from the fact that I exist (ibid., p. 439). The cogito is first un-reflexive and intimate; it is more of a current of existence, a pre-reflexive life than a subjectivity that would constitute the world. The opacity of the tacit cogito is akin to the non-figurability at the basis of affects.

However, in his later works, and particularly in *The Visible and the Invisible*, Merleau-Ponty contests the tacit cogito, refuting both its subjective and silent dimensions (Merleau-Ponty 1960a, pp. 224–225, 232–233). The idea of thinking is inseparable from words: constituent consciousness and the transcendental attitude proceed from words, not as positive but as diacritic significations (Merleau-Ponty 1960a, p. 225). The reference to the self, previously defined in the tacit cogito, stems from a linguistic division. The diacritic meaning results from the fact that the "world of silence" is already inscribed in language: this place, at the base of what we shall now call the "sensitive cogito", an affectivity previously determined by language. Yet what is the extent of this determination? The "Merleau-Pontian Unconscious" seems to be more concerned with affects than ideas: its links with language are not as clear as for the Freudian Unconscious (thing-representations – Sach-Vorstellungen – dissociated from word-representations – Wort-Vorstellungen) or the Lacanian Unconscious, structured as a language. It seems important to try and define whether this affective Unconscious, which I conceive of as an affect search for figurability, is merely non-verbal, and what characterizes its relation to language.

11.3 Non-verbal Unconscious?

11.3.1 Language, Body and Expression

Language is essentially approached by Merleau-Ponty through the category of expressivity. In *Phenomenology of Perception*, the body is compared to a work of art insofar as it realises a fusion between expression and the expressed:

> A novel, poem, picture, musical work are individuals, that is beings in which the expression is undistinguishable from the thing expressed, their meaning accessible only through direct contact, being radiated with no change of their temporal and spatial situation. It is in this

sense that our body is comparable to a work of art. It is a nexus of living meanings....
(Merleau-Ponty 1945, p. 176)

The body is the expression of existence in the sense that speech expresses thought: it realises the sense of existence in a fusion between expression and what is expressed. This notion of expression is precisely what enables Merleau-Ponty to relate sexuality to existence: sexuality "expresses existence" through bodily being, it reveals how corporality produces meaning (ibid., p. 183).

Considering the body as the source of expression, Merleau-Ponty conceives of speech as an articulate continuation of bodily gestures. Linguistic articulation is but a conduct by which the body confers meaning to the world, and which carries on the perceptive organisation. Consequently, for Merleau-Ponty, the level of corporality is not distinct from that of language: it even constitutes its carnal basis. Merleau-Ponty's approach of language ends up reforming it entirely, as he mutually roots it in the body, and institutes the body into language and culture, through the concept of expression.

This conception is resumed in the *Prose of the World*: corporality and perception are already expressive, in a "primordial expression" that happens with and despite me, and can be captured in a "secondary work" of expression (Merleau-Ponty 1969, pp. 106–112). The affect search for figurability I read in Merleau-Ponty's phenomenology is definitely linked to expressivity: what ends up being expressed is one particular figuration of affect.

Yet this body expressivity is quite different from the psychoanalytical conception of the link between body and language. The body expression, an incarnate language, may evoke the way hysterical conversion is a body language; however, it follows a totally different psychic logic. Analysing the pain felt by Fraülen von R… on her leg, Freud asserts that when he pinched her on the painful spot, her features assumed a singular "expression of satisfaction rather than pain" (Breuer and Freud 1895/1971). Elisabeth's body is expressive in a sedimented way: the pain on the thighs and the abasia-astasia experienced by her refer to the conflict between her attraction towards a young man and the necessity to take care of her father, or to the conflict between the concealed desire for her brother-in-law and the moral and social imperatives (Breuer and Freud 1895/1971, p. 116). A compromise between desire and prohibition, the hysterical symptom is an indirect way to realise desire, by disconnecting idea from affect. In the hysterical pain, the idea is repressed and the affect converted: this affect that is "expressed" by the body is the sedimentation of an affect of desire towards a man, moral prohibition and the final satisfaction guaranteed by the symptom.

However, the hysterical symptom appears on a body already invested by language. Let us recall, for instance, how Elisabeth gathers her memories according to the standing, lying or sitting positions of her body, which are themselves lived and felt through verbal categories. Freud reminds how she is literally "riveted" when her father is brought back home ill, or when she is standing still in front of her dead sister's bed. Her abasia-astasia can also be related to her loneliness (the German expression translating exactly into "standing alone") and to her incapacity to carry on. The phenomenological continuity between body and language is reversed here: it's not the body that precedes and induces language through its expressivity, just like speech carries out gestures. On the contrary, language precedes the body, which turns out to be lived and felt only through certain words-representation. Elisabeth's body positions refer to another scene, a space of imaginary jouissance linked to language before any perception takes place. As a matter of fact, every subject perceives her/his body only out of a certain symbolization, which makes perception secondary to language.

The psychoanalytical articulation between body and language is therefore exactly opposed to the phenomenological model: the body proceeds from language. On the contrary, in *Phenomenology of perception*, language is founded on incarnation and draws meaning from it. Actually, for Merleau-Ponty, body and language prove mutually founded; their relation follows the Husserlian Fundierung, a category aiming to overcome any strict separation between founding and founded:

> The relation of reason to fact, or eternity to time, like that of reflection to the unreflective, of thought to language, or of thought to perception is this two-way relationship that phenomenology called Fundierung: the founding term – time, the unreflective, the fact, language, perception – is primary in the sense that the founded gives itself as a determination or explication of the founding, which is what prevents the founded from ever resorbing the founding, and yet the founding is not primary in an empiricist sense, and the founded is not simply derived, for it is through the founded that the founding manifests itself. (Merleau-Ponty 1945, p. 451)

The relation between language and the body is circular: they found each other. Yet Merleau-Ponty's approach suggests that more than any language, intersubjective relations are what determine the fantasmatic construction of the body. This point proves quite important: it concerns the primacy of the Symbolic and the question of whether it is determined only linguistically (in a structuralist approach), and whether it necessarily precedes every phenomenon. Merleau-Ponty's conception of the mutual foundation of language and body through expression and their intersubjective common source then offers a distinct possibility for the Symbolic. I would link the affect quest for figurability to this notion of expression.

Remembering that Merleau-Ponty's conception of sexuality in *Phenomenology of Perception* is closely linked to his theory of expression, I contend that the affect search for figurability (linked here to expressivity) is more likely to give a non-pathologising account of the unconscious processes of non-binary gender and sexuality configurations. To understand how, it seems necessary to discuss the idea of the Symbolic as conceived of by Lacanian psychoanalysis and the controversies it brings about.

11.3.2 A Linguistic Symbolic?

As previously stated, Lacan (1961a, b) reproaches Merleau-Ponty for his failure to comprehend the Symbolic and consider reality as the result of a net of signifiers. For Lacan, the incarnate subject – massively conceived of as an imaginary Ego – is poles apart from the subject constituted by language and resulting from the chain of signifiers.

We are here confronted with two opposite versions of the Unconscious. The phenomenological Unconscious traces back to a primordial perception: it is a stratum that seems previous to codification, and stems from the body impersonalisation. Its paradigm is the passive synthesis (Husserl 1998): it lies in the progressive blurring of impressions, the last step of the disappearing retention, or the zero degree of intuitive donation. Differently, the symbolical Unconscious is articulated by a symbolic institution, basically linked to language. It proceeds from the structure of signifiers and the big Other, does not result from any perception, but precisely from the lacks, gaps and holes of the perceptive system. Its paradigm is the repetition automatism, a missed encounter with perception. It is the reason of the subjective division.

I contend that the affect quest for figurability I find in Merleau-Ponty's phenomenology of affectivity partakes from both the phenomenological and the symbolical Unconscious. Consequently, it may present a version of the Lacanian Symbolic which is neither strictly linguistic nor fixed and eternal.

Merleau-Ponty indeed refuses the primacy of language and often expresses discontent when excessive importance is given to language.[6] This scepticism towards an exclusively structuralist conception of the Unconscious is actually shared by Judith Butler, when she criticises a too rigid Lacanian conception of the Law. She does so in order to try and go beyond binary conceptions of gender and sexuality in Gender Trouble, when questioning the plausibility of a Symbolic "that requires a conformity to the Law that proves impossible to perform and that makes no room for the flexibility of the Law itself, its cultural reformulation in more plastic forms" (Butler 1990).

Butler resumes this critique in *Undoing Gender*, in order to show how the gendered subject emerges insofar as s/he is subjected to the social regulation of norms. Certain Lacanian theorists distinguish between social and symbolic norms, and consider the latter as the universal "realm of the Law that regulates desire". In response to this conception, Butler aims to show that the distinction between the symbolic and social law cannot be maintained, and that the Symbolic is but the sedimentation of social practices (Butler 2012, pp. 61–62).

The Lacanian Symbolic, though, is defined along the conception that linguistic structures are radically irreducible to the social forms of language. Consequently, for many Lacanians, the symbolic norm is conceived of as a-temporal and universal, and should be distinguished from actual social positions (the position of the father, a symbolic paradigmatic position, is not to be mistaken for the socially changing position of fathers, and should not be transformed by any social reorganisation of paternity). If I here take up and resume Butler's reading of Lacanian versions of the Symbolic, I would like, though, to clearly state, as Butler does too, that a strictly linguistic transcendental version of the Symbolic is not Lacan's concern – as the

---

[6] He expresses "discomfort in seeing the category of language take up all the room" (Ey 1966, p. 173), criticizes the "ridiculous plays on words" (Merleau-Ponty 2000, p. 279) in some versions of psychoanalysis, or states, right after Lacan's intervention in the Société française de philosophie, that "language cannot be reduced to puns" (Merleau-Ponty 1960b/2000).

Symbolic cannot be conceived of separately from the Imaginary and the Real, and Lacan's first structuralist perspective gives way to a focus on the Real rather than on the Symbolic. Yet this strictly linguistic universal register of transcendental rules certainly characterizes the reading of various Lacanian theorists. The problem, according to Butler, consists in considering parenthood positions as fundamental linguistic structures, elementary structures of intelligibility (Butler 2012, p. 62). On the contrary, Butler urges to consider every symbolic position as a contingent norm whose contingency was obscured by a theoretic reification. Thinking that the Symbolic may be changed by human practice is not merely voluntaristic, nor is it a way to regress to the Imaginary Ego. It is a way to consider the symbolic norm as mainly historical, and likely to be transformed and subverted from within. This ends up having a highly important consequence on non-binary gender and sexuality configurations, as they are often classified in psychopathological categories for not being in keeping with the usual binary categories of the Symbolic. Therefore, when the Symbolic is not conceived as merely linguistic, permanent and primarily psychic, its components (the phallus, sexual difference, the Name-of-the-Father, and the categories of father, mother, woman and man) appear as non-universal, non-necessary and non-transcendental categories that actually result from sedimented social norms.

The notion of affect quest for figurability that I find in Merleau-Ponty, linked to his questioning of a merely linguistic and an-historical Unconscious, is likely to account for non-binary gender and sexuality configurations. It confirms how Merleau-Ponty's non-binary phenomenology may enable a feminist stance. To analyse how, it seems important, first, to address the feminist critiques directed to Merleau-Ponty, in order to see how his non-exclusively verbal conception of the Unconscious may pave the way for a non-binary feminism.

11.4 Feminist Merleau-Ponty?

11.4.1 Feminist Criticism

Feminist readings of Merleau-Ponty have often set forth the implicit androcentrism of his perspective, and the way he neglects specific feminine embodiment and sexuality experiences. For Luce Irigaray (1984), Merleau-Ponty is in debt to feminity and maternity: the flesh owes many of its aspects to the feminine, which nevertheless remains unspoken and disembodied. Irigaray refutes the primacy of vision in the philosophy of the flesh: replacing other senses, vision partakes from a phallic economy that represents the feminine as a lack or a blind spot. On the contrary, the visible stems from the intrauterine tactile experience, followed by the mother's voice: the per-personal realm of flesh is maternal-feminine, a dimension Merleau-Ponty leaves aside.

For Iris Marion Young (1990) too, though Merleau-Ponty locates subjectivity in the body, providing great insights about the structure of human embodiment, he fails to account for specifically feminine experiences, such as that of the breasted existence or pregnancy. She stresses how the relations between subject and object or subject and other are not the same for women, and discusses the specific motility of the female body.

While Sonia Kruks (2001) resumes the critique of the apparently non-gendered generality of the body thematized by Merleau-Ponty, Michèle Le Doeuf (1998) believes that the visible is a female body seen from the standpoint of a man, within a general structure of power. Shannon Sullivan (1997) pursues Irigaray's critique of Merleau-Ponty's solipsism that results from erasing individual differences: imposing a commonality upon different bodies whose gender, sexuality, class, nationality, race and upbringing have been effaced, Merleau-Ponty impedes the dialogue between embodied subjects.

Last but not least, Judith Butler (1988) pays tribute to Merleau-Ponty's conception of the body as both an historical idea and a set of possibilities to be continually realised. Yet, while phenomenology sets forth the various acts by which cultural and gender identity is constructed, it fails to grasp that collective sedimentation by taking constituting acts to be its point of departure. More significantly, in another text (Butler 1989), after praising Merleau-Ponty for his conception of sexuality as a modality of existence, she denounces the androcentrism of his perspective. The French philosopher considers only male bodies, within unquestioned cultural constructions of sexual normalcy, and never asks whose sexuality and whose bodies are being taken into account.

Most of these analyses underline the phallocentrim of an apparently gender-neutral perspective that turns out to be that of a male, white, straight and cis-centred body. Yet if these readings succeed in presenting phenomenology's aspiration to universalism as one among other possible particularisms, when some of them conjure up a radically different female body, they end up producing binary differentialism. This raises the question of how to escape androcentrism without falling in an essentialisation of sexual difference.

To address these critiques, let us start observing that if Merleau-Ponty perpetuates, most probably unwillingly, the unspoken assumption of masculinity the Western system of philosophy is based on and tries to efface, he does not, however, resume any gender binary. From the Phenomenology of perception to the Visible and Invisible, Merleau-Ponty refuses conceptual or real binary, blurring the boundaries between sensation and intellection, empiricism and rationalism, perception and imagination, reflection and the un-reflexive, the other and the self, being-in-itself and for-itself. Doing so, he destabilizes the traditional oppositions of Western philosophy and refutes the very terrain of dualisms. Just like he is more concerned with the space between the subject and the other rather than by their opposition, his philosophy extends in the space in between binary pairs. It seems fair to ask whether this episteme disruption is not likely to serve for a feminism that wishes to subvert identities and go beyond gender binary, a feminism questioning the idea that naturalised woman is the subject of feminism.

Let us consider that when some of these feminist readers try and found a phenomenology on the specificity of the female body – involving breasts and pregnancy (Young 1990), maternity and the vulva (Irigaray 1984) considered as non-masculine experiences – they essentialise a body-based femaleness. Having breasts or a vulva not necessarily defines femaleness (as shown by trans men for instance), and pregnancy is only a particular use of the body culturally associated with feminity, in a disjunctive oppositional gender order. As a matter of fact, historically, first and second generation feminisms have often summoned the category of woman as a universal. While this category aims to depose the false universal of man, and account for the specificity of women and their oppression, it perpetuates, nonetheless, an essentialisation of woman.

When Merleau-Ponty supposes a pre-cultural, phenomenological primacy of perception, he indeed conjures up the possibility for two conventionally distinct body experiences – female and male – both centred on the pre-reflective lived body. However, when acknowledging that any perception experience is always pre-formated, determined, inscribed in a symbolic organization (this symbolic being not exclusively linguistic, but intersubjective and characteristic of the cultural world), these "male" and "female" body experiences turn out to proceed from cultural assignments of "maleness" and "femaleness" (defined in a discrete opposition). Once again, Merleau-Ponty's use of dialectic thought, and his resorting to the notion of Fundierung may allow to move away from any essentialist or structuralist perspective. More clearly, because it is at the basis of perception, the body is the starting point for having a cultural world. Yet, on the other hand, because my body is not separated from other bodies and always included in an intersubjective context, the cultural world is also the starting point for having a body. In other words, if there are various subjective experiences defined by the specificity of a particular corporality, this corporality is made significant only in a cultural context that assigns functions and meanings to its particularities.

The question that some of the mentioned feminist readings raise is whether we leave aside a particular experience when we don't specifically centre phenomenology on womanly experience. Further on, to which extent is this experience womanly, and to which extent is it missed by those traditionally assigned as men? Let us observe that no large scale "female" or "male" phenomenology is likely to render two global experiences of the body, because there are only multiple ways to be a woman or a man. Merleau-Ponty's focus on lived experience and body proper, poles apart from any universalist and transcendental eidetic, provides a unique way to account for multiple, diverse lived experiences outside of any generalizing theoretical paradigm. Merleau-Ponty's gender-neutrality indicted by those readings does not aim for androcentric universality, but rather for multiplicity. It is true that the historical context of his writings (the forties and the fifties) could hardly allow escaping the general phallogocentrism. Yet his non-dichotomic thought aimed at subverting this very stance. Since Merleau-Ponty does not explicitly tackle the question of gender, and refutes any disjunctive binarity in thought, we could surmise that his phenomenology is more open to gender fluidity and ambiguity, and extends beyond any differentialist definition of female or male body experience.

Merleau-Ponty's phenomenology is then neither androcentric and misogynist nor binarist and differentialist: it seems to give ground to a queer phenomenology. Let us now consider more closely this "gender-trouble phenomenology", addressing Judith Butler's critique of the category of expression and the way Merleau-Ponty could respond to it.

11.4.2 Expressivity, Language and Sedimentation

11.4.2.1 Butler's Criticism of Expressivity

In "Performative Acts and Gender Constitution" (Butler 1988), J. Butler purports to show how gender is a performative accomplishment imposed by social sanction and taboo, using tools drawn from theatrical and phenomenological discourses. Gender is conceived of as a performance, a doing, that follows the strategic aim of maintaining a binary frame. Yet gender is not a fact or an essence externalised by the body: the acts of gender are what creates gender, and conceal its performative genesis in order to produce the belief of gender necessity and naturalness.

In this formulation of gender, the model of expressivity is refuted by Butler, for the risk of essentialism it conveys. To expressivity, she opposes performativity: gender comes into existence only in the very moment of its performative constitution, which means that it does not pre-exist the acts that perform it. As a consequence, performativity is to be distinguished both from performance, which presumes a subject prior to his/her acts, and from expression, which, for Butler, similarly implies an "I" as a disembodied agency preceding and directing its constitutive acts and embodiment.

More precisely, Butler states that expressivity theories that conceive of acts and gestures as expressive of gender "suggest[s] that gender itself is something prior to the various acts, postures and gestures by which it is dramatized and known" (Butler 1988, p. 528). Gender appears then as a "substantial core" or "the spiritual or psychological correlate of biological sex". On the contrary, when gender attributes and acts are not apprehended as expressive but as performative, they effectively constitute the identity they are said to express or reveal. That gender be performative means that it is real only to the extent that it is performed, that there is no pre-existing identity giving sense to acts or attributes, and that the very notions of an essential sex, or a correct, true gender "are also constituted as part of the strategy by which the performative aspect of gender is concealed" (ibid., p. 529).

11.4.2.2 From Expressivity to Discourse

Does this critique of expressivity as a separation of subject and acts apply to Merleau-Ponty? I previously underlined how Merleau-Ponty's notion of expression implies a fusion between expression and what is expressed. If sexuality expresses existence through bodily being, it is because the role of the body is to ensure the metamorphosis of ideas into things. The body is symbolic insofar as it "can symbolise existence because it realises it and it is its actuality" (Merleau-Ponty 1945, pp. 191–192). The claim that the body is responsible for the realisation of existence (and is not only an outward expression of an essence) is quite akin to Judith Butler's refusal to dissociate an "inner identity" from the acts and gestures that express it. As Sylvia Stoller writes, "just as Butler rejects the very assumption that somebody exists before the performative act, Merleau-Ponty rejects the assumption that somebody exists before his or her expressive acts" (Stoller 2010, p. 108).

As a matter of fact, the apparent divergence between Merleau-Ponty and Butler regarding expression lies in the extension of the category of discourse used by Butler. While Merleau-Ponty is apparently more concerned with the lived body than with speech, discourses are central in Butler's concept of performativity. It is, once again, the status of language that is at stake, particularly as far as the Symbolic is concerned. Merleau-Ponty conceives of language as an articulatory gesture, founded in the body. As a result, there is, for Merleau-Ponty, no distinction between a "primary" world of "natural behaviours" and a secondary "cultural, spiritual or fabricated world": both realise the same expressive phenomenon and both are neither natural nor cultural. As a matter of fact, as Merleau-Ponty states:

> It is no more natural, nor less conventional, to shout in anger or to kiss in love than to call a table 'a table'. Feelings and passional conduct are invented like words. Even those which like paternity seem to be part and parcel of the human make-up are in reality institutions. It is impossible to superimpose on man a lower layer of behaviour which one chooses to call 'natural' followed by a manufactured cultural or spiritual world. Everything is both manufactured and natural in man as it were in the sense that there is not a word, not a form of behaviour which does not owe something to purely biological being and which at the same time does not elude the simplicity of animal life and cause forms of vital behaviour to deviate from their pre-ordained direction through a sort of leakage and through a genius for ambiguity which might serve to define man. (Merleau-Ponty 1945, pp. 220–221)

Here, Merleau-Ponty remarkably points out the irreducible symbolic pre-structuration of any phenomenological phenomenon, which gives high priority to the symbolic norms that form our bodies and confer them meaning. In this respect, his conception is very close to Butler's symbolic norms as responsible for body intelligibility – and, thus, for un-intelligible forms of life, considered as abject for not being gender-binary.

Yet, for Merleau-Ponty, what differentiates language form any other expressive modality is sedimentation: "of all the expressive operations, speech alone is capable of sedimenting and constituting an intersubjective acquisition" (Merleau-Ponty 1945, p. 221). With language, the meaning produced by expression does not vanish away when the event of expression is over, but persists, and implies a possibility of indefinite reiteration. This sedimentation characteristic of language seems quite close to Butler's conception of the Symbolic as the sedimentation of social practices (Butler 2012, pp. 61–62). However, in Merleau-Pontian terms, those social practices are rather conceived of as cultural intersubjectivity, and not as discourses.

Furthermore, Merleau-Ponty's theory of expression may even account for Butler's notions of intelligibility and subversion, through the difference he establishes between "speaking speech" and "spoken speech". The former refers to the signifying intention in *statu nascendi*, and the latter to the sedimented acquisition of speech acts. When speaking, I don't begin an absolutely new task, as I rely on established significations, "spoken speech"; yet I am not absolutely determined by a system of which I would be only an effect, and I can indefinitely repeat the expressive operation in *statu nascendi*. This distinction is resumed in terms of "speaking" and "spoken language" (Merleau-Ponty 1969). In literature, spoken language is brought along by the reader, it is a mass of already available significations, and "speaking language" is the new way a text calls out to a reader, an operation by which available significations produce a new one (Merleau-Ponty 1969, p. 20).

Spoken speech is then a sedimentation of speaking speech: this explains how expressive gestures can both be intelligible, constitute meaning (considered as spoken speech), and be creative (as speaking speech). In Butlerian terms, this is why gender, considered of as a performative repetition, may contain the very subversion of this repetition. Gender is conceived of as the mechanism by which the notions of male and female are produced and naturalized, but also by which they can be deconstructed and denaturalized: gender normative positions and non-binary gender-transformations equally belong to gender (Butler 2004, p. 59), precisely because there is room for subversion in repetition, for speaking speech within spoken speech. If, as Butler states, bodies are discursively constructed (as male or female, heterosexual or homosexual) through the reiteration of discursive practices, their queer deconstruction can be apprehended precisely through this Merleau-Pontian distinction between spoken and speaking speech.

As a consequence, it appears that when Butler comprehends social practices as discourses, she not only resumes Foucault's category of discourse, but also extends Merleau-Ponty's conception of language as sedimentation. This extension is actually performed by Merleau-Ponty himself, in his category of institution: speaking and spoken speech are also referred to as "instituting speech" (Merleau-Ponty 1969, p. 170) and "instituted speech" (Merleau-Ponty 1945, p. 214). Hence the importance of asking the question of affect quest of figurability in new terms: considering that Merleau-Ponty's notion of expressivity is larger than language, yet allows for a conception of language as sedimented spoken speech, and considering that Butler's discursive conception of body dwells on an extension of the category of language (discourse is made akin to social practices), how does the affect quest of figurability relate to language? How does it take place between instituted and instituting speech? Genderwise, how can Merleau-Ponty's conception of institution account for the constructiveness of gender not only socially, but also subjectively, through an Unconscious conceived as instituted affectivity, mid-way between affect and discourse? To answer these questions, it seems relevant to analyse Merleau-Ponty's notion of institution.

11.4.3 Institution, Non-verbal Unconscious and Gender

11.4.3.1 The Concept of Institution

Institution is first an historical concept for Merleau-Ponty[7]: in history the meaning of events is neither imposed "from outside", and projected by a constituent consciousness, nor received "from inside" within an all-encompassing determinism. The notion of institution is called upon by Merleau-Ponty to blur the boundaries between "interior" and "exterior". In 1955, Merleau-Ponty defines it as "symbolic matrixes", contact points that relate humans to nature and to the past, events that appear and disappear without being destroyed (Merleau-Ponty 1955, p. 25).

The meaning of institution is widened in the lectures Merleau-Ponty dedicates to the notion in 1954–1955: it expands over multiple areas, from a subject's bodily personal construction to the sphere of social and historical existence, from the Oedipus complex to a starting love, from parenthood systems to the use of perspective in the history of painting. Instituting a feeling, a work, a knowledge, a cultural field, institution is both a founding action and a subjective, social or political situation.

The main dimension of institution Merleau-Ponty stresses is its possible reactivation:

> By institution we were intending those events of an experience which endow the experience with durable dimensions, in relation to which a whole series of other experiences will make sense, and will form a thinkable sequel or a history – or again the events which deposit in me a sense, not as something surviving or as a residue, but as a call to follow, the demand of a future. (Merleau-Ponty 1968, p. 61)

An event awaiting its completion, institution is what cannot be approached through the former rules of a field, but alters this field and introduces new meanings. Yet this new meaning, an "open signification" (Merleau-Ponty 2003, p. 87) is deposited without being created or constituted. Institution reveals a subterranean logic that allows an "interior circulation between past and future" (Merleau-Ponty 1968, p. 64). This notion bridges the gap between past and present, the self and the other, activity and passivity, but also nature and culture.

This neither-nor position, characteristic of Merleau-Ponty's philosophy in general and of institution in particular, is also what may define gender for Butler:

> As a public action and performative act, gender is not a radical choice or project that reflects a merely individual choice, but neither is it imposed or inscribed upon the individual, as some post-structuralist displacements of the subject would contend. The body is not passively scripted with cultural codes, as if it were a lifeless recipient of wholly pre-given

---

[7] The concept first appears in the *Structure of Behaviour*, linked to Hegel and dialectics (Merleau-Ponty 1942, p. 224). It refers to the Husserlian *Stiftung* in *Phenomenology of Perception*. In "Concerning Marxism" (Merleau-Ponty 1996), the notion of institution allows to understand the ambiguity of history beyond the traditional opposition of mechanism and finalism. But this notion acquires its plain meaning in *The Adventures of dialectics* (Merleau-Ponty 1955), where it is used to replace a conscientialist interpretation of history.

cultural relations. But neither do embodied selves pre-exist the cultural conventions which essentially signify bodies. (Butler 1988, p. 526)

Gender is then neither totally deliberate – a vonluntaristic position – since it depends on symbolic norms, nor totally imposed – a deterministic position – since it requires performative acts, and the possibility of subversion through repetition. It may be apprehended through Merleau-Ponty's notion of institution. Last but not least, on a subjective level, institution is, it seems to me, linked to affectivity: the "symbolic matrixes" deposited by institution reactivate a series of sedimentations called "passivity" by Merleau-Ponty.

11.4.3.2 Institution, Passivity and Gender

Merleau-Ponty's course on institution, in the Collège de France, is actually an introduction to the one on passivity (Merleau-Ponty 2003, p. 157). This notion is approached through an analysis of sleep, dreams, the Unconscious and memory, all manifestations of a being previous to the objective being. Merleau-Ponty refutes both a "frontal passivity", implying to consider the body as the "cause" of sleep, the Unconscious as the "cause" of my actions and the past as the "cause" of my memories, and the total activity of a consciousness for which sleep would be only a content of the transcendental subject, the Unconscious only a refusal to be conscious, and memory only a consciousness of the past.

Combining institution to passivity allows Merleau-Ponty to move away from the concept of a constituent consciousness, while not reducing meaning to an anonymous causality. The institution of corporality is a paradigm of the intertwining of institution and passivity: it merges activity and passive sedimented crystallisations, nature and nurture, life and history. In this respect, institution reveals a subject which remains alien to her/himself, and whose reflexivity may never be completed.

Consequently, for Merleau-Ponty, institution is what takes over passivity, and develops a sense awaiting to be completed, beyond any opposition between a natural substratum and a cultural construction. This notion seems relevant to J. Butler's refutation of gender identities based on naturalised sex difference. In *Gender Trouble* (1990), the philosopher resumes the analysis of "Performative acts and gender constitution" (1988) and problematizes the relation between sex and gender outside of the traditional divorce between nature and nurture: gender is not only a social construction founded on a natural biological sex substratum. There is, for Butler, no ontological nature nor essential anatomic sex difference that may be apprehended out of the culturally and historically instituted signification of sex. Gender is "the very apparatus of production whereby the sexes themselves are established": it designates "the discursive/cultural means by which 'sexed nature' or a 'natural sex' is produced and established as 'prediscursive', prior to culture, a politically neutral surface on which culture acts" (Butler 1990, p. 7).

As previously underlined, the issue of nature and nurture is recurring in Merleau-Ponty's work, and treated as an irreducible circularity. The assertion, in *Phenomenology of Perception*, that "it is impossible to superimpose on man a lower layer of behaviour which one chooses to call 'natural' followed by a manufactured cultural or spiritual world" (Merleau-Ponty 1945, p. 221) is made clearer in *The Visible and the Invisible*:

> The distinction of the two levels (natural and cultural) is, besides, abstract: everything in us is cultural (our Lebenswelt is "subjective") (our perception is culturally historical) and everything in us is natural (even the cultural is based on the polymorphism of Wild Being. (Merleau-Ponty 1960a, p. 307)

Years before Butler, Merleau-Ponty stressed the *a posteriori* construction of nature, and the subsequent opacity of nature that lies in the fact that any apprehension of it always proceeds from a symbolical institution.

The institution of gendered bodies may be seen as consisting in cultural constructs of sex produced by gender assignments. Gender performativity, the repetition of gender attributes that produces the idea of an original model – which does not exist per se but results from this very repetition – can than be interpreted as an institution. This institution reactivates passivities – the natural opacity of bodies, but also previously instituted gender attributes – and perpetuates their instituted signification, through repetition, or may found new instituting significations, through subversion. Here, passivity refers to the illusion of an original – a "natural" woman or man, preceding their cultural institution –, an irreducible opacity that exists only through its instituted repetition. It also refers to all the sedimented institutions that are taken up and repeated, the "instituted speeches" that guarantee reiteration, as opposed to new "instituting speeches" that may open up new gender possibilities. That there is no passivity out of institution may mean that no nature can be apprehended out of a cultural particular point of view, and that "the body is not passively scripted with cultural codes" (Butler 1988, p. 526). That there is no institution out of a reactivated passivity may refer to the fact that no "embodied selves pre-exist the cultural conventions which essentially signify bodies" (ibid.).

As a result, when Butler mentions "gender constitution", asserts that the phenomenological theory of acts "seeks to explain the mundane way in which social agents constitute social reality", evokes the phenomenological "doctrine of constitution", claims that "gender is (…) an identity tenuously constituted in time – an identity instituted through a stylized repetition of acts" or "instituted through acts which are internally discontinuous" (Butler 1988, pp. 519–520), she indifferently uses "constitution" and "institution" as synonyms. Merleau-Ponty's reinterpretation of the Husserlian away from cognitive act intentionality, and his notion of institution provide a phenomenology that may adequately account for gender construction.

Merleau-Ponty's phenomenology of affectivity comprehends the body as a junction of institution and passivity: if there always is, as Merleau-Ponty writes, an anonymous corporal life "which precedes my history and will end it" (Merleau-Ponty 1945, p. 399), it is through a constant institution of my corporal passivity. This conception of the lived body stresses out its affective dimension, and allows conceiving every bodily act and experience as a result of the affect search for figurability. Let us now show how this passivity constantly reactivated by institution which Merleau-Ponty calls "Unconscious" is a phenomenological version of the psychoanalytical notion of "affect.

11.4.3.3 Non-verbal Unconscious and Affect

a. Oneiric Symbolism and Affect

At the core of the theory of passivity that refers to what Merleau-Ponty calls "Unconscious", he develops the notion of oneiric symbolism (Merleau-Ponty 2003, p. 197), conceived as an atmosphere that proceeds from the body. The paradigm of expression is here again quite central: a primordial symbolism, merging expressing and expressed, is taken up by a second symbolism, in the same way passivity is reactivated by institution. This oneiric symbolism adds up an affective stream to consciousness, thus establishing continuity between consciousness and the Unconscious. It applies both to dream and perception, since, as Merleau-Ponty writes, the same body sleeps and perceives, not in a Sinn-Gebung (sense donation), but through a different "focus" (mise au point), a variation of "the position of the sensorial apparatus" (Merleau-Ponty 2003, p. 196). Sleeping is an activity of the body withdrawing from the world: the body becomes the subject of a pre-objective organization of the world, and, through a different "focus", elaborates the images of the dream. I would conceive this different "focus" as the dissociation, in dream, of affects from their representations. If in dream symbolism "something means something else" (ibid., p. 200), it is because the affects are not connected to fixed ideas, as they usually are in the focus of a vigilant body. In wakefulness, the dream fantastic symbolism disappears, just as a monocular image is wiped out by a binocular one (ibid., p. 201), because affects are connected to stable ideas. On the contrary, in dream, disconnected from stable ideas, the affects in search for figurability produce "disorientated meanings", and "indirect truths".

When he examines more precisely Freud's *Interpretation of Dreams*, Merleau-Ponty reminds us that the affects remain the same in dreams.[8] In the *Interpretation of Dreams*, Freud sets forth this permanence of affects. Following Spitta's position (Freud 1967, p. 59), Freud asserts that a dream imposes as a psychological experience through its affective content: while ideas yield to displacements and substitutions, affects do not change (Ibid., p. 392). "Affects are always right" (ibid., p. 393), Freud asserts, they allow to account for the whole dream. Yet they vary in intensity when they are disconnected from their ideational contents: the dream work often result in a suppression of affects (ibid., p. 398). However, unlike repression, suppression does not break up affects: the diverse affective sources from which the dream affects proceed are overdetermined or suppressed, depending on whether the ideas linked to these sources are transformed or repressed.

The primary symbolism Merleau-Ponty attributes to dreams then corresponds to the permanence of affects in dreams: impoverished, intensified or suppressed, affects are in search for a meaning lost due to the repression and fragmentations of their ideas. The intentionality he attributes to dreams is not an act intentionality, but "the exhibition of concretions that 'line' our life" (ibid., p. 280): it is akin to the

---

[8] "Feelings are not concealed: ideas yield to censorship, but not feelings; hence dreams in which the feelings are not adapted to the content" (ibid., p. 204).

a-representational desire-like operative intentionality. Dreaming, Merleau-Ponty states, is neither thinking nor knowing, but "letting that affective field play away" (ibid.).

b. Perceptive Symbolism and Affect

In wakefulness too, affect is what relates consciousness to the Unconscious, and, as Merleau-Ponty reminds after Freud, links, through an "oneirism (…) implicit to perceptive consciousness" (Merleau-Ponty 2003, p. 213), Dora's repressed idea of her father to a new idea – each new man she may desire (ibid., p. 217). When he conceives the Unconscious as "sedimentation of perceptive life (originary sedimentation: the fields; secondary sedimentation: the symbolic matrixes)" (ibid., p. 213), Merleau-Ponty apprehends it through the institution/passivity model. Sexuality, the "great supplier of our passivity" (ibid.) infiltrates every perception: this passivity is reactivated by institution every time a new perception is made.

An illustration of this is the premonitory dream Merleau-Ponty takes up from Freud: Mrs. B. states that she dreamt of meeting Dr. K (K2) in front of a shop, and indeed met him the day after. She thought about the dream only after the event, though. Twenty-five years before, she was married to an elderly rich man who bankrupted and she had to give piano lessons in order to provide for her family. Dr. K (K2) took care of her husband and helped her find piano students. Another Dr. K., (K1) a lawyer, who managed her husband's business, fell in love with her. She remembers how he showed up one day as she was thinking about him – which was not so surprising, considering he often visited and she often thought about him… This episode corresponds, according to Freud, to the latent content of the dream. Dr. K2 (the physician), is an idea that replaces the repressed idea of Dr. K1 (the lawyer), and Freud interprets Mrs. B's dream as a disguised desire to meet the lawyer.

For Merleau-Ponty, in this dream, oneirism is neither a lie nor a censorship, but "a perceptive contact which is not a knowledge" (ibid., p. 221). K2 does not conceal K1 but reveals him because he is linked to him: the physician's perception in the street "touches some assemblages, and produces echoes" (ibid., p. 222). The perfect encounter Mrs. B had with K1 "remained in her as a Stiftung" (ibid., p. 222): K1 was instituted as a forbidden love-partner, turned into passivity, and reactivated by K2. Perceiving K2 is a new institution (an instituting institution) that arose the passivities that infiltrate and determine Mrs. B's body map. These passivities are sedimented institutions (instituted institutions) affectively centred on K1. "The Unconscious is a symbolic matrix left by the event" (ibid., p. 223), Merleau-Ponty concludes, and this matrix of passivities is related to every new perception through an affect stream.

Similarly to Mrs. B's sexuality determined through encounters that leave their marks, gender when self-assigned and assigned by the others, is, in every new perception, the reactivation of primary assignments, in order to repeat or contest them. When a new institution reactivates a passivity, to repeat or subvert it, an affect in search for figurability finds a punctual figuration. K2 and the premonitory dream remembered in retrospect is the figuration found by the affect disconnected from K1. In the same way, my gender assignment as male or female, every time I am to state my gender (in whichever intersubjective context) is the figuration found by the affect disconnected from my originary gender multiplicity. The passivity that is constantly reactivated, however, is but an institution itself: I was assigned male or female, a sedimented primary institution that I am asked to reactivate in each of my acts and attributes, but which exists only through this reactivation.

Yet only limited passivities can be reactivated: gender melancholy (Butler 1990, p. 72) designates the operation through which a part of the body erogenous potential is definitively lost and becomes a performative impossibility. When a body amputates itself from a part of its erogenous potential, namely homosexual desire, not named and thus foreclosed rather than repressed, it becomes a gendered body. This naturalized heterosexualisation of the bodies produces the literalising fantasy that sex, the literal penis or the literal vagina, is what causes pleasure and desire, and designates at one and the same time anatomy, "natural identity", and "natural" desire. Only certain passivities can be echoed by new events: gender melancholy precludes both homoerotic and transgender possibilities to emerge as passivities taken up by institutions. They remain pure passivities, non-existent inasmuch as they were nor primarily nor posteriorly instituted, and reactivated. In other words, here, unconscious possibilities remain affects in search for a figurability they may never find, as they settle in more intelligible figurabilities. In non-binary gender and sexuality configurations, the affect quest for figurability stretches over classical binary categories: it looks for a figuration that may not correspond to the instituted possibilities (instituted speech), but rather to new instituting ones, thus introducing a new instituting speech.

11.4.3.4 Gender Multiplicity and Symbolic Narrative Patterns

Laplanche's final version of the theory of generalized seduction (Laplanche 2007) is likely to account for the non-exclusively-verbal Unconscious that appears in this affect quest for figurability. For Laplanche, the Unconscious, induced by the adult in the child, is the residue of the translation by the child of the enigmatic messages passed on to her/him by the adult. These messages are "scrambled" by the adult's own Unconscious, marked by the sexual-infantile, and need to be translated by the child. This translation is what constitutes a pre-conscious/conscious level in the psyche, enabling the child to historicize her/himself. Yet it also produces some remnants, the Unconscious, that escaped this signification ordering. When the translation partly fails, it results in the "classical" neurotic Unconscious. When it totally fails, the original message remains as such in the psyche, and forms what Laplanche calls the "embedded Unconscious" (*inconscient enclavé*), a psychotic non-historicized Unconscious.

To realise this translation, the child needs codes: those possessed are often insufficient, and the child has to summon a new code, both improvised by her/him, and in keeping with the patterns of the cultural environment. The latter provides preformed narrative patterns, "aids to translation" (Laplanche 2007, p. 208): a mytho-symbolic universe that includes "codes such as the (classic) 'Oedipus complex', 'murder of the father' or 'castration complex', but also more modern narrative patterns, partly similar to the previous, but partly innovating" (ibid.). For Laplanche, the "mistake of psychoanalysis" consists in trying to turn these contingent, culturally contextualised narration patterns into truths of the psyche, as it does when it universalises the Oedipus complex. On the contrary, these patterns are not the Unconscious nor the repressed (that is to say that which results from translation), but the repressor (the tools that operate translation); they are not to be considered "as what is primary sexual, but as what orders it, and eventually desexualises it, in the name of the laws of alliance and procreation, etc." (ibid., p. 212).

This position seems crucial as regards both the linguistic dimension of the Unconscious and the consideration of non-binary genders and sexualities. The Unconscious as translation remnants proves not entirely linguistic: language, and linguistic categories of the Symbolic are not the sexual-infantile, but the codes that serve to translate the enigmatic messages. Moreover, these categories, often used to present binary classic gender positions as the Law of psyche, are not the sexual-infantile, but the codes that help translate and desexualise it. Laplanche explicitly argues this in another text. He defines: gender as plural, sex as dual, due to sexuated reproduction and to the human symbolization that rigidly fixes this duality as absence/presence, phallic/castrated, and the sexual (le sexual), which corresponds to the Unconscious, as multiple, polymorphous. He suggests conceiving the sexual as "the unconscious residue of the repression-symbolisation of gender by sex" (Laplanche, p. 153).

I would consider this gender multiplicity as passivities, instituted in the child through the enigmatic messages of the adult, but not all taken up and reactivated by institutions. They form the sexual, a multiple polymorphous Unconscious, that consists in what was not filtered through binary institutions, or constitute and embedded Unconscious when they yield to gender melancholy. They may be reactivated if confronted to new, instituting institutions, which take up and continue their multiplicities. Non-binary gender and sexuality configurations manifest an affect quest for figurability. They are an attempt to symbolise-translate gender multiplicity outside of the binary ideational contents and gender-binary narrative patterns. The latter either repress this multiplicity (producing a translation-rests Unconscious), or foreclose it (forming an embedded gender-melancholy Unconscious). These passivities are reactivated when instituted anew as identificatory possibilities, and therefore find figurability in various new sexuality and gender positions.

Hence the importance, in my opinion, of Merleau-Ponty's non-exclusively-verbal Unconscious. If interpreted as the affect quest for figurability, the non-linguistic part of this Unconscious allows accounting for gender and sexuality possibilities that escape the Lacanian linguistic Symbolic (conceived of as a fixed set of possibilities of alliances, filiations and sexuations). Far from confirming a traditional phallogocentrism, this reading would present us with a feminist Merleau-Ponty, whose phenomenology gives tools to conceive the effects of power-relations on subjectivities. Yet it is a feminism that moves away from any differentialist binary approach, a feminism that refutes any universal category of "woman" (either defined by nature or by the Symbolic) as much as it shuns androcentrism as another false universal, a feminism with no necessary female subject, but with gender multiplicity.

References

Aulagnier, Piera, and Al. 1967. *Le désir et la perversion*. Paris: Seuil.
Ayouch, Thamy. 2009a. Approche de la psychanalyse par la phénoménologie: l'exemple de Merleau-Ponty. *Revue de phénoménologie et de psychologie analytique*. 2009-1: 7–20.
———. 2009b. Body-proper and fantasmatic body: The debate between Merleau-Pontyan phenomenology and psychoanalysis. *The Journal of Theoretical and Philosophical Psychology* 28 (2): 336–355.
———. 2012. *La Consonance imparfaite. Maurice Merleau-Ponty et la psychanalyse*. Paris: Le Bord de l'Eau.
———. 2014. Questionando a teoria psicanalítica das perversões. In *Psicanálise e questões da contemporaneidade* II, 81–95, Curitiba/São Paulo: CRV.
———. 2015. Psychanalyse et transidentités: hétérotopies. *Evolution Psychiatrique* 80 (2). doi:10.1016/j.evopsy.2015.01.004.
Baas, B. 1996. L'élaboration de l'objet a: Lacan avec Kant et Merleau-Ponty. In *Les Cahiers philosophiques de Strasbourg*, tome 4, 13–41, Strasbourg: USHS.
———. 1998. Jacques Lacan et la traversée de la phenomenology. In *Phénoménologie et psychanalyse*. Etranges relations, 32–40. Paris: Champ Vallon.
Barbaras, Renaud. 1999. *Le Désir et la distance*. Paris: Vrin.
Benoist, Jocelyn. 2006. Pulsion, cause et raison chez Freud. In *La Pulsion*, 115–138. Paris: Vrin.
Bergeret, Jean. 1996. *La personnalité normale et pathologique*. Paris: Dunod.
Breuer, Joseph, Freud, Sigmund. 1895/1971. *Etudes sur l'hystérie*. Paris: P.U.F.
Butler, Judith. 1988. Performative acts and gender constitution: An essay in phenomenology and feminist theory. *Theatre Journal* 40 (4): 519–531.
———. 1989. Sexual ideology and phenomenological description: A feminist critique of Merleau-Ponty's phenomenology of perception. In *The thinking muse: Feminism and modern French philosophy*, ed. Allen, Jeffner and Iris Marion Young, 85–100. Indiana: Indiana University Press.
———. 1990. *Gender trouble. Feminism and subversion of identity*. New York: Routledge.
———. 2004. *Undoing Gender*. New York: Routledge.
———. 2012. *Défaire le genre*. Amsterdam: Paris.
———. 2014. *Qu'est-ce qu'une vie bonne*. Paris: Payot.
Castoriadis, Cornelius. 1971. Le Dicible et l'indicible. L'Arc. "Merleau-Ponty" 67–79.
Chiland, Colette. 2005. Problèmes posés par les transsexuels aux psychanalystes. *Revue française de psychoanalyse*. 2005–2/69: 563–577.
Czermak, Marcel. 1982. Précisions sur la clinique du transsexualisme. Discours psychanalytique. 3
———. 1996. Préface. In *Sur l'identité sexuelle: à propos du transsexualisme*, ed. Henri Frignet, 11–24. Paris: Editions de l'Association freudienne.
Dor, Joël. 1987. *Structure et perversions*. Paris: Denoël.
Ey, Henri. 1966. *L'inconscient. VIè Colloque de Bonneval, 1960*. Paris: Desclée de Brower.

Freud, Sigmund. 1915a. *Repression. The standard edition, volume XIV: A history of the psycho-analytic movement, papers on metapsychology, and other works*. London: Hogarth Press.
———. 1915b. *Instincts and their vicissitudes. The standard edition, volume XIV: A history of the psycho-analytic movement, papers on metapsychology, and other works*. London: Hogarth Press.
———. 1900/1967. *L'Interprétation des rêves*. Paris: P.U.F.
Frignet, Henri. 2000. *Le transsexualisme*. Paris: Déclée de Brower.
Green, André. 1964. Du comportement à la chair : itinéraire de Merleau-Ponty. *Critique* 211: 1017–1046.
Husserl, Edmund. 1950. *Idées directrices pour une phenomenology*. Paris: Gallimard.
———. 1998. *La Synthèse passive*. Paris: Jérôme Millon.
Irigaray, Luce. 1984. *Ethique de la difference sexuelle*. Paris: Minuit.
Kruks, Sonia. 2001. *Retrieving experience: subjectivity and recognition in feminist politics*. Ithaca: Cornell University Press.
Lacan, Jacques. 1961a. *Le Séminaire, livre XI, Les quatre concepts fondamentaux de la psychanalyse*. Paris: Seuil.
———. 1961b/2001. Maurice Merleau-Ponty. *Autres écrits*. Paris: Seuil.
———. 1966. *Ecrits*. Paris: Seuil.
———. 2011. Ou Pire. Séminaire, Livre XIX (1971–1972). Paris: Seuil.
Laplanche. 2007. *Sexual. La sexualité élargie au sens freudien*. Paris: P.U.F.
Le Doeuf, Michèle. 1998. *Le Sexe du savoir*. Paris: Aubier.
Merleau-Ponty, Maurice. 1942. *La Structure du comportement*. Paris: P.U.F.
———. 1945. *La Phénoménologie de la perception*. Paris: Gallimard.
———. 1955. *Les Aventures de la dialectique*. Paris: Gallimard.
———. 1960a. *Le Visible et l'invisible*. Paris: Gallimard.
———. 1960b/2000. Préface à l'ouvrage de A. Hesnard, L'œuvre et l'esprit de Freud et son importance dans le monde moderne. Parcours Deux (1951–1961). Paris: Verdier.
———. 1968. *Résumés de cours. Collège de France. 1952–1960*. Paris: Gallimard.
———. 1969. *La Prose du monde*. Paris: Gallimard.
———. 1996. *Sens et non-sens*. Paris: Gallimard.
———. 2000. *Parcours Deux*. Paris: Verdier.
———. 2003. *L'Institution. La passivité. Notes de cours au Collège de France. 1954–1955*. Tours: Belin.
Morel, Geneviève. 2004. *Ambiguités sexuelles*. Paris: Anthropos.
Pirlot, George, and J.-L. Pedinelli. 2009. *Les perversions sexuelles et narcissiques*. Paris: Armand Collin.
Pontalis, J.-B. 1961. La Position du problème de l'inconscient chez Merleau-Ponty. In *Après Freud*, ed. J.-B. Pontalis (1993), pp 76–97. Paris: Gallimard.
Stoller, Silvia. 2010. Expressivity and performativity: Merleau-Ponty and Butler. *Continental Philosophy Review* 43 (1): 97–110.
Sullivan, Shannon. 1997. Domination and dialogue in Merleau-Ponty's phenomenology of perception. *Hypatia* 12 (1): 1–19.
Young Iris, M. 1990. *Throwing like a girl and other essays in feminist philosophy and social theory*. Bloomington: Indiana University Press.

# Chapter 12
The Unconscious and the Non-linguistic Mode of Thinking

Dieter Lohmar

Abstract One of the challenging problems with the unconscious is that it turns out to affect our consciousness and influence our behaviour. This enigma of the effectivity of unconscious contents asks for a theory about how we can at the same time *know* and *not know* about unconscious contents. In my opinion this enigma may be solved partly by pointing out that there is a non-language system of representation still working in our mind. I consider the difference of language and non-language systems of representation to be one of the most important steps in the continuum from conscious to unconscious thoughts. In my opinion we do not only refer to states of affairs in language modes of symbolization but also in a system of scenic phantasma accompanied by feelings. The cooperation of both systems can make us understand how to know and not-know something at the same time.

Keywords Unconscious • Non-language thinking • Phantasma • Neurotic displacement • Daydreams

Freud's psychoanalysis presents some enigmas to the philosophy of consciousness. It proposes the thesis of a powerful and lasting unconsciousness, which mostly is out of reach of conscious thinking but nevertheless it has forceful effects on our behaviour. Thus the unconscious, even when we are not aware of its contents, influences our actions in a way that offers a clear sense – at least in the view of a psychoanalytical hermeneutics. Therefore we have to answer the difficult question how we can know and not know something at the same time.

Psychoanalysis also wants to give an explanation for a strange behaviour of the human mind, the *neurotic displacement*, that in a variety of ways encodes the experienced contents. Neurotic displacement has different forms: shifting, denial,

D. Lohmar (✉)
University of Cologne, Cologne, Germany
e-mail: dieter.lohmar@uni-koeln.de

inversion, compression of contents, etc. One can reconstitute the original contents after the displacing activity only with the help of a psychoanalytical hermeneutics.

Psychoanalysis uses a lot of evidences that we as phenomenologists cannot make use of: The big realm of case studies, the successful curing as well as the sudden insight and revitalized memories of the patients convinces us of the correctness of the psychoanalytic hermeneutics.

But, from a philosophical point of view, psychoanalysis incorporates an alarming insight, viz., the insight that our consciousness is opaque and that in its self-obscuring activity it is oriented to rules that we also do not understand. Looking from the point of view of a subject who understands himself as lucid and rational, this enigmatic activity is a thorn in the flesh of reason.

I would like to make some of the above-mentioned enigmatic aspects more comprehensible by analysing the non-linguistic system of thinking in humans in three steps: (1) The first step is to shortly present the theory of non-language thinking in humans. (2) The second step will be to make clear, why this theory may help us to understand the enigmatic ability of consciousness for neurotic displacement. (3) And the third step will be an investigation in the way non-linguistic thinking manages to memorize experiences in a form that uses the modification and enrichment of the sense of the types (*Typus*) we use in everyday circumstances. This is not a position of Husserl himself, it is only based on the methods of his phenomenology. But it develops some motives that might be helpful to understand the effectivity of unconsciousness.[1]

12.1 Non-linguistic Thinking: A Short Version

My starting point is a phenomenological analysis of human non-linguistic thinking[2] which is ceantered on the mode of *scenic phantasma*. Scenic phantasma are suddenly upcoming short-term visual phantasma that carry sense and allow also for connecting, drawing consequences, making plans on the basis of our knowledge etc.

---

[1] This contribution does not intend to replace Freud's concept of unconscious, it only tries to present an interpretation of the unconscious from a phenomenological point of view that concentrates on non-linguistic forms of thinking. If one like paradoxical wording we may characterize this as an attempt to understanding unconsciousness within consciousness, i.e. within the paradigm of a refined phenomenological analysis of consciousness.

[2] What is thinking? Here every answer depends on the idea of thinking you start with. If you tie thinking exclusively to the use of language concepts by definition, then consequently non-linguistic thinking is not thinking at all. But this is simply the outcome of a definition, not more. If you understand thinking as proceeding your experience, your ideas about possible challenges and useful solutions in a symbolic medium not using language symbols that non-linguistic operations may pass for thinking. I prefer the second understanding because it allows to understand primates and non-linguistic humans (deaf and aphasic persons after stroke) as thinking agents and it harmonizes with the phenomenological analysis of the system of scenic phantasma.

with one word: The non-linguistic System of scenic phantasma allows for thinking.

Often this short-term phantasma unites to what we commonly identify with daydreams. But we should make clear from the very beginning that even these daydreams are not a regressive move, but they are more functioning like normal thinking in language mode. That means: they cause only a short break in our activity guided by the insights and consequences of this thinking.

This alternative is also to be found in Freud, who often interprets wakeful fantasies as a kind of flight from reality, as a regressive way of satisfying insatiable wishes or as a *phantasmatic compensation* of humiliating experiences by free formation of my fantasies of being mighty. But in Freud there is also a distinct recognition of scenic fantasies as a forceful means of reshaping and imaginatively modifying urgent wishes while facing unavoidable obstacles.[3]

In my view, in series of short term phantasies and daydreams, no matter whether they reflect humiliation, fear or fun, we are playing out possible solutions to a problem, mentally testing our options, their usefulness for a solution and their respective consequences. This "life" of scenic phantasma constitutes an important part of our conscious life. Let me mention some every-day examples: Worries about urgent challenges or uncertainties that makes us sleepless at night. There are many fantasies of having success. I would like to mention also empirical-psychological research that suggests that most grown up males think of sex every few minutes, and the mode of this thinking is definitely not conceptual (Cameron and Biber 1973; Hicks and Leitenberg 2001). In these scenic episodes of our conscious life, linguistic expressions emerge in the background in favor of phantasmatic elements.[4] I am not denying that we can also think about our wishes and problems by means of language and that in daydreams both are often merged, but what I want to emphasize is that we also use non-linguistic systems of representation.

Since we regularly suppose that most performances of thinking are bound to the use of language, my starting point calls for some explanations. But I cannot present here my theory of non-linguistic thinking exhaustively.[5] I have even to leave out the part of basic phenomenological theory of knowledge and meaning-giving acts, and this theory-part is essential for phenomenologists to understand that Husserl's theory of meaning leaves open exactly a place for non-linguistic thinking.[6] One way to

---

[3] Cf. for example the impressive analysis of the three phases modifying the characteristic scene in Freud (1919). Cf. also the elucidating discussion of this text by R. Bernet (2012).

[4] This is true also for nightly dreams, cf. Symons (1993).

[5] This starting point arises in the framework of a broad analysis of the central functions of phantasy in our consciousness. As a consequence of this approach, there lies an extension of the concept of thinking to non-linguistic thinking. Cf. Lohmar (2008b, 2012c, 2016).

[6] I have elaborated this in my recent book (Lohmar 2016) Ch: I.1 and I.3 "Husserls Theorie der Bedeutung". The central idea of this theory of meaning is that the meaning of symbols (in language or other media), deeds and objects is not fixed. It asks in every case for an act of consciousness to give a symbol a meaning (the meaning-giving act) and this meaning-giving is usually oriented to the conventions in a communicating society. But meaning-giving may be performed quite freely and spontaneous, completely apart from conventions. Think for example of a child sitting in a

the insight that there is a non-linguistic system is a sober phenomenological analysis of the activity of our everyday Fantasies. Other ways are considerations about the necessity of a functioning non-language system to learn from experience for hominids in the long time between the raise of *homo erectus* 1.8–2.0 Mio. years ago and the begin of a refined language use that cannot be earlier that 120.000 years ago. Beside this also the intelligence of animals hints to their ability to think without language.

We might take an opposite view and suppose that wakeful fantasies deal only with a non-real fantasy-world, i.e. it is only a regressive form of phantasy activity and never concern the real world. This view needs to be given up if daydreaming turns out to be an old, non-linguistic mode of thinking about the present world, about our former experiences, about our wishes and future plans.

Series of short term scenic phantasma turn out to be the medium in which I bind my former experiences with possible future actions and possible events. Even short term daydreaming thus functions as a problem-solving activity.[7]

The scenic phantasma may sometimes seem to be reducible to static pictures that do not entail any kind of narrative. Consider in this regard the following situation: While I am thinking over problematic plans a short term phantasma of a good friend just looking at me sorrowful appears for me. This can let me know that even my friends will not agree with my problematic plans. But scenic phantasma are not to be thought of in terms of pictures through which objects are mediated; they are more like scenes that appear in the same way as though the person was really looking at me. Thus I am also somehow there, right in this scene, but as the spectator who is incorporated in his special perspective. Scenic phantasma are not static: nearly all of them have a narrative element, even though this element may sometimes be hidden in a move of emotions or other dimensions of the scene (for example associate ideas of past or future events) that do not affect the visual dimension directly.

We must first have a rough idea of non-linguistic thinking in its modes and its performances to be able to understand that its performance is almost the same as that of linguistic thinking, even though it is based on a quite different set of rules.[8] However, non-linguistic thinking has some specific limitations and deviations when compared to language-based thinking: Non-linguistic thinking can preserve our experience (whether it is pleasant or not), recall and modify it, and transform it into a form that permits its use in further actions.[9] Human non-linguistic thinking pro-

---

sandy playground using a wooden block with the acoustic expression "Broom, broom." as if it is a car. This is already a meaning-giving activity and it is obvious that there is a long way of communication and agreement until we reach a lexicon of meanings shared by all members of a community.

[7] With this analysis I do not claim a comprehensive understanding of all psychic events in correlation with daydreaming. Such a claim would be disproportionate when compared with my limited knowledge of the psychoanalytical theory-formation.

[8] If the reader is interested in the most important differences of the two systems I would like to refer to the extensive discussion in Lohmar (2016), Ch. III–VI, p. 91–266.

[9] It goes without saying, that the preservation of experience is also possible for a language system, the point of my investigation is that this performance is already possible for the non-linguistic system of scenic phantasma.

ceeds mostly in the mode of short term phantasmatic scenes, sometimes daydreams. On the first view it seems that these phantasmatic scenes only repeat a former pleasant or unpleasant event or a challenging future event.

Is there a link between the two systems? In regard to humans we might suspect that each older and low-level system of representation might be influenced by our language and its concepts. It asks for other studies to find evidences for this. But even if there is an influence of the linguistic system of representation on the non-linguistic system in high developed speaking humans, we can't conclude that the low-level system is generally contaminated by language. My thesis is that the most important thinking performances in everyday concerns are to be done already on a non-linguistic base. That implies that there may be an influence of language concepts on non-linguistic systems of thinking, and it may refine the performance, but language is not the essential basis of non-linguistic systems, they can function independently in non-linguistic thinking highly cerebralized agents like primates or mammals.

One very prominent mode of non-linguistic thinking proceeds in *repetitions* or *replays* of a particular scene in our consciousness. But, and this is very important: *In each repetition the scene undergoes a slight modification.* This means that the circumstances, situations and sometimes even the acting and suffering persons are slightly modified in their constellation, activities and motives. The result of this modifying activity (or: thinking activity) is also a kind of scene. We may call it a *characteristic scene* and – this is another difficulty – it may be regarded as an advantageous but fake memory of my past experience. But it is more appropriate, with regard to its overall function, to consider the result of this modification as a *useful idea of my future actions based on former experience.* Perhaps we may think of a kind of a video clip (resp. a narrative scene) that briefly presents a possibility regarding how, for instance, a painful and passive experience could have been turned into a successful active mastering of experience.[10]

Let me shape this idea of non-linguistic 'thinking' understood as a slow modification of our scenic phantasma with the help of an example. Everyone knows the following situation: In traffic it often happens that you had been pressed hard by an impertinent and aggressive bully and you often give way to his demands due to the situation and circumstances. This annoying situation will repeatedly and furiously remerge in your short term scenic phantasma (or daydreams). But these seemingly identical replays would each time introduce slight modifications and in the end you will find the right solution to get rid of these aggressive demands. Suddenly we gain the insight: This would have been the right reaction; had I done this, it would have stopped him!

---

[10] The characteristic transformations sometimes also include *denying* of former events, because in negation we are still holding on to these former events, *inverting*, or *transferring* my former and future activities to other persons and other objects etc. Because of such far-reaching transformations, which nonetheless preserve the "lessons of experience" while opening up particular future possibilities, I see in this discussion a contribution to the epistemological founding of psychoanalysis.

I am aware of the fact that this is only a very special example. To convince you of the good sense of non-linguistic thinking in scenic phantasma I have to give much more examples of conceiving of situations, consequences, alternatives, past and future events etc.[11]

12.2 Neurotic Displacement

Now the question arises: What is the meaning of these modifications in the context of neurotic displacement? This resulting characteristic scene need not be truthful in all its details regarding the actual experience, because it sometimes incorporates essential modifications of our own behavior (perhaps it simply says: don't be so dogmatic and pigheaded in such everyday affairs, stay cool). The central function of the resulting characteristic scene is to keep the decisive "lesson" of this experience for the future. This seems to be easy and indisputable in this case and we can think about most everyday concerns in a non-linguistic way using scenic phantasma.

But what happens if the situation or event is disgusting, humiliating or even traumatic to a certain degree? We will not be willing to repeat this event on and on – but you know: exactly this is often the case. In these traumatic cases it reveals that the modification takes on a more radical form. It turns out that often situations are transformed in a radical way so that – even in enigmatic forms like denying, inversion or transferring – one could keep and make further use of this "central lesson of experience" without emotional pains. If we are able to reach such an outcome we can easily make productive use of it in future challenges.

To give some examples for these central lessons of experience: I do not have to keep in mind the painful memory of rape to hold on to the essential lesson I have learned from this experience. This lesson should at least enable me to avoid such an event with some security. Similarly, if a robber or a dangerous animal has threatened my life, I do not need to memorize the situation in its full thrilling anxiety. It is enough to remember that "something like this" once has happened to "other persons" to avoid places, situations, things and persons that entail this particular dangers.

Thus to hold on to the essential lesson of experience, I may even forget that it was me who suffered the unbearable humiliation and violation. Even more, it is helpful to forget some of the seemingly central elements of my former experience so as to make successful use of it without being paralyzed by anxiety. The non-linguistic mode of thinking, by introducing slight modifications of my experience, enables me to act without such hindrances.

We wonder why such "untruthfulness" is possible in our consciousness even if it makes perfect sense. In this concern we have to keep in mind that non-linguistic thinking is only useful for the *solitary inner thinking*. It does not have to adjust to

---

[11] For more examples and other modes of non-linguistic thinking cf. Lohmar (2012b, 2016).

the external demand of truthfulness in a communicating society. While the demand of accuracy makes good sense within the public forms of communication, it is not necessary for the solitary non-linguistic thinking.[12] And this is even true for keeping identity of all objects, the avoidance of contradictions etc. "Mistakes" in this concern would immediately devalue our thinking in the view of a second or third person, but they can still keep the central lessons of our experience.

In regard to the essential lessons of experience, there is always a set of equivalent memories. We may regard different characteristic scenes as "equivalent" if they portray the central lesson of experience and also enable us to use this experience in future situations without anxiety. We may therefore paradoxically say that we must be able to forget parts of our experience to become able to hold on to and make further use of the central lessons of our experiences.[13]

In non-linguistic non-public thinking we are capable of keeping the essential lessons of experience; but precisely with such an aim in mind, it may make good sense to change some features of the former experience. Especially if an experience is connected with painful and frightening emotions (bodily pains, humiliation etc.), or with strong defensive reactions like fear, disgust etc., then it can be of decisive importance to change particular elements in order to be able to make further use of this experience. In the case of a mere repetition of the critical situation, we might remain completely paralyzed with fear or disgust. By displacing particular elements of experience, we preserve our ability to act effectively without hindrances.

All of these modifications and transformations are not to be interpreted as lies, because non-linguistic thinking is not happening in a communicative framework. Moreover, the slight modifications in non-linguistic thinking are not even cases of self-deception because the sense of a self-deception carries a social and communicative sense.[14]

One great advantage of the non-linguistic mode of thinking is to start the theoretical understanding of neurotic displacement by analysing normal and psychologically healthy persons. The special characteristics of non-linguistic modes of thinking can be analysed with phenomenological methods through self-observation and reflection. Analysis of non-linguistic thinking in the context of everyday

---

[12] The basic level of non-linguistic thinking can function solitary and private (to organize future action under the information of former experience) but it must not, because it can refer extensionally to other's insights, valuations etc.

[13] The concept of non-linguistic thinking is obviously also of some use to understand thinking in animals. Cf. Lohmar (2008a). The decisive point in my analysis is that humans are using language and the older non-linguistic mode of thinking. And this is the ground of our possibility to manipulate the characteristic scene, and somehow also to manipulate our memories but in doing this to keep the central lessons of our experiences.

[14] Understanding some displacements of contents as a self-deception asks for the contribution of other persons who could show me that my memory is not fully accurate but changed and improved. This also means that we do not have to solve the enigma of a subject who decides to deceive himself and may even be successful in this action. The mechanisms of self-deception are more closely to a strategy of avoiding certain insights, cf. for this Rinofner-Kreidl (2012).

situations enables us to understand why and how neurotic displacement, inversion, denying etc. is possible, and why it makes sense.

Thus the general strategy of my approach is a kind of "approximation" of the phenomenon of neurotic displacement from the functioning of non-linguistic thinking in normal persons. I am also well aware that I should present you more analyses concerning the possibility of concrete neurotic displacements, inversions, negations etc.[15]

12.3 How We Remember in Non-linguistic Modes

Up to now we seem not to have a solution for the second important enigma of psychoanalytic: The fact that in most neurotic displacements the reaction to normal situations, things and events are forcefully changed in a characteristic way. The resulting "neurotic" behaviour nevertheless has a good sense in the view of psychoanalytic hermeneutics. Thus we have to understand how it is possible that we obviously do not remember the offspring of the neurotic displacement but nevertheless we behave as if we know very well about it.

In my opinion the process of keeping experience and knowledge can also be investigated in a new way on the level of non-linguistic thinking. This means: There is also a specific way to keep experiences on the level of non-linguistic thinking. And this level is in fact deeper that the level of usual thinking in language because the result usually is nearly complete out of range of the language based thinking and remembering. What I am thinking of is the way in which our experiences are collected and somehow also sedimented in the so called types (*Typus*).

The concept of type is to be found in the late genetic phenomenology of Husserl. It denotes what we know about a singular thing or a group of similar things on the basis of our former experiences with this object or "objects of this kind". In the framework of the genetic phenomenological theory of perception the type is a necessary tool in performing perceptions. In the type there is preserved what we know about the typical way in which a thing presents itself in perception. For example if we see a yellow object of a certain oval shape and a rough surface and at the same time we register a slight fruity smell we tend to perceive a lemon including this faint smell. If it is the smell of gasoline, we do not tend to interpret this smell as a representant of the object (lemon) in sensibility. During our experiential life we somehow "collect" the specific contents of types and if we perceive an object or event without its usual or essential way to appear our fantasy tends to "fill in" this missing special sensible givenness with the help of phantasma.[16] For example if I know a person who usually uses too much of an obtrusive perfume, I am able to "smell" her in

---

[15] I have done this discussion in Lohmar (2012a). But please keep also in mind that I am not an expert in psychoanalytical theory, therefore it may happen that I have presented some of its parts in a too simplified way.

[16] For an analysis of this function of weak phantasma in perception cf. Lohmar (2008b).

12 The Unconscious and the Non-linguistic Mode of Thinking

modes of olfactory Phantasma even when she arrives from a distance that will usually not allow for smelling the perfume. These essential elements of the way a thing or event appears are produced in the mode of phantasma according to our precise expectations sedimented in our types.

Types are to a certain extend "private", because they are undergoing a slow modification and enrichment during my own experiential life. An inexperienced child that never has tasted a lemon cannot have the strange feeling that we have in our mouth when we see someone else biting in a lemon (the phantasma of tasting a lemon).

I will now start to discuss a kind of paradigmatic standard example for this slow modification of the contents of a type in everyday circumstances. I have the habit to use a certain plate of the electric oven in the kitchen for preparing my coffee using an old fashioned Italian style coffee machine in the morning. It happens someday that the plate of the oven is defect, so that I make up my mind to call for a service man. In the next morning I act like usual, i.e. I following my habits in everyday concerns – and put the coffee machine on the same plate as yesterday. After some minutes I realize that it does not start and in realizing that the plate is defect I remember that I made the same experience yesterday but forgot about it. Perhaps I will even criticise myself: You should have known this, yesterday you have already seen it! Everyone of us has experienced similar events. The important point is: Only after a series of similar disappointments I will slowly change my habits and avoid the use of the defect plate.

This shows that the type of a singular object does not only include information about the usual way the object will appear but also contains intentions on its value and about its working qualities: the plate is helpful for heating the coffee machine. Now suddenly this quality has changed and it turns out that my usual orientation in the world is (1) based on a non-language way of preserving my experiences, i.e. with modified types. And (2) this way of preserving experience is quite conservative and changes only slowly like habits do change in a series of equal experiences. At least (3) this way of preserving knowledge in our types has a kind of "life", because in principle my expectations are changing, but this life is slow and quite conservative (sluggish).

This way to preserve knowledge in types is not dependant on the use of language because the language system of preserving knowledge is obviously reacting much faster – but in fact in most everyday situations we will not make use of this language based system. We realize that there are big differences between the language system based on propositions memorized and the non-language system with types modified. The non-language system is effectively organizing our everyday concerns. With this non-language system we seem to know "A" – but this is only presented by the guidance of our activities – while with the language system we already know that "non A" is the case, but we do not use it for everyday affairs. There is a clear cut paradox of knowing and not knowing in contrast of the two systems of thinking and memorizing.

Additionally language systems make use of the idea of truth: Something is the case or not (yes/no logic) while types are quite differentiated in relation to the *probability* that something is the case. Think of a car that left you in the lurch for some times: You use it with a weak confidence, bad feelings and insecure while remembering the optimistic information of the mechanic that it is repaired and will now work "for a while". Our orientation in everyday concerns does not rely on the yes/no logic of the mechanic but we will tacitly follow the way of a bus line that will bring us further if the car breaks down again.

Thus we might take this difference as a serious hint that our consciousness definitely is not only working on the language level. Moreover: We simply do not "know" in language terms about the contents of the beliefs hidden in the type that in fact guide our actions.[17] This is obviously a case of unconscious knowledge but nevertheless we are able to remember also on the language level about that what we already know. Starting from this example I will in the following try to explore the cases of changing types in experiences that have gradually more traumatic elements in it.

Locking back on our example all of us know also about the next phase of the story: The day after the service man has repaired the plate, we will come into the kitchen in the morning and avoid using the plate which is in fact already repaired. And thus there is another cause to criticize myself for not being up to date and stuck in my changed ("new/old") habits. But you can be sure: Your habits that incorporate knowledge about the usability of things will slowly change back in the next weeks and reign your everyday concerns reliable.

In the example of the defect electric plate we see clearly the usual course of the preserving activity in cases where there is a changing quality of an object. In my opinion we share this system of memorizing with most higher cerebralized animals. Therefore my next example is a well-known fact about dogs – but you might use also your own similar experiences. Hume proposed it as a clear sign for the ability of animals to gain knowledge: No dog will hurt himself twice at a hot oven.

But the example of the dog has an obvious disadvantage in view of our standard example: There is only one experience, but an impressive negative one. Usually we should not expect that a single event can change the contents of a type. Where is the series of similar experiences in this case? We might even speak of a traumatic experience in this case. Perhaps this makes the difference? Or: Will we have to accept that dogs have an ability to think with the performance of a yes/no logic like in language systems? No, I think that it is not necessary to speculate about such high class equipment in the case of dogs, especially because we have own experiences with such hurting events.

The extremely hurting experience of burning his nose has serious after effects on the dog's knowledge: Every time he sees the oven in the room, the hot ace is revitalized in the mode of phantasma – and this is also true for our own experience. Thus the series of similar events that will change the type is also to be found here. But we have to be attentive to the role of phantasma in the replays of the event: There is a

---

[17] The precise contents of types are not explicit and consciously given to us, even if they are functioning in perception. Their contents only manifests in the use of types and the continuously raising expectations in perception. Cf. Lohmar (2008b).

sudden hot reaction like a welling up of ace in phantasma but no real ace. We know this sudden reaction of our fantasy in our own experience and thus we found back the trace of the series of similar experience changing the contents of a type in this case based on a traumatic experience with. – So you have already recognize my strategy in watching the effects of traumatic experiences and trying to figure out their function in the change of our types.

My next example is taken from my wife's rich experience in family therapy: Kevin, a boy aged 13, lives together with his mother and the new partner of her. Kevin has the possibility of meeting his father at the father's place each second weekend. The problem is that Kevin's biological father has a serious problem with alcohol, usually he is drunken. Now it turned out that Kevin is changing his whole everyday interests on the Father's weekends: He does neither visit his friends nor does he invite them to visit him, he does not join the Saturday meetings of his local soccer club etc. Asked why he changes his behavior like this only on the father's weekends he gives quite eloquent reasons: He wants to have these weekends exclusively together with his father. When he was himself engaged in a soccer game he asks his stepfather to accompany him. On the first view Kevin's arguments seems to be quite reasonable: The stepfather is more an expert on soccer. And he sticks to this argument, even if he would have preferred the recognition of his real father much more that of his stepfather. So you see the pattern: Kevin is avoiding every occasion where the appearance of his drunken father would cause an awkward situation in public. But he is simply not able to say this in the form of a sentence, even if he is urged to.

What we see here is that Kevin has a kind of "hidden knowledge" of the good reasons why he wants to avoid a public occasion where his drunken father causes an awkward scene ("hidden" in the sense that it is not explicit known in language mode but explicit in a non-linguistic mode of thinking). But this knowledge takes the form of a non-language element, of a scenic phantasma of his drunken father staggering and speaking thickly in public. But as this scenic phantasma is welling up with hot shame every time when Kevin thinks of a situation in which this may happen he simply avoids this occasions with more or less reasonable – but untrue – language based arguments. But: He will not speak about his true motives because he does not know about this avoiding tendency in language mode.[18] We see that the two systems of language and non-language thinking can depart for a while – even if they generally cooperate quite good.

To mention also some variants of this kind of traumatic events: There are several cases where people are suddenly hurt in an accident or – conversely – it may happen that they hurt someone else in an accident they could not prevent or evade. Especially in the case of engine drivers this leads very often to a disability to perform their profession any longer. Also in the case of so called nearly-accidents this experience has an influence on the further behaviour. But we know that this effect strongly

---

[18] It is surely a promising way of therapy to turn non-linguistic modes of thinking into linguistic modes - but language is not the only way to communicate about contents we do not know in linguistic modes. Cf. D. Lohmar, *Denken ohne Sprache*, Heidelberg 2016, Ch. 7.1.

depends on the self-concept of a person. While a young coward will simply realize that he was lucky not to be hurt, a father of a family will be deeply shocked and perhaps change his life. In all this cases there will be several replays in phantasmatic modes and the non-linguistic system of thinking will try to modify the situation up to a point where the anxiety can be accepted – and the result of this thinking process is a changed attitude to this kind of situation.

Now let us consider a neurotic shifting that changes the situation of the acting persons and actions itself in such a far-reaching way that the original "lesson of experience" is no longer to be recognized. For example, think of Freud's analysis of the "kleine Hans", where the anxiety of castration caused by the casual thread by the mother is transferred on the horse.

How can we understand the fact that neurotic shifting often seems to go beyond this limit of modifications characterized by a preservation of the "central lesson of experience"? Often neurotic shifting drifts away in a completely different, pathological direction and cannot preserve the change of behavior that makes sense from the functional point of view. This may even lead to a pathological blockade of part of my activities. Is there not a natural limit of the iteration of neurotic shifting that restricts this way off the original sense? I do not think so.

The tools of neurotic shifting are used iterative until the scenic phantasma is no longer too frightening, too humiliating, too disgusting etc. These emotions are the restless motor of shifting contents in the non-linguistic mode of modifications in scenic phantasma. Let us take a look on Freud's description of the "kleine Hans" who shifts the mothers more or less casual threatening with castration on the horses on the street, which he fears to be bitten by.[19] There is no real protection against such border-crossing neurotic shift. This process seems to be only to stop when the subject feels to be able to go along with the emotional threatenings still connected with the resulting modification.

But there may be also hidden benefits we did not realize in the first view: Sometimes it may turn out that the resulting neurosis is a complex compromise keeping a balance between costs and benefits like in the case of "Der kleine Hans". Here we find a multitude of factors: the sexual and emotional longing for his mother, the feeling of guilt for masturbation, the casual threatening with castration and the extension of his mother's and father's care about him because of his "irrational" neurotic fears of horse. What we gain as insight in the reflection on these examples of the modification of types can be summed up in four items:

1. The sedimentation of experience in types is different than the memory based on language and revitalizing propositional knowledge. So even in standard cases we have to accept that there is something that remains unknown in the *mode of language* while it is known in a *mode based on types* of objects influencing our actions.
2. The slow work of non-language thinking in modifying replays results in a change of types, so that we can also gain knowledge in the mode of modified types from

---

[19] Cf. Freud (1909).

only one experience. We had to realize that in the standard case a type changes slowly its contents due to a series of similar experiences. But even if there is only one singular event or experience, this might induce a series of phantasmatic replays of this experience – especially if it is traumatic.
3. Even if – on the first view – the replays in the mode of phantasmatic scenes are not productive they slowly modify the scene in which the traumatic event arises. The slow transformation in this non-language mode of thinking ends up in a functioning compromise or in a useful plan for the future action.
4. Sometimes it is not easy to see the way in which a new behavior in special situations is to understand as an overall acceptable solution of the difficulty, a functionary system.

So there is an *unconsciousness* in humans but it coins out more in a difference of our non-linguistic processing and memorizing of experience in contrast to the language system of thinking.

References

Bernet, Rudolf. 2012. Phantasieren und Phantasma bei Husserl und Freud. In *Founding psychoanalysis phenomenologically*, ed. D. Lohmar and J. Brudzinska, 1–21. Heidelberg: Springer.
Cameron, P., and H. Biber. 1973. Sexual thought throughout the life span. *Gerontologist* 13: 144–147.
Freud, Sigmund. 1909. Analyse der Phobie eines fünfjährigen Knaben [Der kleine Hans]. In *Gesammelte Werke. Bd. VII*, 243–377.
———. 1919. Ein Kind wird geschlagen. In *Gesammelte Werke*. Bd. XII, 197–226.
Hicks, T., and H. Leitenberg. 2001. Sexual fantasies about one's partner versus someone else: Gender differences in incidence and frequency. *Journal of Sex Research* 38: 43–50.
Lohmar, Dieter. 2008a. How do primates think? Phenomenological analyses of a non-language system of representation in higher primates and humans. In *Husserl and the non-human animal*, ed. Chr. Lotz and Corinne Painter, 57–74. Heidelberg: Dordrecht.
———. 2008b. *Phänomenologie der schwachen Phantasie*. Dordrecht: Heidelberg.
———. 2012a. In *Founding psychoanalysis. Phenomenological theory of subjectivity and the psychoanalytical experience*, ed. D. Lohmar and J. Brudzinska. Heidelberg: Springer.
———. 2012b. Psychoanalysis and the logic of thinking without language. How can we conceive of neurotic shifting, denying, inversion etc. as rational actions of the mind? In *Founding psychoanalysis phenomenologically. Phenomenological theory of subjectivity and the psychoanalytical experience*, ed. D. Lohmar and J. Brudzinska, 149–167. Heidelberg: Springer.
———. 2012c. Thinking and non-language thinking. In *Handbook of contemporary phenomenology*, ed. Dan Zahavi, 377–398. Oxford: Oxford University Press.
———. 2016. *Denken ohne Sprache*. Dordrecht: Heidelberg.
Rinofner-Kreidl, Sonja. 2012. Self-deception. Theoretical puzzles and moral implications. In *Founding psychoanalysis phenomenologically. Phenomenological theory of subjectivity and the psychoanalytical experience*, ed. D. Lohmar and J. Brudzinska, 213–233. Heidelberg: Springer.
Symons, Donald. 1993. The stuff that dreams aren't made of: Why the wake-state and dream-state sensory experiences differ. *Cognition* 47: 181–217.

Chapter 13
A Broken Self-Possession: Responsive Agency in Habits

Line Ryberg Ingerslev

Abstract A rational agent is someone who knows what she is doing and why; and we hold her responsible for her actions. However, in our everyday lives we often act automatically and even involuntarily. The aim of this paper is to motivate a reconsideration of agency such that we can conceive of basic forms of the unconscious, the involuntary and the unreflective as being part of human *responsive* agency. The paper dwells on the structure of self-experience in habits to reveal how temporal displacements, disintegration and self-alienation are part of human self-experience. The central claim is that the responsive structure of habits form a possibility for re-appropriation of our own actions. This will allow us to acknowledge that a large part of our actions and decisions are less rational and deliberate than we might have hoped, while avoiding the unfortunate conclusion that such behaviour is impersonal and simply a complex form of reflex.

Keywords Ownership • Skilful intentionality • Self-withdrawal • Intransparency • Responsiveness

13.1 Introduction

Many human acts originate beyond our conscious grasp. Sometimes we don't know why we act as we do; it is *as if* we cannot hold ourselves responsible for what happens: "I just did it" or "I couldn't help it" we might say. Such actions range from mere habits like biting one's nails; to repetitive acts like always putting on the left shoe first; and to symptomatic behaviour in psychopathology like constantly checking yourself in the mirror. Actions like these seem to originate elsewhere than in the agent; we act unconsciously, automatically, and even involuntarily.

L.R. Ingerslev (✉)
Universität Wien, Vienna, Austria
e-mail: line.ryberg.ingerslev@univie.ac.at

Actions such as these form a challenge to the philosophical idea of a human agent which characterizes our agency mainly in terms of rationality and accountability. Typically, actions are understood as events that are intentional under some description, and to act intentionally is to act in a way that's intelligible in terms of the agent's reason. What I would like to challenge is not the idea that most of our actions are intelligible in terms of an agent's reason. Rather, what I believe we have to question is the accessibility we have as agents to our own reasons in certain activities of ours, namely habits. Given that an agent is understood as someone who is the conscious author of her actions, we might question the status of the activities in which it appears unclear to us who the author is of our doings. The consequence of characterizing agency exclusively or mainly in terms of rationality in this particular way is that all behaviour for which we cannot provide reasons acquire the status of blind reflexes or blind behaviour that does not belong to the subject: My leg may kick when you tap it at the knee, but it wasn't *me* that kicked.

I would like to dwell on to the idea that we can be responsible for actions that are not rational. Or what I will propose is a meditation on the kind of agency at stake in our habit, as it might provide an entry point for thinking about how we are barred from our self as conscious agents. This does not merely suggest that what we might think of as the unconscious is always defined negatively in relation to what is conscious. Rather, I will suggest that in the responsive structure of habits we will see how a reservoir of possibilities are alive in our habits, as a past that has to be re-appropriated as our own such that we can in fact come to live well with our habits. For, surely, my pathological mirror checking or nervous nail biting is something *I do*. They are habits that I possess as an agent in a much stronger sense than the sense in which the disposition to kick is mine. But how can we account for our unreflective, involuntary and unconscious actions as more than mere reflex, bodily affectivity and passive re-activity? What kind of agency is at stake in the cases where we cannot fully recognize ourselves in our actions? The present paper reflects on the unconscious origin of very basic forms of activities of ours, namely habits in the attempt to answer to these questions.

In order to pursue the idea that habits can be conceived of as a form of responsive agency I will proceed in four steps. First, I will look at some structural characteristics of self-experience in habit. Secondly, I will ask whether responsiveness in habits should be understood as a form of skilful intentionality. Thirdly, I will argue why we lose some of the personal character of habitual agency if we accept this idea. Finally, I will suggest that the important element of self-withdrawal in habit points to our possibility for re-appropriating our habits as our own.

13.2 Self-Experience in Habits. Withdrawal of Self and Displacement in Time

Habits in the broadest sense of being unreflective and non-intended provide an entry point for a reflection on a peculiar kind of agency. We come to experience them as having *already happened*, and as such they are beyond and before our conscious grasp. In this way bodily habits reveal a self-displacement in our experience of agency: as they have already happened, I come to catch myself in my habits, for instance when I realize that I *keep* biting my nails! My habits entail an element of self-surprise: I do not know how they come about, *why* do I keep biting my nails? And what is even more peculiar is that despite their foreign nature, I know my habits very well to be mine, but in a strange way.

In what follows, I will reflect on the structural significance of the kind of self-experience where we do not recognize ourselves as the authors of what happens, but we still assume ownership of our doings. As such, the paper is a meditation on what could be termed a broken self-possession. With this term the aim is to analyse the significant ways in which we escape ourselves and do not seem to recognize ourselves in our actions. A broken self-possession does not mean that we once were in possession of ourselves, but then something happened and now we feel different or cannot recognize ourselves anymore. The broken self-possession does not enter our lives because of illness, chock or other kinds of rupture. Quite on the contrary, the idea is that there is no original dwelling in oneself. A broken self-possession refers to the constitutive lack of unity in the way in which we experience ourselves; I am, but I haven't got myself as we can say with Helmuth Plessner (2003, p. 190). The following is a meditation on what it could mean to *not have oneself*. It is a reflection on the temporal self-withdrawal at the heart of the human self-experience. Such self-withdrawal prevents us from experiencing ourselves as fully unified autonomous agents and thus as the primarily rational source of our own actions. If we attend to the motif of "not having oneself", of not being oneself the conscious author and of being thus experientially displaced, we must ask how bodily habits involve unreflective actions that are nonetheless experienced with ownership. How can bodily habits that are so intimately mine at the same time be experienced in a manner of not-having-myself?

Think of the basic everyday experience of getting up in the morning. When I get up in the morning, bodily habits and several years of practice enable me to reach my bowl of cerials without thinking "right leg out of the bed, left leg out of the bed, brush your teeth in circular movements, open the fridge, pour some milk". Bodily habits can be characterized by the typical embodied way of coping with everyday challenges in an un-reflective manner. Such habits are the discrete helpers that enable me to do other things of which I am aware such as listening attentively to the radio all the time without having to plan or consider how I get up and turn the radio on. The element of compensation in habits prevents everything from being effort, will, and deliberation; without habits everything would be new to me. Habits *transform* the unknown into a world *for me*, something I can deal with as a natural part of my bodily repertoire.

Nonetheless, we might say there is something strangely alienating in such habits, namely in the way that I actually don't know what I am doing when I get up in the morning. As if I didn't decide myself what to do. As if my habits help me being and becoming myself; Line who is capable of getting up in the morning, although she doesn't know how to. We might say that I have to trust the habitual me in order to become me every morning: my habits are always there before I get up, so to say, and in actually getting up, I respond to the temporal displacement within me. The displacement namely that I am thrown into my own habits; I only discover my habits with a certain delay. I am not aware of their beginning; they always show up before me. This element of displacement in habits shows how my agential origin is somehow before me and how, at the same time, I am ahead of myself. Habits reveal an ecstatic self-relation.

If we accept that this structure entails self-withdrawal tied to the origin of my own habitual agency, we introduce the motive of knowing without knowing, or of a subject that is bared from itself in understanding and authoring its own actions. The idea of self-withdrawal can be further spelled out as a form of bodily anonymity: "The body affects me *but I can't initiate that it does so*: how the body feels and what it does is how I feel and what I do, but I have no grasp upon where it comes from: the fact that my body's past affects me escapes me. I am not the origin of whether or not I have a trauma, whether I love or hate, whether I am attracted or repulsed – but all this is nonetheless part of *my* body, part of *me*." (Ingerslev and Legrand 2017b) Here the structure of responsiveness in habit share the same temporal structure of the symptom, in the way that the bodily traces of my past anonymously repeat themselves: they " irremediably show up *before me*, deciding *for me* before I decide to decide myself" (Ibid) What I will unfold under the heading of re-appropriation of agency at stake in the responsive structure of habits will share with psychopathological symptoms the repetitive bodily manifestation that "reveal an anonymity at the very heart of me, while at the same time [show how] I embody this anonymity *as mine*. [And in this way], my self-possession is broken, not contingently but constitutively, in the sense that I don't identify my name with an anonymity so inherently mine" (Ibid). This means that when we embark on the responsive structure of habits, we will at the same time indirectly reflect on the role of the unconscious in symptoms at least to the extent of pursuing the motif of not-having-oneself and of ecstatically finding oneself having already acted while not understanding why or how so. Importantly, this does not imply that a habit repeated long enough will automatically turn into a symptom or that a symptom in any thinkable way is reducible to a bad habit; rather, the claim is that the responsive structure of habit will tell us something important about reclaiming ownership in the therapeutic striving, be it on the side of the patient or the clinician, towards understanding the meaningfulness of symptoms.

The need, however, to develop a notion of responsive agency in habits doesn't arise out of a lack of theories that tell of the role of habit in relation to human agency in general, but all these accounts suffer from the same flaw: habit is excluded from the sphere of the personal. Philosophically, habits somehow play the less heroic part in characterizing the human condition. Habits glue together the otherwise contingent happenings of our lives (Hume 1978). Habits unburden us from the constant struggle of reasoning (Gehlen 1986): We just do what we always do or what seems the easiest and most convenient thing to do, as we live in the inauthentic ways of das man (Heidegger 1993), embodying ideals of docility (Foucault 1977). We think we know all we need to know or at least enough to have the opinions we have (Lear 1998). Moreover, we live with people that are like us so that we need not question our own grounds for acting as we do (Bourdieu 1977), this might even turn into some kind of unreflective moral habitus (Mahmood 2004; Rietveld 2008a, b). When reasoning, we create short cuts and act out of habit (Tversky and Kahlman 1974). Following these latter lines of thought it seems that human actions are at most rarely rational or even not at all.

Unless we develop a theoretical framework for understanding how lack of conscious, rational authorship in human agency differs from mere reflexes and pre-reflective doings, we are left with no choice but concluding that we rarely perform actions that are *ours* in the stronger sense suggested above. And to this end, we need some kind of notion of responsive agency that can account for the many actions we perform that somehow originate beyond our conscious grasp but that still come with ownership. With the notion of responsive agency, the aim is to show how we come to view our actions as our own but importantly with a significant delay and by experiencing them through a certain kind of self-alienation. To better understand the role that temporal displacements, disintegration and self-alienation play in human self-experience, we must correct the idea of rational agency such that we become able to conceive of basic forms of the unconscious, the involuntary and the unreflective as being part of human responsive agency.

Thus having introduced some aspects of self-experience in habits we can say that although habits are strangely intentional at the same time seem to escape our will, effort, and control; they direct us towards the world, form it, shape it and give it to us; however, at the same time, we only come to realize this in a form of re-appropriation of this world, so I will argue. I am concerned with the kind of self-experience at stake in habits in order to show how self-withdrawal and temporal self-displacement in habits calls us into question as responsive agents. My claim is that we rely on something strangely other than ourselves in order to become ourselves. Importantly, becoming oneself does not ease, erase or cancel out the broken self-possession in mention. Moreover, the idea of becoming oneself is to be understood as a form of learning to live well with the affective habituality that ongoingly addresses us with anonymity and intransparency characteristic of so many of our actions. Habits are therefore not only a matter of skilled intentionality; they further come with an opening for re-appropriation in the way we deal with taking over our own past. If we focus mainly on how habits as skill or embodied familiarity shape our world, we forget how we are temporally already shaped by them and thus have to surrender to them in the mode of responsive re-appropriation. These ideas will be developed in what follows, which is why I will not be focusing on how we acquire habits as skills, but on self-experience in habits that we already have.

By this short introduction to habit, I will leave it up to the single bodily pattern to be decided whether we see in it as a random tic, a compulsory act, a personal habit or a designed manner of self-presentation. The aim is not to ignore these differences, but to point at a structural phenomenon; namely that of how we come to experience these doings of ours that go beyond ourselves and escape us in their agential origin. Although we might explain why someone tends to always accept yet another phone call from a family member, another person plays the violin in a certain characteristic way, and a third person eats too many cakes, the idea is here to look at the experience of not knowing yourself why you do as you do while at the same time responding to these habits in your own name.

13.3 Responsive Agency: Unreflective Skilful Actions?

Now, can't we do without experiential broken self-possession and temporal displacement and instead give an account of habitual agency as a mode in which we are responsive to the affordances of the world? Isn't skilled intentionality in unreflective action what we should be looking for in order to understand what responsive agency could be?

In phenomenology the lived body is often referred to as the medium of having a world. The close relation between embodiment and inhabiting a world suggests that bodily habits are a way of acquiring this world, getting to understand it, to feel and know it through the body. The body is the total field of my motivations; it is imbued with meaning in so far as my body is the lived capability and skill that answers to the affordances of the world. Although we also react to the world, the lived body is first and foremost directed towards the world, as Merleau-Ponty writes: "[T]o move one's body is to aim at the things through it, or to allows one's body to respond to their solicitation, which is exerted upon the body without any representation." (Merleau-Ponty 2012, p. 140) The world calls the body into moving and the body inhabits felt motivation to answer these calls (Kiverstein and Rietveld 2015). Standing in front of a door, I responsively open it with ease; and being next to a person I like, I responsively stand close to that person. Bodily movements can be seen as responses to affordances of the world. The body is constituted by its *capacity* to move and respond; when it moves, it responds to the world by inhabiting it.

If we follow this rough outline, being a bodily subject per se means being a responsive subject. I will look at Erik Rietveld's writings on what he calls the phenomenology of affordances, since here we find not only the idea that the world moves us to respond, but also that this responsiveness entails freedom and normativity. Rietveld thus avoids opposing habit and freedom, however, his notion of responsiveness is too generic to actually account for the experience of (dis)-ownership in habits and the possibility for self-understanding at stake in them.

According to Rietveld, affordances are described as bodily responses to being in the world:

13 A Broken Self-Possession: Responsive Agency in Habits

> Affordances are [...] understood as an organism's possibilities for action in some situation. I focus on the phenomenology of affordances. Or better, on the phenomenological description and analysis of an individual's responsiveness to affordances. [...] Part of the first-person experience of such responsiveness is that affordances are not *mere* possibilities for action but are experienced as *potentiating* and having *affective allure*. (Rietveld 2008b, p. 468)

The individual's responsiveness to affordances is experienced as an affective allure, which means that we are simply either drawn or repulsed by something, without or before being consciously aware of this. It is not the case that we are self-aware of self-conscious while running after busses or getting up in the morning like me, we are merely affected by being attracted to move in a certain way (Rietveld 2008a, p. 132). Rietveld's argument for pre-reflective affective self-awareness builds on the internal link between the living body and the world: in unreflective actions it is not the case that we possess as it were a numb experiential point of view from nowhere; rather, we simply allow ourselves to respond to the calls of the world as we experience such calls affectively. We are clearly engaged as ourselves, but there is no representation of this engagement apart from a pre-reflective affective self-awareness tied to the experience of the body as mine.

Since it is not the case that we are completely absorbed and thus blindly dictated by the surrounding world and its objects, Rietveld raises the question what *freedom* might be in unreflective skilful action, independent of any possible later reflection and linguistic articulation (ibid., p. 128, 149).

> This freedom does not require anything outside unreflective engagement with things in the context of a socio-cultural practice, let alone the detached attention of a noticing or choosing reflective ego, because the affective allure of another relevant affordance may induce the switch from responding to one affordance to another without the mediation of linguistic articulation, reflection or detached attention. [...] unreflective freedom simply *is* being situated in a field of multiple relevant affordances. Freedom in unreflective action is therefore inherent in (or constituted by) the concernful system of possible actions that the situated skilful body is. (Rietveld 2008a, p. 128)

If we follow Rietveld, unreflective freedom simply means to be in a situation where we receive several potentiating calls from the surrounding world. As if we were over-determined by the possibilities of a situation, like we are when confronted with a fruit basket; an apple, a pear, a peach or a banana? The fruits all symbolize relevant affordances and unreflective freedom consist in the way we are situated in front of this fruit basket, not so much in each of the single possibilities, but being situated in this very field of a multiplicity of relevant affordances is what unreflective freedom is, since here we experience the affectivity of being called and we experience, although unreflectively, that we are somehow able to answer this call by giving in to one of the calls.

In this way, because the body is a 'concernful system of possible actions' unreflective freedom translates into the idea that within this field it is always possible to start something new by responding to the multiplicity of affordances, without being reflectively aware of this. So in giving in to the solicitations of the world, we always have the possibility of being differently bound, to begin something new, to unreflectively make a transition from one activity to another, (Rietveld 2008a, p. 148,149). Shifting from one absorbed, unreflective way of skilful coping to another, say from walking to running, requires *no reflection* or is not motivated by thought or the awareness of an 'I do': "normally the nature of one's first-person experience of responding to affordances is not that 'I do', since there is no reflective subject or ego having the experience. In most cases the individual will not reflect (neither now, nor later) on her experience of the solicitation but simply respond to it." (ibid., p. 133).

The important point is that we are affected when we respond, and the "felt solicitation" (ibid., p. 134) arises on the background of a tension, which according to Rietveld is normative. When I go from walking to running, I experience unreflectively a normative tension that moves me; I am literally being "moved to improve" the situation (ibid., p. 151, Kiverstein and Rietveld 2015, pp. 211–2). In cases like catching a bus or watching a big painting in a museum, we unreflectively feel a tension: our pace is too slow for catching that bus, so we start running; likewise, we stand too close to the picture to see its motive or colours, so we step back. This is what Rietveld terms contextual normativity: "A basic sense of distinguishing in context between better or worse, optimal and suboptimal, appropriate and inappropriate, what is significant and what is less significant" (Rietveld 2008a, p. 151, note 136). In a specific context we are sensitive to perceptual norms of optimums, and thus, we are being moved to improve, when we change from one form of response to another. Freedom in this minimal sense means to be able make such shifts within a field of relevant affordances determined by skill (ibid., p. 151) and thus to answer freely to the felt tension.

On this account, responsiveness and bodily habits provide us with a socio-cultural sensitivity to certain situation and practices. How close we stand to people in an elevator or how well we, say as architect's, measure the size of a door depends on situated normativity (Rietveld 2008b). The way we are affectively sensitive to a normatively significant field of affordances matters to the possible changes in our concern for being ready to act, and this action guiding sensitivity is essential to unreflective freedom. What separates this unreflective freedom from regulative automatism is the fact that we *allow* ourselves to respond and that this allowance depends on skill and education, we do not just simply respond, we have acquired and cultivated a sense for responding in a certain way.

13.4 Habits and How We Answer to Them in Our Own Name

If by every bodily move we make we already respond to affectively felt tensions or to relevant field of affordances, responsiveness seem to translate into some sort of *reactive sensitivity*; when it is too hot I open the window, if it is too cold I put on a sweater. If the objects and surfaces of the world elicit our movements and attract our attention, is responsiveness not just another word for plain reactivity? Does being responsive translate into being a sensuous being whose responses are pulled or drawn out by the world? Am I responsive *because* I can take the cup *or* the glass, walk to the bus stop or run to catch it? Am I responsive to a certain field because I excel in that field? Yes, skill gives us access and practical understanding of the world we inhabit. But when it comes to responsive agency in habit we cannot overlook the experience of self-displacement constituted by an anonymous embodied activity that I answer to in my own name. If responsiveness is reduced to a sort of bodily openness to the world as such, we compromise the experience of *having* to respond or *having* to deal with our own responses as they are shaped in form of our habits. I am a responsive being because I find myself already being in the habit of… and *this* I have to deal with, as it calls me into questions as an agent; the embodied anonymity of my habits go on in my name, and only by re-appropriating them as mine, can I take responsibility for who I am. Taking over one's past provides access to the future, not only in the sense that it opens up a field of relevant affordances, bodily habits also come with anonymity, involuntary and unconscious acts that we have to re-appropriate as our own, so I will argue in the last section of the paper. These latter aspects are left out in Rietveld's account since they do not concern skilled intentionality. My habits not only provide access to the world, they also question and provoke my self-understanding, commitment and responsibility as an agent. Even skill comes with openness to disruption in a fundamental way (see Lear 2011).

Further, we might ask how the tension that makes me move to improve can be normative in the first place. When confronted with the fruit basket, is the felt tension really a normative tension? It is certainly not the case that an urge to or concern for acting is gratified when I do in fact pick up an apple. It is not the case that I can say to myself, I have done something wrong, inappropriate or incorrect, by choosing the apple and not the banana. Thus, we might ask whether habits and unreflective action can be experienced as right or wrong. Isn't it rather the case that habits come with no rules and no norm, – unless they have turned into neurotic compulsory behaviour -? When I get up in the morning, I do not blame myself or hold myself guilty if I change the order of brushing my teeth and eating my cereals. There are no standards of correctness inherent to habits themselves. We might say that habits are indeed habituating, they reinforce themselves and they are self-generating, and thereby they provide a fundament for certain lifeforms, but in and of themselves they generate no rules. Habits occur as part of the social realm, of course, and as such they appear in a realm of norms. But the order built by habits themselves is not subject to moral evaluation. However, the way in which I experience them as anonymous on-goings in my name, might call me as an agent into question. This means that responsiveness has to be tied to agency not simply as a matter of skilled intentionality. We need a stronger notion of (dis)-ownership tied to self-experience in habits if we are to account for the urge to respond to what goes on in one's name. When I move in the elevator to adjust the uncomfortable lack of distance between me and others I do so without referring to any normative standards. To say that my situated normativity tells me to step back deflates the idea of norms as something *agents* respond to; there might be a socio-cultural institutionalized norm as to how close we stand, but it seems to be Rietveld's point that such objective standards are not what moves us, rather it is the affected unreflective agent that has an internalized norm experienced as personal discomfort relative to his agential skills. How can discomfort or pleasure in and of itself be a norm?

To sum up; in Rietveld's account responsiveness becomes another word for an affective embodied reaction, skilled or not. Therefore the following questions remain unanswered by Rietveld: What if our bodily material nature is something we have to surrender to and that this having to surrender to is experienced as such? What if we are not in the safe zone of skilful unreflective action but irreducibly exposed to the tension of having to deal with too many affordances, of having to deal with conflicting habits and of having to deal with a bodily material nature that is not only present to us when we fall ill or reflect upon it in a detached way? What if already in our embodied habits the tension we experience is one that is not normative, but rather one that is constitutive of being human? The theory of responsiveness is not reducible to a theory of the affective and feeling body as such; rather, it is a theory of self-withdrawal and disintegration or dis-union at the heart of human self-experience. These questions remind us of the existential dimension of responsive agency that I will turn to in what remains of the paper.

13.5 Responsive Agency as Re-appropriation. To Begin Something New Is Done by Taking Up One's Habits

So far, we have seen that a skilled intentionality framework reduces responsiveness to mere affective reactivity, and thereby leaves aside the idea that *someone* is responding to the calls of the world in her own name. In the following I will argue why it is of further therapeutically relevance that we keep the connection between an existential level of self-understanding in habits and a motor intentional level of what bodily habits might reveal.

My suggestion is that the key to understanding responsive agency in habit is to grasp how we deal with the alienness that habit makes manifest to and in us. This alienness is *not only* something we meet, say, when our habits break down (like in cases of illness, traveling, or rupture) *or* in exceptional and extra-ordinary situations (in situations of death, grief, or divorce, say); *rather,* the alienness is pervasive, which is why the force of habit is not only alienating when we find ourselves in new places or when our daily rhythm breaks down; on the contrary, there is an important alienness inherent to the very way we experience ourselves on a daily basis. To put it with the words of Bernhard Waldenfels; when it comes to self-experience we escape ourselves on a daily basis:

> We could continue in this way and show that all our behaviour arises from a sort of self-affection we undergo and respond to. We are older than ourselves, and as a result of the fact of our birth and a further series of second births we are incapable of making up our *Selbstvorsprung*, our precedence to ourselves or lead on ourselves.[...]. My original delay

or posteriority generates an irreducible sort of alienness which I call *ecstatic alienness*. I get outside myself, not by chance, illness or weakness, but by being who I am. (Waldenfels 2004, p. 242)

What Waldenfels describes here as 'birth' and a 'series of second births' refers to the way in which we confirm, take on and commit to the temporal displacement that we are (see also Waldenfels 1994, 2006). Finding myself thrown into my habits, I come to realize myself as a responsive agent, and thereby I give birth to being who I am by taking over my habits. It is only by way of the experience of alienness that I come to find myself, stretched in time, displaced, withdrawn from being the conscious author of my doings: I find myself already being in the habit of....

Therefore, it is not the case that because I fall ill or feel uncomfortable in the elevator I move; rather, the tension in mention is pervasive. I am already ecstatically alienated from myself through my habits. They already possess me; I am already thrown into them. However, receiving them as ecstatic alienness and surrendering to them is a way to respond to oneself as someone who can take responsibility for who I am. What would it mean, then, to practically surrender to one's own habits? It would mean that rather than paying attention to whether they are good or bad, whether they can be learned, unlearned or improved; I belong to my habits as they urge me to respond to what I have become. Surrendering consist in the way I give myself over to already having acted, while at the same time taking up this agential urge of having to respond to this displacement. In this way, we find in habits not only automatizations of skilful action but an inherently creative self-alienation that helps us becoming who we are. The creative moment is the moment that Waldenfels refers to as birth and that Maria Talero describes when she describes the past of habits being a reservoir for the possible:

> Freedom lies in the *rediscovery* of my habitual past as a *reservoir of possibilities*, indeed, as a vigorous force actively shaping my future at every moment. It lies in our ability to enter into this force, both past and futural, intrinsically rigid and intrinsically flexible, with the stance of one who approaches the world as a place where meaning grows. (Talero 2006, p. 203, italics added, LRI)

Importantly, if we simply outsource the cause of my actions to a relevant field of affordances, we lose the personal character of *re-discovery* and of taking over one's habits and thereby we merely have the unreflective skilful responsiveness, but no sense of *how* I appropriate these otherwise anonymous actions as going on in my name. The idea of rediscovering oneself is essential to what Talero calls the openness for transformation:

> [O]ur body's capacity to hold onto the past in its habits is what situates us in a meaningful world in the first place, and the phenomenon of being-in-the-world itself is understood in terms of a permanent power of escape, *an essential non-presence at the heart of our existence*. But this very holding, this very structure of repetition and compulsion and escape that appears in habit as well as in the traumatic experiences of repression, *is essentially open to transformation* – it is our very openness to transformation – and this through the very strength by which it seems stubbornly to repeat the past. The pastness of habit […] is intrinsically futural, and the very rigidity of habit stems from the way in which it is always cleaving to a certain future. (Talero ibid., italics added, LRI)

The creativity, the possible birth, and the intrinsic futural aspect of habit consist in the possibility for *re-appropriation*. We might say that responsiveness without some personal grasp of alienation remains blind, because it can merely answer to the potentiating calls of the world, but cannot come to grasp the absence of authorship and self-withdrawal in habits as something that concerns how I live well with my habits – or my symptoms. Therefore, responsive agency is the kind of agency that I have to re-appropriate as mine, and by doing so, I respond to what is most intimately me but in a most unrecognizable way, since I cannot find myself as the author of such agency, and thus I am delivered over to realizing and rediscovering that this is me. Contrary to Rietveld's idea that freedom in unreflective action consists in the possibility to begin something new relative to a field opened by one's acquired skills, the point is here that none of these possibilities could occur as new out of nothing, which Rietveld would agree to. However, freedom is not only experienced relative to a field determined by skill, but importantly also by the experience of delay, echo and displacement such that there is no re-appropriation without alienation, and no freedom without becoming an echo in taking over one's habits and thereby becoming the second answer to a broken self-possession. Freedom has to mean more than grasping a fruit or standing in the optimal way in front of a picture. The Self-brokenness is not turned into a balanced well-being simply when we stop smoking or learn to live with anxiety, say. The temporal displacement and the ecstatic alienness will remain addressing us as will the way in which we have to take over our past as a possibility for re-appropriation. It will remain an open to transformation, but the transformation will not cancel out the fundamental self-withdrawal that we live with as responsive agents.

What we introduced in the beginning as a broken self-possession is what Paul Ricoeur means by a nascent alienation of not coinciding with oneself: "The path of automatization lies open, representing at the same time a temptation to sleep and sloth, as if habit were a weak point offered to what is perhaps the most perfidious of passions, the passion to become a thing. A nascent alienation presents itself. For all these reasons, even our most familiar abilities are up to a certain point distinct from us, as a 'having' which does not exactly coincide with our 'being'" (Ricoeur 2007, p. 297) According to Ricoeur, I am not distinct from my ownmost capacities, but neither are they completely mine: the alienated existence that confronts me in my habits is nature, "but a nature at the very core of myself" (ibid., p. 295) To be able to be me, I have to surrender to the answer my habits already give to the question of who I am, however, at the same time, they are delivered over to me in such a way that I creatively have to deal with; I *keep* becoming me. The alien nature at the very core of myself is the second nature that is alien to me because there was never a first one; I only receive myself – ecstatically – mediated through what I already am. I have to respond to not being the conscious author of so many of my acts; otherwise the alienation becomes total and not simply ecstatic.

13.6 Concluding Remarks

Summing up, we can say that the notion of responsive agency allow us to see habits in a new light. Habits are indeed second nature, they come to us as already existing; and further, they appear to us as answers we have already given, but that we can only discover as such by giving them again, namely as a second answer to who we are. Habits do show that we are affective beings, committed to the world, but in a stronger sense they reveal something else, namely the existential response to who we are that only come to us as something that we can follow. My habits do not simply confirm, reinforce or articulate a certain mode I might be in, say my nail biting or mirror-checking does not simply reflect existential anxiety. Rather, if we follow the present reflection, habits confront us with having to deal with *not* being at one with ourselves; we have to respond to our own answers to whom we are by taking over, following, and re-appropriating ourselves through our habits. As a result of the present reflection on responsive agency, we might reclaim some of the personal character at stake in unreflective, involuntary and unconscious actions. Rather than seeing this as a "hyper-reflective trap" where one's second nature breaks down (de Hahn et al. 2013a, b), the positive claim is that only by analysing the self-withdrawal and ecstatic alienness in habit can we understand in which way agency in habits is responsive and how we might come to assume ownership of some of the things that we do and know unknowingly. In a therapeutic context these ideas could help us in understanding how psychopathological symptoms are not merely objective signs of pathology or that they should be recognized primarily in order to be relieved. Rather, symptoms can be listened to and responsively attended to by the patient herself as well as by the clinician in order to be re-appropriated *as responsive agency*; I come to answer to this incomprehensibility going on in my name, and I surrender to it by responding to it (Ingerslev and Legrand 2017a). We do not respond blindly or with a good enough practice of skilfully being who we are. The question of my habits constantly breaks my self-possession and reveals how the alien nature at core of myself accompanies my actions as an intransparency that I have to learn to live well with. Our habits are the answers we have already given and that we are still to accomplish as our own.

References

Bourdieu, Pierre. 1977. *Outline of a theory of practice*. New York: Cambridge University Press.
De Hahn, S., E. Rietveld, and D. Denys. 2013a. Being free by losing control: What obsessive-compulsive disorder can tell us about free will. In *Free will and the brain: Neuroscientific, philosophical, and legal perspectives on free will*, ed. Walter Glannon. Cambridge: Cambridge University Press.
———. 2013b. On the nature of obsession and compulsions. In *Pharmacopsychiatry -anxiety disorders*, ed. David S. Baldwin and Brian E. Leonard. Basel: Karger. pp. 1–15.
Foucault, Michel. 1977. *Discipline and punish. The birth of prison*. New York: Vintage Books.
Gehlen, Arnold. 1986. *Der Mensch. Seine Natur und Stellung in der Welt*. Wiesbaden: Aula.

Heidegger, Martin. 1993. *Sein und Zeit*. Tübingen: Niemeyer.
Hume, David. 1978. In *A treatise on human nature*, ed. L.A. Selby-Bigge and P.H. Nidditch. Oxford: Clarendon Press.
Ingerslev, L.R., and D. Legrand. 2017a. Clinical response to bodily symptoms in psychopathology. *Philosophy, Psychiatry, and Psychology* 24(1): 53–67.
Ingerslev, L. R., and D. Legrand. 2017b. Responding to incomprehensibility – On the clinical role of anonymity in bodily symptoms. *Philosophy, Psychiatry, and Psychology* 24(1): 73–76.
Kiverstein, J., and E. Rietveld. 2015. The primacy of skilled intentionality: On Hutto and Satne's the natural origins of content. *Philosophia* 43: 701–721.
Lear, Jonathan. 1998. *Open-minded. Working out the logic of the soul*. Cambridge: Harvard University Press.
———. 2011. *A case for irony*. Cambridge: Harvard Univeristy Press.
Mahmood, Saba. 2004. *Politics of piety*. Princeton: Princeton University Press.
Merleau-Ponty, Maucrice. 2012. *Phenomenology of perception*. Transl. by Landes, D. A. London: Routledge.
Plessner, Helmuth. 2003. Die Frage nach der Conditio humana. In *Gesammelte Schriften VIII*, ed. Güunther Dux et al. Frankfurt am Main: Suhrkamp Verlag.
Ricoeur, Paul. 2007. *Freedom and nature the voluntary and the involuntary*. Evanstone: North Western University Press.
Rietveld, Erik. 2008a. *Unreflective action. A philosophical contribution to integrative neuroscience*. Amsterdam: University of Amsterdam, ILLC Dissertation Series.
———. 2008b. Situated normativity: The normative aspect of embodied cognition in unreflective action. *Mind* 117: 973–1001.
Talero, Maria. 2006. Merleau-Ponty and the bodily subject of learning. *International Philosophical Quarterly* 46 (2): 182.
Tversky, A., and D. Kahneman. 1974. Judgment under uncertainty: Heuristics and biases. *Science* 185 (4157): 1124–1131.
Waldenfels, Bernhard. 1994. *Antwortregister*. Frankfurt am Main: Suhrkamp Verlag.
———. 2004. Bodily experience between selfhood and otherness. *Phenomenology and the Cognitive Sciences* 3: 235–248.
———. 2006. *Grundmotiven einer Phänomenologie des Fremden*. Frankfurt am Main: Surhkamp Verlag.

Part V
Beyond Phenomenology

Chapter 14
Surprise as a Phenomenal Marker of Heart-Unconscious

Natalie Depraz

Abstract In this contribution I would like to make a room for another unconscious, which I name the "heart unconscious". To me it appears as a remarkable possible thread in order to bridge, more, to weave together two already well-known threads; that is, broadly speaking, the physical and the subjective, which first appear ontologically irreducible. Why? Well, one initial argument in favour is that the heart-unconscious allows a pre-conscious continuity of our experiential dynamics because of its very twofold structure, organic (the heart-muscle) and lived (heart-affectivity). In order to reveal the specificity of such an experiential pre-conscious heart-unconscious, I will put to work a very simple and daily experience; namely, the experience of surprise. Why surprise? My idea is that surprise is a remarkable marker of heart-unconscious, insofar as, in a similar structural way, it also appears as a twofold objective-subjective pre-conscious, easily conscious becoming occurrence, manifesting as a physiological-cardiac startle as well as a lived perplexity.

Keywords Unconscious • Heartl • Surprise • Emotion • Pre-conscious • Explication interviews • First-person methods • Micro-phenomenology • Neuro-phenomenology • Cardio-phenomenology

14.1 Introduction

It is usual today to talk about a cognitive, a bodily neural or a psychic unconscious (Kihlstrom 1987; Buser 2005; Dehaene et al. 2006). These forms of unconscious all appealing to a sub-personal level where automatic processes, be they neural, biological or psychic-libidinal occur as not directly accessible to my first personal introspective lived experience.

N. Depraz (✉)
Université of Rouen (ERIAC), Rouen, France
e-mail: pr.natalie.depraz@gmail.com

Now, there is an increasing interest in trying to cross the data-experimental dynamics of such automatic events with the subjective experiential micro-processes of my lived experience (Petitmengin and Lachaux 2014; Desmidt et al. 2014; Depraz and Desmidt 2015). There is a correlatively growing awareness of the abstract character of the dichotomy unconscious/conscious and of the still external distinction between third- and first-personal approaches (even though both latter distinctions only partially map), and also consequently of the necessity to provide a more gradual description of the fined-grained continuum of pre-conscious states and dynamics.

In this contribution I would like to make a room for another unconscious, which I name the "heart unconscious". To me it appears as a remarkable possible thread in order to bridge, more, to weave together two already well-known threads, that is, broadly speaking, the physical and the subjective, which first appear ontologically irreducible. Why? Well, one initial argument in favour is that the heart-unconscious allows a pre-conscious continuity of our experiential dynamics because of its very twofold structure, organic (the heart-muscle) and lived (heart-affectivity).

In order to reveal the specificity of such an experiential pre-conscious heart-unconscious,[1] I will put to work a very simple and daily experience, the experience of surprise. Why surprise? My idea is that surprise is a remarkable marker of heart-unconscious, insofar as, in a similar structural way, it also appears as a twofold objective-subjective pre-conscious, easily conscious becoming occurrence, manifesting as a physiological-cardiac startle as well as a lived perplexity.

14.2 The Hard Problem of Unconsciousness

When one broaches the issue of unconsciousness, one immediately has in mind various forms of unconscious that are already well known. In experimental neurosciences and in cognitive psychology, we face a cognitive unconscious: it amounts to a neuronal processing of perceptions, memories, learning activities or verbal expressions with no subjective awareness of any possible kind but it can be measured through different technics (EEG/Fmri); in psycho-physiological sciences, we investigate a bodily unconscious made of non- or pre-verbal organic (cardiac, breath-frequency, skin-temperature) and behavioural expressions (face and motor-gestures). Such parameters may also be measured and traced back when video-recorded; in psycho-analytic approaches, the unconscious is said to be purely "psychic": it is made of repressed feelings, subliminal perceptions, train of thoughts, habits, and also complexes, hidden phobias and desires, symbolized in dreams and

---

[1] With « unconscious » here in the expression « heart unconscious », I mean a structural meaning of unconsciousness: what is not directly accessible to consciousness, but needs to be triggered or paid attention to.

The heart unconscious may therefore easily emerge to consciousness, hence be « pre-conscious », awaiting for being conscious, insofar as my heartbeats are easily « conscientisable » (consciousizable), if I pay attention to them.

in slips of the tongue, thus only indirectly identifiable in language or behaviour and sometimes best revealed thanks to an analytic therapy.

These different aspects of unconscious take place at a sub-personal level of the mind, of consciousness or of psychism and refer to automatic neural, biological or libidinal processes. They share an indirect way of identification through neuronal electric measures, video-recordings, language or behavior. As I already mentioned, they are not directly accessible to my introspective subjective lived experience.

We thus face the "hard problem", not of consciousness as it has being long claimed since David Chalmers, but of the unconscious itself: indeed these forms of accessibility to unconscious are third-personal ones (neuronal/behavioural/linguistic). The question is: what is and *is there* a first-personal unconscious?—If yes, it will be an unconscious that could directly be accessible to consciousness. But to what extent would it still be a full-fledged unconscious if it is meant to change itself into its reverse, that is consciousness, or again, if it is "consciousizable"? Thus stated, the problem has an unsolvable paradoxical structure which is due to the apparent but in fact misleading too clear-cut distinction between conscious (first) and unconscious (third) or if not, to the confusional mixture of both dimensions going one into the other, which makes unconscious disappear into its contrary.

We know some recent thrusts in cognitive sciences which aim at unfolding the dynamics of the becoming aware of such automatic events of the mind: this was the pioneering goal of Varela with neurophenomenology (1996/1999), where the author makes the hypothesis of the fertility of mutual generative constraints of third person data and first person subjective experiences for a better understanding of consciousness. It was early applied to visio-motor-time-perception (Lutz et al. 2002), who shows how first person data can be used to detect and interpret neural processes, while the latter help control the variability of subjective fluctuations. In a far more reductionist way, S. Dehaene and his team (Marti et al. 2010) showed how introspection is not necessarily to be dismissed as an inappropriate measure but can be used in experimental work in a quantified way while taking into account the detailed descriptions of the subjects of the time and effort spent on a task.

Such theoretical thrusts however only account for a dynamic going from a third-personal unconscious to a possible first-person consciousness, either by using co-generative constraints between first person lived events and third person brain data, on the joint-basis of Husserl's conceptual dynamics of the living present and of an experiment of anticipatory time-dynamics of visuo-motor perception (Varela), or by indicating not only the formal correlation between objective and subjective data but the gradual processing of consciousness out of unconscious subliminal processes (Dehaene). Such endeavours therefore still claim to "bridge a gap" between two heterogeneous ontological realities, the physical and the subjective-conceptual (à la Descartes), with at best the location of a "pre-conscious" intermediary step within the process, as it is exemplified with vegetative states such as coma, anæthesia and sleep (Naccache), which only succeeds in providing a last resort. Of course, an alternative statement (Damasio) is the ontological non-dual monism (à la Spinoza), where conscious and unconscious events unfold parallel in their own dynamics as co-dependent aspects of an only reality. Indeed, Damasio's statement relies on the ontological contention of the unity and the continuity of our only reality as brain-subject. So the methodological epistemic question of access consciousness is not fitting here, since the unconscious is a neurophysiological one, that can only be registered through measures. It is therefore completely inaccessible to the subject as a conscious and self-conscious subject. But in this latter case there is no felt need whatsoever to articulate any different kinds of data (first personal vs. third personal), since we have to do to a unique and homogeneous ontological reality, as W. James would have early claimed it. In the following, my claim therefore is methodological and epistemic, not ontological.

14.3 Heart Unconscious as the Index of Cardio-phenomenology: An Integrative Approach

My proposal therefore is the following: we observe a phenomenal difference in the *mode of givenness* of subjective lived experiences and physical data, and such an observation is theoretically argued by phenomenological accounts, in Husserl and Merleau-Ponty mainly ; we also observe the felt unity of our reality as an individual, attested for example by Descartes both in the sixth Meditation and in his Letters to the Queen Elizabeth, on the basis of which we also experience dis-functioning between our body and our mind. How can we think together such a felt unity and our experience of modal differences in our way of knowing and experiencing?

My suggestion is that a heart-centred model provides such an opportunity to think together both modal differences of the givenness of our self and its immediate felt unity. The advantage of the heart-unconscious against a neural-cognitive or an analytic psychic unconscious lies in its experiential first-personal accessibility. Unconscious is here the fact that the heart beats without my being necessarily conscious of it, though I may easily access to its beating while simply putting my hand on my chest.: whereas I am thus able to directly feel my heart beating, I will never feel directly my neurons activating, neither my libido processing: I have direct organic sensations of my heart (I feel it pulse), I don't experience as such my libido, even though I may bodily experience a sexual desire (orgasm) as an indirect manifestation of my "libido". With the heart rhythmic movements, we get a phenomenal spontaneous accessible and light experiential *continuum* in the organic-subjective dynamics. We neither need to go against our common observation of the difference of the structural givenness of first personal (subjective) and third personal (physical) data.

One objection still exists though: what about the bodily unconscious? It seems that we do not need to promote a specific heart unconscious, since: (A) the heart is a bodily organ: a muscle in the body; (B) I can feel the sensations of my body (painful, pleasant) as much as the beatings of my heart (and sometimes even more directly). So what? What is the need for a "cardio-phenomenology", since phenomenology is as such a bodily-somatic-phenomenology? Indeed there is a general experiential continuum sensation-feeling. My contention is directly against the discontinuity between brain and consciousness, and puts the heart to the fore as a central organ which offers a specific case for such a continuity. The heart unconscious therefore does not go against the bodily unconscious but offer a complementary dimension more specifically dedicated to emotions-affects and able to interact with subjective experience more smoothly than the brain: (A) it suggests thanks to the heart-organ a refined, focused and also easily measurable access to our organic-subjective continuous dynamics; (B) it allows to identify more precisely the proper affective dimension of the lived body; (C) it provides a more integrative system of the self-including emotions as full-fledged components and not only as derived from the body or from the brain.

The idea therefore is to make a room for the heart unconscious—not to promote it as an exclusive system—but in order to braid together with it the two already better well-known threads, that is, the physical-bodily and the neuronal-cognitive. An epistemology of the braid thus emerges with *three* threads instead of two: brain, body, heart, originally linked together. Such a triangular model is more complex et flexible and therefore helps going beyond the limitations of such dualities as subjective/objective, or consciousness/brain.

Cardio-phenomenology therefore appears as a nice experiential phenomenology initially operating with a very simple common sense argument, since we have a direct first person sensation of our heartbeats: you feel your pulse, you feel your heart beat in your breast, in your head, your pulse races when you get anxious or after running, you feel your pulse reduce at rest, the rhythm of your heart always beats faster when you have drunk too much coffee or when you fall in love. You can feel it at the very moment with a minimum of trained attention… Or even without it! Hence the remarkable experiential 'automaticity' of the heart-rhythm: it beats *within myself without myself* but I can spontaneously 'turn' to my heart beating and "feel" it. This is the very amazing thing of the pre-conscious modality of my being aware, its light peculiarity: unceasingly "running" in myself without having to be reflected upon to be effective but easily "coming" to me if only I turn my attention to it.

This being said, it is clear how much with cardio-phenomenology we make a step beyond neurophenomenology (Varela 1996). The latter provided mutual generative constraints between the time-embedded experience of the subject and her subpersonal neuro-dynamics. Now, the limitation of this approach proceeds from the ontological time-discrepancy existing between a priori timeless philosophical categories (here the living present as a constant overlapping of protention, impression and retention) and the subpersonal milliseconds neurodynamics: my hypothesis is that in fact we have to do here to an interaction between two theoretical third person approaches (the Husserlian a priori generic structures of subjectivity and of experience vs. the sub-personal generic structures of the brain), which both leave out the experiential lived 1st personal approach. Cardiophenomenology instead (Depraz 2015; Depraz and Desmidt 2015) apply generative constraints to a twofold continuous unitary pre-conscious experience, both organic (heart beating) and lived (emotional-affective). The so-called gap therefore disappears as an ontological problem while being reduced and then phenomenally seamed thanks to one common experienced time-dynamics both measurable and qualitative. With more appropriate tools, that is, physiological/cardiac measures and 'explication' interviews, we favour a real effective productive crossing between a third-person approach and a first-person approach, with the goal of synchronizing the timing of the cardiac-organic-physiological components *and* of the lived heart/affective experience into a common shared seconds-scaled time. Thus it is based on a correlation between cardiac and lived components but it is going beyond it while co-producing potential new aspects of the affective experience and of the physiological one, that would remain unseen if you used only one level of approach.

In short, the heart system results more integrative than the brain system. It is more integrative because it includes a dimension, the heart-dimension revealing the emotional aspect, that was not taken into account in the previous systems, hence less integrative. Cardiac rhythmicity thus appears as a genuine clue to "sew" together the discrepancy of the explanatory gap generated by the irreducible ontological discontinuity between consciousness and brain.

A first step was already made with the introduction of body and context as two-fold dimensions, both lived and measurable: the two-fold unity *Leib/Körper*) (Husserl 1912–1915, 1918–1936) on the one side; the autopoiesis of the living being as a circular coupling of the living body and its environment (Varela 1989, 1991) on the other side.

Husserl's *modal* distinction of object-body (*Körper*) and subject-body (*Leib*) is innovative insofar it questions both the Cartesian *substantial* duality of body and mind but also the naive view of a sheer ontological unity of our bodily experience. Husserl thus encompasses the unity of our bodily experience while insisting on the multifarious way of bodily appearings, along a graduality between strong objectified bodily automatisms and quite subtle subjective lived bodily proprioceptive sensations.

Varela's contention with *autopoiesis* is the self-organisation of the living being as emerging from its constant inter-actions with its environment. The notion of "operational coupling" describes the double move at work between an individual organism and its motor-perceptive context of action, which is both an activity directed towards objects and a reception from them. The organism and the environment thus mutually build and produce each other.

The next present step consists in proposing the heart-system as an experiential "remedy" to the explanatory gap. We have different kinds of arguments at our disposal: (1) an embryogenetic argument. The heart self-organizes during the first weeks of the embryo as spontaneous contractions independently of the brain (Coghill and Gesell as quoted by Merleau-Ponty in his *Nature Lessons*). (2) A linguistic indication. Parallel to the twofold unity of the body as physical/lived revealed for example in German language as *Körper/Leib*, we have a similar twofold unity with the heart respectively with the words *Herz* and *Gemüt* (Ricœur 1950). (3) A phenomenological argument. The heart is the matrix of the person as both lived (affection) and organic (muscle) and it is therefore at the core from which emerge the first- and third-person experiences of the subject (Husserl 1908–1914). In short, the heart-rhythmicity results an interactive circular dynamics at three levels at least: (1) the circular organicity of cardiac pulsation; (2) the mobility of emotional micro-fluctuations; (3) the structural breath-rhythm (Depraz 2008, 2009).

14.4 Surprise as an Experiential-Experimental Remarkable Clue for Accessing Heart Unconscious

The theoretical and methodological framework being settled, I will explore further its relevance while putting it to work thanks to a nice and easy enough case study. My hypothesis is that surprise is an interesting subjective phenomenon that reveals parts of our pre-conscious heart-functioning (both cardiac and affective) and opens the way for its emotionally specific temporality. The fact that it is pre-conscious is crucial because then it can become conscious (for example also thanks to explication interviews for a more articulated explicit consciousness). Surprise is here a specific case study that allows to exemplify the general more structural statement about the hypothesis of a heart unconscious.

Surprise is quite a common and ordinary variable[2] and experience,[3] at once easy to measure through physiological startle and immediately lived in most daily situations, be they relational or individual: I am waiting for a friend and I am surprised at his coming to me with my worst enemy. Here surprise emotionally associates with disappointment, anger and irritation, or even with fear; I am looking forward to going to theatre with my lover and he calls to tell me that he finally got tickets for the opera: my surprise then associates with an overflow of joy, gratefulness and euphoria. In each case, surprise, though not being an emotion as such, immediately *associates* with different kinds of state-emotions defined by their valence (Smith 1795: "surprise of joy/of grief"[4]; Husserl 1908–1914: "Freudenüberraschung"[5]; Depraz 2015); surprise is embedded into a bodily succession of cardiac-, breath-rhythms and peripheral temperature oscillations, in relation with attentional or emo-

---

[2] D. Dennett (2001, p. 927): "Surprise is a wonderful dependent variable, and should be used more often in experiments; it is easy to measure and is a telling betrayal of the subject's having expected something else".

[3] Ch. S. Peirce (1903, p. 295): "Experience is learning us through surprises".

[4] A. Smith (1795, p. 295): "Surprise is not to be regarded as an original emotion of a species distinct from all others. The violent and sudden change produced upon the mind, when an emotion of any kind is brought suddenly upon it, constitutes the whole nature of Surprise. (…) The change produced by a Surprise of joy is more sudden, and upon that account more violent and apt to have more fatal effects, than that which is occasioned by a Surprise of grief. " It thus brings about a heart-temporality of surprise, where the surprise of joy may be temporally distinct from the surprise of grief: "The heart springs to joy with a sort of natural elasticity, it abandons itself to so agreeable an emotion, as soon as the object is presented (…) But it is otherways with grief; the heart recoils from, and resists the first approaches of that disagreeable passion, and it requires some time before the melancholy object can produce its full effect. Grief comes on slowly and gradually, nor ever rises at once to that height of agony to which it is increased after a little time. But joy comes rushing upon us all at once like a torrent" (*op. cit.,* p. 295).

[5] E. Husserl (1908–1914) : « [A VI 12 II/131 „53"]Die Schwierigkeit ist es, der Schicht gerecht zu werden, in der die Unterschiede <zwischen> der „still beseligten", der „stürmischen", leidenschaftlichen Freude, der Freudenüberwältigung und -überraschung – das Herz steht still und eine große Woge der Seligkeit strömt in das weitgeöffnete Herz hinein, dann Aufregung oder Freudenschmerz, <das> Herz droht zu zerspringen vor Freude – <und> der ausgeglichenen sonstigen Liebe ohne Leidenschaft usw. <liegen>."

tional physiological increases or decreases, though it is not exclusively explainable by the bodily structure ; surprise unfolds as an experiential organic-lived time-continuity made of multifarious pre-conscious micro-ruptures and organized in a recurrent model of three phases: anticipation/crisis/aftermath, which are mapping each other in turn (Depraz 2001; Desmidt et al. 2014), though it is not reducible to such a time-dynamics. Furthermore it may appear as a micro-rupture within a cognitive perceptive temporal process (Peirce 1903; Husserl 1938), irreducible to an instant-shock but manifesting as an articulated process qua dynamics of phases (Husserl 1905): (1) an awaiting phase characterized as an implicit anticipation and affective tension; (2) an aftermath phase made of reminisce and affective resonance; (3) a crisis phase identifiable as an affective zero point of rupture.

Along previous investigations (Depraz 2008, 2015), I was led to question the one-sidedness of such approaches of surprise. In physiology indeed, surprise is reduced to its bodily startle reaction basis (Darwin); in psychology, it is considered as a primary emotion among others (Ekman 1971); in cognitive sciences, it is seen as the upsetting of my beliefs within a cognitive process (Davidson, Dennett); in neuro-computational ones it is identified to a brain mismatch, that is, as an error within a predictive coding which tends minimize surprise (Friston); in ontological metaphysics finally, which would reject surprise as too much empirical in favour of an astonishment (*thaumadzein*) only referable to man (Heidegger), it equates to the very source of questioning proper to philosophy (Plato, Aristotle). My contention instead is to consider surprise as a multivectorial process that has it inner duration, therefore not reducible to an instant-abstract shock, including a three-phased micro-dynamic and associating emotional and bodily dimensions that need to be described and articulated precisely (Depraz 2015). Thus, in phase 1, we have a valence with specific emotions associated (hope/anxiety), inner thoughts and discursive processes; in phase 3 a valence with other specific emotions associated (disappointment/satisfaction), perseverative memories, and phase 2 an emotional blank associated with a latency time (silence, interjections or exclamations and intense bodily cardiac reaction).

Such an integrative non-linear approach obviously does *not* exclude startle, admiration, wonder, astonishment, upsetting of beliefs or even mismatch, but rather situate them into a more articulated complex scheme not reducible to any of them, be that physiological, emotional, neural, cognitive or ontological. If we stuck to an approach involving a subpersonal unconscious, we would only understand surprise as a startle, a neural mismatch or a cognitive upset; if on the contrary, we contended a philosophical approach of surprise, we would favour an underlying reflective or questioning self-conscious meaning of surprise as wonder, admiration or astonishment (Aristotle, Smith, Maldiney, Heidegger).

Now, both levels of approach capture only one aspect of surprise: with the heart-unconscious on the contrary, we have a two-fold experience of surprise encompassing an organic cardiac response and a psychic affective reaction. Contrary to neural or cognitive inner processes it is directly accessible to consciousness, and contrary to the philosophical reflexive consciousness, it is embodied as a lived experience. Besides, heart-unconscious is not opposed to bodily unconscious, which is also pre-conscious. It is rather embedded into a lived bodily approach but suggests a more focused approach of cardiac affectivity.

With such an integrative model as a background we currently lead a startle/lived surprise experience-experiment, both in the psychiatric framework of depressed patients (at the Tours CHU, with Th. Desmidt) and with students taking part in a psycho-linguistic task (at Paris-Diderot University, with P. Goutéraux). In both cases, strong emotional images are shown to the subjects, either shocking photos (injury/erotic images from the IAPS base-date) contrasting with neutral ones (objects), or contemporary disturbing paintings alternating with more classical ones. In one case we electronically measure physiological cardiac, breath, skin temperature reactions and brain-activity and, in parallel with these third person physiological measures, which provide significant markers of the reactivity to surprise and to associated emotional valence, I am leading explication interviews, in the course of which I guide the subject back to the lived moment of the specified and situated appearing of one particularly shocking image chosen by herself, with the goal of collecting a refined first person account of the lived bodily, verbal, emotional and cognitive micro-time-embedded pre-conscious experience of surprise of the patient during the three phases; in the second case, we record the verbal spontaneous verbal reactions of the students and I lead explication interviews with them about one chosen art-image. In each case, I was led to unexpected discoveries regarding surprise, for example, either concerning its peculiar pre-conscious disturbed time- and language-process or about its specific emotional content and dynamics irreducible to the standard distinction between affection and cognition.

14.5 The Psychotic Depressive Heart-Unconscious: Circular Repetitive Time-Dynamics, Emotional Peaks and Stammering Non-elaborative Language

The leading hypothesis of the experimental physiological task (at the Tours-CHU) is the following: in contrast with a standard-subject group, depressed patients would undergo a hypo-reactivity to surprise (Kaviani et al. 2004). An intermediary remission group might help modulating such a contrast. Commonly speaking, the idea to test is: the more you are depressed, the less you are surprised! It truly matches a type of depression linked to a melancholic coming back to oneself, with a diminished opened fear linked to the indeterminacy of the future, a secure self-coiling into the past (Tellenbach) and a tendency to anhedonia. Some other patients I interviewed though manifest a different form of depression with an increasing anxiety, which gives way to the exact reverse of hypo-reactivity: hyper-reactivity, and is often linked with a will to control. Whatever the form of depression is, it results that the implicit protentional awaiting time of the surprise is disturbed, either because protention quasi-disappears as a process, like in the melancholic closure of my coming horizons, or, on the contrary, because it is hyper-pathologically mobilised, like in anxiety.

So the temporality is highly relevant for the study of unconsciousness: in the first person descriptions I gathered already, the time of surprise indeed is not successive nor linear like in explicit consciousness where sequentiality is dominant, but it is circular, and in some cases, in depressive subjects, it is blurred, with gaps, holes in sequences or at least difficulties to identify them.

The pathological time of surprise in depression may also be characterized in a broader way as disturbed or blurred with regard to its standard dynamics of its three articulated micro-phases, anticipation/crisis/aftermath, as described above. In order to characterize more precisely some modalities of disturbance of the depressed time-dynamics of surprise I was able to notice till now, I will present two accounts of depressed patients at the visual perception of an image of mutilation, that is, during the crisis-phase.

A. <u>D-03's map of depression at the heart-unconscious level</u>

- Time: blurring of micro-sequentialities: unnoticed synchronizing of sensations, motor-reactions and emotions
- Language: strongly bodily-emotional echolalia, obsessive-compulsive and denial-laden
- Emotion: dynamic ambivalence of immediacy and distantiation

One crucial indication of the temporality at work for patient D-03's experience of surprise is the recurrence of one obsessive *leitmotiv*, which crystalizes in one ever-repeated expression when seeing an image of mutilation: "it is only an image!".[6]

Such an exclamatory expression occurs at an uncountable number of times. And the ever and ever coming back of "it is only an image" produces a feeling of blurring and even confusion of the sequences corresponding to phases 2 (crisis) and 3 (aftermath). Such a nagging repetition helps the patient so it seems distancing from the deep emotional shock generated by a face where no distinctive feature appears ("a melted face"[7]) and takes the recurrent formal "it is not"[8] structure of a denial: "I have a jolt, *but I...mean, it's not, um... I have no* jolt, it is, yes, I have empathy, yes that um... that seizes me somewhere, *but I mean it's not...* here, *it's not something that I*...that that... really gets under my skin...um... that I... um… sss... *I don't have...* um... yes, um... surprise, *not* a jolt, but a small movement backwards".[9] Or again :

---

[6] « c'est qu'une image ! »

[7] « un visage fondu ». Recurrence of the adjective *melted* : "a melted face without expression, without eyes, without mouth, without nose, all was melted, as though it were plastic"; "yeah, melted, um... which didn't have a human shape, which, without form, without eyes...we can guess it is a face, but after one doesn't see the eyes anymore, one doesn't see anymore"; "in the end, we guess that it is a man, we guess, but it is...um...his traits have melted...it's, it's not..." (no mention of colors, nor of spatial disposition center/periphery); "no, I don't see, no I don't see the hair, I see nothing, no I only see this face"(« ben un visage fondu sans expression, sans yeux, sans bouche, sans sans nez, quoi, tout était fondu, comme si c'était du plastique... »; « waouais fondu, fin qu'avait plus de forme humaine, que, voilà, sans forme sans yeux. fin on devine que c'est un visage, mais après on voit plus les yeux, on voit plus... »; « voilà, fin on devine que c'est un homme, on devine, voilà, mais c'est... euh... ses traits sont fondus, voilà, c'est... c'est pas... » [pas de mention des couleurs, ni de la disposition spatiale centre/périphérie] : « non, je vois pas, non j'vois pas de cheveux. j'vois rien, non je vois que ce visage »).

[8] « C'est pas... »

[9] « ben j'ai un sursaut, *mais je... veux dire, c'est pas, fin j'ai pas* un sursaut, c'est, oui, j'ai de l'empathie, oui ça m'a fin ça me saisit quelque part, *mais j'veux dire c'est pas. voilà, c'est pas...*

"and I have difficulty bursting into tears, or anything like that because *it's only* an image... um... here... it is, here it it it it's not beautiful to see, *but it isn't*... here... there, *it's only* a photo, an image... a photo, here, it's... um... it's... it's not beautiful to see, here, but it's...ugh, but *it's only* an image...after, here, *it's only a...it's not* reality... yes, *it's only* an image... here, um... well... there... well... here... it's, um... I have difficulty to express myself with respect to an image, there...*it's it's not* that, but it's here there's (silence for a few seconds), *it's only* an image, here, um... well... in brief, but, *it's only* an image... and ugh... and then ugh... (silence for 4–5 seconds)... *it's only* an image... it's it's... but *it's only* an image. It was a *photo* (she stresses the word) of a *person* (she stresses again) no, I don't see, no I see no hair... I see nothing, no *I see only* this face! Ah, I feel fine."[10] The recurrence and repeated alternation of the syntagms "it is that... it is not... " strongly refers to a language of denial mixed with concessive and defensive tones (example: "Ah, I feel fine"), forms and contents: "there nonetheless a barrier that puts itself in place".[11] In a nutshell, we can speak of an important global emotional shielding both in language and in contents expressed.

Besides, the intensity and the anxious-character of the enduring emotion during the task is strongly expressed by a repeated phonetic "sss" expression, which may also refer to a bodily sensation of stomach-spasm and to an emotional anxious feeling, here re-lived in such a direct bodily language, and also by an important difficulty of speaking, best expressed in the repeated echolalic expressions: "it's, it's, it's..." as well as in her recurrent stammering. In short, she gives the clear impression of strong endeavouring to control her emotions while trivializing the vision of horror she mentions though: "it is horrible to see someone who is totally disfigured".[12]

To summarize, we can underline three main aspects, one regarding the language, the other related to time, the last concerning her relation to emotions. Concerning the former, I already mentioned her difficulty to verbalize: "I have difficulty to describe,"[13] she says. Here is an exemplary verbal sequence of it: "it's it's not that I am heatless, but it there's (silence for a few seconds), it's only an image there... it's perhaps a... it's it's it's perhaps a woman that has been burnt, um... sprayed, um... well... but, well... it's only an image...and... er..., and then... er... (silence for

---

pas quelque chose qui me... qui qui ...me prend vraiment aux tripes...fin qui m' euuuuuuuh, sss... *J'ai pas de euh*... oui fin surpris, *pas un* sursaut, mais un peu de recul quoi.... »

[10] « et j'ai du mal à fondre en larmes ou quoi que ce soit parce que *ce n'est. qu'*une image euh voilà c'est... voilà c'est c'est c'est c'est pas beau à voir, *mais c'est pas voilà*. ... là *c'est qu'*une photo, fin une image. une photo, voilà, c'est fin ça, c'est pas beau à voir, voilà, mais *c'est... euh mais c'est qu'*une image...après, voilà *c'est qu'une... c'est pas* la réalité.. oui, *c'est qu'*une image, quoi, fin, bon après fin voilà c'est, fin j'ai du mal à m'exprimer par rapport à une image, voilà... *c'est c'est pas* que, mais c'est voilà y a (silence for a few seconds), *c'est qu'*une image voilà.... fin bon, bref, mais, bon moi *c'est qu'*une image... et euh, et puis euh (silence for 4–5 s) ouais, *c'est qu'*une image... c'est c'est... mais *c'est qu'*une image, C'était une *photo* (she stresses the word) d'une *personne* (she stresses again) non, je vois pas, non j'vois pas de cheveux. j'vois rien, non *je vois que* ce visage ! Ah, ben je me sens très bien fin. ». I underline.

[11] « y a *quand même* une *barrière* qui s'instaure »

[12] « c'est horrible de voir quelqu'un qui est. complètement défiguré »

[13] « J'ai du mal à décrire »

4–5 seconds) yeh, it's only an image... it's it's...".[14] Her stammering shows here its climax: she speaks in monosyllables, in stereotypes, keeps reciting in a drone; her predicative sentences are full of holes, hence often very poor and simplified, negative and mostly bodily and emotional. In short, we have to do with frequent nominalizations and with no descriptive-predicative language, except for the contextualisation of the experience at the beginning. Furthermore, no inner discursive thoughts are to be found during phases 2 (Crisis) and 3 (Aftermath) in the form of "I said to myself ", which would mean a certain degree of elaborative-cognitive distanced attitude. The only moment of inner discourse is be to found in Phase 1 (anticipation, during the 6 s when she is expected an image related to the word "mutilation" she already saw: here it is interesting to note that her expectation is higher than what she will see, so that she accounts at once or successively for the inner resonance of the word in her mind (Phase 1b: "I think that it was really serious mutilations, well... I expect... I expert... er... I don't know... as if it was in the series of burns, I waited for something.... more...",[15] and for ideas than come to her mind, in form of hypothesis she makes, linked to the meaning of the word "mutilations" and its inner visualizing power (Phase 1c : "mutilation," "burnt people," perhaps they are burnt, um... I know not, after, there, because "mutilation" it is something, yes, that we *can* impose upon oneself, or that we can impose upon another, to damage him psychologically".[16]

Regarding the time-sequentiality of the experience, if the macro-dynamic of the three phases Anticipation/Crisis/Aftermath is broadly identified by the patient, the micro-sequentialities inherent in the Crisis-Phase 2 are mostly blurred: not only doesn't she sub-sequence it spontaneously, but she does not when asked by me,[17] even if it means

---

[14] « c'est c'est pas que je suis pas quelqu'un sans cœur, mais c'est voilà y a (silence for a few seconds), c'est qu'une image voilà…. c'est peut-être un c'est c'est c'est peut-être une femme qui a été brûlée, fin, aspergée, fin bon, bref, mais, bon moi c'est qu'une image… et euh, et puis euh (silence for 4–5 s) ouais, c'est qu'une image… c'est c'est… »

[15] « je pensais que c'était vraiment des graves mutilations, ben j'm'attends à … j'attends à… euh, je sais pas euh…comme c'était dans la série des brûlures, j'm'attendais à quelque chose de… plus… ».

[16] « 'mutilation', 'personnes brûlées', peut-être qu'on les a brûlées, fin je sais pas, après, voilà, parce que, 'mutilation' c'est quand même quelque chose, oui, qu'on *peut* s'infliger à soi-même, ou qu'on inflige à l'autre, pour le détruire psychologiquement… » (I underline the hypothetical register called upon by the occurrence of the verb *can*).

[17] At different moments of the interview, I ask her what appears to her first, and I can never get a clear and constant answer :

1. A "see, when the image appears on the screen… err…What does happen?" (« voyez, quand l'image apparaît sur l'écran, euh qu'est-ce qui se passe? »). B "errm… nothing happens, because it's… um... I have I have… I have some empathy, I have some, but, hm… err… It's difficult… It's difficult to grasp" (« ben y s'passe rien, parce que moi c'est…. fin si, j'ai j'ai de la…j'ai de l'empathie, j'ai de la, mais après euh…euh… c'est difficile… c'est difficilement palpable »).
2. A « Ok, so, when you see the image appearing… Hm…errr…" (« d'accord, donc quand vous voyez l'image apparaître…euh… euh…»). B "well, I am startled, but I … I mean, it's not, well, I am not startled, it's, yes, I feel empathy, yes, it, well, it is startling somewhere, but I mean, it's not… There you go, it's not…" (« ben j'ai un sursaut, mais je… veux dire, c'est pas, fin j'ai pas

hesitating or saying you do not know what came first.[18] It is therefore difficult to know if she startles first, or if nothing happens (like a silence) as she also says, or if she has first this inner talk about it is only an image. Hence the confusing feeling of a strong temporal ambivalence about the non-successivity of the different micro-moments of Phase 2. If we wish to restore some experiential coherence at the very appearing of the image, we might want to suggest an initial threefold quasi-simultaneous model formed by lived body/ verbal latency/emotion associated with differences of duration and partial mapping for each: according to neuro-scientific evidence it is consistent to hypothesize (1) a very short time of the motor bodily startle (cardiac reaction) and pulse reaction; (2) a short time enough of silence and bodily language made of stammering's and hesitations, and finally (3) a longer time of the raw emotional reaction. Such a three-dimensional emergent lived experience of surprise seems to be nicely clear-cut and complex enough. Nevertheless the experience of surprise for this depressed person shows in reality a great confusion in her account of the three levels with no specific spontaneous temporal sequentiality: what I nicely reconstituted in terms of a three-dimensional differential duration with partial mapping is a nice but partly false reconstruction of something that is probably far more chaotic and mixed up. Furthermore, we would normally tend to consider the inner distancing reaction about "it is only an image" as a next micro-sequence following this initial threefold emerging sequence, where also a physical bodily distance and a feeling of empathy emerges. But the problem is that such a process is at work in a anticipatory way at the very beginning of the appearing of the image with this expression "it is only an image " as well as her empathetic move. In short, the temporal process is confused, blurred, for the best part highly circular, in any case hardly a sequence.

As for emotions finally, they permeate as we saw time and language. Beyond the obsessive negative valence linked to the shocking "mutilation", the inner dynamics

---

un sursaut, c'est, oui, j'ai de l'empathie, oui ça m'a fin ça me saisit quelque part, mais j'veux dire c'est pas »).

3. A "Right, so you have a, a, a movement in which you are surprised, you have a startle, you're startled... You said" (« d'accord, donc vous avez ce ce ce mouvement où vous êtes surprise, vous sursautez, vous avez un sursaut...vous avez dit »). B "yes, well surprised, it's not a startle but more of a setback, right..." (« oui fin surpris, pas un sursaut, mais un peu de recul quoi... »).

4. A "there you go you have this movement... First a movement of surprise, then, you say, there, it's just an image..." (« voilà vous avez ce mouvement... un mouvement d'abord de sursaut, ensuite vous dîtes, voilà, c'est qu'une image... »). B "That's it" (« voilà »).

5. A "Are you startled at this very moment, or, on the opposite, do you have this "it's just an image!" movement?" (« euh est-ce que vous avez ce sursaut à ce moment là, ou bien au contraire, vous avez ce mouvement de 'ce n'est qu'une image! '? »). B "Yes, well, it's only an image, right, well, then you see, well, it's hard to express myself on an image, there..." (« oui, c'est qu'une image, quoi, fin, bon après fin voilà c'est, fin j'ai du mal à m'exprimer par rapport à une image, voilà... »).

[18] Indeed such an inner reflexive discourse about the difficulties and possibilities of sequencing is a good indication of the ability to step back from the lived experience and evaluate its temporal articulation. See for example S-010 of the linguistic task about which I will tell more below: B': "(...) the image appears, I feel reassured, err, and all that, the internal smile let's say, and half a second later, that's when I start questioning more the image, that's when, when, simultaneously, I realize it's a sculpture (...)" (underlined by the author).

is characterized by a contradictory ambivalence. It expresses itself as a concrete antinomic double movement of a strong immediate intensity of being struck and a neutralizing distance coupled with a co-occurring passive overflow and active control. Such an ambivalence appears as object-linked, relational and internal: (1) as object-linked, the emotional valence (−/+) is blurred and twisted: "yes, it's a calm image nonetheless, err, a quiet being, which is lying down, um... yes, it's it it it would be like quietness, but... instead, it's actually torture err...physical torture, right... um... it's sss it is an amputation... it is a mutilation, it's...".[19] Or again: Or again: "it's not pretty to look at, but it's not, right... There it's only a picture, well an image (...)"[20]; (2) On the relational aspect, the ambivalence mixes empathy and neg-empathy: "Yes, I feel empathy, yes, it did, err, strike me somewhere, but, I mean, it's not... Right, it's not... not something that.... that that... really strikes me to the core..."[21]; "It's disturbing, it's, there... but I feel compassion, but err, I don't have..."[22]; "Well nothing happens, because for me it's... well... um... yes, I have I have some... I have some empathy... I have some... but, then, err... err... it's difficult... it's difficult to grasp... so, err, right, I have... there is. Nonetheless that I fix to myself err...".[23] Finally, as an internal tension, the emotional ambivalence refers to a controlled defensive shield, which permits all the more a surge of emotional overflow to happen: "Whereas here, it was *rather*... it was *awful* (she accentuates this word) because the person was... because the person was burnt, but it was *rather* soft... I mean the image, it was not... filled with blood, filled with... violent, yes... yes, it's not trivialised, but err ... it's, err... right, it's err... it's, it's, it's a terrible image, it's someone who has no face anymore, who's completely disfigured, but it's err...there's no blood, I mean... there's no... there, it's not... (long silence for several seconds) err, I don't know (prolonged excessive laughter), no, it's, it's... normal, I mean, normal, *um... shocked, right... but not shocked*".[24] Or again: "I find it hard to break down in tears or something because it's only a picture".[25]

---

[19] « oui, c'est une image calme quand même euh, un être qui est. reposé, qui est. étendu, qui est. calme, enfin oui, c'est, ça ça ça s'apparenterait à de la quiétude, mais… sauf que c'est de la torture euh… de la torture physique quoi… fin c'est sss c'est une amputation. c'est une mutilation, c'est… »

[20] « c'est pas beau à voir, mais c'est pas voilà. … là c'est qu'une photo, fin une image (…) »

[21] « oui, j'ai de l'empathie, oui ça m'a fin ça me saisit quelque part, mais j'veux dire c'est pas. voilà, c'est pas… pas quelque chose qui me… qui qui …me prend vraiment aux tripes »

[22] « C'est troublant, c'est voilà mais je compatis mais euh…. J'ai pas »

[23] « ben y s'passe rien, parce que moi c'est…. fin si, j'ai j'ai de la…j'ai de l'empathie, j'ai de la, mais après euh…euh… c'est difficile… c'est difficilement palpable, donc euh voilà j'ai … y a quand même une barrière que je m'instaure euh… »

[24] « alors que là, c'était *quand même* assez… c'était terrible (elle accentue le mot) parce que la personne était… parce que la personne était brûlée, mais c'était *quand même* assez soft… fin l'image, c'était pas… plein de sang, plein de. violent oui… oui c'est pas banalisé, mais euh… c'est euh. fin voilà c'est euh…c'est c'est c'est terrible comme image, c'est quelqu'un qui a plus visage, qui est complètement défiguré, mais c'est euh. y a pas de sang, fin y a pas…voilà, c'est pas… (silence de plusieurs secondes) euh, je sais pas (rires prolongés et excessifs), non, c'est c'est… normale, fin normale, *fin choquée, mais pas choquée* »

[25] « j'ai du mal à fondre en larmes ou quoi que ce soit parce que c'est qu'une image »

B. D-05's map of depression at the heart-unconscious level

- Time: spring fall/domino effect of repeated surprises of different kinds generating each time specific emotions and bodily reactions
- Language: appears as strongly bodily-emotional, silence laden with no inner discourse nor rational elaboration during the crisis-phase
- Emotion: repeated immediate emotions triggered by external perception, inner associations and moral judgments

During the vision of the image of mutilation below (crisis-phase), what becomes salient for the patient D-05 is the domino effect of surprises that overlap and generate each time a distinct emotional effect; such an overlapping of surprises then carries on in the phase 3 (aftermath phase), with a specific emotional coloration due the strong impact of the image: the patient says the image remained persistently in her mind even after disappearing physically from the screen: "I was stuck…",[26] "there, she is in my mind, yes",[27] and the enduring emotional intensity completely absorbs her visual attention, so that she does not see nor remember having seen crosses, the word "réagir",[28] etc., and also misidentifies the next object-image : "it felt to me that it was a plate, but I wasn't so sure".[29] In fact, the next image was a person with white shoes carrying a bag with apples and the image of a plate she mentions was shown earlier.

Phase 2 is the place of a repeated overlapping of a visual focal perception and emotion, a bodily motor-reaction of startle and emotion, an inner memory-association and emotion, a second bodily reaction and emotion, and finally a peripheral perception with moral judgement and emotional flashback. In short, each cognitive event (be it perceptive, memorial or moral) gives way to an immediate emotion overflow, as if it was impossible to contain it.

The general scheme of Phase 2 (Crisis) is as following:

Phase 2: emergence of the photo, a few seconds:

(a) Focal vision: "the head!"
(b) Sudden emotion: "horrible!"
(c) Startle: "already that made me jump!"[30]
(d) Sudden emotion: "that shocked me!"[31]

Phase 2': inner lived duration when the image still being seen (a few seconds)

(a) Memory association: "right away, that reminded me of my brother"[32]

---

[26] « ben j'étais restée dessus quoi… »

[27] « ah ben là, elle est. dans mon esprit, oui »

[28] To react

[29] « il me semble que c'était une assiette, mais j'suis pas trop sûre… »

[30] « déjà ça m'a fait sursauter! »

[31] « ça m'a choqué! »

[32] « ça m'a tout d'suite fait penser à mon p'tit frère »

(b) Bodily reaction: "my eyes are full of tears"[33]
(c) Empathic emotions: "this is sad, he was small... one can do nothing"[34]

Phase 2''': Swaying look of the image as a visual duration (a few other seconds)

(a) Peripheral perception: "there was someone with a shovel to exhume"[35] (silent emotion in the voice)
(b) Moral judgement: "this is macabre!"[36]; "dead people must rest in peace"[37]
(c) Re-emergence of emotions: "it is too much!"[38]

The process of the spring fall of surprises is as follows:

I. Emergence: vision-emotion-startle-emotion:

—> Cardiac reaction (somatic)

II. Inner duration while seeing: memory-bodily emotional reaction (crying)-empathic emotion

—> Lived surprise (inner)

III. Swaying look: peripheral perception-emotion in the voice-moral judgement-emotion

—> Perplexity (cognitive) and stronger cardiac reaction

We have to do with an embedded micro-temporality of many micro-phases both successive and mapped together alternating perceptive (focal or peripheral)-inner associative and emotional phases. As far as language is concerned, the bodily-emotional language is dominant (especially in the crisis-phase 2), genuinely reactivated in her evocation of the just lived moment, which attests a strong presence to the lived experience. The only room for an inner discursive thought is to be found in the awaiting phase 1: "I thought gold, I thought 30. Money, it is the first word that I said which came into my head"[39]; "it is the size of ingots that we find, um... ordinary things, which we see on television, things like that, um... this is what I've said to myself when I saw them...".[40] Then it completely disappears and gives way to an immediate bodily emotional language with no elaborative rational distance.

Provisional conclusion: we have to do with two distinctive forms of circular temporality, either taking the obsessive form of a continuous loop or having the dynamic

---

[33] « ben ça m'a donné les larmes aux yeux quoi »

[34] « triste quoi! Il était p'tit. On peut rien faire... »

[35] « y avait quelqu'un avec une pelle qui déterrait... »

[36] « macabre... quoi! »

[37] « les morts ça doit r'poser en paix »

[38] « c'est trop... »

[39] « j'ai pensé or, j'ai pensé 30. argent, c'est le premier mot que j'ai dit qui m'est passé par la tête »

[40] « oh ben c'est la taille de lingots qu'on trouve, fin ordinaires, qu'on voit à la télé, des choses comme ça, fin, c'est que j'me suis dit quand j'les ai vus... »

of a repeated self-generating spring fall. In both cases, the time of surprise is disarticulated, non-linear, be it blurred, disturbed, or spontaneously self-unfolding along the generic image of the chaos, with contrast with the standard ordered and articulated micro-dynamics of the three anticipation-crisis-aftermath phases.

14.6 The Standard 'Normal' Emotional Dynamic of Heart Unconscious: An Intriguing Case of "Mixed Emotions" Associating to Surprise

The linguistic task of the Emphiline study (ANR EMCO) guided by Pascale Goutéraux at the University Paris-Diderot invites the selected students to look at work of art pictures (paintings and sculptures mainly). Among the 80 students who will be included mid-2015, I could already lead 60 interviews. A certain number of expressions of surprise mention clear valence laden-emotions, either positive (wonderful, marvellous) or negative (horrible, disgusting). Some other stress cognitive expressions of non-understanding, of questioning, of difficulties of identification or mis-identification. Some other underline bodily expressions of startle or shivering. Finally I discovered some other emotional expressions that do not seem to strictly fit into the valence, the cognitive or the bodily components of surprise. I would like to inquire more precisely into these unexpected emotions associated to surprise insofar as they account for a peculiar experiential dynamics that might have to do with the heart unconscious process, especially if we want to think it in its specificity, that is, in its irreducibility either to a clear-cut polarized valence, or to cognition or again to the bodily cardiac basis of the heart. I call such unfitting emotions "mixed emotions" in order to underline their displaced character with regard to clear expected bodily, here negative (disgust) or inner, here positive (marvel) ones.

So the idea and expression of mixed emotions is directly drawn from the first person interviews and descriptions I led and analysed: their evidence is experiential. I rely on the statements of interviewed subjects who talked about the pictures they are shown using adjectives such as "weird", "strange", and talking about their own emotions while seeing them as having been "stunned" or "captured". Such mixed emotions are related to an unconscious functioning, insofar as our explicit standard consciousness would rationally chose to favour one or the other, while our unconscious functioning does not chose, keeps both and thus generate lived tensions, what is ultimately called for example in psychiatry a 'double bind' functioning (Bateson 2008; Wittesaele 2008; Elkaïm 1989). They are related to the heart-unconscious in the sense that, as emotions, they are the manifestations of the heart both as a cardiac rhythm and as the affective core of my subjectivity.

Let me start with mentioning some of such unfitting or displaced occurrences of emotions linked to a surprise reaction in the first eleven interviews. While staring at contemporary paintings, some students indeed express themselves in the following way:

First of all, I was surprised, I told myself ... it was... that it is a *very uncanny* choice of representation... especially since the other character doesn't have a real head either, like I tell you it's a kind of balloon...[41] (Giorgio De Chirico, *Disquieting Muses*, 1918)

I was maybe a bit more, err, I wouldn't go as far as saying stressed, but I was all in all err, *curious* at this point[42] (Camille Claudel, *Sakountala*, 1905)

So, I was immediately surprised, err, I thought this was *very weird*, because it reminded me of... It looked like many things... At the same time, I didn't really know... In the middle it looked like something had been eaten, at the same time, err, devoured, I don't know, it looked like a croissant that would have been devoured, like a *weird croissant*, err, (laughter) like many things, I don't know (laughter)... I was asking myself questions, I was wondering what it was because it looked like some precise thingy, and at the same time it was abstract... So... (...) it was a bit, well, not scary, it did not scare me either, but it was *a bit weird*, right, so, well, yes...[43] (Louise Bourgeois, *Janus fleuri*, 1968)

Then I started to look more closely, I looked at the shape of the body, let's say, well, maybe I didn't look at it well, but it seemed *just a bit twisted*, a bit ...(sigh) it's not a real spider's body...[44] (Louise Bourgeois, *Spider*, 1996)

I also used the expression *"twisted"*. "It's twisted", it's rather vulgar, sorry, but this is *twisted to see*, that thing is sick, really, right...[45] (Paul Rebeyrolle, *Implosion*, 1994)

In these different extracts of explication interviews, what appears is a vocabulary of the weird (*étrange*), the curious (*curieux*), the strange (*étrange*), the unseemly (*incongru*), which is sometimes directly linked to the disturbed cognitive process of not being able to identify what it is ("It looked like many things... At the same time, I didn't really know... In the middle it looked like something had been eaten, at the same time, err, devoured, I don't know"), or to the production of an effect of global lived ill-at-easiness in relation with the structural ambivalence attraction-repulsion ("it's rather vulgar, sorry, but this is *twisted to see*, that thing is sick, really, right..."). These mixed emotional-cognitive trans-valence laden features are intriguing: they

---

[41] « j'étais étonnée avant tout, je me suis dit… que c'était…, c'est *très étrange* comme choix de représentation…., surtout que l'autre personnage n'a pas non plus une vraie tête, c'est je vous dis un genre de ballon… »

[42] « j'étais peut être un petit plus euh, j'irais pas jusqu'à dire stressé, mais en tout cas euh, *curieux* sur le moment »

[43] « Alors, j'étais immédiatement surprise, euh j'ai trouvé ça *très bizarre*, parce que ça me rappelait, ça ressemblait à plusieurs choses… à la fois, je savais pas trop… avec le milieu qui semblait être quelque chose qui était mangé, en même temps, euh, dévoré, je sais pas, cela ressemblait en même temps à un croissant dévoré, à un *croissant bizarre*, euh, (rires) à plein de choses, je sais pas (rires)… je me posais des questions, je me demandais ce que c'était, parce que ça ressemblait à qu'chose de précis, et en même temps c'était abstrait…donc. […] c'était un peu fin pas ef-fray-ant, ça m'a pas fait peur non plus mais c'était *un peu bizarre*, donc du coup, fin oui…»

[44] « après j'ai commencé à regarder plus précisément, j'ai regardé la forme du corps, on va dire, fin, j'ai peut être pas bien regardé, mais ça m'a semblé *juste un peu tordu*, un peu…(soupir) c'est pas un vrai corps d'araignée… »

[45] « j'ai aussi eu l'expression « *tordu* ». « C'est tordu », c'est assez vulgaire, désolé, mais c'est, c'est *tordu à voir*, c'est malsain comme truc, vraiment fin. »

refer to a dimension of the *different* experience of surprise, which drives confusion, perplexity, puzzlement or bafflement, unsettling, disconcerting.

Contrary to the lived surprise of the two patients, who manifest a circular repetitive time-dynamics, emotional peaks and stammering-non elaborative language characteristic of a mainly psychotic depressive heart-unconscious, we have to do here to students who account for a standard 'normal' emotional dynamic of heart unconscious. In that respect, the time-dynamics is mainly clearly sequenced and articulated, and the discursion lets appear multifaceted aspects ranging from bodily and emotional expressions to inner discourse and rationalizing judgments. The mixed emotions I just mentioned above appear in such a standard experiential context all the more intriguing. My hypothesis is that they provide us with remnant expressive conscious traces of the normo-pathetic neurotic functioning of my unconscious as manifested at its heart emotional pre-conscious level. With such non-clear-cut emotional-cognitive transvalenced reactions, we may become aware of small breaches of disruptions in our habitual rational-controlled way of behaving-reacting.

Of course surprise is in itself, as a direct bodily and inner reaction to an unexpected event, a nice marker (both physiological and lived) of a rupture into the ongoing flow of my pre-conscious lived experience. It first appears as an easy somatic *and* inner marker of unconscious processes, be they pre-conscious or strictly unconscious. In that respect, from a psycho-analytic viewpoint, surprise could be characterized as a symptom or as an indirect manifestation of hidden and veiled processes, equivalent in its structure to slips of the tongue or subconsciously deliberate mistakes, through which it is commonly said since Freud that unconscious reveals itself. More precisely, surprises would be the micro-conscious revelation of light disturbances, tiny breaches in our inner life, dubious felt senses, diffuse ill at ease feelings, which remain most of the time pre-conscious and are commonly identified in psycho-analysis through the common expression of *Unheimlichkeit*. But is it doing genuine justice to surprise to reduce it to such a conscious instant revelation of unconscious processual events? Not really, especially if we understand surprise as we articu lated it above as a dynamic three-micro-phased anticipatory-crisis-aftermath process and not as a still abstract instant symptom.

If we leave as we did above one-sided approaches of surprise which limit it to a cognitive process, to an emotional reaction or to a bodily response and move to integrative perspectives of surprise, we find researchers and research projects who account for the embarrassment about the way to name and categorize surprise: is it a "cognitive emotion" (Ortony), is it a global process (Reisenzein), is it irreducible to valence because it may be pleasant or not (Depraz 2015)? We agree with integrative approaches that surprise includes and articulates all these components and require a temporal finely articulated dynamics favouring an interplay at different moments between emotional peaks, cognitive events, bodily and verbal reactions (Depraz and Desmidt 2015). However, along explication interviews (Vermersch 1994/2001) I came across first-person descriptions that do not completely fit into the picture of surprise as a multivectorial process. Not that it reveals a contradiction, but it may require so it seems to search for complementary models of understanding.

In that respect, I would tend to interpret such mixed emotions as neurotic colorations of surprise understood as a multivectorial process, which reveal a peculiar pathological figure of surprise.

14.7 Conclusion

Beyond the peculiarities of surprise at the heart unconscious level for depressed patients and for standard students, a common feature for both of them with the two different tasks appears in the ambivalent structure of mixed emotions. As a still tentative conclusion about the heart unconscious, we could say – according to what we could explore thanks to the explication interviews—, that is not so far away from the psychic unconscious, but probably not so deep anchored, that is, more lightly occurring at the surface and in experiential continuity with conscious events. In that respect, either emotional peaks in depression or mixed emotions in standard experience are vivid manifestations of our heart-unconscious. Even if the case of the two psychotic depressive experiences of surprise we studied also brings about a circular repetitive time-dynamics and a stammering-non elaborative language, the standard experiences with the students we mentioned let emerge a peculiar form of surprise laden with the ordinary neurotic dimension of mixed ambivalent emotions.

References

Bateson, Gregory. 2008. *Vers une écologie de l'esprit*. Paris: Seuil.
Buser, Pierre. 2005. *L'inconscient aux mille visages*. France: Odile Jacob.
Dehaene, Stanislas, J.-P. Changeux, L. Naccache, J. Sackur, and C. Sergent. 2006. Conscious, preconscious, and subliminal processing: A testable taxonomy. *Trends in Cognitive Sciences* 10: 204–211.
Dennett, Daniel. 2001. Surprise, surprise. Commentary on O'Regan and Noe. *The Behavioral and Brain Sciences* 24 (5): 982.
Depraz, Natalie. 2003. Looking forward to being surprised.—At the heart of embodiment. *Theoria et Historia Scientiarum: International Journal for Interdisciplinary Studies* 7: 5–11.
———. 2008. The rainbow of emotions: At the crossroads of neurobiology and phenomenology. *Continental Philosophy Review* 41: 237–259.
———. 2010. Phenomenology of surprise. Levinas and Merleau-Ponty in the light of Hans Jonas. In *Advancing phenomenology. Essays in honor of Lester Embree*, ed. T. Nenon and Ph. Blosser, 223–235. Heidelbeg: Springer.
———. 2011. Phénoménologie de la surprise. In *L'héritage de la phénoménologie et le problème de la vie*, ed. D. Rocchi. Roma: Lithos editrice.
———. 2013. The surprise of non sense. In *Enactive cognition at the edge of sense making*, ed. M. Cappuccio and T. Froese. Baskingstoke: Palgrave MacMillan.

———. (to appear). Surprise, valence, emotion. The multivectorial integrative cardio-phenomenology of surprise. In *Surprise, an emotion?*, ed. Depraz, N. and Steinbock, A. Heidelberg: Springer.

Depraz, Natalie and Thomas Desmidt. 2015. Cardiophénoménologie. Cahiers philosophiques de Strasbourg, La neurophénoménologie vingt ans après, 38.

Desmidt, Thomas, M. Lemoine, C. Belzung and N. Depraz. 2014. The temporal dynamic of emotional emergence. *Phenomenology and the Cognitive Sciences, Emotion Special Issue*. Heidelberg: Springer.

Elkaïm, Mony. 1989. *Si tu m'aimes, ne m'aime pas. Approche systémique et psychothérapie*. Paris: Le Seuil.

Husserl, Edmund. 1908–1914. Studien zur Struktur des Bewußtseins, Volume III, edition in preparation in german at the Husserl-Archives in Leuven under the responsability of Üllrich Melle and Thomas Vongehr.

———. 1938. *Expérience et jugement (1970, §21, a. L'origine de la négation)*. Paris: P.U.F.

———. 1999. *De la synthèse passive (1918–1926)*. Grenoble: J. Million.

Kihlstrom, J.F. 1987. The cognitive unconscious. *Science* 237: 1445–1452.

Lutz, Antoine, J.-Ph. Lachaux, J. Martinerie, and F.J. Varela. 2002. Guiding the study of brain dynamics by using first-person data: Synchrony patterns correlate with ongoing conscious states during a simple visual task. *PNAS* 99 (3): 1586–1591.

Marti, S., J. Sackur, M. Sigman, and S. Dehaene. 2010. Mapping introspection's blind spot: Reconstruction of dual-task phenomenology using quantified introspection. *Cognition* 115 (2): 303–313.

Ortony, A., G. Clore, and A. Collins. 1988. *The cognitive structure of emotions*. Cambridge: University Press.

Peirce, C.S. 2002. Sur la phénoménologie (Conference de Harvard, 1903). In *Pragmatisme et pragmaticisme*, 295–296. Paris: Cerf.

Petitmengin, C., and J.-Ph. Lachaux. 2014. Microcognitive science: Bridging experiential and neuronal dynamics. *Frontiers in Human Neuroscience* 7: 617.

Reisenzein, R., W.-U. Meyer A. Schützwohl. 1996. Analyse von Reaktionen auf überraschende Ereignisse: Ein Paradigma für die Emotionsforschung. In *Bericht über den 40. Kongreß der DGPs in München*, ed. H. Mandl, 830–836. Göttingen: Hogrefe.

Reisenzein, R., W.-U. Meyer, and A. Schützwohl. 1997. Reactions to surprising events. A paradigm for emotion research. In *Proceedings of the 9th conference of the international society for research on emotion*, ed. N. Frijda, 292–296. Toronto: ISRE.

Smith, A. 1982. Wonder, surprise, and admiration one feels when contemplating the physical world. In *Lecture on astronomy, section I: Of the effect of unexpectedness, or of surprise, glasgow edition of the works and correspondence vol. 3 essays on philosophical subjects (1795)*, ed. W.P.D. Wightman and J.C. Bryce. Indianapolis: Liberty Fund.

Varela, F.J. 1996. Neurophenomenology: A methodological remedy for the hard problem. *Journal of Consciousness Studies* 3: 330–349.

Varela, F.J., and J. Shear. 1999. First-person methodologies: Why, when and how. *Journal Conscious Studies* 6 (2–3): 1–14.

Wittesaele, J.-J. 2008. *La double contrainte. L'héritage des paradoxes de Bateson*. Bruxelles: De Boeck Université.

Chapter 15
This Immense Fascination with the Unconscious: Psychoanalysis and Surrealism

Alphonso Lingis

Abstract Psychoanalysis appears to intellectual historians and anthropologists as a general theory of dreams, trances, hallucinations, and certain physical symptoms that derives from nineteenth-century German Romanticism and arrogates scientificity to itself. It embodies a further stage of metaphysical subjectivism, attributing what is seen in dreams, trances, hallucinations, and certain physical symptoms to unconscious drives, desires, anxieties, and conflicts in the subject. These are posited, deduced, by interpretation. The interpretations vary with different psychotherapeutic schools and criteria for the reliability of interpretations are in question. Anthropologists find that psychoanalysis does not succeed in explaining all the phenomena covered by the general conceptions of other cultures. The Surrealists devoted themselves to the products of the unconscious, but instead of using them for therapy, set out to integrate them into conscious life. This led them away from metaphysical subjectivism and revealed the ethnocentric character of psychoanalytic doctrine.

Keywords Phenomenology • Genius • Surreality • Base materialism • Metaphysical subjectivism

15.1 Phenomena and Their Unconscious Causes

In the course of the nineteenth century discourse concerning the unconscious mind was elaborated by philosophers and psychiatrists; it organized and explained a number of representations, emotions, behaviours, and actions some of which previously had, in the West, been conceptualized as spirit possession (Ellenberger 1970). They include trance, dreams, glossolalia, fugues, automatic writing, maladies of memory,

A. Lingis (✉)
Pennsylvania State University, State College, PA, USA
e-mail: allingis@hotmail.com

hallucinations, and telepathy. The analysis of hysterical symptoms led Sigmund Freud to posit unconscious drives, desires, anxieties, and conflicts as their cause. These unconscious forces are not observed; they are posited to explain physical symptoms, delirious discourse and hallucinations, dreams, parapraxes such as slips of the tongue, misreadings, and mislaying objects. The drives, desires, anxieties, and conflicts can become manifest only in a disguised form. Consciousness has access only to a remembered dream, most often to but fragments of the dream. A remembered dream is a second disguise of the disguised representation of unconscious desires and conflicts that is the actual dream.

Freud claimed that psychosomatic symptoms disappeared when the unconscious conflicts were brought to light. Yet this took time, sometimes a long time, and sometimes they disappeared and then recurred. Dreams and free association were taken to be correctly interpreted when the patient endorsed the interpretation. But the patient is susceptible to suggestions perhaps inadvertently offered by the interpreter. The conflicting schools of psychotherapy pursue different interpretations and infer different unconscious drives, desires, anxieties, and conflicts.

The various methods of interpretation each reduce the complexity and individual variation of dreams, deliriums, hallucinations, parapraxes, and psychosomatic symptoms to a limited number of symbols and unconscious drives, desires, anxieties and conflicts. This has resulted in the discredit of psychoanalytic interpretations of literature and of art among literary critics and art historians and critics.

A scrupulous account of physiological symptoms, dreams, and visions within psychoanalysis is thus compromised by the theoretical presuppositions as to their causes. They are taken as disguised and false representations of frustrated and conflicted unconscious intentions. If we suspended their alleged causes or purposes from the account, would they appear differently?

15.2 Liberating the Unconscious from the Medical Gaze

The vivid imagery, the poetry, in the delirious utterances of shell-shocked soldiers fascinated André Breton. Breton (b. 1896) was a medical student who had been drafted into the French army in February 1915 and after basic training assigned first to a military hospital and then to a neuropsychiatric hospital in Saint-Dizier in northeastern France. There he read psychiatrists Jean-Martin Charcot, Emil Kraepelin, Constanza Pascal, and in the works of Emmanuel Regis and Angelo Hesnard discovered the theories of Sigmund Freud. "Completely occupied as I still was with Freud at that time, and familiar as I was with his methods of examination which I had had some slight occasion to use on some patients during the war, I resolved to obtain from myself what we were trying to obtain from them, namely, a monologue spoken as rapidly as possible without any intervention on the part of the critical faculties, a monologue consequently unencumbered by the slightest inhibition and which was, as closely as possible, akin to *spoken thought*" (Breton 1972, pp. 22–23).[1]

As free association was for Freud the principal method in therapy, automatic writing—and drawing—was for Breton the basic method to access the unconscious. Dreams and hypnogogic states likewise represent the spontaneous movements of the mind. Breton and his friends practiced speaking in hypnotic trance. They were not following Freud's early practice; after René Crevel encountered a medium, the Surrealists staged séances as done by mediums (but without crediting any communication with the dead).

The goal was to explore and take possession of the vast realm of what is actively repressed by rational, moral, and aesthetic concerns of the conscious mind. "Everything tends to make us believe that there exists a certain point of the mind at which life and death, the real and the imagined, past and future, the communicable and the incommunicable, high and low, cease to be perceived as contradictions" (Breton 1972, p. 123).

Breton found that in automatic writing there often erupt unpredictable marvellous meetings of images with no logical or causal relation between them. "The marvellous is always beautiful, anything marvellous is beautiful, in fact only the marvellous is beautiful" (Breton 1972, p. 14).

Breton associated himself with poets and artists, and starting in 1924 the "Surrealists" met daily in a café for automatic writing and automatic drawing, recounting dreams, inducing hypnotic trances, and discussion. Over the years they included Louis Aragon, Hans Arp, Antonin Artaud, Jacques Baron, Luis Buñuel, René Char, René Crevel, Salvador Dali, Giorgio de Chirico, Robert Desnos, Jean Dubuffet, Marcel Duchamp, Paul Eduard, Max Ernst, Alberto Giacometti, Michel Leiris, Georges Limbour, Georges Malkine, André Masson, Jean Miró, Max Morise, Pierre Naville, Benjamin Péret, Francis Picabia, Jacques Prévert, Raymond Queneau, Man Ray, Philippe Soupault, Yves Tanguy, Tristan Tzara, and Roger Vitrac. They were possessed with an immense fascination with the unconscious.

That such extraordinarily gifted and individualist thinkers, poets, and artists were brought together testifies to the force of Breton's character and intellect and to the concentrated attention with which he listened to them. Maurice Nadeau wrote that "All these men loved him madly [...] Those who enjoyed the moments of his unforgettable friendship, which he begrudged no one, were ready to sacrifice everything to him: wives, mistresses, friends" (Nadeau 1989, p. 86).

The group issued manifestos, announcements, group questionnaires, political tracts, exhibition catalogues, glossaries, definitions, litanies, canonical texts. They staged debates and trials.

---

[1] Breton obtained his auxiliary doctor certification in 1919, but abandoned his medical studies in 1921. On the eve of the Second World War Breton was inducted into army on Sept 29 1938 as an assistant medical officer, then put in reserves after 10 days. He was called back on August 22, 1939, and discharged in July 1940.

15.3 Phenomenology of Manifest Representations

While Freud took the manifest images that are remembered to cover over latent content which is accessible only to interpretation, Breton was interested in the manifest images for their irrational and marvellous, poetic character. He asked Freud for a contribution to a book *Trajectoire du rêve* that he was editing. Freud declined, writing "The superficial aspect of dreams, what I call the manifest dream, holds no interest for me. I have been concerned with the 'latent content' which can be derived from the manifest dream by psychoanalytical interpretation. A collection of dreams without associations and knowledge of the context in which it was dreamed does not tell me anything, and it is hard for me to imagine what it can mean to anyone else" (Polizzotti, 1995, pp. 452–3).

In *Communicating Vessels* Breton did work out a very detailed analysis of one of his dreams, very like Freud, bringing up the latent content beneath the manifest content and connecting each detail with events of his waking days. He also pursued a thorough explication of the social and practical context of the dream event (Breton 1990, pp. 28–44). But it was the manifest content of dreams and hypnotic trances that Breton found marvellous. The marvellous appears in the world but reveals things in webs of connections that are not functional or causal. Marvellous beauty erupts when things meet without cause or utilitarian finality, "beautiful as the chance encounter of a sewing machine and an umbrella on an operating table," according to the Comte de Lautréamont. "Convulsive beauty will be veiled-erotic, fixed-exploding, circumstantial-magical" (Breton 1988, p. 19).

The Surrealists tracked down the lines of connection, of encounter and of parody, of a manifest appearance with other manifest appearances, without positing lines of causality issuing from latent appearances. Georges Bataille found that things double into parodies of themselves:

> An abandoned shoe, a rotten tooth, a snub nose, the cook spitting in the soup of his masters are to love what a battle is to nationality.
>
> An umbrella, a sexagenarian, a seminarian, the smell of rotten eggs, the hollow eyes of judges are the roots that nourish love.
>
> A dog devouring the stomach of a goose, a drunken vomiting woman, a sobbing accountant, a jar of mustard represent the confusion that serves as the vehicle of love (Bataille 1985, p. 6).

These pairs, the one a parody of the other, are not couplings only contrived by the unconscious; they are found in the world where the most remote things are connected.

Psychoanalytic interpretation reduces the complexity and individual variation of representations generated by the unconscious to a limited number of symbols and unconscious drives, desires, anxieties and conflicts. Surrealist artists, ignoring interpretation, moved by the unconscious, unendingly multiplied images of things never seen or imagined, unendingly new images in any individual. With the Surrealists the unconscious becomes inexhaustible abundance that never weakens its power to astonish.

15.4 Paranoia and Genius

In 1932 Jacques Lacan (b. 1901) published *De la psychose paranoïaque dans ses rapports avec la personnalité* (*Paranoid Psychosis and its Relationship with Personality*), his doctoral dissertation in psychiatry. Of some 40 psychotics he had observed, half of them paranoid psychotics, he selects one for extensive examination. He calls her "Aimée A."—the name she gave to the heroine of her first (unpublished) novel. Aimée A. had stabbed an actress, Huguette Duflos, at the entrance of a theatre. Lacan recounts all he could discover about Aimée's family and childhood, her work as a railroad company employee and her colleagues, her husband, her first child stillborn, her widowed and domineering sister who moved into her house, and a delirious episode after the live birth of her second child for which she was interned in a private psychiatric clinic for 6 months. He locates the origin of Aimée's paranoid psychosis in the death of her first child and the arrival of her widowed sister. This sister is both Aimée's ego ideal and a tyrannical figure who takes over the care of Aimée's infant son. The actress Huguette Duflos whom Aimée stabbed is for her a displacement of this sister.

Twenty days after her imprisonment, Aimée's paranoid delirium abruptly disappeared and did not return in the year and a half that Lacan observed her in the asylum to which she had been transferred. He notes that such abrupt cures are observed among the perpetrators of crimes of passion; after the murder they experience relief and their delirium abruptly dissolves. In the prison Aimée had found herself in the company of delinquents and experienced their cynicism in her regard; she suffered the blame of all those who knew her and their abandon of her. She experienced the relief of being punished, and her delirium abruptly dissolved. Lacan's diagnosis is that she was a self-punishing paranoid psychotic. Aimée's guilt over the death of her child motivates the aggression that produces punishment that she required.

Lacan incorporates almost twenty pages of the two novels Aimée A. wrote into his dissertation. He is intent on detecting in them evidence of his patient's state of mind, the foci of her paranoid obsessions, and the affectively charged personages about her. But he also finds here the positive yield from the psychosis.

> Certain traits of exquisite sensibility of our patient, her comprehension of the sentiments of infancy, her enthusiasm for the spectacles of nature, her Platonic love, and her social idealism (which we should not take to be empty because it remains without effective engagement)—all that appears to us to be evidently virtualities of positive creation which the psychosis has not merely spared but directly produced […] She was able to complete the best and most important of her writings only during the most acute phase of her psychosis and under the direct influence of delirious ideas. The end of the psychosis seems to have made her pen sterile (Lacan 1975, pp.288–9).

Lacan here invokes Jean-Jacques Rousseau, bearer of a childhood trauma and "paranoid and a genius." He says that not only Rousseau's sensibility and his style, but also his addiction to work, training, his exceptional memory, excitability, and resistance to fatigue may owe much to his paranoid condition.

Lacan's article "*Le problème du style et la conception psychiatrique des formes paranoïaques de l'expérience*" (*The Problem of Style and the Psychiatric Conception of the Paranoid Forms of Experience*) (Lacan 1975) was published in 1933 in the first number of the magazine *Minotaure* edited by Surrealists André Breton and Pierre Mabille (also a doctor and an anthropologist). Here Lacan says that the delirium of paranoid psychotics express social and instinctual complexes directly; thus their delirium is essentially communicable. He affirms that the delirium of paranoid psychotics is characterized by a profound feeling for nature, an idyllic and utopian sense of humanity and of antisocial demands that are the equal of those of the greatest artists. He affirms that features of their delirium such as images of cyclic repetition, multiplication in different places, periodic return of the same events, doubles or triples of the same personage, and doubling of the person of the subject are typical of poetic creation.

Lacan met Salvador Dali in 1929 and attended meetings of the Surrealists until he was excluded; he continued to attend meetings of dissident Surrealist Contre-Attaque, the Collège de Sociologie, and Acéphale until the war. He became Pablo Picasso's personal doctor.

15.5 Madness as a Method

In the psychiatric hospital in which Breton worked during the war, one of the tasks of the psychiatrists was to determine whether soldiers were simulating mental breakdowns in order to avoid being sent to the front. Breton and Paul Éluard practiced simulating deranged mental states—mental debility, acute mania, general paralysis, interpretative delirium, dementia praecox; the results they published in *The Immaculate Conception*. They saw that no lasting ill effects ensued from these practices. "We all know, in fact, the insane owe their incarceration to a tiny number of legally reprehensible acts and that were it not for these acts their freedom (or what we see as their freedom) would not be threatened" (Breton 1972, p. 5).

In 1922 Dr. Hans Prinzhorn published *Bildnerei der Geisterkranken (Artistry of the Mentally Ill)* in which he reproduced and analysed 187 from the more than 5000 paintings, drawings, and carvings he had collected from various asylums in and around Heidelberg, mostly from patients diagnosed as schizophrenic. André Breton and Max Ernst looked upon the works reproduced in Prinzhorn's book with awe and admiration; Paul Éluard called it "the most beautiful book of images there is."

Salvador Dali (b. 1904) joined the Surrealists in 1929. He practiced the surrealist methods of automatic writing and drawing, speaking and drawing under hypnosis, *cadaver exquis,* and painted images that emerged in his dreams, nightmares, and hypnogogic states. Monstrous figures, with bloated, limp, and melting body parts, populated his canvases. He affirmed that the images were not deliberately contrived; he was the first to be surprised by what emerged. He set out to paint them with the clarity and precision of seventeenth-century Dutch still lifes.

In paranoid delirium connections and relationships are posited between the most remote things and events and quite insignificant objects and events are taken to be signs and omens. As Breton was fascinated with the delirium of shell shocked soldiers whom he attended in the Saint-Dizier hospital, Dali was fascinated with the paranoid delirium of a neighbour woman in the village of Port Llegat named Lidia Noguer i Sabà. Like Lacan's patient Aimée A., who believed that she was being ridiculed in the plays of Pierre Benoit and by the actress Hugette Duflos who performed in them, Lidia believed that she was being depicted in the novels of Eugeni d'Ors. Dali set out to put himself in a paranoid state and to experience how things remote from one another come into contact, overlap, and coincide. He painted the images that emerged, images frequently combining or overlaying two radically different objects. He called his method "paranoiac-critical," contrasting it with the passivity of dreams and automatic writing and drawing; it consists in actively making remote things overlap and objectifying them in paintings that are "handmade photographs." He said, "The sole difference between myself and a madman is that I am not mad." He did not probe beneath the images to stage the gory, lascivious, or cruel drives of the unconscious. The images instead are like the manifest content of dreams, produced by desires seeking to mask themselves to elude the censor. Freud told him, "It is not the unconscious I seek in your pictures, but the conscious…your mystery is manifested outright. The picture is but a mechanism to reveal itself" (Ades 1974, p. 49).

15.6 Self-Analysis as Integral Self-Affirmation

After the death of his father in 1896, Sigmund Freud suffered heart irregularities, disturbing dreams, and periods of depression; to understand this disturbed state he undertook an exhaustive self-analysis, and found that his discoveries were directly applicable to the treatment of his patients. Could such an intense self-analysis become absorbed in itself and issue in the opposite of therapy?

Salvador Dali discovered Freud's work in 1924 and it became the central matrix of his thought. In *The Secret Life of Salvador Dali,* the first and most elaborated of his three autobiographies, he recounts his complex emotions in events of his early childhood in meticulous detail. He writes long about his relationship with his father, a veritable psychoanalytic exploration, and later with Picasso, a second father. His repeated disparagements of André Breton, especially in his last autobiography *Diary of a Genius,* makes evident that Breton too was a father. He makes Freud's dictum that a hero overcomes his father the leitmotif of his career. He sets out to verbalize all his impulses and feelings about body movements, excretion, and masturbation; he writes of his shame over the inferior size of his penis and of his hatred of being touched. In *Diary of a Genius* (1962) he devotes pages of his diary to discussion of his feelings while defecating and of the amount, consistency, texture, and color of his stools. He expands long on perceptions of dead animals, putrefaction and corruption. He tells of childhood aggression against his younger sister, whom he kicked in the head, and against other members of the household. In his childhood he learned to throw tantrums to get his will. He illustrates his youthful timidity, and details how as a young adult he overcompensated by ostentation and braggadocio. The reader soon senses that it would take a Freudian to be interested in all that in an autobiography. And it is hard to see what else a professional psychoanalysis would uncover in Dali's relations with his dead brother, his mother, his enthrallment with certain fetish objects, his anal eroticism, and fascination with excrement.

This exhaustive autoanalysis is nowise at the service of therapy. Instead Dali affirms that he is not only a painter of genius but also a genius as a human being. He takes all his cravings, compulsions, and obsessions to be so many aspects of his exceptional nature, sensibility and gifts, his genius.

15.7 "Transform the World," Marx Said; "Change Life," Rimbaud Said. These Two Watchwords Are One for Us[2]

Breton was nowise interested in gaining access to the drives and forces of the unconscious in view of neutralizing them or subjecting them to the exigencies of the reality principle. Yet to liberate the processes of the unconscious within oneself from moral, aesthetic, and rational concerns and control is to change one's life fundamentally, and this the Surrealists pursued with visionary exultation. "Surrealism . . . has provoked new states of consciousness and overthrown the walls beyond which it was immemorially supposed to be impossible to see; it has . . . modified the sensibility, and taken a decisive step towards the unification of the personality, which it found threatened by an ever more profound dissociation" (Breton 1978, p. 138).

Breton abjured the dictum art for art's sake. "It is a question, not . . . of producing works of art, but of casting light upon the unrevealed and yet revealable portion of our being wherein all beauty, all love, all virtue that we scarcely recognize in ourselves, shine with great intensity" (Breton 1972, p. 162n).

For Breton this eruption of the marvellous is one with the liberation of all the possibilities and forces of life. "The depths of our mind contain within it strange forces capable of augmenting those on the surface, or of waging a victorious battle against them" (Breton 1972, p. 10). The Surrealists played Truth or Consequences, in which players were required to answer all questions, no matter how private or embarrassing. Between 1928 and 1932 they held twelve meetings devoted to answering every question about their sexual tastes and practices (Pierre 2014).

"Freud is again quite surely mistaken in concluding that the prophetic dream does not exist—I mean the dream involving the immediate future—since to hold that the dream is exclusively revelatory of the past is to deny the value of motion" (Breton 1990, p. 13). Dreams may well follow from one another night after night; the realm of the dream is continuous and internally organized. "Can't the dream also be used in solving the fundamental questions of life?" (Breton 1972, p. 12).

---

[2] Breton (1972), p. 241.

15 This Immense Fascination with the Unconscious: Psychoanalysis and Surrealism

For Freud the dream's manifest content is a mask, produced by displacement, condensation, visualization, dramatization, symbolization, etc., of the true unconscious desires. How then shall this manifest content guide our lives, resolve problems? Dreams should be set on the same plane as waking perceptions; Breton demonstrated this in *The Communicating Vessels*. Breton and his friends composed dream résumés, like employment résumés, but listing their employments and achievements in dreams. To put side by side the artistry of dreams with the perceived environment is to make life, every life, poetry.

The Surrealists integrated chance into everyday life. They practiced wanderings in the streets and trips to places chosen by chance where they roamed aimlessly. While walking with friends, Philippe Soupault would borrow the hat of a street beggar and solicit passersby for him, get on a bus and ask the passengers their birth dates, offer to swap drinks with strangers in a bar, and enter a building at random and ask the concierge if Philippe Soupault lived there (Polizzotti 1995, p. 65).

The liberation of unconscious forces issues in the sovereignty of desire, of libido—which in its integral form is mad love. Breton identified it to be the total devotion to someone met by chance. Mad love requires absolute trust and also unrestricted honesty.

Breton combatted the morality based on oppression and hypocrisy in the name of lucidity and integrity. He did not hesitate to call attention to failings of integrity and to greed and commercialization and in meetings enlisted the group's agreement to exclude an individual from surrealism.

> I say without hesitation that some painters who set out with high purposes are today being tracked on their path by a vile, stinking beast named money. It is only too possible that after years of disinterested effort and the winning of general esteem they may find themselves attacked by this creature. I am not talking about those who rush into its jaws. But in the guise of that monstrous thing, success, which will come to anyone who waits long enough, the beast will literally hurl itself on its reluctant victims ... What degradation of the human spirit, in Europe at least, can have played its part in establishing a market value for works of art? (Breton 2002, pp. 20–1).

During Dali's trip to the United States in 1934, his paintings were exhibited and sold and he was received as a celebrity. Department stores, fairgrounds, and advertisers solicited works from him for which he received large sums of money. When he returned to France the Surrealists held a meeting to hear his explanations and justifications, and voted to exclude him for his greed as well as for his sympathy for Franco and Hitler. Henceforth Breton cited him only as "Avida Dollars" (Greedy for Dollars), an anagram made with the letters of his name.[3] Jacques Lacan's relations with the group ended in 1934 when he sent Breton an invitation to his church wedding: Breton ripped the card into pieces and mailed them back (Polizzotti 1995, p. 390n).

---

[3] During World War II Dali lived half the year in the United States, half the year in Paris. When the war was over he returned to Spain and Port Llegat. He publicly praised and flattered Franco, espoused the Catholic Church. He also abandoned surrealism in art; he launched his Catholic, then Nuclear Mysticism styles. He induced the Spanish government to purchase a theatre to be made into a museum devoted to his works.

Liberation of the unconscious forces entails liberation from family, church, and state. "One can understand why Surrealism was not afraid to make for itself a tenant of total revolt, complete insubordination, of sabotage according to rule, and why it still expects nothing save from violence. The simplest Surrealist act consists of dashing down into the street, pistol in hand, and firing blindly, as fast as you can pull the trigger, into the crowd. Anyone who, at least once in his life, has not dreamed of putting an end to the petty system of debasement and cretinization in effect has a well-defined place in that crowd, with his belly at barrel level" (Breton 1972, p. 125). But proletarian revolution would be the effective liberation from oppression, and Breton was a member of the Communist Party from 1927 until he was expelled in 1933. "Everything remains to be done, every means must be worth trying, in order to lay waste to the ideas of *family, country, religion*" (Breton 1972, p. 128).

15.8 Fantasy or Surreality

Freud's psychoanalytic theory figures as a culminating moment in modern metaphysical subjectivism.[4] Much that in prior culture and in other cultures was taken to be exterior, that indeed appears to be exterior—chance and the marvellous, spirits of the dead, ghosts, demons, deities—are declared to be projections engendered within our unconscious subjectivity. The alien forces that seize control and torment or overwhelm the conscious self are taken to be located within and to be in fact one's own forces. It is the reality principle, in fact the rational principle, that determines what will be rejected from outside reality and relocated within the sphere of unconscious projections. What modern Western culture rejects as incompatible with its physic-chemical, electromagnetic representation of reality is relocated within the subjective sphere.

Yet there are outside events and forces that contribute to the apparition of irrational representations. The unconscious is found to contain a stock of idiomatic expressions, slogans, and common-sense opinions, which, when set free and randomly expressed can have poetic force. A poetry that, in Isidore Ducasse's words, is "made by all, not by one." There are the laws and norms of society that are incarnate in the figure of the father and his successive representatives, a figure that is interiorized in the superego. There are the representations set up in the language of a culture

---

[4] Freud's psychoanalysis figures within the vast movement of subjectification in modern ontology. Teleology, with Francis Bacon, and efficient causality, with David Hume, were relocated from the "outside" to the "inside," that is, they are conceived in the mind and projected outside; space and time were, with Immanuel Kant, taken to be apriori forms of the mind. The secondary qualities of observed things were, with Descartes and Locke, relocated "inside."

> Sensations ... properly speaking, are qualities of the mind alone. These sensations are projected by the mind so as to clothe appropriate bodies in external nature. Thus the bodies are perceived as with qualities which in reality do not belong to them, qualities which in fact are purely the offspring of the mind ... Nature is a dull affair, soundless, scentless, colourless; merely the hurrying of material, endlessly, meaninglessly. (Whitehead 1967, p. 54)

and a time and that figure as paradigms for identifications and relationships. There is the language that structures the conscious processes and also, according to the later Jacques Lacan, the associations of representations in the unconscious. We noted above that Lacan had found in the novels of his paranoid patient Aimée and in paranoid Jean-Jacques Rousseau an exceptionally refined and penetrating experience of nature.

The Surrealist project was not only to integrate the unconscious with the conscious, to take possession of the whole range of the mind. It was to integrate the world that the unconscious addresses and reveals with that perceived by the conscious mind. "I believe in the future resolution of these two states, dream and reality, which are seemingly so contradictory, into a kind of absolute reality, a *surreality.*" (Breton 1972, p. 14). "Surreality, the state where these concepts are fused by the mind, is the shared horizon of religion, magic, poetry, dreaming, madness, intoxication and this fluttering honeysuckle, puny little life, that you believe capable of colonizing the heavens for us," Louis Aragon wrote (Aragon 2013, p. 5).

Surrealist thinking oscillates between subjectivism and ontological revelation. Between taking dreams, hallucinations, and irrational, marvellous meanings in things to be contents of the mind, projections, creations, of the mind—and assigning ontological status to the surreal realm, which is encountered in surrealist objects and objective chance events. Breton recognized this ambiguity:

> Without attempting to judge what direction surrealism will ultimately take,…its most recent advance is producing a *fundamental crisis of the 'object.'* It is essentially upon the *object* that surrealism has thrown most light in recent years. Only the very close examination of the many recent speculations to which the *object* has publicly given rise (the oneiric object, the object functioning symbolically, the real and virtual object, the moving but silent object, the phantom object, the discovered object, etc.), can give one a proper grasp of the experiments that surrealism is engaged in now (Breton 1978, p. 138).

Surrealist practices involve a repudiation of the concept of an individual of exceptional talent or genius, indeed repudiation of the concept of individual subjectivity as creative. *Cadavre exquis* drawings and sentences were collective products, bypassing the intentions of a single creator. Surrealist practices belie the subjectivist thesis that the marvellous is projected by the mind onto objectively neutral things. Surrealist objects—found, readymade, natural, interpreted, incorporated or irrational—are put on the same level as works painted or sculpted by human intention. The Surrealists collected incongruous, bizarre, objects and artefacts. They did rubbings of wood grain, plastered walls, leaves, and other textured substances. They practiced aerography, using a three-dimensional object, such as their genitals, as a stencil in spray-painting. Dali shot ink onto a blank sheet of paper and elaborated the image thus produced. They practiced coulage— dropping molten metal, wax or chocolate into cold water to produce sculptural forms involuntarily. They set out to make the objects that appeared in dreams.

The Surrealists were on the lookout for "objective chances," that is, encounters with objects and events that cannot be anticipated or understood from the environment in which they are found. The importance of such encounters motivated their practice of aimless wandering in the streets and in the country. These surrealist objects and events were assigned the same ontological index of reality as the objects and events that compose the coherent and cohesive environment that common sense calls reality.

"It is the universe which should be interrogated about man and not man about the universe" (Breton 2002, p. 321). Jacques Lacan valued the novels of "Aimée A." not simply for their literary and aesthetic qualities, but instead for "her exquisite sensibility…her comprehension of the sentiments of infancy, her enthusiasm for the spectacles of nature, her Platonic love, and her social idealism." In his vast survey of surrealist painting, Breton does not simply admire the ingenuity of the unconscious mind that fabricates phantasms; he sees so many searchlights projected upon a domain, a surreality, more vast than that the rational intellect knows. "Once in New York, for example, when I witnessed that superb phenomenon known as 'northern lights', I felt exactly as though Tanguy's skies were being unfolded before me at a dizzy speed; since neither he nor I had ever seen these lights before, one can only conclude that Tanguy's mind is in permanent communication with the earth's magnetism" (Breton 2002, p. 71).

15.9 Base Materialism

In writings by Georges Bataille we find a movement from metaphysical subjectivism, from the unconscious as simply productive of unreal phantasms, to the unconscious as in contact with and revealing material reality.

Georges Bataille (b. 1897) spent his childhood in Reims. His father, afflicted with syphilis, was blind for 20 years and paralyzed for 15, and finally insane the last years. Georges had to help caring for him, cleaning him. In 1915 the mother with her two sons fled Reims as the German front approached, leaving the father to be looked after by a neighbour; he died as the Germans shelled the city. In 1914 Georges Bataille had converted to Catholicism, and in 1917 he spent a year in a seminary. He renounced Catholicism 9 years later. He graduated from the Ecole de Chartres in 1922 with a dissertation on a medieval manuscript. Except for a few years leave when he had tuberculosis, Bataille was employed as archivist at the Bibliothèque National. Initially drawn to Breton and the Surrealists, he never joined the group, but remained close to Michel Leiris, Roger Caillois, André Masson, and Pierre Klossowski throughout his life.

Bataille underwent psychoanalysis with Dr. Adrien Borel in 1926. He wrote out his most perverse fantasies in *Story of the Eye*, which he published in 1927 under the nom de plume of Lord Auch. He maintained close relations with Borel, and thereafter sent him the first numbered copy of each of his books (Surya 2002, p. 99). In 1929 he published a psychoanalytic analysis of the castration complex and its sequels in Salvador Dali's painting *The Lugubrious Game*.

Dali wrote out his excremental obsessions, aggressions, and lusts in three autobiographies and one novel; Bataille wrote eight debauched pornographic novels, which he published under pseudonyms or not at all. Throughout his life, and even during his two devoted marriages, Bataille frequented brothels, indulged in drunkenness and orgies, gambled huge sums and even with his life in Russian roulette.

His first published texts under his own name, "The Solar Anus," "Eye," "The Big Toe," "Rotten Sun," "Mouth," and especially "The Jesuve" and "The Pineal Eye" elaborate images drawn from the unconscious. They reveal the formless materiality of reality and the unstable and monstrous images that take form in it. This materiality Bataille called base materiality, distinguishing it from the materiality represented with abstract concepts and mathematical forms in the natural sciences and materialist philosophies, and which Bataille therefore characterized as a materialism that is thus in fact idealist. The rational categories of regularity, determinism, and causality do not apply to the base materiality that Bataille explored in dreams, nightmares, and delirium.

Base materiality is also seen in certain cultural images such as the Gnostic stones that Bataille studied that depicted acephalic gods with animal heads, gods with the legs of a man, the body of a serpent, and the head of a cock. Bataille saw in Gnosticism the conception of matter as an active principle of darkness and evil, and in the Gnostics a sinister love of darkness, a monstrous taste for obscene and lawless forms (Bataille 1985, p. 48).[5]

Bataille subsequently opposed two movements in a living system: appropriation and excretion. A living organism appropriates, assimilates air and nutrients, and also resources and implements that enable it to stabilize, augment, and secure itself. Humans appropriate clothing, furniture, dwellings, and instruments of production; they appropriate land divided into parcels. Humans, with common sense and science, appropriate objects and events of the external world with concepts and relations (Bataille 1985, p. 95).

An organism also expels excrement, sweat, laughter, sighs, sobs. It releases excess energies in sexual activity and competitive sports. Resources and the products of labor are wasted in the production and wearing of jewels of precious stones for which fortunes are sacrificed and in gambling. Resources are expended unreproductively in mourning, cults, and the construction of sumptuary monuments, on music and dance, and on sculpture and painting. Theatre and literature provoke dread and horror in the representation of tragic degradation and death.

---

[5] André Breton was repelled by this preoccupation with the vulgar and the base, and called Bataille an obsessive and an excremental philosopher – while Bataille called even Breton's adhesion to dialectical materialism idealist. Breton wrote:

> M. Bataille's misfortune is to reason: admittedly, he reasons like someone who 'has a fly on his nose,' which allies him more closely with the dead than with the living, but *he does reason*. He is trying, with the help of the tiny mechanism in him which is not completely out of order, to share his obsessions: this very fact proves that he cannot claim, no matter what he may say, to be opposed to any system, *like an unthinking brute* (Breton 1972, p. 184).

Comedy produces the gratuitous release of energies in laughter. The whole body is expelled from life in death and in the decomposition of the corpse.

The sacred is what is separated from the zone of work and reason. It is the outer zone of formless substance and forces that mark the limit of the zone of work and reason. It is marked off with prohibitions and taboos. The sacred is what attracts and repels, what induces awe and anxiety. It is the outer zone of impersonal forces, incalculable, ungraspable, uncomprehendable. Bataille calls this zone the impossible, that is, that which offers us no possible objectives, paths, implements, or obstacles. It is where the zone of the profane, of reason and work, come to an end.

The sacred also encompasses all that is expelled from the zone of work and reason. Thus spilt blood, sperm, menstrual blood, and cadavers, which arouse disgust and anxiety, are also sacred. "The identical nature, from the psychological point of view, of God and excrement should not shock the intellect of anyone familiar with the problems posed by the history of religions. The cadaver is not much more repugnant than shit, and the specter that projects its horror is *sacred* even in the eyes of modern theologians" (Bataille 1985, p. 102).

Philosophy is concerned with the waste products of intellectual appropriation. It has most often envisaged these with abstract concepts of nothingness, infinity, the absolute. But as what is expelled from appropriation is sacred, the thought dealing with it will have a religious form[6]—although not the form of the world religions that separate the sacred domain into a superior divine sphere and a lower demoniacal sphere (Bataille 1985, p. 95). Bataille calls this "science of what is completely other" heterology and scatology (Bataille 1985, p. 102n). His thought thus veers far from the metaphysical subjectivism for which the unconscious is the set of internal forces that fabricate dreams, delirium, parapraxes. For Bataille the unconscious opens upon base materiality and the sacred.

The mind that pushes itself beyond the farthest limits of the known is not seeking to apprehend, appropriate, to annex the unknown. The mind that plunges into the darkness of the impossible, the inapprehendable, the uncomprehendable finds itself without support, pulsating with its own energies, condensed in the state of extreme anxiety and exhilaration. No longer servile, no longer an implement to serve the system of implements and objectives, it finds itself to be sovereign. "A burst of laughter is the only imaginable and definitively terminal result—and not the means—of philosophical speculation" (Bataille 1985, p. 99).

What Breton designated as the realm of surreality is here taken decisively outside a subjectivist metaphysics, and conceived as base materiality and the sacred.

---

[6] "Systematic sexual education can only be meaningful if it leaves intact the incentive toward 'sublimation' and finds the means of transcending the mere lure of 'forbidden fruit'. The only possible approach is that of initiation, with the whole aura of sacredness—outside all religions, of course—which the word implies, an initiation providing the impulse for that spirit of quest which the ideal constitution of each human couple demands. *This is the price of love*" (Breton 2002, p. 408).

15.10 Anthropological Relativism

The movement away from a metaphysical subjectivism leads Breton and Bataille to acknowledge the marvellous in other cultures, and to acknowledge with respect the sacrifices, ceremonies, and rituals of other cultures. The Surrealists pursued explorations of exotic or "primitive" cultures; Breton repudiated the Greco-Latin heritage in Western culture to the point of refusing to visit Greece or Italy. Associated with the Paris Surrealists were Martiniquan writer Aimé Césaire, Chilean painter Roberto Matta, Cuban painter Wilfredo Lam, and the Mexican painters Diego Rivera and Frida Kahlo. Breton visited Mexico, Haiti, and Hopi reservations in the US. Michel Leiris traveled with an anthropological study group across North Africa for a year. Bataille was fascinated by the human sacrifices performed by the Aztecs. Alfred Métraux, who become a renowned anthropologist specialized in pre-Columbian American cultures was a close and lifelong friend.

The Surrealists found the marvellous in the most ancient cultures, Breton in the art of the Gauls, Bataille in the carved stones of the Gnostics. They prized images and artefacts from other cultures, placing them on the same level as those made or found by Surrealist artists, but they did not, as Freud did, attribute them to infantile or primitive stages of life.

But logically putting images and artefacts from other cultures alongside those of Western culture leads to putting the ideology behind and in those images and artefacts alongside the ideology behind and in the images and artefacts of Western culture. Putting the ideologies behind and in images and artefacts of other cultures alongside of psychoanalysis.

The scientific study of the unconscious as established by Sigmund Freud, Alfred Adler, and Carl Gustav Jung constituted the unconscious as a universal structure of the human mind, and set out to identify the instincts, drives, desires, and conflicts in it. Later Jacques Lacan set up to again construct an encompassing science of the unconscious. Critics such as Adolf Grünbaum complained that reliably tested empirical data on psychoanalytic treatments and rate of cure are still lacking.

The data attributed to effects of the unconscious have been conceptualized differently in diverse ancient and contemporary cultures, by Chinese practitioners, in Vedic India, by the Morita psychology in Japan created in the 1930s. Claude Lévi-Strauss compared shamanist treatment among the Cuna people of Panama to psychoanalysis, and conceded that it produced cures (Lévi-Stauss 1974, pp. 186–205). Vincent Crapanzano wrote that to declare these conceptualizations inadequate is "an act of intolerable cultural arrogance."[7]

---

[7] "Much of what we in the West call psychological and locate in some sort of internal space ('in the head,' 'in the mind,' 'in the brain,' 'in consciousness,' 'in the psyche') is understood in many cultures in manifestly nonpsychological terms and located in other 'Spaces.' ... To declare such articulations inadequate, as some Western thinkers . . . have done, is, in my view, an act of intolerable cultural arrogance ... Sudden blindness, mutism, and paralysis, aphonia, tics, and other motor disturbances, anaesthesias and paraesthesias, glossolalia and echolalia, mimetic behavior, all accompanied by a *belle indifference*. For all of these a demon (with a particular character and desires) was held responsible. Cures were spectacular: communal exorcisms with elaborate trance dances, possession crises, and acts of self-mutilation" (Crapanzano 1992, p. 142).

Medical anthropologists complain that accumulation of data on treatments across cultures are lacking. Even thorough studies of the relative correspondence between Western psychiatric categories and those in other cultures are lacking. Does the conceptual system of psychoanalysis cover all the medical cases covered by other conceptual systems? The confrontation of the metaphysical presuppositions and methods of psychoanalysis with other cultures is suspended before us as an essential task.

References

Ades, Dawn. 1974. *Dada and surrealism*. London: Thames and Hudson.
Aragon, Louis. 1953. *Le paysan de Paris*. Paris: Gallimard.
———. 2013. *A wave of dreams*. Trans. Susan de Muth. London: Thin Man Press.
Bataille, Georges. 1985. *Visions of excess: Selected writings, 1927–1939*. Trans. Allan Stoekl, Carl R. Lovitt, and Donald M Leslie, Jr. Minneapolis: University of Minnesota Press.
———. 1986. *Erotism: Death and sensuality*. Trans. Mary Dalwood. San Francisco: City Lights Books.
Bourguignon, Erika. 1968a. World distribution and patterns of possession states. In *Trance and possession slates*, ed. R. Prince. Montreal: R. M. Bucke Memorial Society.
———. 1968b. *A cross-cultural study of dissociational states: Final report*. Columbus: Ohio State University Research Foundation.
———. 1973. Introduction: A framework for the comparative study of altered states of consciousness. In *Religion, altered states of consciousness, and social change*, ed. Erica Bourguignon. Columbus: Ohio State University Pres.
Breton, André. 1960. *Nadja*. Trans. Richard Howard. New York: Grove Weidenfeld.
———. 1972. *Manifestoes of surrealism*. Ann Arbor: University of Michigan Press. Ann Arbor Paperback.
———. 1978. In *What is surrealism? Selected writings*, ed. Franklin Rosemont. New York: Monad.
———. 1988. *Mad love*. Trans. Mary Ann Caws. Lincoln: Bison Books.
———. 1990. *Communicating vessels*. Trans. Mary Ann Caws and Geoffrey T. Harris. Lincoln: University of Nebraska.
———. 2002. *Surrealism and painting*. Trans. Simon Watson Taylor. Boston: MFA Publications.
Breton, André, and Paul Éluard. 1990. *The immaculate conception*. London: Atlas Press.
Carstairs, G.M., and R.L. Kapur. 1976. *The great universe of Kota: Stress, change, and mental disorder in an Indian village*. Berkeley: University of California Press.
Caws, Mary Ann. 2009. *Salvador Dalí*. London: Reaktion Books.
Claus, Peter J. 1979. Spirit possession and spirit mediumship from the perspective of tulu oral traditions. *Culture, Medicine, and Psychiatry* 3 (1): 29–52.
Crapanzano, Vincent. 1980. *Tuhami: Portrait of a Moraccan*. Chicago: University of Chicago Press.
———. 1992. *Hermes' dilemma and Hamlet's desire: On the epistemology of interpretation*. Cambridge: Harvard.
Dali, Salvador. 1992. *50 secrets of magic craftsmanship*. Trans. Haakon M. Chevalier. Mineola: Dover.
———. 1993. *The secret life of Salvador Dali*. Trans. Haakon M. Chevalier. Mineola: Dover.
———. 2007. *Diary of a genius*. Trans. Richard Howard. Solar Books.
Dali, Salvador, and Alain Bosquet. 1969. *The great masturbator: Conversations with Salvador Dali*. Boston: Dutton.

Dali, Salvador and André Parinaud. 1976. *The unspeakable confessions of Salvador Dali*. Trans. Harold J. Salemson. New York: William Morrow.
Ellenberger, Henry F. 1970. *The discovery of the unconscious*. New York: Basic Books.
Gibson, Ian. 1997. *The shameful life of Salvador Dali*. New York: Norton.
Lacan, Jacques. 1975. *De la psychose paranoïaque dans ses rapports avec la personnalité*. Paris: Éditions du Seuil.
Lévi-Stauss, Claude. 1974. *Structural anthropology*. Trans. Claire Jacobson and Brooke Grundfest Schoepf. New York: Basic Books.
Magee, Jeannette Marie. 2003. *Dreaming and the self: New perspectives on subjectivity, identity, and emotion*. Albany: State University of New York Press.
Mauriac, Claude. 1970. *André Breton*. Paris: Bernard Grasset.
Nadeau, Maurice. 1989. *The history of surrealism*. Trans. Richard Howard. Cambridge: Belknap Press.
Pierre, José, ed. 2014. *Investigating sex: Surrealist research 1928–1932*. London: Verso.
Polizzotti, Mark. 1995. *Revolution of the mind: The life of André Breton*. New York: Farrar, Straus & Giroux.
Prinzhorn, Hans. 1995. *Artistry of the mentally ill: A contribution to the psychology and psychopathology of configuration*. Trans. Eric von Brockdorff. Wien: Springer-Verlag.
Soler, Colette. 2014. *Lacan: The unconscious reinvented*. Trans. Esther Faye and Susan Schwartz. London: Karnac.
Surya, Michel. 2002. *Georges Bataille, an intellectual biography*. London: Verso.
Thurlow, Clifford. 2011. *Sex, surrealism, Dali and Me*. London: Yellow Bay Books.
Tythacott, Louise. 2003. *Surrealism and the exotic*. London: Routledge.
Valentine, Daniel E., and Judy F. Pugh, eds. 1984. *South Asian systems of healing*. Leiden: E. J. Brill.
Whitehead, Albert North. 1967. *Science and the modern world*. New York: The Free Press.

Index

A

Alterity, 27, 28, 37, 109–111, 114, 115, 123, 128, 129, 151, 154, 158
Anxiety, 10, 12, 149, 151, 163–178, 214, 215, 220, 234, 235, 246, 247, 274
Architectonic, 27, 30, 35–36
Asubjectivity, 96, 99, 103, 106–108

B

Base materialism, 272–274
Body, 10, 18, 20, 21, 42–45, 48–58, 62–73, 76–80, 83, 85–87, 102, 103, 105, 108, 128, 147, 149–152, 154, 155, 168, 171, 172, 182, 185–187, 189–192, 194–198, 200–204, 226, 228, 229, 232, 233, 242, 244, 251, 256, 266, 267, 273, 274

C

Cardio-phenomenology, 242–244
Cogito, 4, 19, 21, 44, 58, 148, 189
Consciousness, 5–8, 10, 12, 13, 16, 17, 21, 22, 26–30, 32–36, 42–46, 50, 54–56, 61, 65, 67, 70–72, 76–78, 80, 83–86, 88–90, 96–103, 105–109, 111, 113–116, 123, 134–138, 140, 142–145, 147–149, 151–158, 164–167, 169, 171, 172, 174, 177, 178, 184–189, 199, 200, 202, 203, 209, 210, 213, 214, 218, 241, 242, 244–246, 248, 255, 262, 268
Corpse, 150–152, 154, 274

D

Daydreams, 7, 49, 211–213
Dreaming, 13, 164, 165, 170, 172, 175, 178, 202, 212, 271

E

Emotion, 4, 9, 22, 23, 53, 73, 212, 215, 220, 243–258, 261, 267
Ethics, 17, 109, 111, 122, 129–131, 141–158
Event, 7, 11, 18, 45, 64, 72, 98, 107, 116, 117, 120, 121, 126, 127, 129, 134, 135, 137–139, 144, 145, 149, 151, 197, 199, 203, 212–214, 216–219, 221, 224, 240, 241, 253, 257, 258, 264, 266, 267, 270, 271, 273
Explication interviews, 245, 247, 256–258

F

First-person methods, 17, 21, 176, 229, 230, 240–242, 244, 257
Freud, S., 4–6, 8–13, 15, 16, 19, 22, 30, 44, 47, 51, 53–56, 62, 64, 70, 72, 76–78, 80, 81, 83–86, 88, 90, 91, 96, 98, 99, 101, 114, 115, 151–153, 185, 186, 188, 190, 202, 203, 209, 211, 220, 257, 262, 264, 267, 268, 270, 275

G

Gender, 181–205
Genesis, 19, 29, 30, 35, 36, 196
Genius, 91, 197, 265–268, 271

H

Heart, 3, 7, 47, 50, 73, 90, 117, 129, 134, 142, 143, 154, 157, 169, 184, 225, 226, 232, 233, 239–258, 267
Husserl, E., 3–23, 25–37, 43–58, 62, 65, 67, 68, 76, 96, 116, 135, 136, 138, 142, 143, 146–149, 182, 186, 187, 192, 210, 211, 216, 241, 242, 244–246

I

Imagination, 7, 16, 22, 30–32, 36, 46, 64, 69, 70, 73, 76, 166, 167, 175, 187, 194, 263, 264, 274
Inapparent, 96–99, 113–131, 140
Intransparency, 227, 235
Invisibility, 86, 88, 115, 117, 121–125, 127–129

L

Lacan, J., 11, 51, 55, 56, 89–91, 137, 152–154, 182, 185, 188, 191, 193, 265, 266, 269, 272, 275
Levinas, E., 28, 36, 37, 68, 95–111, 115, 122–127, 147, 155–158
Logos, 85, 98, 99, 104, 105, 110, 152

M

Meillassoux, Q., 144, 145, 150, 151, 153, 154
Memory, 4, 6, 7, 22, 23, 78, 84, 151, 173, 175, 200, 213, 214, 220, 253, 254, 261, 265
Merleau-Ponty, M., 6, 9–12, 41–58, 62–73, 75–91, 95–111, 113–131, 147, 164–167, 171–178, 181–205, 228, 242, 244
Metaphysical subjectivism, 270, 272, 274
Micro-phenomenology, 240, 246
Mourning, 273

N

Neuro-phenomenology, 241, 243
Neurotic displacement, 209, 210, 214–216
Night, 107, 110, 133–140, 170, 211, 268
Non-language thinking, 182, 210, 212, 217, 219, 220
Non-verbal unconscious, 76, 86, 88, 89, 183, 186, 189

O

Ontology, 31, 42, 50, 57, 81, 85, 97, 99, 101, 106, 107, 109, 111, 116, 122, 136, 148, 151, 154, 156
Otherness, 95–111, 115, 122, 124, 128, 136, 167
Ownership, 225–228, 231, 235

P

Passivity, 7, 22, 48, 49, 57, 108, 110, 124, 125, 136, 139, 149, 199–201, 203, 267
Past, 7, 11, 16, 17, 62, 63, 66, 69–73, 121, 127, 138, 144, 154, 171, 173, 174, 184, 199, 200, 212–214, 224, 226, 227, 231, 233, 234, 247, 263, 268
Phantasma, 210–214, 216–221
Phenomenology, 4, 5, 10, 26, 42, 62, 76, 90, 96, 100, 101, 113, 134, 142–143, 164–166, 182, 210, 228, 242, 264
Phenomenon, 10, 28, 31, 43–45, 56, 77, 81, 84, 96–98, 113, 115, 116, 118, 119, 121–125, 129, 130, 150, 155–157, 164, 191, 197, 216, 228, 233, 245, 272
Pre-conscious, 6, 27, 32, 184, 204, 240, 241, 243, 245–247, 257
Psychoanalysis, 4–13, 23, 26, 36, 42, 48, 62, 64, 70, 72, 73, 76–78, 80, 81, 83, 86, 89–91, 96, 99–101, 104, 114, 152, 153, 182, 184–186, 191, 192, 204, 209, 210, 213, 261–276

R

Reflexion, 32
Responsiveness, 224, 226, 228–234

S

Secret, 52, 88, 107, 115, 121, 125–131, 152, 184, 267
Self, 15, 17, 18, 21, 26, 33, 35, 85, 108, 119, 127, 128, 136, 137, 139, 164, 165
Self-consciousness, 32–34, 36, 108
Self-withdrawal, 224, 226, 227, 232, 234, 235
Sense, 5, 7, 14, 16, 18, 20–22, 26, 28, 32, 35, 36, 44, 55, 64–67, 69, 72, 80, 82, 85–88, 91, 98, 103, 106, 107, 109, 114–116, 118, 124, 125, 128, 129, 135–137, 139, 140, 142, 144, 145, 148, 164, 165, 167–171, 173–178, 184, 185, 187, 190, 191, 193, 196, 197, 199, 200, 209, 210, 214–216, 219, 220, 224–227, 230, 231, 233, 235, 243, 255, 257, 266, 268, 270, 272, 273

Index 281

Skilful intentionality, 224, 228–230, 233
Spectrality, 139, 140
Subjectivity, 16, 17, 27, 29, 34, 35, 67, 86, 96, 98, 99, 101, 103, 106–109, 111, 115, 135, 137–139, 142, 148–149, 156, 164, 171, 173, 174, 177, 182, 189, 194, 205, 243, 255, 270, 271
Surprise, 100, 127, 239–258, 266
Surreality, 270–272, 274
Symbolic, 29, 103, 151, 153, 182, 185, 191–193, 195, 197, 199–201, 203–205, 271

T

Temporality, 10, 28–30, 33, 166, 167, 173, 174, 176, 245, 247, 248, 254
Time, 10, 16, 18, 21, 22, 26–30, 33, 35, 44, 52, 57, 61, 63, 73, 79, 82, 86, 97, 102, 103, 115, 116, 118–120, 123, 127, 130, 136, 138, 140, 146, 148, 153, 164, 165, 167, 170–172, 174–176, 191, 201, 203, 212, 213, 218, 219, 225–228, 233, 234, 241, 243, 246–249, 251, 253, 256, 262, 271
Transcendental field, 5, 26, 28, 34

U

Unconscious, 4, 6, 26, 30, 31, 42, 62, 76, 81, 96, 114, 134, 142, 144, 164, 182, 209, 223, 239, 261–262
Unconsciousness, 54, 61–73, 77, 80, 95–111, 113–131, 134, 151, 164, 177, 209, 210, 221, 240–242, 247

W

Waking, 6, 12, 84, 133, 134, 137, 164, 165, 167, 170, 176–178, 264, 269

Printed by Printforce, the Netherlands